# NEW
# GEO

Junior Certificate Geography

Liam Ashe

Kieran McCarthy

**THE EDUCATIONAL COMPANY OF IRELAND**

First published 1999
The Educational Company of Ireland
Ballymount Road
Walkinstown
Dublin 12
Reprinted September 2010

A member of the Smurfit Kappa Group plc

The paper used in this book comes from Managed Forests in Northern Europe For every tree felled, at least one new tree is planted

Editor: Kate Duffy
Design and layout: Brendan O'Connell
Illustration: The Unlimited Design Company, Compuscript Limited, Helmut Kollars, Daghda, Brian Fitzgerald
Cover design: The Design House

**Ordnance Survey maps and aerial photographs**
Based on Ordnance Survey Ireland Permit No. 8554
© Ordnance Survey Ireland/Government of Ireland

**Acknowledgements**
The authors and publisher wish to thank the following for permission to reproduce photos and other material: Airticity, Ballymun Regeneration Ltd, Boliden Tara Mines Limited, Bord na Móna, Bóthar, Cobh Heritage Centre, Department of Foreign Affairs – Irish Aid, Fáilte Ireland, Fairtrade Mark Ireland, Fatima Regeneration Board, Harper Collins, Indaver Ireland, Irish Dairy Board, Mellon Housing Initiative, NRA, NUI Galway, Roche Ireland Limited, RUSAL Aughinish, Shannon Development, Slattery Communications, Suas, White Young Green

The authors wish to acknowledge their debt to the series editor Kate Duffy and designer Brendan O'Connell.

05M15

# Foreword

This edition of *New Geo* is designed to meet the needs of the Junior Certificate Geography syllabus. There are many new features in this edition. These include the following:

◎ The text has been extensively rewritten to take account of recent developments in the world of geography.
◎ The language has been simplified.
◎ It has a one-column page layout.
◎ Photographs, maps, graphs and diagrams have been amended and updated.
◎ Cartoons have been updated and are extensively used to illustrate particular points.
◎ Case studies, many of them new, are used widely throughout the book to bring realism and relevance to it.

The syllabus framework is common to both Ordinary and Higher level courses.

This book covers both the Ordinary and Higher level courses. Where options exist within the syllabus, they are clearly indicated. Each chapter begins with brief learning outcomes for that chapter. All sections end with a summary. Exercises and revision questions are placed at the end of each section. Short additional questions are included throughout the text.

A complementary workbook containing examination-based material is available.

# Contents

# Section 3 Social Geography

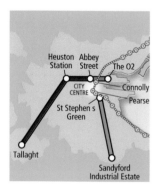

# Section 4 Economic Geography

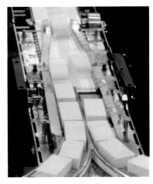

# 1 THE EARTH

**Learning Outcomes**

In this chapter you will learn that:

◎ Planet Earth is part of the Solar System.
◎ Earth consists of three layers.
◎ The plates of the Earth's crust move.

◎ This movement results in volcanoes, earthquakes and fold mountains.
◎ People are affected by the results of plate movement.

## 1.1 The Solar System

The Solar System consists of the sun, eight planets and their moons.

### The sun

The planets follow a regular pattern (orbit) around the sun. **Earth** is one of these planets.

The sun is a huge ball of extremely hot gas at the centre of the Solar System. About 4 million tons of gas is burned each second. This produces **solar energy**, some of which reaches Earth, giving it heat and light.

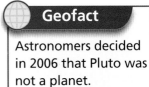

**Geofact**

Astronomers decided in 2006 that Pluto was not a planet.

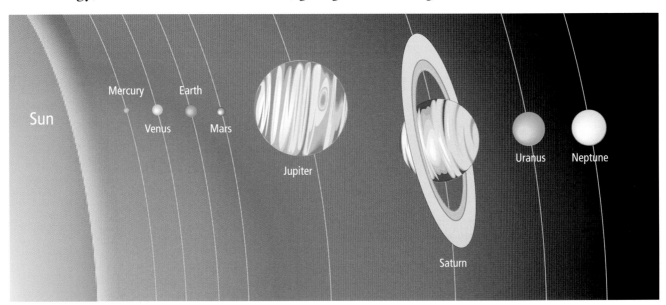

Fig 1.1 The Solar System, with the sun at its centre

**Geofact**

It is only 400 years since the surface of Earth was proven to be round. Before the 1600s, most people thought it was flat.

# Planet Earth

Earth is shaped like a sphere that is slightly flattened at the North and South Poles and bulges slightly at the equator.

Earth is the only planet that is known to support life and, as a result, is sometimes called the **miracle planet**. It is able to support life because it has water and air. Earth is also just the right distance from the sun. If it were closer to the sun, it would be too hot to support life. If it were further away, it would be too cold to support life.

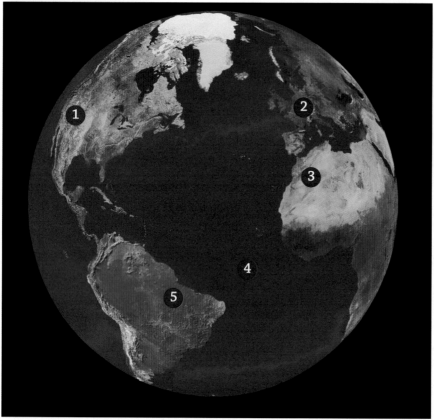

Seen from space, Earth is a bluish disc with swirling white clouds. It looks blue because so much of its surface consists of water

1 Mountains cover almost one tenth of Earth's surface.

2 Earth is home to more than 6 billion people.

3 Deserts cover almost one-eighth of Earth's surface.

4 Water covers more than two-thirds of Earth's surface.

5 Forests cover almost one quarter of Earth's surface.

## SUMMARY

◎ The Solar System consists of eight planets that orbit the sun.
◎ Earth is shaped like a sphere.
◎ Earth is the only known planet that is able to support life.

## QUESTIONS

1 How many planets are there?
2 Why is Earth called the miracle planet?
3 Describe Earth's shape.

# 1.2 The Structure of Earth

Earth was formed about 4.5 billion years ago.

At first Earth was a giant, boiling sea of molten (melted) material. As it began to cool, the heavier material sank, while the lighter material floated to the surface. As a result, Earth is made up of a number of different layers. These layers are called the **crust**, the **mantle** and the **core** (outer and inner).

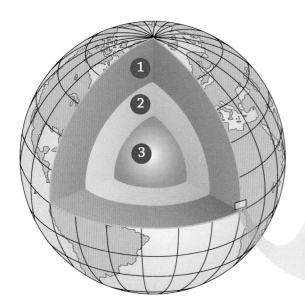

**1 The crust**
The **crust** is Earth's outer skin and consists of solid rock. It can be up to 60 km (kilometres) thick beneath the continents, but as thin as 10 km under the oceans.

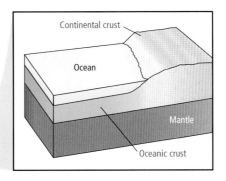

**3 The core**
The **core** (inner and outer) is at the centre of Earth. It is made of iron and nickel. Its temperature reaches over 5,000°C. The heat that the core generates causes the magma in the mantle to move upwards.

**2 The mantle**
Beneath the crust is a layer of hot, soft rock called the **mantle**. The temperature in the mantle is about 4,000°C. As a result, the rock is in a molten (melted) or semi-molten state and is called **magma**. The crust floats on top of the magma.

Fig 1.2 The structure of Earth

## SUMMARY

◎ Earth is made up of three different layers: the core (inner and outer), the mantle and the crust.
◎ The crust consists of solid rock, while the mantle consists of molten rock.

## Definition

**Magma:** The molten or semi-molten material that makes up Earth's mantle.

## QUESTIONS

1 Name the outer layer of Earth.
2 Which of Earth's layers is the hottest?
3 Which of Earth's layers is made up of melted rock?
4 Write three sentences to describe Earth's crust.

# 1.3 Plate Tectonics

The theory that Earth's crust is broken into a number of constantly moving plates is called plate tectonics. The plates move in different directions and at different speeds.

## The Earth's crust

The crust of the Earth is broken into a number of separate **plates**. There are seven large plates and several minor plates. These fit together like a jigsaw, floating on the semi-molten magma of the mantle. The plates meet at plate boundaries.

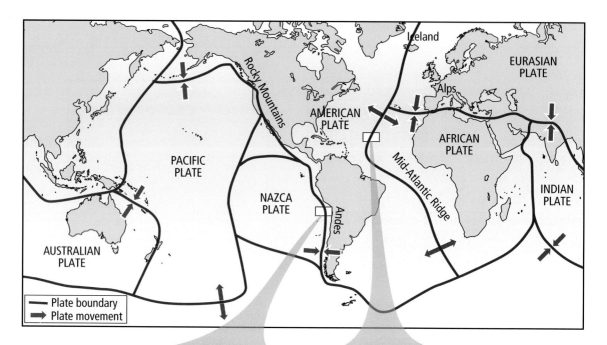

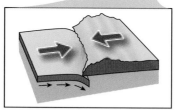
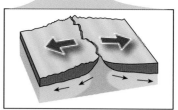

### Question

Name the plates on which Ireland, the USA and South Africa lie.

When two **plates collide**, they build up huge pressure. The heavier plate is forced downwards into the mantle, where it melts. Since some crust is destroyed, this is called a **destructive boundary**. In this example, the Nazca Plate and the American Plate are in collision.

When **plates pull apart**, molten magma rises up from the mantle, where it cools and new crust is formed. As a result, this is called a **constructive boundary**. In this example, the American Plate and the Eurasian/African Plates are moving apart.

### Geofact

North America and Europe are drifting further apart at a rate of about 2 cm per annum.

Fig 1.3 The major plates of the Earth's crust and their boundaries

## Plate boundaries

The plates appear to move at different speeds and in different directions. Even so, the whole jigsaw puzzle of plates is linked together. No single plate can move without affecting the other plates.

When the large plates move, enormous energy is let loose. As a result, a lot of activity takes place at plate boundaries. These activities include:

◎ Volcanic activity

◎ Earthquake activity

◎ Mountain building activity

> You will deal with these topics in sections 1.4 to 1.6.

## Plate movement

Why do the plates move as they float on top of the mantle?

The very hot core heats the **magma** in the mantle. This sets up **convection currents** in the mantle. Molten magma moves upwards from the core towards the crust. Here it cools and sinks back down towards the core, so that the cycle can start all over again.

There is friction between the convection currents and the plates. This causes the plates to move slowly on top of the mantle. As a result, the plates may pull apart from one another or collide with one another.

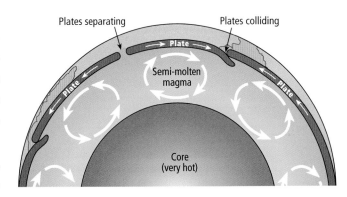

Fig 1.4 Convection currents in the mantle cause the plates of the crust to move

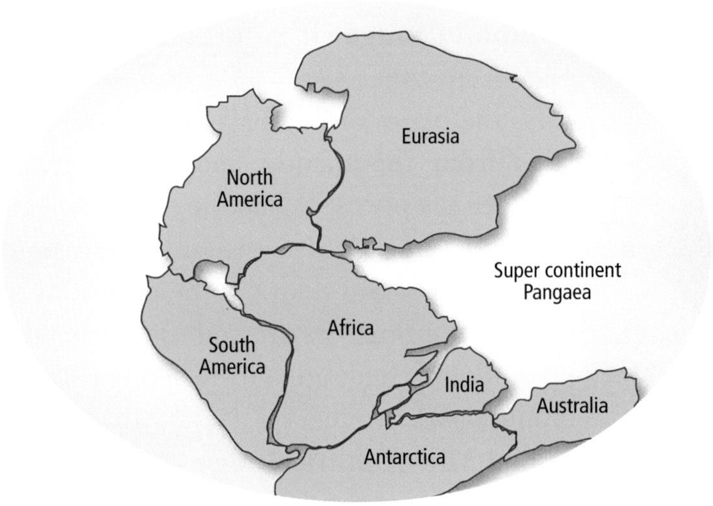

**Continental drift**

The Earth's continents are passengers on the plates that float beneath them. As the plates move, they carry the continents with them. This movement is very slow and it has taken millions of years for the continents to reach where they are today.

The continents began as one large landmass, called **Pangaea**. It gradually began to break up. The individual sections started to drift apart, carried along on the moving plates. This process is known as **continental drift**.

Continental drift continues today. For example, Europe is slowly moving away from North America, while India continues to push northwards into Asia.

Fig 1.5 The continents, as they might have looked about 200 million years ago, before continental drift. Compare this to a present-day map of the continents

### 📄 SUMMARY

- ◎ The Earth's crust is broken into plates.
- ◎ The plates are in constant motion, either colliding or moving apart.
- ◎ As the plates move, they carry the continents with them.
- ◎ Plate boundaries are associated with earthquakes, volcanoes and fold mountains.

### 🖐 QUESTIONS

1. What name is given to the sections into which the crust is broken?
2. What is magma?
3. Name two plates that are in collision.
4. Name two plates that are pulling apart.
5. With the aid of a simple diagram, explain why the plates move.
6. Which activities might take place at the boundary of two plates?

## 1.4 Volcanic Activity

### 👆 Definition

**Lava:** Molten magma when it reaches Earth's surface.

Most volcanic activity takes place along the margins or boundaries of plates. Volcanic activity can result in:

- ◎ Mid-ocean ridges and islands
- ◎ Volcanic cones

### Mid-ocean ridge

A mid-ocean ridge is an underwater **mountain range**. It is formed where two plates separate.

As the plates move apart, molten magma rises from the mantle and fills the gap between the plates. When the magma meets the cold seawater, it cools and solidifies to form a new ocean floor. As the eruptions of magma continue in an endless cycle, the ocean floor is built up to form a long ridge of mountains.

The **Mid-Atlantic Ridge** runs north to south (N-S) for the full 16,000 km length of the Atlantic Ocean. It is so high in places that it is exposed above sea level. One such place is **Iceland**.

Fig 1.6 The Mid-Atlantic Ridge runs N-S on the floor of the Atlantic Ocean. It breaks the surface in places to form islands such as Iceland

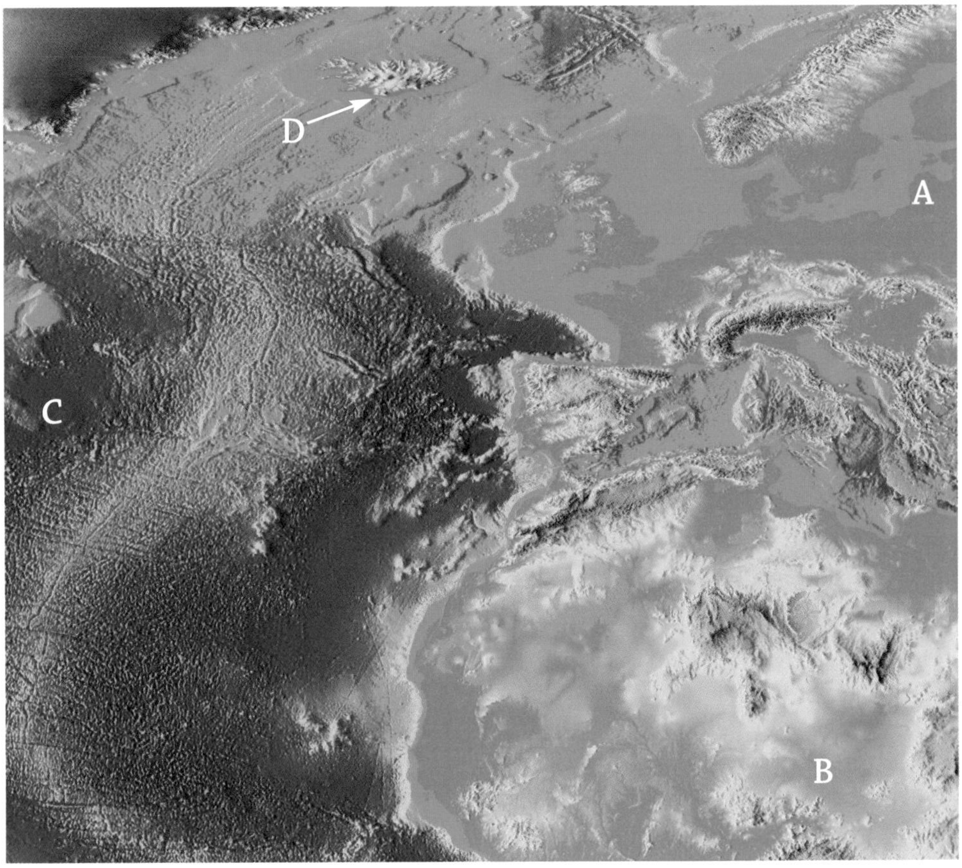

The Mid-Atlantic Ridge

Questions

### Questions

1 Identify the three plates marked A, B and C, shown in the picture on the left.
2 Name the country marked D.

# Case Study

# Iceland: A volcanic island

Iceland is one of the few places where the Mid-Atlantic Ridge is exposed above the ocean. It is only about 20 million years old, making it the youngest country on Earth.

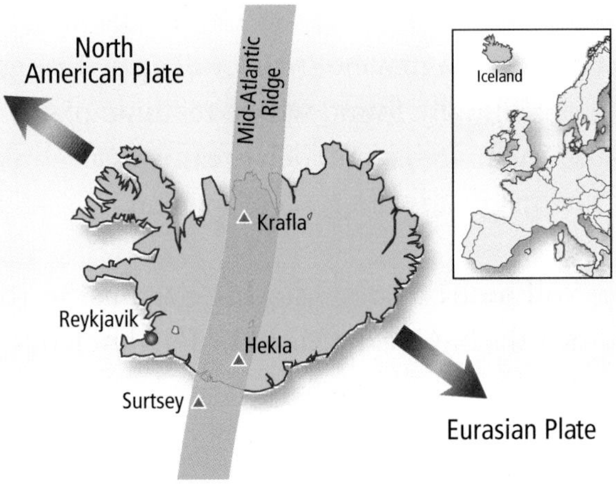

**Krafla** has been erupting regularly for over thirty years. The magma spews out through a crack or fissure that is about 20 km long.

**Hekla** is the most active volcano in Iceland.

**Surtsey** is the newest of the volcanic islands. It first appeared above the sea during an eruption in 1963.

### Geofacts

◎ The Antrim-Derry Plateau is the result of volcanic activity. Magma spewed out through a crack or fissure in the Earth's crust, spread out and cooled.

◎ The Giant's Causeway is the best-known section of the plateau. Its six-sided columns of rock are a major tourist attraction.

Fig 1.7 Iceland is a volcanic island lying on the Mid-Atlantic Ridge

Steam rises from a fissure in Iceland, where the American and Eurasian Plates are pulling apart

 **Question**

With the aid of Fig 1.4, on page 5, explain how the plates shown in the picture drift apart.

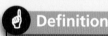 **Definition**

**Geothermal energy:** Hot water or steam from deep beneath the Earth's surface is converted into electricity.

The magma heats underground water. Some of this water comes to the surface as hot springs and geysers. These are said to have healing powers and attract many tourists to spas such as the Blue Lagoon.

The hot springs are used to:

◎ Generate **geothermal energy**.
◎ Centrally heat houses in urban areas such as Reykjavik.
◎ Heat greenhouses for growing vegetables.

## Volcanic mountains

Volcanic mountains are formed when molten magma emerges or **erupts** through a hole in the crust called a **vent**. They are generally found where tectonic plates are pulled apart or are in collision. Because the magma is under great pressure in the mantle, many eruptions are violent. The magma is often accompanied by ash, gas, steam, rocks and boiling mud.

More than half of the world's active volcanoes are found along the **Pacific Ring of Fire**. This is a zone that encircles the Pacific Ocean. Many of Earth's plates are in collision here.

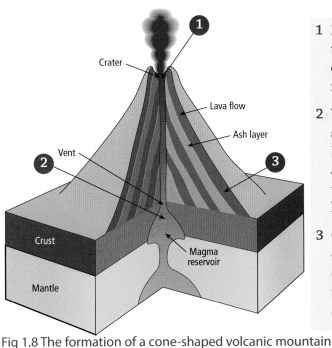

Fig 1.8 The formation of a cone-shaped volcanic mountain

1  Magma reaches the surface through a vent. It may erupt violently, blasting material into the sky.

2  When magma reaches the surface, it is known as lava. Lava pours out of the crater and flows down the side of the cone. It cools and hardens.

3  Other materials may also come out during the eruption. Layers of these materials build up to form a cone-shaped mountain.

**Question**

Explain each of the following terms:
◎ Mantle
◎ Lava flow
◎ Vent
◎ Crater

**Geofact**

Stromboli, located off Italy's Mediterranean coast, is a volcano that erupts so frequently that sailors have named it the Lighthouse of the Mediterranean.

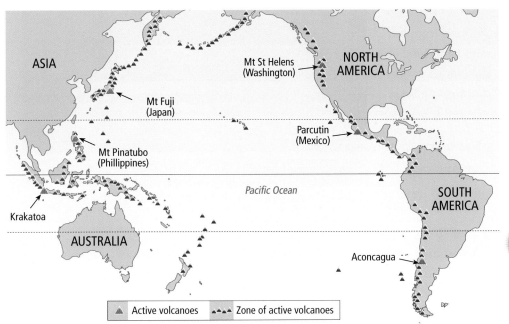

Fig 1.9 Some of the most active volcanoes of the world are found along the Pacific Ring of Fire

**Question**

Why, in your opinion, is the Pacific Ring of Fire so named?

# Life cycle of a volcano

Volcanoes do not erupt forever. Some have long ceased to erupt. Volcanoes can be classed as:

◎ **Active**: The volcano is still erupting at regular intervals, e.g. Mount Etna, Mount Vesuvius and Mount St Helens.

◎ **Dormant**: The volcano has been quiet for hundreds of years but may erupt again. Mount St Helens had not erupted for over 120 years when it became active again in 1980.

◎ **Extinct**: The volcano has not erupted in recorded times (thousands of years). Slemish Mountain in Co. Antrim is the remnant of an extinct volcano.

**Geofacts**

◎ Pumice is a volcanic rock that is so light that it can float in water. It is used as an abrasive.

◎ When volcanic ash is weathered it makes a fertile soil.

# Case Study

## Mount St Helens

Mount St Helens is a mountain peak in the Rocky Mountains, in the USA. It was formed by a series of volcanic eruptions over thousands of years. By 1980, it had been dormant for so long that people living in the region thought it would never erupt again.

A series of earthquakes early in 1980 indicated that the mountain was beginning to rumble again. Soon steam and small lava flows began to appear from the crater. One side of the mountain began to bulge as pressure built up. It swelled outwards by over 100 metres before a massive eruption took place. Clouds of steam, gas and ash escaped in a tremendous volcanic eruption.

A snow-capped Mount St Helens shortly before the eruption

- ◎ The force of the eruption reduced the height of the mountain by 400 metres. A new crater, almost 3 km wide, was created.
- ◎ Forests were stripped from hills. Trees 2 metres in diameter were mown down like blades of grass up to 25 km from the volcano.
- ◎ The eruption melted glacial ice and snow at the summit. This water combined with ash to form mudflows that clogged shipping channels in nearby rivers.
- ◎ The force of the blast and poisonous gas killed more than sixty people. Some were geologists, but the majority were so-called 'disaster tourists'.

 **Question**

Why, in your opinion, was the eruption on Mount St Helens so violent?

Mount St Helens shortly after the eruption

## SUMMARY

◎ Most volcanic activity occurs at plate boundaries.
◎ Mid-ocean ridges are formed when plates separate beneath the ocean.
◎ If the ridge breaks the surface of the ocean, it creates new islands.
◎ Volcanic cone mountains form after eruptions.
◎ The most active volcanic zone is the Pacific Ring of Fire.
◎ Lava, dust, ash, steam and gas are among the materials that come to the surface during an eruption.
◎ Volcanoes can cause death and destruction.

## QUESTIONS

1  (a) What is a mid-oceanic ridge?
   (b) Describe, with the aid of a diagram, how a mid-oceanic ridge is formed. (JC)
2  Draw a diagram of a volcanic cone. On it show and label the following:
  ◎ Crater
  ◎ Vent
  ◎ Magma reservoir
  ◎ Lava and ash flows
3  Choose one feature associated with colliding plates and one feature associated with separating plates. In the case of each:
   (a) Name the feature and
   (b) Describe how the feature was formed.
4  Describe:
   (a) The negative impact and
   (b) The positive impact of volcanic activity, referring in each case to an example you have studied. (JC)

# 1.5  Earthquakes

An earthquake is a sudden movement or trembling of the Earth's crust. This movement takes the form of a series of shocks or tremors.

Earthquakes occur at boundaries where plates collide. As the plates push into one another, pressure builds up until one of the plates slips. This eases the pressure and a huge amount of energy is released. The earthquake has occurred.

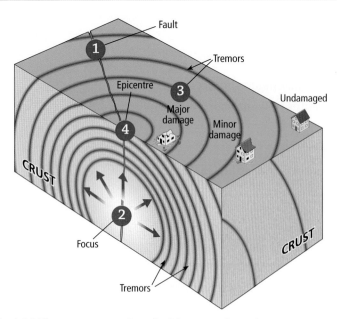

Fig 1.10 The terms associated with an earthquake

1 The **plates** move along the fault line.

2 The **focus** is the point deep in the Earth's crust where the earthquake begins.

3 The **tremors** spread out from the focus.

4 The **epicentre** is the point on the surface directly above the focus. It is the place where tremors are strongest.

 **Question**

Why are aftershocks as dangerous as the original tremors?

 **Geofact**

While more than 500,000 earthquakes occur each year, only about fifty are strong enough to cause damage.

**Question**

If earthquake A measures 8 on the Richter Scale and earthquake B measures 7 on the Richter Scale, how many times stronger is earthquake A?

## Aftershocks

Earthquakes rarely last for longer than one minute. Smaller tremors, called **aftershocks**, may occur in the hours or days following an earthquake. They often cause more damage than the original earthquake because buildings and structures are already weakened by the first tremors.

## Measuring earthquakes

Tremors from an earthquake can be detected and measured by a **seismometer** or **seismograph**. A pen on the tip of the seismometer records the tremors on a rotating drum.

The **Richter Scale** is used to describe the strength or force of an earthquake. Each increase of one unit on the scale means that the strength of the earthquake is ten times more powerful.

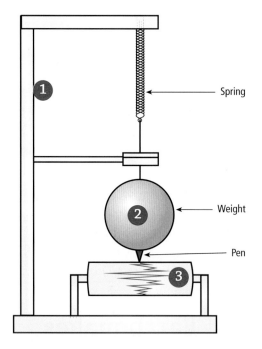

1 The frame of the seismograph vibrates during the earthquake.

2 The weight does not move because it is hanging from a spring

3 A pen, attached to the weight, records the tremors on a rotating drum.

Fig 1.11 A seismograph recording earthquake tremors

# Case Study

## Sichuan earthquake (2008)

Sichuan Province in China was hit by an earthquake in May 2008. It measured 7.9 on the Richter Scale. It was followed by more than fifty aftershocks over the following three days. The plates moved up to 9 metres in distance along a fault line that was about 250 km long.

The earthquake occurred where the Indian Plate pushes against the Eurasian plate, building up stress. When the rock slipped, the stress was released and the earthquake occurred.

Rescue efforts were held back by the roughness of the landscape and the bad weather. The Chinese authorities were slow to permit foreign aid to be brought in.

The effects of the earthquake included the following:

◎ More than 70,000 people were killed, including 10,000 school children. Many buildings collapsed due to poor building standards. Over 20,000 people are still missing.

◎ Five million people were made homeless as over 500,000 homes were destroyed.

◎ Over 12 million animals were killed.

◎ Landslides blocked valleys, disrupting communications as well as creating earthen dams that were likely to burst.

◎ The spread of diseases was a major cause of concern due to polluted water and poor sanitary conditions.

Fig 1.12 The earthquake took place where the Indian Plate collides with the Eurasian Plate. When the plates collided, one was forced downwards beneath the other, causing the earthquake

 **Geofact**

The collision of the Indian Plate and the Eurasian Plate was responsible for the formation of the Himalaya Mountain Range.

**Question**

Why is an earthquake in a developing country likely to cause more damage than one in a developed country?

**Definition**

**Tsunami:** A huge wave that is caused by an underwater earthquake.

# Tsunamis

When a strong earthquake occurs under the sea, a giant wave, called a **tsunami** can result. It travels rapidly towards the shore.

A major tsunami occurred in South-east Asia in 2004, when, once again, the Indian Plate pushed under the Eurasian Plate. The wave, up to 30 metres in height, hit the coast at speeds of up to 800 km per hour.

Over 200,000 people were killed and 1 million people made homeless by the tsunami.

People's livelihoods were destroyed. Coastal communities lost their boats and equipment. The local tourist industry was wiped out. Epidemics were a major concern. Food aid had to be provided for almost 2 million people.

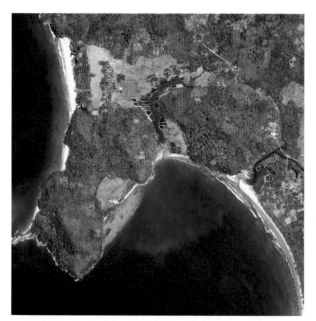 

Satellite images showing the Indonesian coastline before and after the tsunami

## SUMMARY

- ◎ Most earthquakes occur at boundaries where plates collide.
- ◎ Earthquakes take the form of seismic waves or tremors.
- ◎ An underwater earthquake may cause a tsunami.
- ◎ The strength of an earthquake is measured by a seismograph and described on the Richter Scale.
- ◎ Earthquakes cause great destruction and loss of life.

**QUESTIONS**

1 With the aid of a diagram, explain how earthquakes happen. (JC)
   Write one sentence to describe each of the following terms that are associated with earthquakes:
   ◎ Tremor
   ◎ Aftershock
   ◎ Focus
   ◎ Epicentre
2 Describe how the strength of an earthquake is measured and recorded.
3 Describe the negative effects of an earthquake on an area that you have studied.

## 1.6 Fold Mountains

**Fold mountains are found along plate boundaries.**

When two plates move towards each other and collide, the rocks tend to buckle and crumple upwards into a series of folds. This happens in the same way as a tablecloth wrinkles as it is pushed across a table.

◎ The Nazca Plate and the South American Plate collide.
◎ The Nazca Plate is pushed down into the mantle.
◎ The rocks that lie on the plates are compressed and forced upwards.
◎ The layers of rock buckle and crack into a series of upfolds and downfolds.

 **Definition**

**Fold mountains:** Mountain formed when rocks buckled and folded as two plates collided.

**Question**

Fossils (skeletons of sea creatures) have been found thousands of metres up in the Andes. How might this have happened?

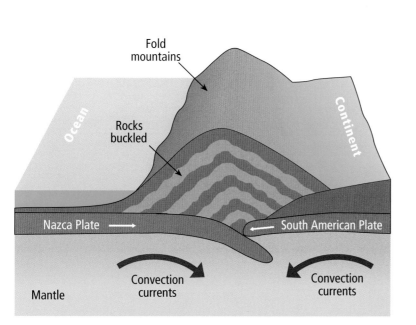

Fig 1.13 The Andes were formed where the Nazca plate collides with the South American plate

**Question**

Examine the picture on the right. What evidence suggests that the rocks have been put under pressure?

Folding has buckled and cracked these sedimentary rocks

## Periods of folding

The world's **young fold mountains** formed only about 30 to 35 million years ago. They include the Andes in South America and the Rockies in America, the Himalayas in Asia and the Alps in Europe. All mountains formed during this period of folding are called **Alpine Fold Mountains**. These mountains are very high and steep, as they have not yet been worn down as much as other fold mountains.

Alpine peaks rising above cloud cover

## Fold mountains of Munster

Folding in Ireland took place on a number of occasions. The most recent fold mountains in Ireland were formed in Munster about **250 million years** ago when the Eurasian Plate and African Plate collided. They include Magillicuddy's Reeks, the Galtees, the Comeraghs and the Knockmealdowns. Mountains that were formed during this period of folding are known as **Armorican Fold Mountains**. While they were once as high as the Alps, they have been severely worn down over the years.

**Question**

With the aid of an atlas, can you identify the mountain ranges A, B, C and D?

Fig 1.14 The fold mountains of Munster have a west-east trend. The pressure that folded them came from the Africa Plate as it pushed northwards

---

### SUMMARY

- Folding takes place at plate boundaries where plates collide.
- The crust is compressed and buckles into upfolds and downfolds.
- The Alps, Andes and Rockies are young fold mountains.
- Irish fold mountain ranges include the Comeraghs and Magillicuddy's Reeks.

### QUESTIONS

1. Name four ranges of fold mountains in Ireland.
2. With the aid of a diagram, explain how fold mountains are formed. (JC)
3. Write a brief account of fold mountain building in Ireland.

# 2 ROCKS

## 2.1 What Is Rock?

Rock is the hard material that forms Earth's crust.

Rocks are made up of various **minerals** that are held together by natural **cement**. Rocks differ from each other in their:

◎ Mineral content
◎ Colour
◎ Hardness
◎ Texture (how they feel to the touch)

Rocks are divided into three groups, according to how they were formed. These groups are:

◎ Igneous
◎ Sedimentary
◎ Metamorphic

There are many different rock types in each group.

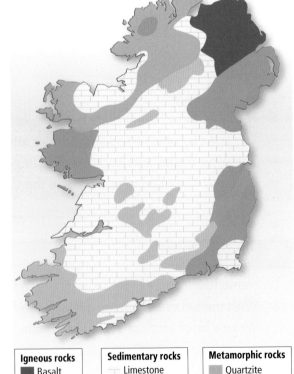

## Question

Examine the map in Fig 2.1. What is the most common type of rock found in Ireland?

Fig 2.1 The locations of the most common rock types in Ireland

| Igneous rocks | Sedimentary rocks | Metamorphic rocks |
|---|---|---|
| ■ Basalt | Limestone | Quartzite |
| Granite | Sandstone | Marble |
| | Shales | |

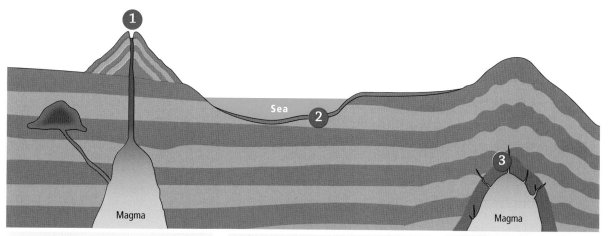

1 **Igneous rocks** are formed as a result of volcanic activity. Hot molten magma cooled down and solidified, either on the surface or within the crust. The word igneous comes from the Latin word for *fire*.

2 **Sedimentary rocks** were formed from the remains (sediments) of other rocks, plant life and animal life. These sediments were deposited on the beds of seas and lakes as well as on land. They were then compressed and cemented together.

3 **Metamorphic rocks** are those that have been changed in shape or form by great heat and pressure. They already existed as igneous or sedimentary rocks before being changed.

Fig 2.2 The settings in which the three different rock groups are formed

**Question**

Which rock group formed first? Why did you select that group?

📄 **SUMMARY**

◎ Rocks are made up of minerals that have been cemented together.
◎ There are three groups of rocks: igneous, sedimentary and metamorphic.

**QUESTIONS**

1 Name the three groups of rocks.
2 How are rocks classified or grouped?
3 Name one example of each group of rocks.
4 With the aid of your atlas and Fig 2.1, opposite, identify the main rock type found in each of the following locations:
   (a) Counties Derry and Antrim
   (b) The Central Plain and North Clare
   (c) County Kerry and West Cork
   (d) County Donegal
5 Select any one rock of your choice.
   (a) Name the rock.
   (b) To which rock group does it belong?
   (c) Name a location where it is found.
   (d) Describe how it was formed. (JC)

## 2.2 Igneous Rocks

The two most common igneous rocks are granite and basalt.

### Granite

Granite formed when molten magma forced its way into the crust. It **cooled very slowly** over millions of years, allowing **large crystals** to form. These crystals include quartz. It eventually came to the surface when the overlying rocks were worn away.

Granite varies in colour from black or grey to pink. It is used in the building industry and for monuments. Granite is found in the Mourne and Wicklow Mountains.

### Basalt

Basalt formed when lava spread out across the Earth's surface. It **cooled very quickly** and solidified because it was exposed to the air. As a result, it has **tiny crystals** that cannot be seen by the naked eye.

Basalt varies in colour from dark grey to black. It is found in the Antrim-Derry plateau. The most famous section of it is the **Giant's Causeway**. Here, as the lava cooled, it shrunk and cracked to form six-sided columns.

Close-up of pink granite, showing large crystals

There are about 40,000 hexagonal (six-sided) blocks of basalt at the Giant's Causeway in Co. Antrim

**SUMMARY**

◎ Igneous rocks are formed when molten magma and lava solidify and cool.

**QUESTIONS**

1  Explain the terms molten magma and lava.
2  Select one igneous rock and explain how it was formed. (JC)

# 2.3 Sedimentary Rocks

Sedimentary rocks include limestone, sandstone and shale.

## Limestone

Limestone formed on the beds of shallow, warm seas from the **skeletons of tiny sea creatures**, **fish** and **shells**. These piled up over millions of years. The particles were **compressed and cemented** together. The remains of some of the skeletons are preserved in the rock as fossils.

Limestone varies in colour from white to grey. It is **permeable** (allowing water to pass through it) and is laid down in strata.

Limestone is found in the Burren (Co. Clare) and under the soil and bogs that cover the Central Plain of Ireland. Limestone is used to make monuments and is the raw material for cement. Many public buildings are constructed of limestone.

Farmers use ground limestone to improve soil fertility.

Limestone containing fossils

**Geofact**

Limestone is the most common rock in Ireland and is found in thirty-one of the thirty-two counties.

## Sandstone

Sandstone formed when large amounts of sand were worn away from the surface of the Earth and transported by wind and rivers. The sand was then deposited on the beds of lakes and seas as well as in deserts. Layers of sand built up and these were **compressed** and **cemented** to form sandstone.

Sandstone varies in colour from **brown** to **red**. It is sometimes used as a building material. The mountains of Munster, including Magillicuddy's Reeks, the Galtees and Comeraghs are made of sandstone.

Sandstone laid down in layers (strata)

**SUMMARY**

◎ Sedimentary rocks are formed from the remains of other rocks, as well as plant and animal life.

**Geofact**

Coal is a sedimentary rock that formed from decayed vegetation.

**QUESTIONS**

1 Select one sedimentary rock and explain how it was formed. (JC)
2 Explain how limestone is formed. (JC)

# 2.4 Metamorphic Rocks

Metamorphic rocks include marble, quartzite and slate.

## Marble

When molten magma forces its way into a body of limestone, it puts it under great heat and pressure. This alters the make-up of the limestone and it changes into marble.

**Pure marble** is white in colour, but, when other minerals are present, it can vary to red, green or black. Marble is a hard rock that also contains **crystals**.

Marble can be easily cut and polished. As a result, it is in demand for fireplaces, gravestones and ornaments. Marble is found at Rathlin Island (white), Connemara (green) and Cork (red).

> **Geofact**
>
> The so-called black marble of Kilkenny is in fact a form of limestone.

Quarrying large slabs of marble at Carrara in Italy. The artist, Michelangelo, used Carrara marble

A pilgrim makes her way up the quartzite slope of Croagh Patrick

## Quartzite

Quartzite was formed when sandstone was changed into a metamorphic rock as it came into contact with magma deep in the Earth's crust. This usually happened during periods of **folding**.

Quartzite consists mainly of grains of quartz that are packed tightly together. It varies in colour from grey to white.

It is an extremely hard rock so it remains as a cap on some of Ireland's mountains. These include Croagh Patrick (Co. Mayo), Errigal (Co. Donegal) and The Great Sugarloaf (Co. Wicklow).

> **SUMMARY**
>
> ◎ Metamorphic rocks are formed when existing rocks are changed by heat or pressure.

> **Geofact**
>
> Slate is a metamorphic rock that has been used for roofing and on billiard tables.

> **QUESTIONS**
>
> 1 Select one metamorphic rock and explain how it was formed. (JC)
> 2 Select one metamorphic rock and describe its characteristics. (JC)

# 2.5 Resources from the Earth

Rocks provide us with a wide range of natural resources that can be extracted or mined.

The Earth's **natural resources** include:

◎ Metal ores: iron ore, copper, lead and zinc
◎ Precious metals and stones: gold, silver and diamonds
◎ Building material: stone, sand and gravel
◎ Energy source: uranium, oil, natural gas and coal

## Mining

Minerals are recovered by **quarrying** and **mining**.

Quarrying is used in Ireland to extract stone, sand and gravel for the building industry.

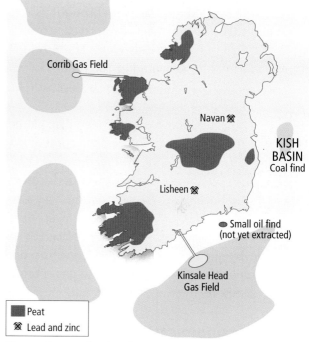

Fig 2.3 Some of Ireland's mineral resources

**Drilling** is used to extract oil or gas from an underground reservoir. Most drilling takes place on land, but some takes place offshore. A pipeline on the seabed then brings the fuel ashore.

**Open-cast mining** is used where the resource is on or close to the surface. It is a cheap method of mining but it is not environmentally friendly. It can be noisy, give off dust and scar the landscape.

**Shaft mining** is used where the resource lies in seams deep beneath the surface. They are reached by constructing shafts to reach the seams.

Shaft mining is used to extract lead and zinc ores from mines in Navan and Lisheen.

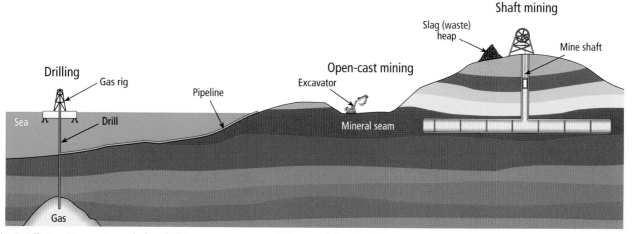

Fig 2.4 Extracting minerals by drilling, open-cast mining and shaft mining

# Case Study

## Natural gas production in Ireland

Offshore **drilling** takes place when natural gas is found under the seabed. The drilling is done from a rig and the gas is brought ashore through an underwater pipeline.

Natural gas has been brought ashore in this way for over twenty years from the **Kinsale Head Gas Field**. The production platform is located in 100 metres of water and it pumps gas from a depth of 1,000 metres below the seabed.

Natural gas has also been discovered in the **Corrib Gas Field**, off the coast of Mayo. The water here is very deep, so all the production equipment will be located on the seabed and production will be by remote control. Production was due to commence in 2005, but it has been delayed by planning issues and concerns about health and safety when the gas is brought ashore.

An offshore gas production platform

### Economic benefits

The discovery of natural gas off our coastline has major benefits for the Irish economy:

◎ It provides direct employment in the exploration and production stages as well as in constructing the pipeline network.
◎ It is a native source of energy, thus cutting down on energy imports.
◎ It is used as a raw material in the artificial fertiliser industry.

---

### 📄 SUMMARY

◎ Rocks provide us with mineral and energy resources.
◎ Ireland's energy sources are of major economic benefit to the economy.

### ✍ QUESTIONS

1 (a) Name one resource that is extracted from the Earth.
  (b) Explain briefly how it is extracted.
2 Imagine that a quarry is to be opened near where you live. Explain why some people would be in favour and some would be against it. (JC)

# 3 SHAPING EARTH'S CRUST

## 3.1 Denudation: An Introduction

The processes of weathering and erosion constantly wear away the rocks on the Earth's surface. The two processes as a whole are known as denudation.

**Denudation**
occurs by **weathering**
and **erosion**.

### Weathering

**Weathering** is the breakdown and decay of rocks that are exposed to the weather. There are two types of weathering:

◎ Mechanical weathering
◎ Chemical weathering

Weathering takes place on site and the resulting waste material is not moved.

### Erosion

**Erosion** is the breaking down of rocks and the removal of the particles that result. Erosion is caused by:

◎ Moving water (rivers and sea)
◎ Moving ice (glaciers)
◎ Moving air (wind)

The rock particles that have been broken down are **transported** and eventually **deposited** (dumped) elsewhere.

As weathering and erosion gradually wear down the surface of the Earth, they reshape it. Many distinct landscapes and landforms develop as a result.

**SUMMARY**

◎ Weathering and erosion have shaped the surface of the Earth.
◎ The main agents of erosion are rivers, the sea and ice.

**QUESTIONS**

1 Explain the terms (a) weathering and (b) erosion. (JC)
2 Name the two types of weathering.
3 Name the agents that cause erosion.
4 List two differences between weathering and erosion.

# 3.2 Mechanical Weathering

Mechanical weathering causes rock to be broken up into smaller pieces. The most common type of mechanical weathering is freeze-thaw.

## Freeze-thaw

**Freeze-thaw** is the break-up of rock by **frost action**. It occurs where:

◎ There is **precipitation** (rainfall) and
◎ The **temperature** rises above and falls below freezing point (0°C).

These conditions occur in Ireland during winter months, especially in upland areas. They also occur in snow-covered mountain ranges such as the Alps.

**Question**

Why does freeze-thaw not occur when the temperature does not drop below freezing point (0°C)?

**By day**
During the day, water seeps into joints (cracks) in the rock.

**By night**
The temperature drops below freezing point (0°C). The water freezes and expands. This makes the crack bigger and puts strain on the rock.

**Over time**
After repeated freezing and thawing, the rock splits. Sharp, jagged pieces break off. These pieces of rock are called **scree**. They roll down the mountainside and collect in piles at the bottom of the slope.

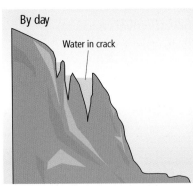
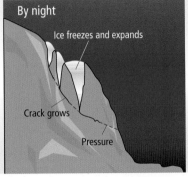
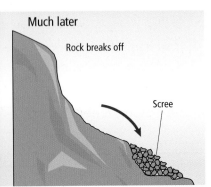

Fig 3.1 How rocks are weathered by the process of freeze-thaw

The pile of **scree** on the mountain slope is the result of freeze-thaw action

## SUMMARY

- Freeze-thaw occurs mainly in upland areas.
- Freeze-thaw shatters rock into particles called scree.
- Piles of scree gather at the foot of mountain slopes.

## QUESTIONS

1. Explain the terms (a) freeze-thaw and (b) scree.
2. In Ireland, freeze-thaw is more likely to occur in upland areas. Why?
3. Describe, with the aid of a labelled diagram, how freeze-thaw occurs. (JC)

## 3.3 | Chemical Weathering

Chemical weathering occurs when rocks decay or dissolve because of a chemical change. Carbonation is one example of chemical weathering.

### Carbonation

- When rain falls it takes in carbon dioxide as it passes through the atmosphere.
- The carbon dioxide mixes with the rainwater, turning it into a weak carbonic acid.
- Limestone contains calcium carbonate. The weak acid rain reacts with the carbon dioxide and slowly dissolves it. This process is called **carbonation**.

The make-up of the limestone makes this easier. It is **permeable**, so the rainwater can easily pass through it. It also has vertical cracks called **joints** and horizontal **bedding planes**, easing the passage of water (see Fig 3.3, page 28).

**Definition**

**Bedding plane:** The line in rocks that separates two layers or strata.

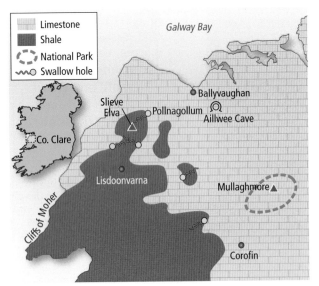

Fig 3.2 The Burren region of North Clare has a limestone landscape that has been shaped by chemical weathering

# Karst landscapes

The effects of carbonation are best seen on a limestone landscape, especially one where the soil cover has been removed and the rock is exposed to the weather. These landscapes are better known as **karst** landscapes, called after the limestone region of Slovenia. Ireland's best-known karst region is the Burren in Co. Clare.

## The Burren landscape

The Burren is a karst landscape of world importance. Its name comes from the Irish word for **rocky place**.

Most of the soil cover of the Burren was removed by erosion, leaving the limestone exposed. Weathering by carbonation has created a remarkable landscape, both on the surface and underground.

### 1 Limestone pavement

The large area of exposed limestone is called a **limestone pavement**. It generally takes the form of almost flat terraces, but also may have steep edges.

As the rainfall seeps through the rock, it picks out the weakest points, weathering them by **carbonation**. The joints or cracks in the limestone are widened and deepened to form deep gashes called **grikes**. The blocks of limestone that remain are called **clints**.

### 2 Swallow hole

When rivers flow onto a bare limestone surface, the water begins to dissolve the limestone by carbonation. The water widens the joints and bedding planes, opening them up. Soon the river disappears from the surface and begins to flow underground. The passage through which the river disappears is called a **swallow hole**. The largest swallow hole in the Burren is Pollnagollum.

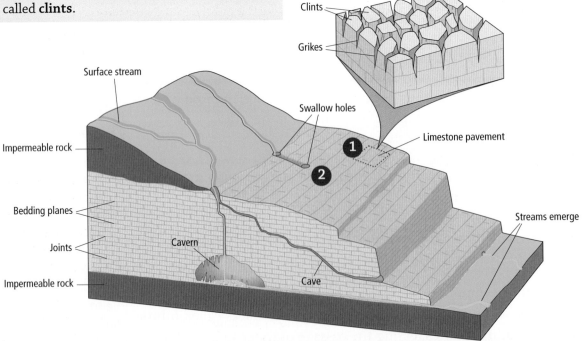

Fig 3.3 Surface landforms of a karst region include limestone pavement, clints, grikes and swallow holes

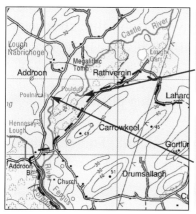

Fig 3.4

The Castle River disappears through a swallow hole at Poulduff (black hole).

It emerges further downstream at Poulnacally and flows into the River Fergus.

Clints and grikes on a limestone pavement in the Burren

**1** As the river flows underground, the carbonic acid in the water dissolves the limestone to cut out long tunnels, called **caves**.

Sometimes the cave is enlarged to form a large chamber called a **cavern**.

**3** When drops of water fall to the floor and evaporate, they also deposit some calcite. These deposits build up in a conical shape to form a **stalagmite**.

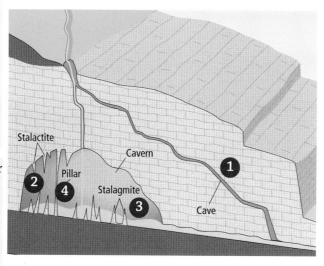

**2** When water containing dissolved limestone (calcium carbonate) seeps through to the cave or cavern, some drops hang from the roof for a while.

Some of the water evaporates, leaving behind tiny deposits of calcite (dissolved calcium carbonate) attached to the roof. These deposits build up slowly over thousands of years and hang from the roof in icicle-like shapes called **stalactites**.

**4** In time, the stalactites and stalagmites grow and join up to form **pillars**.

Fig 3.5 Underground features of a karst region include caves, caverns, stalactites, stalagmites and pillars

Underground landforms in a limestone cavern

| Hint |
|---|
| Stalactites: **c** for ceiling. Stalagmites: **g** for ground. |

**Questions**

1 Explain how the landscape shown in the picture above was shaped.
2 What evidence is there in the picture above that karst regions have some soil?
3 Examine the picture on the left and identify the features labelled A, B and C.

A rubber tree growing in tropical red soil

## Weathering in tropical regions

Chemical weathering is also very active in tropical regions such as the Amazon Basin and the Congo Basin. This is mainly because:

◎ The climate is hot, wet and humid.
◎ There is an enormous amount of decaying plant litter.

These conditions give rise to **tropical red soil**. This is dealt with in more detail in Tropical Red Soils, pages 130–31.

# Case Study

# The Burren National Park

The Burren is one of Ireland's most important tourist destinations. Part of it, centred on Mullaghmore Mountain (see Fig 3.2, page 28), has been designated as a national park.
   It has a wide range of attractions for tourists, including:

◎ **Flora:** The Burren is remarkable because of its varied plant life. Alpine, Mediterranean and native plants grow side-by-side. Orchids, ferns and avens are among the rare plants found there.
◎ **Fauna:** The Burren's wildlife includes the green moth (not found anywhere else in Ireland and Britain), butterflies, pine martens and wild goats.
◎ **Landscape:** The Burren has a wide variety of scenery for tourists. Attractions include the karst landforms, Aillwee Cave and the Cliffs of Moher. Cavers and rock climbers are also attracted to the Burren.
◎ **History:** The Burren's monuments and archaeological sites provide evidence of a long history of settlement. They include dolmens, ring forts, churches and carved crosses.

The Burren is noted for its wild flowers, such as red valerian

The Burren has many historical monuments, such as Poulnabrone dolmen

### ✍ Question

List four reasons why tourists might visit the Burren.

## Benefits of increased tourism

◎ Increased tourism creates a rise in local employment, both in permanent and seasonal jobs.

◎ This, in turn, reduces out-migration.

◎ There are spin-off benefits for shops, coach owners, craftspeople and pubs.

◎ Both locals and visitors benefit from improved facilities, such as roads and recreational facilities.

## Disadvantages of increased tourism

◎ Tourism increases the damage to flora, as people pick or trample on the rare flowers.

◎ The quiet, unspoilt nature of the Burren is changed by noise and air pollution.

◎ Road widening results in increased traffic, thus destroying the environment that attracted people in the first place.

◎ There is an increased risk of damage to ancient monuments.

### SUMMARY

◎ Chemical weathering of limestone is caused by small amounts of carbonic acid in rainfall.

◎ Chemical weathering is effective in karst regions, where the limestone is exposed.

◎ Surface landforms of a karst region include swallow holes and limestone pavement with clints and grikes.

◎ Underground features include caves and caverns, stalactites, stalagmites and pillars.

◎ The Burren is a karst region in Co. Clare that is noted for its scenery, flora and fauna.

◎ The Burren is a sensitive landscape that needs to be protected from mass tourism.

### QUESTIONS

1 Explain the terms (a) chemical weathering and (b) karst.

2 Select any two of the following and explain how they were formed: (a) swallow hole, (b) clint and grike, (c) cave and (d) stalactite.

3 Describe, with the aid of a labelled diagram, one way in which chemical weathering shapes the landscape. (JC)

4 The Burren is a major tourist attraction.

   (a) Describe any two of these attractions.

   (b) Describe two benefits that tourism brings to the Burren.

   (c) Describe two problems that increased tourism might bring. (JC)

# 3.4 Mass Movement

Mass movement refers to the movement downslope of any loose material under the influence of gravity. This loose material is known as regolith. It includes soil, mud and loose rock produced by weathering.

## Influences on mass movement

◎ **Gradient**: Mass movement is fastest when the slope is steep.
◎ **Water content**: Water makes the regolith heavier and acts as a lubricant. This enables it to move quickly and easily.
◎ **Human activity**: People often make cuttings into the sides of hills. This leaves a steeper slope and may cause material to collapse.
◎ **Vegetation**: The roots of trees and plants bind the regolith together. This slows down the rate of mass movement.

### Questions

1  What is mass movement?
2  List three factors that influence mass movement.

## Types of mass movement

Mass movements are grouped according to the speed at which they occur. The main types are listed opposite.

| Speed | Type of mass movement |
|-------|----------------------|
| Slow  | Soil creep |
| Fast  | Landslides, bogbursts, mudflows |

## Soil creep

**Soil creep** is the downslope movement of soil under the influence of gravity. It is the slowest form of mass movement, occurring at speeds of less than 1 cm per year. It is very hard to notice soil creep unless you can see the effects on the landscape. Soil gathers in a series of steps called **terracettes**. Poles and fences bend in the direction of the soil movement. Walls crack and collapse. Tree trunks are curved.

### Question

Examine Fig 3.6. List three pieces of evidence that show soil creep has taken place.

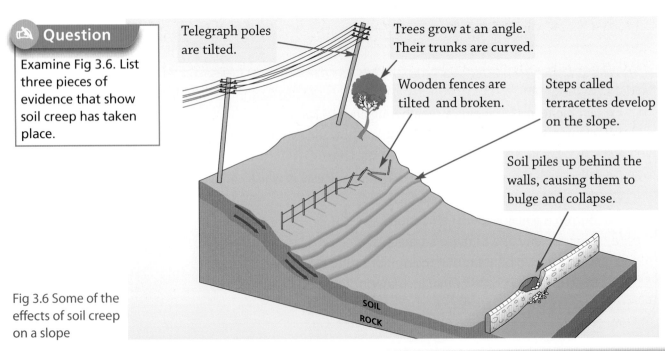

Telegraph poles are tilted.

Trees grow at an angle. Their trunks are curved.

Wooden fences are tilted and broken.

Steps called terracettes develop on the slope.

Soil piles up behind the walls, causing them to bulge and collapse.

SOIL
ROCK

Fig 3.6 Some of the effects of soil creep on a slope

# Landslides

A landslide is the very rapid movement of earth and rock (regolith) down a steep slope.

Landslides occur when a slope becomes unstable. They often occur after heavy rain. Slopes can become unstable when they are undercut by quarrying, road building or by coastal erosion.

In 2003, a landslide in Co. Mayo ripped up roads, destroyed farmland and damaged bridges and houses.

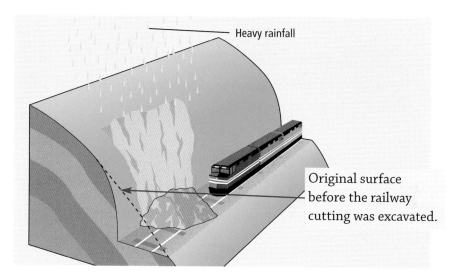

Heavy rainfall

Original surface before the railway cutting was excavated.

Fig 3.7 Landslides have blocked the DART line between Bray and Greystones on a number of occasions

> ## Question
> Examine Fig 3.7 and the photograph below. Describe how a landslide might occur.

# Mudflows

Mudflows are moving rivers of rock, soil and water. They are the fastest forms of mass movement. The debris can travel several miles from its starting point.

Mudflows are often triggered by heavy rainfall when the soil becomes saturated and turns into a river of mud.

Mudflows can also occur following a volcanic eruption on a snow-covered mountain.

## Bogburst

A bogburst is a form of mudflow. It occurs in upland areas when peat becomes saturated with water after heavy rainfall. The liquid peat is capable of blocking roads, demolishing trees and polluting rivers.

Earthquakes can trigger landslides. The tremors are capable of loosening and dislodging large quantities of rock and loose material

# Case Study

## Mudflow: The volcano of Nevado del Ruiz

The volcano of Nevado del Ruiz, a snow-capped mountain high in the Colombian Andes, erupted in 1984. On that night, the mountain was cloud-covered, so the eruption went unnoticed.

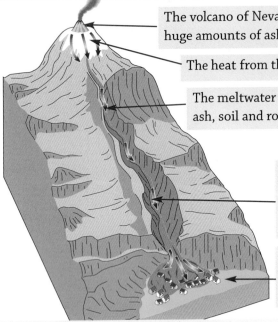

The volcano of Nevado del Ruiz erupted, throwing out huge amounts of ash and steam.

The heat from the eruption melted the snow on the volcano.

The meltwater cascaded down the mountainside, picking up ash, soil and rocks on its way.

Water + ash or soil = mudflow.
The mud was up to 20 metres deep in places. It raced through the valley at speeds of up to 80 km per hour. Heavy rains also increased the size of the mudflow.

The town of Armero was built on the plain at the foot of the mountain. It lay directly in the path of the mudflow which struck just before midnight.

Fig 3.8 From eruption to **lahar** to destruction

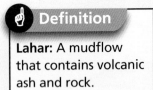

**Definition**

**Lahar:** A mudflow that contains volcanic ash and rock.

### Impact of the mudflow

It was the world's most deadly mudflow in the last century. More than 21,000 people were killed. The death toll was so high because it occurred when people were asleep. More than 5,000 homes were destroyed and a further 6,000 people were made homeless. The cost of the disaster was $1bn, about 20 per cent of Colombia's GNP.

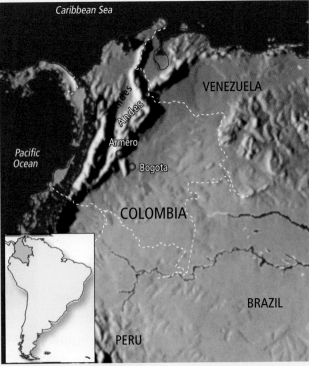

Fig 3.9 Nevada del Ruiz is a volcano high up in the Andes in South America

The town of Armero after its destruction by a mudflow

## SUMMARY

◎ Mass movement refers to the movement of loose material downslope under the influence of gravity.

◎ Soil creep is the slowest form of mass movement.

◎ The fast forms include landslides and mudflows.

◎ Fast forms of mass movement can cause serious damage to property and lead to loss of life.

## QUESTIONS

1 Explain how volcanic activity can cause a mudflow or how earthquakes can cause landslides. (JC)

2 (a) Describe how a landslide might occur, using the following headings:
   ◎ Gradient
   ◎ Water content
   ◎ Vegetation cover
   ◎ Human activity

 (b) Describe the effects of a landslide on an area. (JC)

3 (a) List two reasons why mudflows are so destructive.

 (b) Describe the effects of a mudflow on each of the following:
   ◎ Towns and villages in its path
   ◎ Farmland
   ◎ Roads and bridges

# 3.5 Rivers: Shapers of our Land

Most of the rain that falls on Earth is drained from the land to the sea by rivers. In doing so, the rivers shape the landscape, creating landforms along the way.

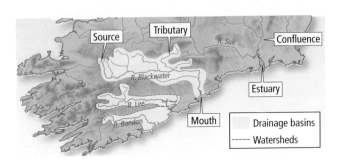

Fig 3.10 The features of a river

| Term | Definition |
|------|------------|
| **Source** | The point where a river begins |
| **Course** | The route taken by a river as it flows into the sea |
| **Tributary** | A small river or stream that joins up with a larger one |
| **Confluence** | The point at which a tributary joins the river |
| **Mouth** | The point where a river enters the sea |
| **Estuary** | The part of a river mouth that is tidal |
| **River basin** | The area of land that is drained by a river and its tributaries |
| **Watershed** | The high ground that separates one river basin from another |

The **gradient** (slope) and **valley shape** change as the river flows from its source towards its mouth. There are three stages in the course of a river:

- The upper or youthful stage
- The middle or mature stage
- The lower or old stage

**A: Youthful stage**
- The river has a steep gradient (slope).
- The valley has a narrow floor and steep sides.

**B: Mature stage**
- The river has a gentler gradient.
- The valley has a wider floor and the sides are more gently sloping.

**C: Old stage**
- The river has an almost flat gradient.
- The valley has a wide, flat floor and gentle sides.

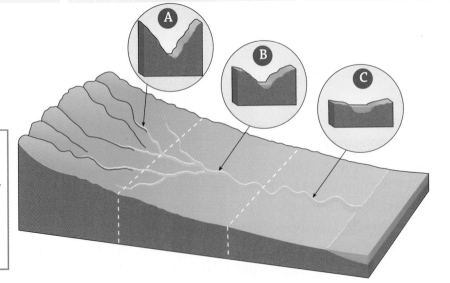

### Question

At which stage of the river is it likely to flow (a) fastest and (b) slowest? Give one reason to explain each answer.

Fig 3.11 The gradient and valley shape of a river change as it flows downstream

# The work of rivers

The work of rivers includes:

◎ **Erosion** (wearing away the landscape).
◎ Transportation (removing the material that it erodes – called its load).
◎ Deposition (laying down or dropping its load along the way or in the sea).

> **Definition**
>
> **Erosion:** The breaking down of rocks and the removal of the resulting particles by rivers, waves and ice.

## River erosion

The river erodes when:

◎ The force of the moving water breaks off material from the banks and bed of the river (**hydraulic action**).
◎ The material carried along by the river hits its banks and bed, wearing them away (**abrasion**).
◎ The material is worn down, smoothed and rounded as the particles bounce off each other (**attrition**).
◎ Acids in the water dissolve some rocks such as limestone (**solution**).

## Transportation

A river is also an agent of transport, carrying material (load) from upland areas to lowland areas. It does this in the following ways:

◎ The larger particles – pebbles and stones – are **rolled** along the bed of the river.
◎ The smaller, sand-sized particles are **bounced** along the bed of the river.
◎ The lightest particles – silt and clay – are carried along, **suspended** in the water.
◎ The dissolved load (such as limestone) is carried in **solution**.

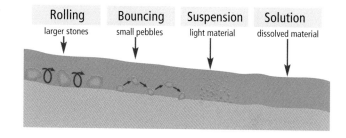

Fig 3.12 A river transports its load

## Deposition

The river drops or **deposits** its load when:

◎ It loses speed and has less energy.
◎ The river's volume decreases.
◎ It enters a flat or gently sloping plain.
◎ When it flows into a lake or sea.

> **Question**
>
> At which stages of the river do (a) most erosion and (b) most deposition occur? Give one reason to explain each answer.

# The youthful river

The **youthful (or young) river** has a small volume of water and flows down a steep gradient. It may turn into a raging torrent after heavy rainfall. It uses most of its energy to **erode** the landscape. As a result, a number of features (or **landforms**) are created.

## V-shaped valley

A **V-shaped valley** has a narrow floor and steep sides.

The river carries stones and rocks in its water. The force of the water and the grinding of rocks and stones cut down into the riverbed, deepening it by **vertical erosion**. Meanwhile, weathering breaks up rock and soil on the valley sides. They eventually collapse and the debris slides into the river. This gives the river its 'V' shape. The debris is eventually worn down and transported by the river. Examples are seen in the youthful stage of the rivers Moy, Lee, Liffey and Slaney.

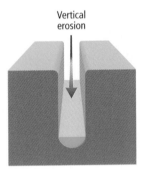 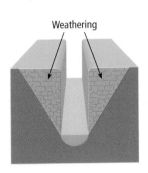 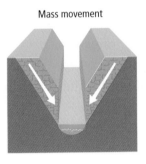 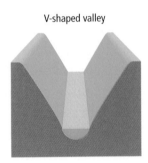

Fig 3.13 The formation of a V-shaped valley

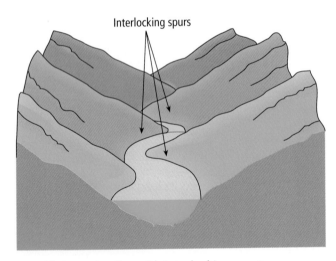

Fig 3.14 V-shaped valley with interlocking spurs

## Interlocking spurs

**Interlocking spurs** are a series of ridges that jut out from both sides of a young river valley and lock into one another like the teeth of a zip.

When the river meets hard or resistant rocks, it is unable to erode through them. Instead, it winds and bends to avoid them. At the same time, the river continues to erode downwards. In this way, the river develops a zigzag course. Examples are seen in the youthful stage of the rivers Moy, Lee, Liffey and Slaney.

## Waterfall

A **waterfall** is a feature where the river flows or falls over a vertical slope.

Waterfalls form when a layer of hard or resistant rock lies on top of a band of soft rock. Over thousands of years, the soft rock is eroded more quickly than the hard rock. Over time, the slope becomes steeper and a waterfall is formed.

As the water drops over the waterfall, it carries its load with it. This helps the waterfall to erode a deep hole called a **plunge pool**.

The falling water also cuts under the waterfall to form an overhang of hard rock. This eventually collapses. The process repeats itself and the waterfall retreats upstream. Examples include Aasleigh Falls (Mayo), Torc Waterfall (Killarney) and Glencar Falls (Sligo).

**Geofact**

Niagara Falls is one of the world's most famous waterfalls. It is only about 50 metres high but is over 1 km wide. It retreats upstream by about 1 metre per year.

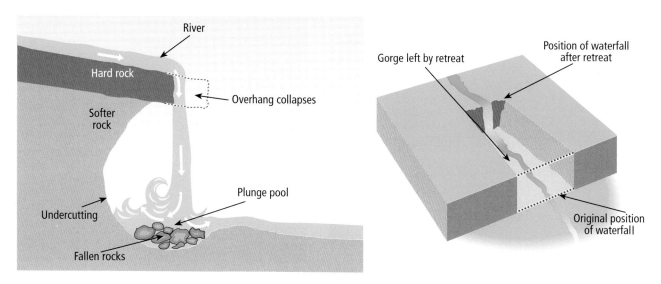

Fig 3.15 A waterall with a plunge pool. When the overhang collapses, the waterfall retreats upstream

## The mature river

The **mature river** has a greater volume of water, now that many tributaries have joined it. It flows over a gentler slope (gradient) and has a large load of material to transport. As a result, it flows more slowly than in the youthful stage.

## Landforms of a mature river

### Wider valley

The sides of the mature valley are less steep. The valley floor is wider and is almost flat.

At this stage, the river begins to swing from side to side, removing the interlocking spurs. As a result, the valley floor is widened. Weathering and mass movement continue, so the valley sides become less steep.

A wider valley may be seen in the mature stage of the rivers Nore, Boyne and Barrow.

 **Question**

Examine the photograph on page 40. On which bank of the river is erosion taking place? What evidence supports this?

### Meanders

**Meanders** are curves or bends that develop along the mature (and old) course of a river.

Meanders are formed by a combination of **erosion** and **deposition**. As the water flows around a slight bend, the water at the outer bank is deeper and flows more quickly. As a result, it has more power to erode the bank.

The water at the inner bank is shallower and flows more slowly. As a result, the river deposits some of its load there. Erosion and deposition continue and the meander becomes more prominent.

Meanders are found along the course of the rivers Shannon, Moy and Avoca.

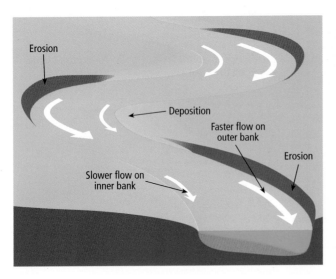

Fig 3.16 Erosion on the outer bank and deposition on the inner bank lead to the formation of meanders

Meander and floodplain on the River Severn

## Floodplain

**Definition**

**Alluvium:** Material transported and deposited by a river when it floods.

A **floodplain** is the level area of land on either side of a mature (or old) river. It has a covering of very fine clay called **alluvium**.

The river may become swollen and overflow its banks after a period of heavy rain. As it spreads over the level land on either side of the river, it quickly loses its energy and deposits its load of alluvium. Over many periods of flooding, a thick layer of alluvium builds up to form the floodplain.

Floodplains have developed along the rivers Shannon, Liffey, Boyne and Suir.

**Geofact**

Well-developed meanders and wide floodplains are found in the old stage of a river.

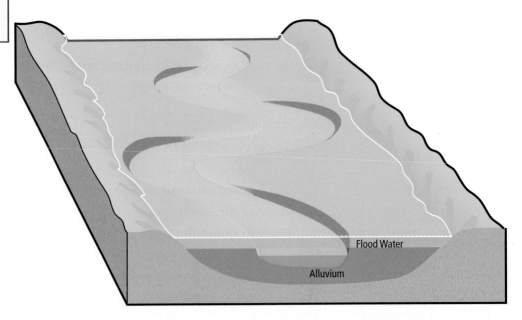

Flood Water

Alluvium

Fig 3.17 River in flood and depositing its load of alluvium to form a floodplain

# The old river

The **old river** transports a large load of alluvium as it flows over land that is almost level. As a result, it flows slowly and has little spare energy. If some of this energy is lost or if the load becomes too great, the load is deposited.

## Oxbow lake

An **oxbow lake** is a horseshoe-shaped lake that was once part of a river meander, but is now cut off from the river.

Erosion continues to take place on the outer bank of the river and the neck of land between the two meanders, as it gets narrower. During a flood, when the river has more energy, the neck of land is finally cut through. When this happens, a new straighter river channel is created.

The river has little energy at this stage and deposits some of its load of alluvium. Both ends of the meander are cut off from the river channel to form an **oxbow lake**.

Oxbow lakes can be seen at the old stage of the rivers Mississippi, Liffey and Moy.

> **Question**
>
> How is the meander loop cut off from the river to form an oxbow lake?

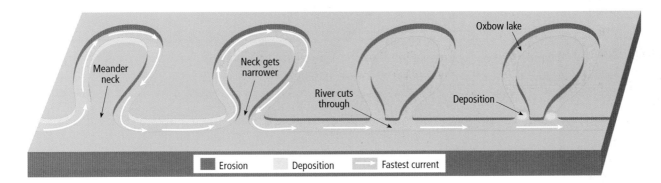

Fig 3.18 Stages in the formation of an oxbow lake

## Levees

**Levees** are raised banks of alluvium that are found along the banks of some rivers in their old stage.

When a river floods and begins to spread out over the floodplain, it quickly loses its energy and begins to deposit its load. Most of the load, especially its heavier particles, is deposited close to the riverbanks. The lighter particles are carried further. After many periods of flooding, these deposits build up to form levees.

Levees are found along the old stage of the rivers Mississippi, Moy and Liffey.

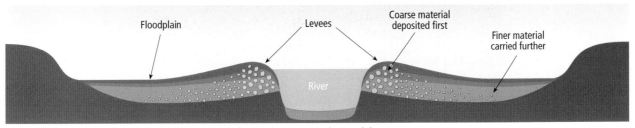

Fig 3.19 Levees are found on the banks of some rivers in their old stage

## Delta

A **delta** is a triangular or fan-shaped area of land found where a river flows into the sea (or a lake).

When a river flows into the sea, it loses its speed and deposits its load. If a river has a big load, the tides and currents may not be strong enough to carry it all out to sea. The mouth of the river becomes clogged and the river breaks up into smaller channels called distributaries. The deposits build up gradually and eventually rise above sea level to form a delta.

Deltas are found at the mouths of the rivers Nile, Po, Mississippi and Amazon.

**Geofact**

The delta is named after the Greek letter delta, which is written as Δ.

**Question**

Why do some rivers not have a delta at their mouths?

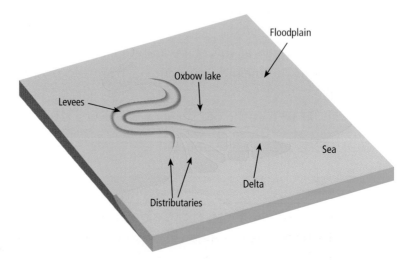

Fig 3.20 A delta forms at the mouth of a river

**Geofact**

The Amazon is the world's greatest river. It discharges almost 150 billion litres of water into the Atlantic Ocean every minute.

A river depositing its load to form a delta

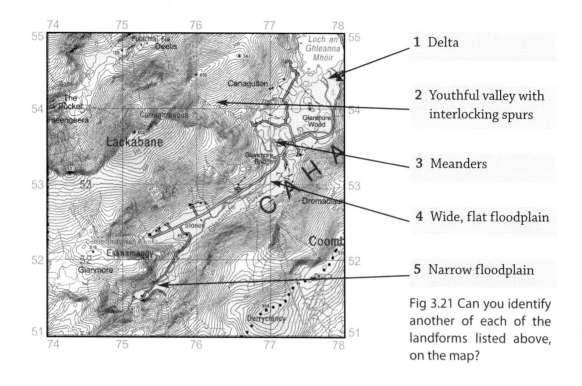

1 Delta

2 Youthful valley with interlocking spurs

3 Meanders

4 Wide, flat floodplain

5 Narrow floodplain

Fig 3.21 Can you identify another of each of the landforms listed above, on the map?

## SUMMARY

◎ Rivers pass through youthful, mature and old stages.

◎ Rivers shape the landscape by erosion, transportation and deposition.

◎ Rivers erode by the processes of hydraulic action, abrasion and attrition. Most erosion occurs in the youthful stage.

◎ Landforms formed by erosion include V-shaped valleys, interlocking spurs, waterfalls and meanders.

◎ The river transports its load by rolling it, bouncing it or carrying it in suspension.

◎ Features of deposition are found in the mature and old stages of the river.

◎ Landforms that result from deposition include meanders, floodplains, levees and deltas.

## QUESTIONS

1  (a) Explain three ways by which rivers erode the landscape.
   (b) At what stage of the river does most erosion occur? Give one reason for your answer.
2  (a) Name three features found on the course of a river that result from erosion.
   (b) Select one of the features you have named and, with the aid of a diagram, explain how it was formed. (JC)
3  (a) Name three features found along the lower course of a river.
   (b) Select one of the features you have named and, with the aid of a diagram, explain how it was formed. (JC)
4  (a) Draw a diagram of one feature of river erosion. Explain how this feature is formed.
   (b) Draw a diagram of one feature of river deposition. Explain how this feature is formed. (JC)

## 3.6 Rivers and People

Humans interrupt or interfere with the natural processes of rivers in a number of ways. Some are of benefit to people, while others can be harmful.

We will examine two ways in which humans work with rivers:

◎ Building artificial levees
◎ Building dams

## Case Study

## The Mississippi floods of 2001

The Mississippi and its tributaries drain nearly 40 per cent of the land surface of the USA. Following periods of heavy rainfall, excess water from a flood spread out and covered the river's floodplain, destroying crops and property.

Over time, people have interfered with the natural course of the river.

◎ Man-made levees, often up to 8 metres in height, have been built to prevent the river flooding the surrounding farmland and towns.
◎ Meanders have been cut off in order to straighten the river and make it suitable for shipping.

These human actions interfered with the natural processes of the river.

◎ The river was now confined between the man-made levees. Since the river could not overflow its banks, it deposited its load on its bed. This raised the level of the river further.
◎ The reaction of the authorities was to raise the levees even higher. Soon the river flowed above the level of the surrounding landscape.

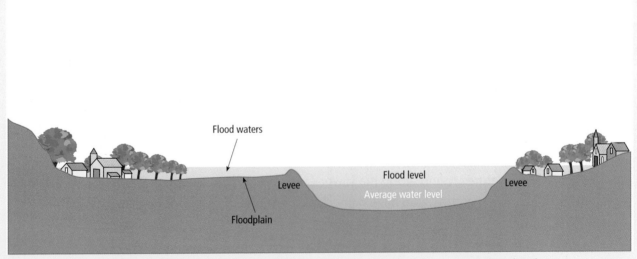

Fig 3.22 Man-made levees resulted in the river flowing above the level of the surrounding landscape

In the spring of 2001, the level of the river began to rise to dangerous levels. There were a number of reasons for this.

◎ Many areas received three times the normal amount of rainfall.
◎ The river and its tributaries were also fed by snow-melt from the mountains.

The river level rose to 7 metres above normal level and the levees were put under extreme pressure. They soon gave way in several places and the water swept across the floodplain. The worst flooding took place near the confluence of the Missouri and Mississippi rivers.

The effects of the flood were very serious.

◎ Nearly sixty people died.
◎ Houses, shops and factories were flooded.
◎ Crops were ruined and animals were drowned.
◎ Water supply and sewage systems were interrupted.
◎ Shipping ceased along the river for several months.

 **Question**

Why was the flooding at its worst near the confluence of the two rivers?

Water pouring out from a breach in the man-made levee of the Mississippi

 **Geofact**

The River Colorado in the USA does not reach the sea. Much of its water is removed for irrigation and water supply for urban areas. The rest is lost by evaporation.

**Geofact**

Clonmel has been hit by severe floods on four occasions in the last decade, with the water of the River Suir rising 2 metres above its normal level. Much of the flooding is blamed on development that has taken place on the floodplain.

# Case Study

## Dam building in Ireland

A **dam** is a barrier constructed across a river to control the flow or raise the level of water.

Dams have been built on a number of Irish rivers. Three dams have been built on the River Liffey. The largest of these is at Poulaphouca. The water trapped behind it has given rise to a reservoir called the Blessington Lakes.

### Advantages of the dam

◎ The ESB station, built into the dam, generates hydroelectricity (HEP). This is a clean source of renewable energy.

◎ The reservoir that built up behind the dam supplies over 400 million litres of water each day to Dublin and its environs.

◎ The reservoir is a major amenity for the people of Dublin. It offers a large variety of water-based leisure activities, including fishing, sailing and windsurfing.

### Disadvantages of the dam

◎ More than 2,000 hectares of farmland and bogland, as well as one village, were flooded as the level of the reservoir rose.

◎ More than 100 families had to evacuate their homes and be relocated.

◎ New roads and bridges had to be constructed to replace those that were flooded.

The HEP station built into the dam at Poulaphouca

Blessington Lakes offer water sport facilities

A section of the Three Gorges Dam on the Yangtze River in China. The dam is 2.4 km long. Its construction resulted in the drowning of 1,000 sq. km of land and the loss of 1,500 towns and villages. Almost 1.5 million people were forced to relocate.

## SUMMARY

◎ People interfere with river processes by building dams and man-made levees.
◎ People's interference with rivers has both positive and negative impacts.

## QUESTIONS

1  (a) Name one way in which people have interfered with the course of a river.
   (b) Describe one benefit that results from human interference.
   (c) Describe one harmful effect of this interference.
2  Rivers can cause problems for people. Describe one example of this. (JC)
3  Rivers are used by people for many different purposes. Describe one of these uses. (JC)
4  Describe one advantage and one disadvantage of building hydroelectric power (HEP) stations. (JC)
5  Describe the damage that serious flooding might cause to:
   (a) An urban area
   (b) A rural area

The syllabus requires that students study either the work of the sea or the work of ice.

# 3.7 The Sea: Builder and Destroyer

The coastline is constantly changing. This is due to the action of waves as they erode, transport and deposit material along the coastline.

## Waves

When wind blows over the smooth surface of the sea, it causes ripples in the water and these grow into waves. The size of the wave increases with the **strength of the wind** and the **length of sea (fetch)** over which it passes.

When waves reach shallow water, they **break** or tumble onto the shore. The frothy water that rushes onto the shore is called the **swash**. The water that runs back out from the wave is called the **backwash**.

Storm waves pounding the coast of the West of Ireland

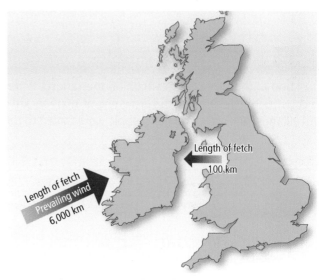

Fig 3.23 The western and southern coasts of Ireland are affected by strong winds. The winds may have been blowing for days as they crossed the Atlantic Ocean

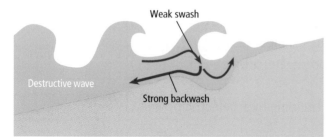

Fig 3.24a Destructive waves operate during stormy weather. They have a lot of energy and a strong backwash. As a result, these waves cause erosion

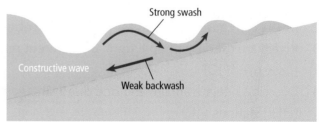

Fig 3.24b Constructive waves operate in calm weather. They have limited energy and most of it is used by the swash to transport and deposit material

# How waves erode

Waves **erode** by the following four methods (or processes).

## 1 Hydraulic action

Hydraulic action is the power of the water as it pounds against the coast. Hundreds of tons of water may hit the coast when the waves break.

## 2 Compressed air

Compressed air is trapped in cracks in the rock by the incoming waves. This increases the pressure on the rock. When the wave moves out, the air expands like an explosion. This can shatter the rock.

## 3 Abrasion

Abrasion occurs when the waves pick up rocks and stones and hurl them against the coast, breaking off even more rock.

## 4 Attrition

Attrition occurs when rocks and stones carried by the waves collide with and rub off one another. They are broken down and smoothed over time into sand-sized particles.

Rocks and stones are broken down and smoothed by attrition

 **Geofact**

Storm waves hit the coast with forces of up to 30 tons per square metre.

# Landforms of coastal erosion

## Cliffs

A **cliff** is a vertical or steep slope on the coast.

Destructive waves attack the coast and cut into the rock, eroding a notch. They do this by the processes listed above. When the notch becomes deeper, the overhanging rock above it will collapse under its own weight. As the processes of undercutting and collapse continue, the cliff slowly retreats and usually increases in height.

As the cliff retreats, a gently-sloping rock surface is created between the high water mark and the low water mark. This is called a **wave-cut platform**.

The best known cliffs in Ireland are the Cliffs of Moher in Co. Clare. The highest cliffs in the country are at Slieve League in Co. Donegal.

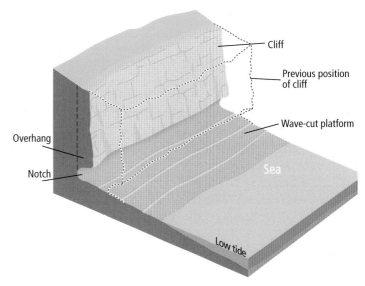

Fig 3.25 As the cliff retreats inland, a wave-cut platform is formed

### Geofact

Headlands are also known as 'points', e.g. Rosses Point.

### Question

What processes (methods) of erosion are active when bays and headlands are formed?

## Bays and headlands

A **bay** is a wide, curved opening into the coast. A **headland** is a neck of high land that juts out into the sea.

Bays and headlands are formed where there are different bands of rock along the coast. If the rock is soft, such as shale, it eroded very quickly and a **bay** is formed. If the rock is hard, such as sandstone, it is eroded much more slowly and stands out as a **headland**. If the headlands are big, they shelter the bay and a small beach may form in the bay.

Examples of bays include Dublin Bay and Galway Bay. Examples of headlands include Mizen Head and Malin Head.

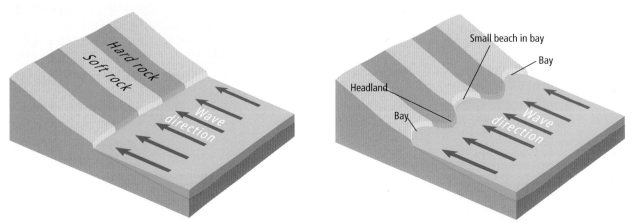

Fig 3.26 Headlands and bays are formed when soft rock is eroded more quickly than hard rock

### Sea cave

A **sea cave** is a tunnel or passage in the rock at the foot of a cliff. If the rock has a weak spot such as a crack, the waves will attack it by hydraulic action, compressed air and abrasion. The crack gets larger and develops into a small cave.

### Sea arch

A **sea arch** is a passage that runs right through a headland. If the cave is deepened and enlarged by erosion, it may cut through to the other side of the headland to form a sea arch. A sea arch may also form if two caves on opposite sides of a headland meet.

### Sea stack

A **sea stack** is a pillar of rock that is cut off from the headland or cliff. When the waves erode the base of the sea arch, they widen it. Eventually the roof is unable to support itself and it collapses, leaving the former tip of the headland cut off as a sea stack. If the base of the sea stack is eroded, it will collapse to leave a **stump** of rock that is visible at low tide.

Sea caves, sea arches and sea stacks can all be seen close together at Hook Head in Co. Wexford and at the Bridges of Ross in Co. Clare.

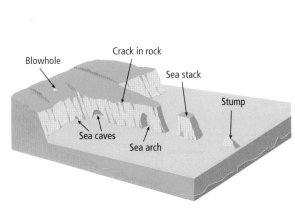

Fig 3.27 Features of erosion found on a headland

Landforms of coastal erosion. Identify the features of erosion marked A to E in the picture

## Blowhole

A **blowhole** is a passage that links the roof of a cave with the surface of the cliff top.

Air is trapped and compressed in the cave by powerful storm waves. This builds up pressure and helps to loosen and shatter the rock at the back of the cave. The rock eventually collapses, forming a blowhole. During stormy weather, sea spray may spurt out from the blowhole.

Some blowholes have very descriptive names such as 'The Two Pistols' and 'McSweeney's Gun' on the Co. Donegal coast.

## Transport by the sea

All the material that is transported by the waves is called the **load**. The load includes pebbles, sand and silt.

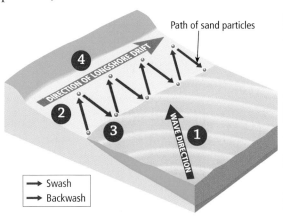

1 The waves approach the shore at an angle.

2 The swash from the breaking waves moves material up the shore and deposits some of it there. Because of the direction of the waves, the material is also moved along the shore.

3 The backwash brings some of the material straight out, following the slope of the beach.

4 These processes are repeated over time and the material is gradually moved along the shore in a zigzag fashion.

Fig 3.28 Waves move their load by swash, backwash and longshore drift

The waves transport the load in two types of movement:

1 Up the shore by the **swash** and back down the shore by the **backwash**.
2 Along the shore by **longshore drift**. This occurs when the waves approach the shore at an angle.

> **Question**
>
> Would longshore drift occur if the waves came straight in towards the shore? Explain your answer.

# Landforms of coastal deposition

The sea deposits most of its load in sheltered areas where the waves have less energy. This may occur in a bay or where the shore slopes very gently out to sea.

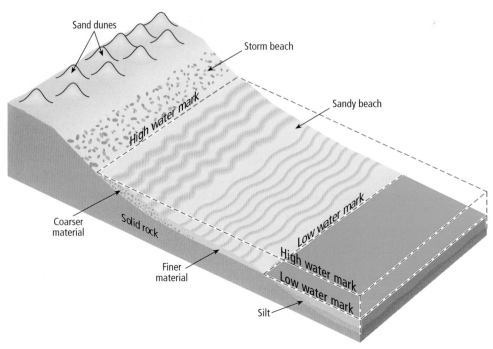

Fig 3.29 A beach is a build-up of material between low and high tide levels

A storm beach and a sandy beach

## Beach

A **beach** is a build-up of sand and shingle (small pebbles), deposited by waves between low and high tide levels.

When waves break, the swash carries its load of both coarse and fine material up the shore and deposits it. The backwash is weaker and it drags some of the finer material back towards the sea. As a result, finer beach materials are found at the lower beach, while coarser beach material is found at the upper beach.

In stormy weather, the swash is strong enough to be able to hurl large stones and rocks up past the normal high tide level, where they remain to form a **storm beach**.

Sandy beaches and storm beaches can be seen at Greystones (Co. Wicklow), Keel (Achill Island) and Tramore (Co. Waterford).

## Sand dunes

**Sand dunes** are hills of sand that pile up on the shore, just beyond the high tide level.

When winds blow in from the sea, they dry the sand on the beach, making it lighter. It then blows the dry sand inland until it is trapped by a wall or vegetation. The sand then piles up to form low hills or dunes.

**Marram grass** is sometimes planted on the dunes. It has deep roots that help bind the sand particles together, preventing them from blowing further inland and covering farmland and buildings.

Sand dunes are found at Inch (Co. Kerry), Rosslare (Co. Wexford) and Tramore (Co. Waterford).

Sand dunes at Ardara, Co. Donegal. Some of the protecting cover of marram grass has been removed by erosion

## Sand spit

A **sand spit** is a ridge of sand or shingle that is connected to the land at one end and extends into a bay.

A spit begins where there is a change in the direction of a coastline. Large amounts of material are moved along the coast by longshore drift. Where there is a break in the coastline, the longshore drift loses some of its energy and deposits material at a faster rate than it can be removed. These deposits gradually build up above the level of the water. As deposition continues, the spit extends further across the bay.

Sand spits stretch across the bays at Tramore (Co. Waterford), Inch (Co. Kerry) and Portmarnock (Dublin).

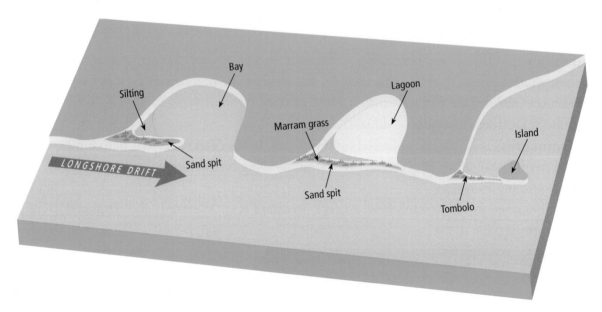

Fig 3.30 A sand spit grows across a bay. It may also lead to the formation of a lagoon or a tombolo

A sand spit growing across a bay in Kerry

 **Question**

Examine the photograph and identify three landforms of coastal deposition.

## Lagoon

A **lagoon** is an area of water that has been cut off from the sea by a bank of sand.

If a sand spit continues to grow, it eventually reaches the far side of the bay to form a sand bar. Some of the bay is now sealed off from the sea. A lake, called a **lagoon**, is formed. Over time the lagoon begins to fill with silt and mud from rivers that may flow into it.

Lagoons have formed at Our Lady's Island (Co. Wexford) and Lough Gill (Co. Kerry).

## Tombolo

A **tombolo** is a ridge of sand or shingle that leads from the mainland to a nearby island.

A tombolo is formed when a sand spit grows outwards from the mainland. Material is moved by longshore drift and is deposited in the sheltered waters between the mainland and the island.

Howth was once an island but it was then connected to the mainland by a tombolo. The suburb of Sutton is built on the tombolo.

A tombolo linking an island to the mainland

 **Question**

Examine the photograph and identify three coastal landforms.

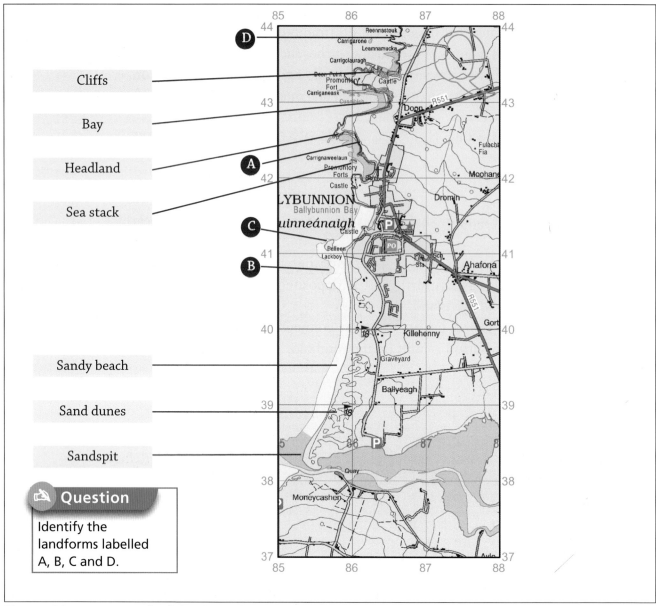

Cliffs

Bay

Headland

Sea stack

Sandy beach

Sand dunes

Sandspit

**Question**

Identify the landforms labelled A, B, C and D.

Fig 3.31 OS map extract of Ballybunion. What attractions does Ballybunion have for tourists?

**SUMMARY**

- ◎ Coastlines are constantly changing as a result of erosion, transportation and deposition by waves.
- ◎ Destructive waves erode by hydraulic action, compressed air, abrasion and attrition.
- ◎ Landforms of erosion include cliffs, bays, headlands, caves, arches and stacks.
- ◎ The sea transports its load along the coast by longshore drift.
- ◎ Constructive waves deposit their load in sheltered areas where they have less energy.
- ◎ Landforms of deposition include beaches, sand dunes, sand spits, lagoons and tombolos.

### QUESTIONS

1 Explain the following terms:
   (a) Swash
   (b) Backwash
   (c) Constructive wave
   (d) Destructive wave
   (e) Longshore drift

2 (a) Examine the diagram showing features of sea erosion. Name each of the landforms labelled A to D.
   (b) Describe two ways by which waves erode the coast.
   (c) Name two landforms that result from coastal erosion and give one Irish location where each may be found.
   (d) Select one of the landforms named above and, with the aid of a labelled diagram, explain how it was formed. (JC)

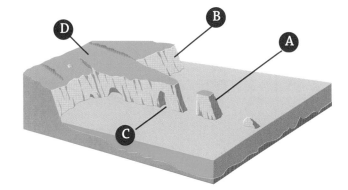

Fig 3.32

3 (a) Name two landforms that result from coastal deposition and give one Irish location where each may be found.
   (b) Select one of the landforms named above and, with the aid of a labelled diagram, explain how it was formed. (JC)

## 3.8 People and the Sea

The sea plays an important role in human activities.

◎ People attempt to protect themselves and their property from erosion.
◎ People look to the sea as the source of many economic activities.

## Coastal protection

### Sea walls

Concrete sea walls are built to protect coastal towns from attack by the sea. They have a curved top to deflect the waves back out to sea. However, the sea may also destroy these walls, especially during severe storms. Sea walls have been built at Bray, Tramore and Galway.

Large boulders help prevent coastal erosion

Groynes help to reduce longshore drift and build up beach deposits

### Boulders

Large boulders (or **rock armour**) are placed at the base of soft cliffs or in front of sand dunes. They help to prevent erosion because the power of the waves is reduced as they hit the boulders. Rock armour has been used to protect the coastline in Tramore and Youghal.

### Groynes

**Groynes** are low walls, often of wood, that are built at right angles to the coast. They reduce longshore drift by trapping sand. The sand accumulates and builds up the level of the beach. Groynes have been constructed at Youghal and Rosslare.

### Gabions

**Gabions** are wire cages that are filled with small stones placed in front of beaches or sand dunes. They break the power of the waves and help to slow down the rate of erosion. Gabions protect sections of beach at Rosslare, Tramore and Lahinch.

## The sea and economic activity

### Recreation

The sea and beaches provide a recreational area for a wide range of activities, including sailing, fishing and sunbathing. Irish resorts include Salthill, Kilkee, Ballybunion and Rosslare.

### Transport

Bulky goods are carried by ship over long distances. These include oil, ores and containers. Ferries also transport people, cars and trucks.

### Food supply

Fish caught by trawlers provide food. Fish farms, located in sheltered bays, rear a wide variety of fish in cages. Many of these fish are then processed onshore, creating more jobs.

# Case Study

## Rosslare

Rosslare has two distinct settlements that lie just five miles apart.

◎ **Rosslare Strand** has been a major holiday resort for nearly a century. It is situated along five miles of safe, sandy beaches with Blue Flag status. The area enjoys the most hours of sunshine in Ireland and has a wide range of attractions for tourists.

◎ **Rosslare Harbour** is the site of Rosslare-Europort, a major ferry terminal. It has roll-on roll-off (RORO) passenger and freight services to Britain and France.

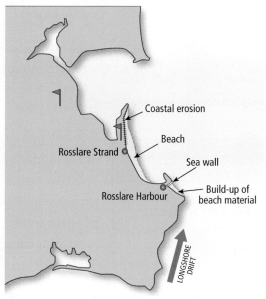

Fig 3.33 Human influences on coastal erosion and deposition in the Rosslare area

While both settlements make use of the sea and the coast, each has different needs. Sometimes, there is a conflict of interest in these needs.

A sea wall was built at Rosslare Harbour, protruding out into the bay. It was built to provide shelter for the ferry terminal and to prevent the harbour from silting up. The wall was extended over the years as the port expanded to become the thriving international transport hub it is today.

◎ The sea wall acted like a huge groyne, trapping sand that was being moved up along the coast by longshore drift. As a result, a new beach began to develop at the foot of cliffs near the harbour.

◎ The supply of sand to Rosslare Strand, to the north, was interrupted. Erosion of the beaches and sand dunes resulted. Parts of the golf course were flooded and some of the course was washed away.

◎ Expensive measures were taken to prevent further erosion. These include placing gabions, boulders and groynes along the coast.

◎ Beach nourishment was also undertaken. Sand was dredged from the seabed about 6 km offshore and placed on the beach to build it up.

### SUMMARY

◎ People attempt to reduce erosion with sea walls, boulders and gabions.
◎ People attempt to reduce longshore drift by building groynes.
◎ The sea is important to people in many ways, including tourism, transport and food supply.

### QUESTIONS

1 Describe two ways by which people attempt to reduce the destructive power of the sea.
2 Explain two ways by which coastal areas are important to people. (JC)
3 Describe two ways by which people can have a negative effect on a coastal area.
4 People see coastal areas in different ways, each according to their own needs. (JC)
   (a) List two priorities that each of the following people would require in a small coastal town: (i) trawler owner, (ii) hotel owner and (iii) environmentalist.
   (b) List two factors on which there would be disagreement between these people. (JC)

The syllabus requires that students study either the work of the sea or the work of ice.

# 3.9 Glaciation: The Work of Ice

About 2 million years ago, the climates of many countries became much colder. There was only one season – winter – and all precipitation took the form of snow.

Snow began to collect on colder upland areas. As more snow fell, the weight of the upper layers compressed the bottom layers into ice.

Great rivers of ice, called **glaciers**, moved down from the uplands under the influence of gravity. While some glaciers melted, others joined together to cover lowland areas with **ice sheets**. Another **Ice Age** had begun.

At one time, almost one-third of Earth's surface was covered with ice. Today, Antarctica and Greenland are still covered with ice sheets. Glaciers are found in the upper areas of high mountains such as the Alps and Himalayas.

**Definition**

**Ice Age:** A period when large parts of several continents were covered by ice sheets.

**Geofact**

The ice sheets of the Arctic and Antarctic are now under threat from climate change.

Glaciers in the Rocky Mountains

## How ice erodes the landscape

As the ice moves, it erodes the landscape by the processes of **plucking** and **abrasion**.

### Plucking

As the ice moves, there is some friction between it and the ground. This causes some melting at the base of the glacier. If the ice stops, this meltwater freezes again and sticks to the rock. As the glacier moves forward again, it pulls or plucks chunks of rock away with it.

### Abrasion

As the ice carries the plucked rocks away, they scrape or scratch the rock surface over which the glacier passes. This sandpaper effect wears down and smoothes the rock. The scratches are called **striae** and they tell us the direction in which the ice moved.

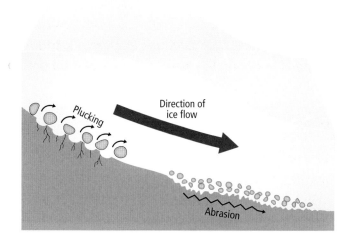

Fig 3.34 Glaciers erode by the processes of plucking and abrasion

# Landforms of glacial erosion

Most landforms of erosion are found in upland areas.

## Cirques

A **cirque** (or coom) is a large hollow that is found high up in a mountain. It has three steep sides and may contain a lake. It is the birthplace of a glacier.

A cirque was formed when snow collected in mountain hollows and was compressed to form ice. The ice **plucked** rocks from the side of the hollow, causing the walls to become steep. These rocks were then used as a tool to deepen the hollow by **abrasion**. The ice built up until it overflowed the hollow and began to flow downhill under its own weight. When the ice finally melted, a lake, called a **tarn**, was trapped in the hollow (cirque).

Coomshingaun, in the Comeragh Mountains, is the largest cirque in either Ireland or Britain. Other cirques include The Devil's Punchbowl near Killarney and Lough Nahanagan in Co. Wicklow.

## Arête

An **arête** is a narrow, steep-sided ridge.

When two cirques developed side-by-side or back-to-back, the ground between them was gradually eroded backwards until just a narrow ridge, called an **arête**, remained.

When three or more cirques formed around a mountain, only a steep-sided peak, with several arêtes, remained as a result of erosion. This is called a **pyramidal peak**.

Arêtes can be seen at Coomshingaun and the Devil's Punchbowl. The upper slopes of Carrauntoohill form a pyramidal peak.

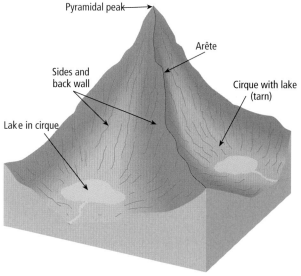

Fig 3.35 Cirques, arêtes and a pyramidal peak

**Question**

Link each of the following with a letter in the picture: arête, cirque, ribbon lake, pyramidal peak.

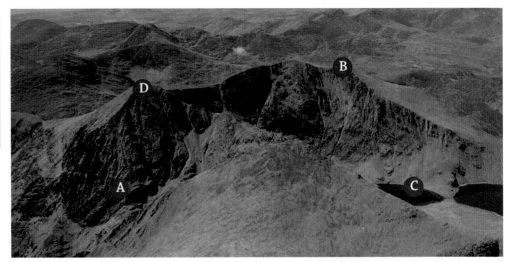

A mountain landscape shaped by glaciation.

### U-shaped valley

A glaciated or **U-shaped** valley has a wide, flat floor and steep sides.

When the glacier moved out of the cirque, it took the easiest route down the mountainside. This was usually through an existing river (V-shaped) valley. The glacier used its load to reshape the river valley by **plucking** and **abrasion**.

The glacier widened, deepened and straightened the V-shaped valley, changing it to a U-shaped valley. In doing this, it cut the heads off the interlocking spurs, leaving them as truncated spurs.

Glendalough (Co. Wicklow), Doo Lough Valley (Co. Mayo) and the Black Valley (Co. Kerry) are amongst the best examples of glaciated valleys in Ireland.

### Ribbon lake

A ribbon lake is a long, narrow lake that occupies the floor of a glaciated valley. If a river links a number of them, they are called **paternoster** (or rosary bead) lakes.

They were formed when the glacier scooped out hollows in the valley floor. This happened where the rock on the valley floor was badly shattered and the glacier was able to pluck and remove large amounts of rock. When the glacier melted, the hollows filled with water to form lakes.

Ribbon lakes occupy the floors of glaciated valleys at the Gap of Dunloe and Black Valley (Co. Kerry).

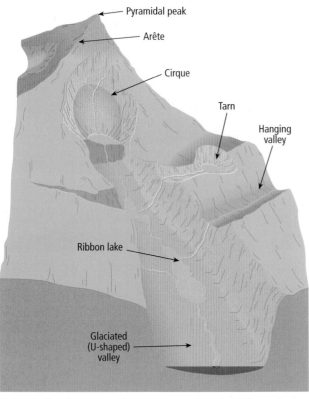

Fig 3.36 The features that are associated with a glaciated valley include hanging valleys and ribbon lakes

## Hanging valley

A **hanging valley** is a small tributary valley that hangs above the main glaciated valley.

This valley was occupied by a small glacier that was unable to erode as deeply as the main glacier did. When the ice melted, the floor of the tributary valley was left high above the floor of the main valley. When a stream leaves the hanging valley, it enters the main valley by means of a waterfall.

The Polanass Waterfall in Glendalough is located where a hanging valley meets the main valley.

## Fiords

**Fiords** are long, narrow inlets that are very deep and have steep sides.

Fiords were once glaciated valleys that ended as the glacier reached the coast. When the Ice Age ended, the glaciers melted. Enormous amounts of water were released. This caused sea levels to rise, drowning glaciated valleys near the coast.

Killary Harbour (Co. Mayo) is the best example of a fiord in Ireland.

Glaciated valley with other landforms of erosion. Can you identify a glaciated valley and truncated spurs? Which letters identify an arête, a ribbon lake and a hanging valley?

A fiord is a drowned glaciated valley

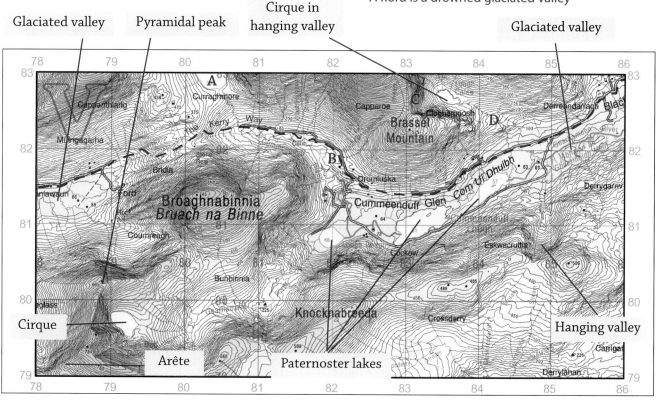

Fig 3.37 Landforms of glacial erosion. Examine the map and identify the glacial landforms lettered A, B, C and D

## How glaciers transport their load

Glaciers are able to carry large amounts of eroded material. The term **moraine** describes the load of loose rock that is transported and later deposited by the glacier.

1 **Lateral moraines** are carried along the side of the glacier. They consist of material that was broken off the upper slopes by freeze-thaw. The material then rolled down the valley side onto the glacier.

2 **Medial moraines** are ridges of material carried along the middle of the glacier. They were formed when two glaciers met and two of their lateral moraines joined together.

3 **Ground moraines** consist of material that was plucked from the valley floor. They are carried along beneath the glacier.

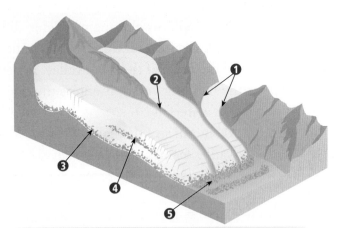

4 **Some material** is carried inside the glacier. It was on the surface of the glacier but fell through crevasses (cracks) in the glacier.

5 **Some material** is pushed ahead of the glacier as it advances.

Fig 3.38 How glaciers transport their load

## Landforms of glacial deposition

Landforms of deposition are usually found in lowland areas because it is here that the glacier melts and loses its energy, depositing its load.

### Boulder clay plains

Boulder clay plains are lowland areas that have been covered by a layer of boulder clay. This is a mixture of boulders, stones and clay.

As the ice sheet melted, it lost some of its energy and began to deposit its load on the lowland areas over which it passed.

All the fertile farming areas of Ireland, including the Golden Vale, have a covering of boulder clay.

Moraines on a glacier. Note that the snout of the glacier is beginning to melt

---

**Geofact**

As glaciers move, the ice can bend like plasticine if it is forced to change direction or gradient.

## Drumlins

**Drumlins** are oval-shaped hills that are made of boulder clay.

Drumlins were formed when the melting ice deposited boulder clay. As the remaining ice moved over the boulder clay, it smoothed and shaped it, forming small hills called drumlins. As a result, one end of a drumlin is steep, while the other end has a gentle slope. Drumlins occur in groups or swarms, forming a 'basket-of-eggs' landscape.

The largest drumlin region in Ireland stretches from Clew Bay (Co. Mayo) through to Strangford Lough (Co. Down).

## Erratics

**Erratics** are large boulders that are deposited by ice in an area where the rock type is different.

Moving ice is capable of transporting very large loads. When the ice begins to melt, it loses its energy and deposits its load. Erratics can tell us how far the ice travelled and the direction from which it came. Erratics made of Connemara marble have been found perched on limestone in the Burren.

> **Definition**
>
> **Drumlin:** The Irish word for narrow hill.

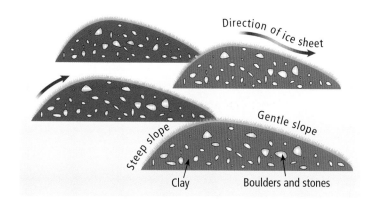

Fig 3.39 Drumlins are oval-shaped hills made of boulder clay

Melting ice deposited this erratic, made of granite, on a limestone surface

Some drumlins, such as those at Clew Bay, have been drowned following a rise in sea level

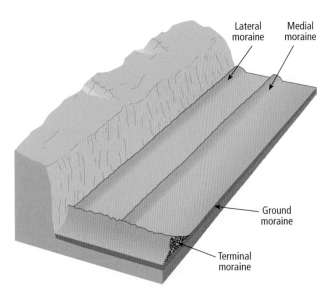

Lateral moraine

Medial moraine

Ground moraine

Terminal moraine

Fig 3.40 Moraines are named according to where they are deposited on the landscape

## Moraines

**Moraine** is the name given to the load of rock, stones and clay that was transported and later deposited on a valley floor by a glacier.

When the glacier began to melt, it deposited its load. There are four main types of moraine, named according to where they were deposited by the melting glacier (see Fig 3.38, page 64).

Moraines are found in most glaciated valleys, including Glendalough (Co. Wicklow). Lough Leane (Killarney) was dammed by a terminal moraine.

## Landforms of meltwater deposition

As glaciers began to melt at the end of the Ice Age, vast quantities of meltwater flowed away from them. It carried away the smaller particles (sand and gravel) and spread them over the landscape to form **eskers** and **outwash plains**.

### Eskers

**Eskers** are long, narrow ridges made of sand and gravel.

When the ice began to melt, huge rivers of meltwater flowed through tunnels beneath the ice, transporting sand and gravel. Some of this material was deposited on the beds of the meltwater streams if the load got too great. As the water escaped from the tunnels, it lost more of its energy and deposited the remainder of its load. The deposited material built up to form ridges called eskers.

The Esker Riada runs through the bogs of the Midlands, where it provides a dry foundation for the Dublin-Galway road.

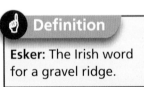

**Definition**

**Esker:** The Irish word for a gravel ridge.

Eskers winding their way across the landscape

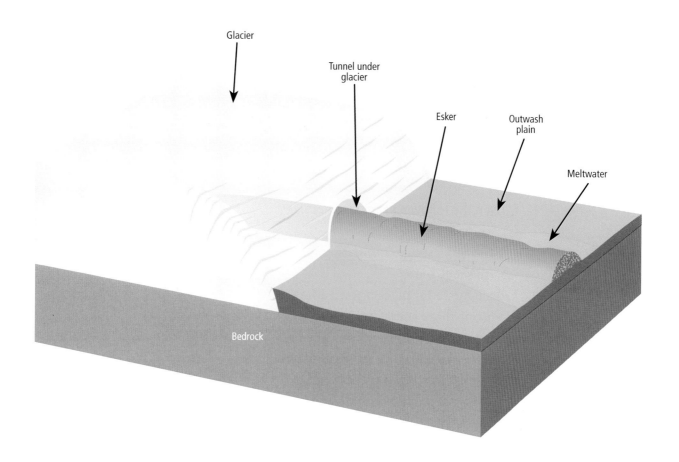

Fig 3.41 Eskers and outwash plains are formed from deposits of sand and gravel deposited by meltwater from glaciers

## Outwash plains

An **outwash plain** is a low, flat area made of sand and gravel deposits, which are found in front of a terminal moraine.

When the ice sheet began to melt, huge quantities of meltwater flowed away from its front. The meltwater carried large amounts of sand and gravel with it. As the meltwater spread out, it lost most of its energy. It then deposited most of its load, spreading it over the landscape.

The Curragh of Kildare is an outwash plain.

## SUMMARY

◎ Glaciers have shaped the landscape by erosion, transportation and deposition.

◎ Glaciers erode by the processes of plucking and abrasion.

◎ Most features of erosion are found in uplands and include cirques, glaciated valleys and ribbon lakes.

◎ Glaciers transport material from upland areas to lowland areas, mainly in the form of moraines.

◎ Most features of erosion are found in lowlands and include moraines, drumlins and eskers.

## QUESTIONS

1 Explain the following terms:
   (a) Ice Age
   (b) Glacier
   (c) Ice sheet

2 Explain the terms plucking and abrasion.

3 (a) Name three landforms that result from glacial erosion.
   (b) Select one of the landforms named above and, with the aid of a labelled diagram, explain how it was formed. (JC)

4 (a) Name three types of moraine.
   (b) Write one sentence to describe each type of moraine.

5 (a) Name three landforms that result from glacial deposition.
   (b) Select one of the landforms named above and, with the aid of a labelled diagram, explain how it was formed. (JC)

6 Identify the landform referred to in each of the following:
   (a) A narrow ridge between two cirques.
   (b) A lake on the floor of a glaciated valley.
   (c) A small, tributary glaciated valley.
   (d) The steep-walled hollow where the glacier was born.
   (e) Debris found at the side of a glacier or valley.
   (f) A ridge of sand and gravel deposited by meltwater.
   (g) Egg-shaped hills that occur in swarms.
   (h) A flat region covered by sand and gravel. (JC)

# 3.10 Glaciation and Human Activity

The effects of glaciation have had a huge influence on human activity. These influences have had both positive and negative effects.

County Wicklow is one region of Ireland that has been influenced by glaciation.

## The positive effects of glaciation

### Hydroelectricity

The steep slopes and water supply available in the cirque has been used to generate hydroelectricity. Lough Nahanagan is a tarn (cirque lake) that is used along with a man-made reservoir, as part of the ESB's Turlough Hill pumped storage scheme.

Fig 3.42 Some of the effects of glaciation in Co. Wicklow

1 Lough Nahanagan (see Fig 3.42 for location)

### Farming

Large areas of south Wicklow have a thick coating of boulder clay. This makes a very fertile soil, giving high yields.

2 A view of South Wicklow (see Fig 3.42 for location)

3 Glen of the Downs (see Fig 3.42 for location)

## Transport

Fast-flowing streams of meltwater from glaciers cut gaps through the mountains. The Bray-Arklow road follows one of these gaps through the Wicklow Mountains at the Glen of the Downs.

## Industry

Large glacial lakes provide water supply for urban areas. Blessington Lakes provide water for the greater Dublin area. The lakes are also used for recreation purposes, including boating and fishing.

4 Blessington Lakes (see Fig 3.42 for location)

5 The lakes of Glendalough (see Fig 3.42 for location)

There are enormous deposits of sand and gravel in the Blessington area. These are quarried for the building industry.

## Tourism

Glaciation has also created some wonderful scenery. This includes the valley occupied by two lakes at Glendalough. It is one of the most popular tourist attractions in the country.

# The negative effects of glaciation

## Environmental impact

Ice removed much of the soil cover from the higher parts of the Wicklow Mountains. These areas are suited only for forestry or sheep farming. A cover of blanket bog now covers much of the area.

The impact of glaciation on the Wicklow landscape may not yet be over. As the ice sheets of the Arctic and Antarctic melt, sea levels will rise. Low-lying coastal areas, such as those near Wicklow town, are at a risk of flooding.

6 The Wicklow Mountains (see Fig 3.42 for location)

7 Broad Lough near Wicklow town (see Fig 3.42 for location)

---

**SUMMARY**

◎ Glaciation has had positive and negative impacts on the landscape. Agriculture, transport and tourism have all benefited from the effects of glaciation.

---

**QUESTIONS**

1 Describe one way in which glaciated landscapes are of benefit to people. (JC)
2 Describe one way in which glaciated landscapes may have a negative impact on people.
3 Describe one way in which glaciated landscapes are attractive for:
   (a) Tourism
   (b) Agriculture

# THE RESTLESS ATMOSPHERE

## 4.1 The Atmosphere

A blanket of air, which we call the atmosphere, surrounds planet Earth. The atmosphere is made up of various gases, including nitrogen and oxygen.

### Why the atmosphere is important

Without the atmosphere, there would be no life on Earth.

◎ The atmosphere provides us with the air we breathe.
◎ It absorbs heat from the sun by day.
◎ It retains heat at night.
◎ It protects us from harmful rays from the sun.

### Geofact

The ozone layer is part of the atmosphere. It protects us from the sun's harmful ultraviolet (UV) rays.

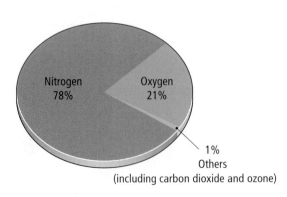

Fig 4.1 The main gases of the atmosphere

### Troposphere

The bottom layer of the atmosphere is called the **troposphere**. It is approximately 12 km thick. Over 75 per cent of Earth's gases are found in the troposphere. Almost all the water vapour and clouds are found here. As a result, the troposphere is the layer of the atmosphere in which **weather** forms.

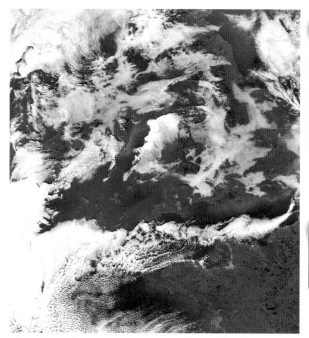

Clouds and water vapour are found in the lower layer of the atmosphere

📄 SUMMARY

◎ Earth is surrounded by the atmosphere.
◎ The gases of the atmosphere include nitrogen and oxygen.
◎ Life on Earth could not survive without the atmosphere.

❓ QUESTIONS

1   Name four gases that make up the atmosphere.
2   List two reasons why the atmosphere is important.

## 4.2 The Heat Machine

The sun is a huge mass of burning gases that give off solar energy. This energy provides heat and light to the atmosphere and to Earth's surface. It also influences our climate and weather.

 **Geofact**

Snow-covered areas and ice caps reflect much of the solar energy that reaches them.

About 25 per cent of solar energy is reflected by clouds and dust in the atmosphere, as well as by the ozone layer.

About 25 per cent of solar energy is absorbed by the atmosphere and the dust and water vapour that it contains.

Just half of the solar radiation gets through the atmosphere and reaches the surface of Earth, where it is absorbed by the land and oceans.

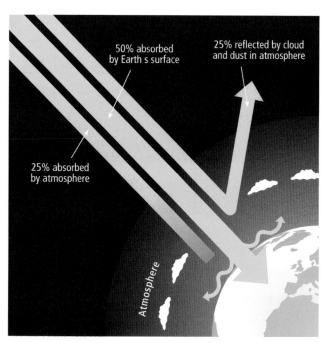

50% absorbed by Earth s surface

25% reflected by cloud and dust in atmosphere

25% absorbed by atmosphere

Atmosphere

Fig 4.2 Not all solar energy reaches the surface of Earth

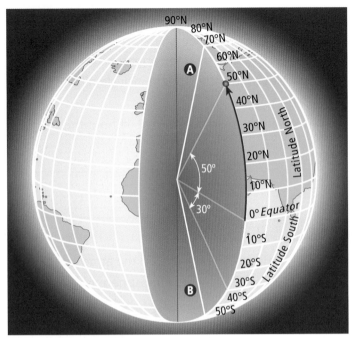

Fig 4.3 Latitude is the angular distance north or south of the equator. It is measured in degrees

## Uneven heating of Earth

The surface of Earth is unevenly heated by the incoming solar energy. The amount received at any place on Earth's surface depends on the latitude of that place and the tilt of Earth's axis.

## Latitude and heat

Places that are near to the equator (low latitudes) are much warmer than places that are near to the poles (high latitudes). This is due to:

◎ The angle of the sun in the sky
◎ The curve of Earth's surface
◎ The layer of atmosphere that surrounds Earth

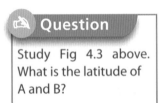 **Question**

Study Fig 4.3 above. What is the latitude of A and B?

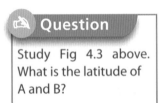 **Question**

Use your atlas to find the latitude between which Ireland lies.

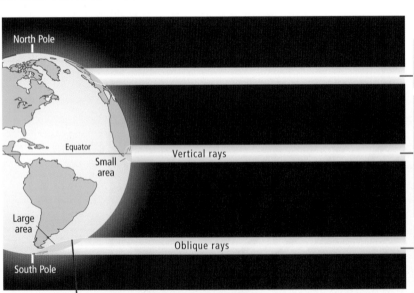

Ireland's position is in the mid-latitudes.

At or near the equator, the sun is at a high angle in the sky. It shines vertically downwards so its rays have less ground to cover. As a result, it warms up rapidly and becomes very hot.

Closer to the poles, the sun is at a lower angle in the sky. Its rays have to spread their heat over a larger area due to the curve of Earth's surface. As a result, these places get much less heat than at the equator.

The sun's rays pass through a greater depth of atmosphere near the poles, so they lose even more heat than at the equator.

Fig 4.4 Solar energy varies with latitude

## Seasons and the sun

Earth orbits the sun once every 365¼ days. During this orbit, different parts of Earth are tilted towards the sun at different times of the year. These parts receive more direct sunlight than those that are tilted away from the sun.

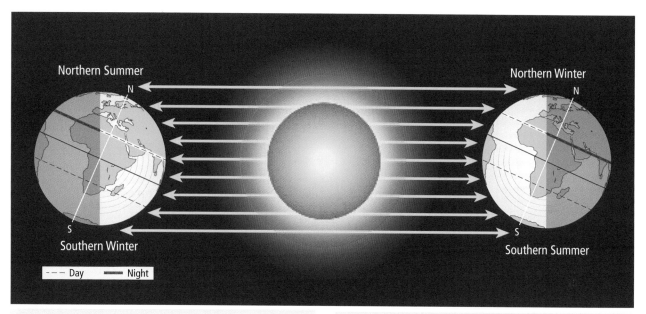

**Summer in the northern hemisphere**
◎ The northern hemisphere is tilted towards the sun.
◎ Days are long, while nights are short.
◎ It receives much more solar energy, so its weather is warmer.

**Winter in the northern hemisphere**
◎ The northern hemisphere is tilted away from the sun.
◎ Days are short, while nights are long.
◎ It receives much less solar energy, so its weather is colder.

Fig 4.5 In the northern hemisphere, summers are warmer than winters

### SUMMARY

◎ Earth receives energy (heat and light) from the sun.
◎ The sun's energy is distributed unevenly over Earth.
◎ The distribution is influenced by latitude and the tilt of Earth's axis.

### QUESTIONS

1 Describe what happens to the sun's energy as it reaches Earth's atmosphere.
2 Explain why equatorial areas receive more solar energy than areas nearer to the poles. (JC)
3 Use your atlas to find the latitudes between which Ireland lies.
4 What effect does the tilt of Earth's axis have on summer and winter in Ireland?

# 4.3 | Wind: The Atmosphere on the Move

The lower layer of the atmosphere is always in motion. This moving air is called wind. The faster the air moves, the more wind there is. And, as the winds move around the globe, they transfer heat.

## How winds form

Winds form because the sun heats different parts of Earth unequally. Places closer to the equator get much more heat than places near the poles (see Fig 4.4, page 74).

**Definition**

**Atmospheric pressure:**
The weight of the air pressing down on Earth's surface.

◎ When air is heated, it expands and becomes lighter. It rises and creates an area of low atmospheric pressure (LP).
◎ When air is cooled, it becomes heavier and descends. It presses down on Earth's surface and creates an area of high atmospheric pressure (HP).
◎ Air moves from high pressure areas to low pressure areas.

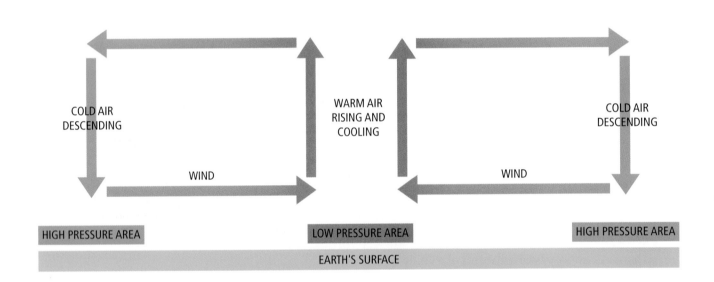

Fig 4.6 Warm air rises to create a low pressure area.
Cold air from a high pressure area moves in to take its place

## Some facts about winds
◎ Winds are named after the direction **from which they blow**.
◎ The wind that is most frequent in an area is called the **prevailing wind**.
◎ Winds that blow from the equator towards the poles are **warm winds**.
◎ Winds that blow from the poles towards the equator are **cold winds**.

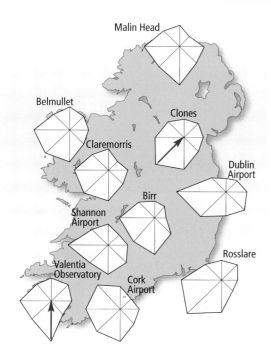

Fig 4.7 The prevailing wind direction at Valentia Observatory is southerly. The prevailing wind direction at Clones is south westerly

 **Question**

What is the direction of the prevailing wind at:
◎ Dublin Airport?
◎ Malin Head?
◎ Shannon Airport?
◎ Rosslare?

**Geofact**

If heat were not transferred around the globe, Ireland would be frozen over all year round.

# Global wind patterns

Winds blow from high pressure areas to low pressure areas (see Fig 4.6, page 76). These differences in pressure result in the development of a global wind pattern.

The same wind pattern develops in the southern hemisphere. The winds in the northern and southern hemispheres are divided into three wind belts. We will now examine how the wind belts of the northern hemisphere develop.

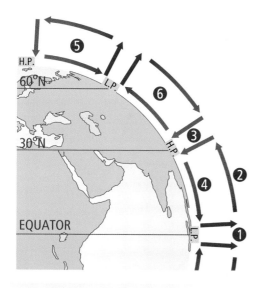

1 Near the equator, the air is heated and rises. As it does so, it creates a belt of low pressure (LP).

2 The warm air begins to move in a polar direction. As it does so, it begins to cool.

3 The air is now cooler and heavier. It begins to sink, producing an area of high pressure (HP) at about 30°N.

4 The cool air then blows along the surface of Earth, away from the area of high pressure, to replace the rising air at the equator. The first wind belt has now developed.

5 Cold polar air sinks to form an area of high pressure (HP). Winds begin to blow out from this high pressure area. At latitude 60°N they meet winds from the south in an area of low pressure (LP). The air rises up again to complete another wind belt.

6 A third wind belt develops between the high pressure (HP) belt at latitude 30°N and the low pressure belt at latitude 60°N.

Fig 4.8 The wind belts of the northern hemisphere

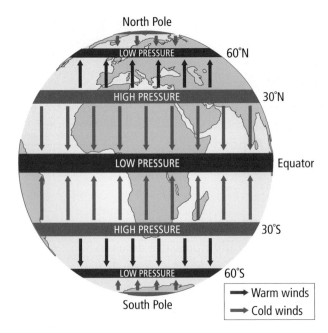

Fig 4.9 Global wind pattern if Earth did not spin on its axis

The differences in pressure tend to push winds in straight paths. Thus, if Earth did not spin on its axis, the global wind system would be like that shown in Fig 4.9. All the winds would blow straight from the north or straight from the south.

## Coriolis effect

Earth spins on its axis from west to east. This changes the direction of the winds, making them follow curved paths across Earth.

◎ Winds are deflected to the right of their direction in the northern hemisphere.
◎ Winds are deflected to the left of their direction in the southern hemisphere.

This is called the **Coriolis effect**.

 **Definition**

**Doldrums**: Areas close to the equator where the wind speeds are very low or where they have died out entirely.

**Geofact**

The **Trade Winds** were named as a result of their ability to quickly drive trading ships across the ocean.

**Questions**

1 Which wind belt affects Ireland most frequently?
2 What is the direction of these winds?
3 Are they warm or cold winds?

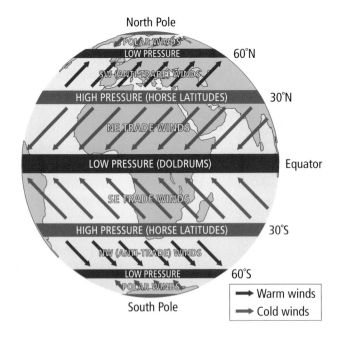

Fig 4.10 The Coriolis effect on wind direction

### 📄 SUMMARY

◎ Warm air is light and rises, creating an area of low pressure.
◎ Cold air is heavy and descends, creating an area of high pressure.
◎ Air moves from high pressure areas to low pressure areas, forming winds.
◎ Winds result from unequal heating of the atmosphere.
◎ A global pattern of winds has developed.
◎ The Coriolis effect refers to how winds are deflected as Earth spins on its axis.

### QUESTIONS

1  (a)  What is wind?
   (b)  What type of air conditions do you find at
       ◎ High pressure areas?
       ◎ Low pressure areas?
2  (a)  How are winds named?
   (b)  What is meant by the term 'prevailing wind'?
   (c)  What is the Coriolis effect? (JC)
3  With the aid of a labelled diagram, explain how any one
   wind belt developed. (JC)

## 4.4 | Ocean Currents

The water of the ocean surface moves in a regular pattern called surface ocean currents. These currents are like giant rivers that flow slowly through the oceans.

The movement of ocean currents results from:

◎ Unequal heating of the oceans
◎ The prevailing winds
◎ The rotation of Earth

## Unequal heating of the oceans

Solar heating causes the ocean water to heat and expand. Near the equator the water is about 8 cm higher than in middle latitudes. This causes a very slight slope and water wants to flow down the slope. By the time it reaches the poles, it is cold and heavy so it sinks.

## The prevailing wind

As the winds blow over the surface of the oceans, there is friction between the water and the wind. This causes some of the water to be dragged along, roughly following the global wind pattern.

## The rotation of Earth

As Earth rotates on its axis from west to east, it causes the currents of the northern hemisphere to move to the right. As a result, a clockwise pattern has developed in the currents of the North Atlantic.

## Impact of ocean currents

The most important impact of ocean currents is their effect on climate. They transfer heat around the globe.

Currents that flow from the equator towards higher latitudes bring warm water and are called **warm currents**. Currents that flow from the direction of the poles bring cold water and are called **cold currents**.

# Case Study

## Currents of the North Atlantic

The **Labrador Current** is a cold current that flows south from the Arctic Ocean. It passes the coasts of Greenland, Canada and the north-east USA.

It lowers the temperature of the oceans and, as a result, many ports in Canada and the USA are frozen over for several months of the year.

It also brings icebergs into the shipping lanes of the Atlantic. As it mingles with the Gulf Stream, it produces coastal fog.

The **North Atlantic Drift** is a warm current that begins as the Gulf Stream. It flows in a north-easterly direction from the Gulf of Mexico and passes by the coast of Western Europe.

The North Atlantic Drift raises the temperature of the waters off the coasts of Ireland, Scotland and Norway by about 8°C. This keeps them ice-free all year round, as well as creating a milder climate throughout the winter. It also brings rainfall

The **Canaries Current** is a cold current that flows in a southerly direction off the coast of West Africa.

When winds blow over this cold current, they lose their moisture. As a result, they bring very little rainfall to the Sahara, thus adding to the desert conditions.

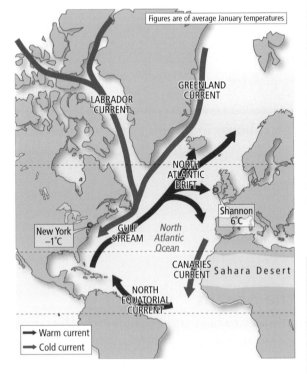

**Question**

Even though it is closer to the equator, New York has colder winters than Shannon. Give one reason why this is so.

Fig 4.11 Currents of the North Atlantic

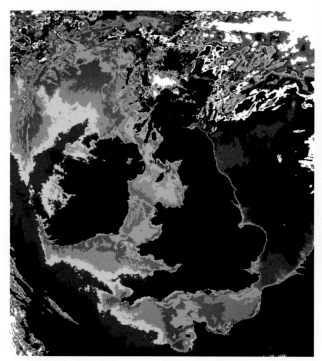

A satellite image showing sea temperatures around Ireland and Britain. The generally warmer (red and yellow) seas to the west are caused by the influence of the warm North Atlantic Drift

Icebergs after breaking off from the Arctic ice sheet

 **Geofact**

The Gulf Stream moves 100 billion litres of water per second.

## SUMMARY

◎ Ocean currents are caused by unequal heating of the oceans and the prevailing wind.

◎ Ocean currents form a circular pattern in the Atlantic, as a result of Earth spinning on its axis.

◎ Ocean currents influence the climate of the coastal areas they flow past.

## QUESTIONS

1 Explain how ocean currents develop. In your answer, refer to the unequal heating of Earth's surface and the prevailing winds.

2 Which current affects:
   (a) The west coast of Ireland?
   (b) The coast of north-east USA?

3 Select one current in the North Atlantic.
   (a) What type of current is it?
   (b) How does it influence the coast by which it passes?

## 4.5 | Air Masses and Weather Systems

Air masses are large bodies of air that have similar temperature, pressure and moisture throughout. They can be thousands of kilometres across.

Air masses move around and influence the weather that a country experiences.

◎ Maritime air masses tend to bring rain.
◎ Continental air masses tend to be dry.
◎ Polar air masses are cold.
◎ Tropical air masses are warm.

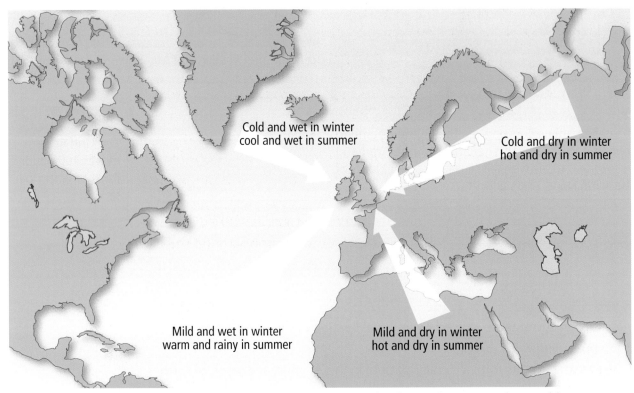

Cold and wet in winter
cool and wet in summer

Cold and dry in winter
hot and dry in summer

Mild and wet in winter
warm and rainy in summer

Mild and dry in winter
hot and dry in summer

Fig 4.12 Four main air masses meet around Ireland. As a result, Ireland's weather is very changeable. Polar maritime air is the most common type of air mass affecting Ireland

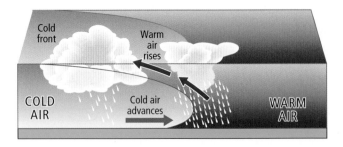

Fig 4.13 The development of a cold front

## Fronts

When two air masses meet, they do not mix very well because of the differences between them. The boundary area between two air masses is called a **front**. Fronts can be cold or warm.

### Cold front

◎ A **cold front** occurs when a cold air mass pushes in and replaces a warm air mass. Warm air mass is lighter so it is forced to rise rapidly into the atmosphere.

◎ As the warm air rises, it cools and condensation takes place. Masses of cloud develop. Heavy rain falls along the front.

## Warm front

◎ A **warm front** occurs when a warm air mass approaches a cold air mass. The warm air is lighter so it rises up over the cold air.

◎ As the warm air rises, it cools and condenses to form dark, rain-bearing clouds. Continuous rain soon follows.

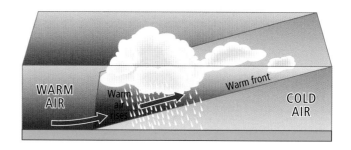

Fig 4.14 The development of a warm front

# Depressions (low pressure)

A depression is an area of **low pressure** and is associated with unsettled weather, including rain, cloud and wind.

In the case of Atlantic depressions, warm, moist tropical air from the south meets colder, drier polar air from the north. Due to these differences, the air masses do not mix easily. The warm air is lighter and is forced to rise, creating an area of low pressure at ground level.

At the same time, the air begins to move in an anticlockwise direction in the northern hemisphere. The cold front begins to wrap itself around the back of the warm air. The warm air is now trapped in a **warm sector**.

The cold front travels faster than the warm front and gradually begins to catch up with it. Eventually, it lifts the warm air completely off the ground. The ground air now consists entirely of cold air and the depression is over.

Ireland's weather is dominated by depressions that pass over the country for much of the year. The depressions develop in the mid-Atlantic and move eastwards towards Ireland.

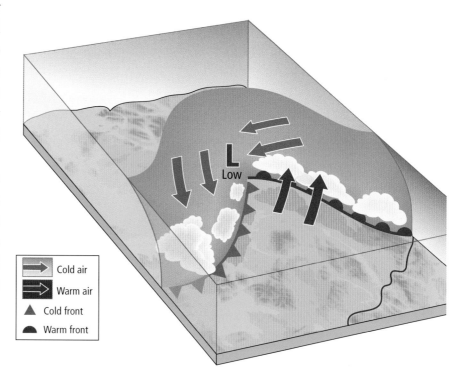

Fig 4.15 The development of a frontal depression

# Weather in a depression

Every depression is different and hence the weather associated with each depression is also unique. However, the weather associated with the passage of depression does follow some general trends.

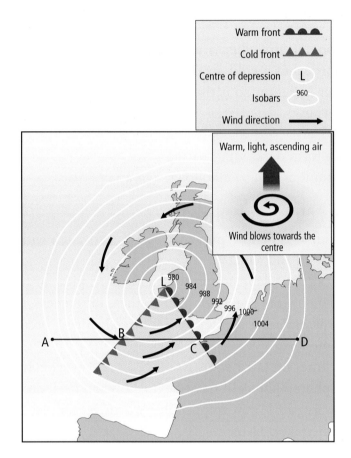

Warm front ●●●
Cold front ▲▲▲
Centre of depression  L
Isobars  960
Wind direction  ➡

Warm, light, ascending air

Wind blows towards the centre

L 980  984  988  992  996  1000  1004

A  B  C  D

Fig 4.16 Weather map showing a depression

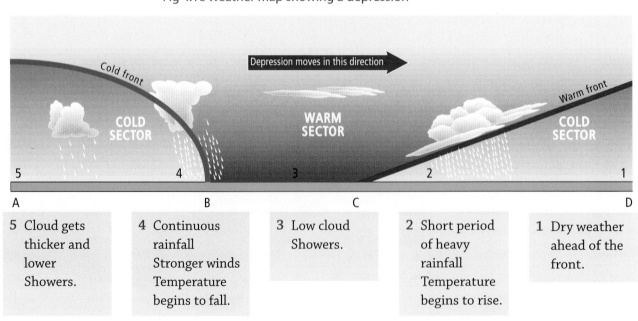

Cold front

Depression moves in this direction

COLD SECTOR

WARM SECTOR

Warm front

COLD SECTOR

5  4  3  2  1

A  B  C  D

5  Cloud gets thicker and lower Showers.

4  Continuous rainfall Stronger winds Temperature begins to fall.

3  Low cloud Showers.

2  Short period of heavy rainfall Temperature begins to rise.

1  Dry weather ahead of the front.

Fig 4.17 Profile across a depression (between A and D in Fig 4.16 above), showing the general weather conditions that occur

# Anticyclones (high pressure)

An anticyclone is an air mass with **high pressure** at the centre. It is also known as a **high**. Since an anticyclone consists of a single air mass, there are no fronts.

In the centre, the air is descending slowly on to Earth's surface, where it is compressed to form an area of high pressure.

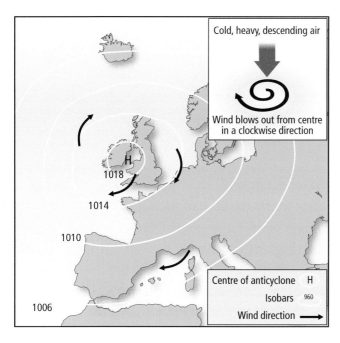

Fig 4.18 Weather map showing an anticyclone

| Questions |
| --- |
| 1 What is the atmospheric pressure along the west coast of Ireland? |
| 2 Is the pressure at H likely to be 1016 or 1020? Explain why. |

## Weather in an anticyclone

Anticyclones bring **settled weather** for days, sometimes even weeks.

◎ The weather conditions include **clear**, **cloudless skies**. This is because the descending air is warmed and condensation is unlikely to occur.

◎ Winds, if any, are very light and blow in a **clockwise** direction in the northern hemisphere.

◎ In summer, the clear skies bring **hot**, **sunny weather**.

◎ In winter, the clear skies bring low temperatures. The lack of cloud cover causes nights to be **cold** and **frosty**.

A satellite image of Europe. Land appears green, water is blue and clouds are white and pink. Swirling clouds mark the position of a depression, an area of low atmospheric pressure, in the Atlantic Ocean at the upper left. A cloudless area of high pressure lies over Ireland and Britain

## SUMMARY

- Air masses are large bodies of air that have similar temperature, pressure and moisture throughout.
- Air masses meet at fronts, which can be warm or cold.
- Depressions have low pressure and ascending air at the centre and bring wet, cloudy and windy conditions.
- Ireland's weather is dominated by depressions that move on from the Atlantic.
- Anticyclones have high pressure and descending air at the centre and bring settled weather with clear skies.

## QUESTIONS

1. (a) What is an air mass?
   (b) Name two air masses that affect Ireland.
   (c) Describe the weather associated with each of them. (JC)
2. (a) What is a front?
   (b) With the aid of a labelled diagram, describe how a warm front or a cold front develops. (JC)
3. (a) Draw a weather map to show a depression. On it show and label the warm front, the cold front, the centre of the depression (L) and the direction of the winds.
   (b) Describe the weather that is associated with a depression.
4. (a) What is an anticyclone?
   (b) Describe the weather conditions associated with an anticyclone. (JC)

## 4.6 | Water in the Atmosphere

Water is a renewable, natural resource, vital for the survival of life on the planet. Less than 3 per cent of Earth's water is fresh water; the remainder is salt water.

### The water cycle

The water cycle is Earth's way of recycling water. It describes the journey water takes as it constantly passes between the atmosphere, the oceans and the land.

**Geofact**

If water were not a renewable resource, Earth would run out of fresh water in a month.

### Clouds

When water vapour in the atmosphere condenses, it forms tiny water droplets or ice crystals. These are so small and light that they can float in the air. When billions of them come together they become a visible **cloud**.

1 **Evaporation**: Energy from the sun changes water from a liquid to a gas (water vapour) in the atmosphere.

2 **Condensation**: As the water vapour rises, it cools and condenses into tiny water droplets to form clouds.

3 **Precipitation**: Water is released from clouds and returns to Earth in the form of rain, sleet, snow or hail.

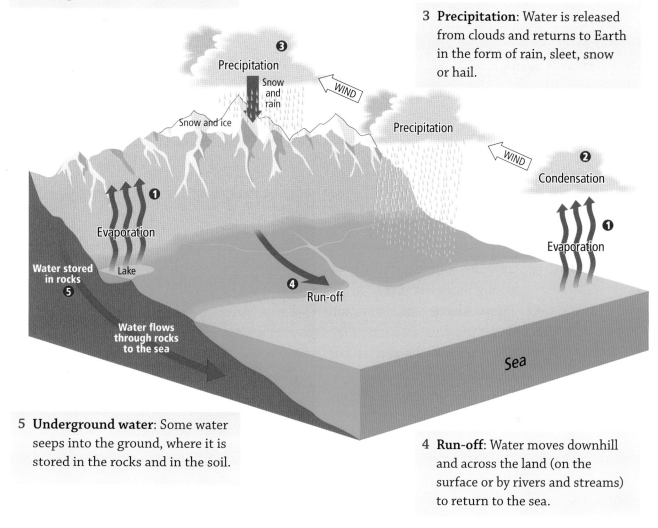

5 **Underground water**: Some water seeps into the ground, where it is stored in the rocks and in the soil.

4 **Run-off**: Water moves downhill and across the land (on the surface or by rivers and streams) to return to the sea.

Fig 4.19 The water cycle is also called the hydrologic cycle

Clouds are grouped according to their **shape** and the **height** at which they occur. The darker the colour of the cloud, the more likely it is that precipitation is about to occur. The main cloud types are:

◎ Cirrus
◎ Cumulus
◎ Stratus

### Cirrus

The word **cirrus** comes from the Latin word for curl.

◎ Cirrus clouds are wispy like a lock of hair.
◎ They occur at high altitude.
◎ They are made of ice crystals.
◎ They are associated with fair weather.

Cirrus clouds

### Cumulus

The word **cumulus** comes from the Latin word for heap.

◎ Cumulus clouds are fluffy or woolly in appearance.
◎ They occur at medium altitude.
◎ They are also known as fair weather clouds.
◎ They can bring rain if they darken in colour.

Cumulus clouds

### Stratus

The word **stratus** comes from the Latin word for layer.

◎ Stratus clouds occur at low altitude.
◎ They form thin layers and can block out the sky.
◎ If they reach ground level, they are called fog.
◎ They bring continual drizzle and light rain.

Stratus clouds

# Precipitation

When cloud particles become too heavy to remain suspended in the air, they fall to the earth as precipitation. Precipitation occurs in a variety of forms: rain, hail, sleet or snow.

**Rainfall** is by far the most common form of precipitation. There are three types of rainfall:

◎ Relief rainfall
◎ Cyclonic (frontal) rainfall
◎ Convectional rainfall

## Relief rainfall

Relief rainfall occurs when an air mass is forced to rise over a **mountain range**.

◎ Warm, **moist air** blows in from over the sea.
◎ If it meets a coastal **mountain range**, it is forced to rise.
◎ This causes the air to **cool** and **condensation** occurs.
◎ Clouds form and eventually rain falls on the windward side of the mountain.
◎ The air that descends on the sheltered (leeward) side of the mountain has very little moisture left. Condensation ceases and a **rain shadow** is created.

**Definition**

**Rain shadow:** A dry area on the sheltered (leeward) side of a mountain.

Ireland receives relief rainfall throughout the year; most of it falls in the mountainous areas of the west coast.

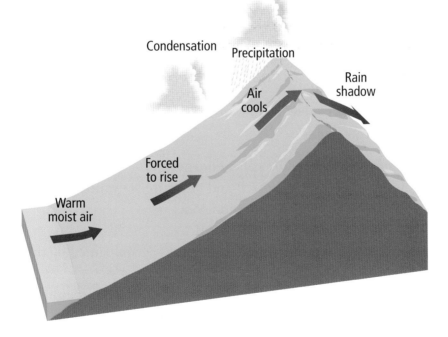

Fig 4.20 Relief rainfall

## Cyclonic (frontal) rainfall

Cyclonic (frontal) rainfall occurs when an air mass is forced to rise at a front.

◎ Cold, polar air and warm, moist tropical air masses meet at a front.
◎ The lighter, warmer air mass rides up over the cold, heavy air mass.
◎ This causes the warm air to **cool** and **condensation** occurs.
◎ Clouds form and eventually rain falls.
◎ Rain is light at first, but eventually becomes heavier.

Fronts develop over the Atlantic and, when they move in, they bring changeable weather to Ireland. Rainfall is most frequent during winter.

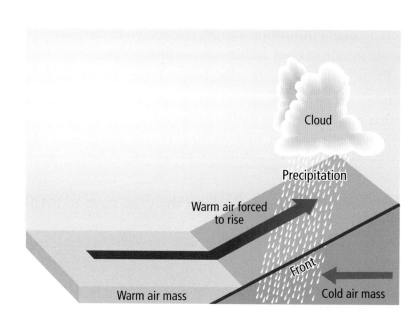

**Geofact**

The West of Ireland receives over 2,000 mm of rainfall annually, while parts of the East and Midlands receive as little as 800 mm.

Fig 4.21 Cyclonic (frontal) rainfall

## Convectional rainfall

Convectional rain occurs when the surface layer of the atmosphere is heated causing moisture-laden air to rise.

◎ Earth's surface is heated by **solar energy**.
◎ The land warms the air above it and moisture is **evaporated**.
◎ This warm, moist air then rises and cools.
◎ Condensation occurs and clouds form.
◎ Heavy showers follow. They are sometimes accompanied by thunder.

Convectional rainfall occurs each afternoon in equatorial regions. It also occurs in Ireland, but only in summer during hot and sunny days.

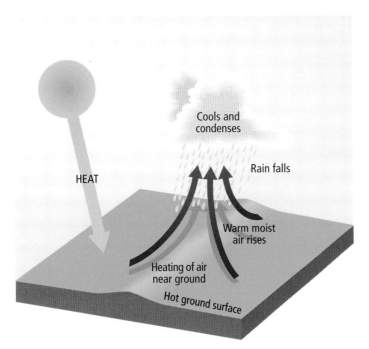

Fig 4.22 Convectional rainfall

---

### SUMMARY

◉ The water cycle is the continual movement of water between the atmosphere, the land and the oceans.

◉ The processes involved are evaporation, condensation and precipitation.

◉ Clouds consist of tiny water droplets or ice crystals.

◉ Precipitation occurs when moisture-laden air rises and cools, leading to condensation.

◉ Rainfall is the main form of precipitation. The three types of rainfall are relief, cyclonic and convectional.

---

### QUESTIONS

1  Explain each of the following terms:
   ◉ Evaporation
   ◉ Condensation
   ◉ Precipitation
2  Briefly describe, with the aid of a simple labelled diagram, how the water cycle works. (JC)
3  (a) Name the three types of cloud.
   (b) Select one cloud type and briefly describe it.
4  (a) What is precipitation?
   (b) Name three types of rainfall.
   (c) With the aid of a labelled diagram, describe how one type of rainfall occurs.  (JC)

# 4.7 Weather

Weather is the word used to describe the state of the atmosphere at any particular time and place. Weather conditions can change every day and can vary over short distances.

## Elements of weather

The study of weather is called **meteorology**. It involves measuring the elements of weather at least once a day. These include:

◎ Temperature
◎ Atmospheric pressure
◎ Humidity
◎ Wind speed and direction
◎ Precipitation
◎ Sunshine

## Weather forecasts

A weather forecast predicts what the weather will be for a particular place. **Meteorologists** prepare weather forecasts. They study information that is collected from a number of sources. These sources include weather stations, satellites, radar stations, gas rigs and shipping.

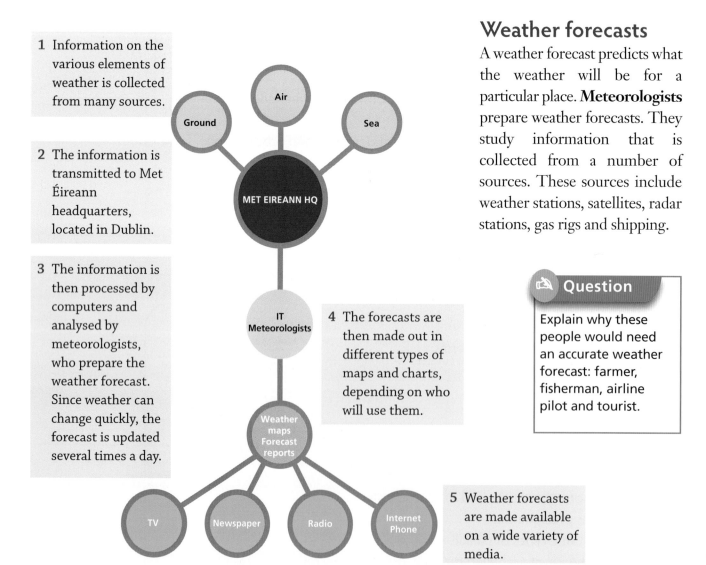

1 Information on the various elements of weather is collected from many sources.

2 The information is transmitted to Met Éireann headquarters, located in Dublin.

3 The information is then processed by computers and analysed by meteorologists, who prepare the weather forecast. Since weather can change quickly, the forecast is updated several times a day.

4 The forecasts are then made out in different types of maps and charts, depending on who will use them.

5 Weather forecasts are made available on a wide variety of media.

**Ground** **Air** **Sea**

**MET EIREANN HQ**

**IT Meteorologists**

**Weather maps Forecast reports**

**TV** **Newspaper** **Radio** **Internet Phone**

Fig 4.23 Preparing a weather forecast

### Question

Explain why these people would need an accurate weather forecast: farmer, fisherman, airline pilot and tourist.

## The importance of weather forecasts

We are all interested in the weather forecast for our local area. The upcoming weather will influence what we wear and the activities that we undertake. It may even affect our mood.

Some occupations require very accurate weather forecasts, e.g. farming, fishing, tourism, air traffic and sport.

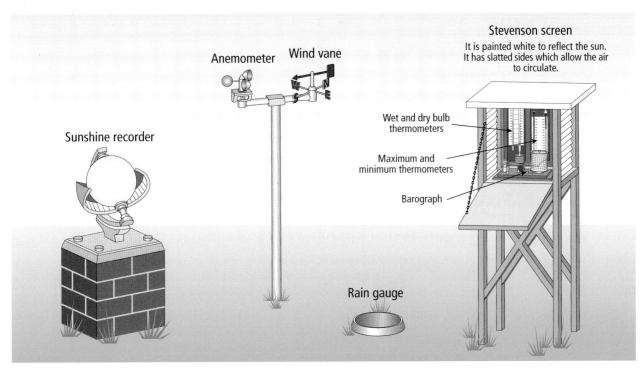

Fig 4.24 A weather station

## The weather station

The land-based instruments and equipment used to measure the elements of the weather are kept in a weather station. The map in Fig 4.7, page 77, gives the location of many of the weather stations used by Met Éireann. Readings are taken hourly at these stations.

## Measuring temperature

Temperature is the degree of hotness or coldness of the atmosphere.

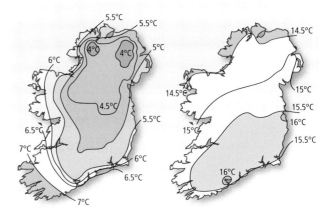

Fig 4.25 Isotherms showing average air temperatures for Ireland in January (left) and in July (right)

◎ Temperature is measured with a **thermometer**.

◎ The unit of measurement of temperature is degrees **Celsius/Centigrade** (°C).

◎ **Isotherms** are lines on a weather map that join places of equal temperature.

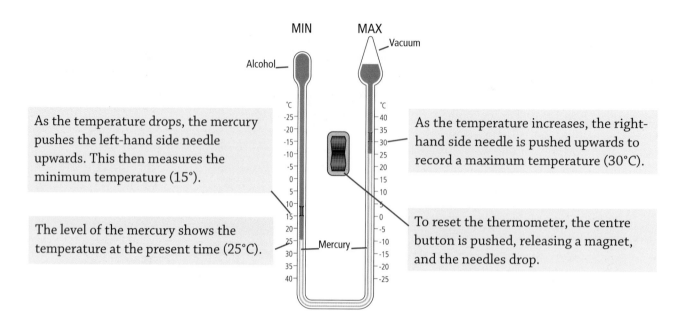

As the temperature drops, the mercury pushes the left-hand side needle upwards. This then measures the minimum temperature (15°).

As the temperature increases, the right-hand side needle is pushed upwards to record a maximum temperature (30°C).

The level of the mercury shows the temperature at the present time (25°C).

To reset the thermometer, the centre button is pushed, releasing a magnet, and the needles drop.

Fig 4.26 Maximum-minimum thermometer

## Calculating mean annual temperature and temperature range

| Temperature table | | | | | | | | | | | | |
|---|---|---|---|---|---|---|---|---|---|---|---|---|
| **Month** | Jan | Feb | Mar | Apr | May | Jun | Jul | Aug | Sept | Oct | Nov | Dec |
| **Mean monthly temperature (°C)** | 10 | 13 | 16 | 18 | 20 | 23 | 25 | 27 | 22 | 16 | 14 | 12 |

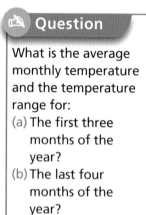

**Question**

What is the average monthly temperature and the temperature range for:
(a) The first three months of the year?
(b) The last four months of the year?

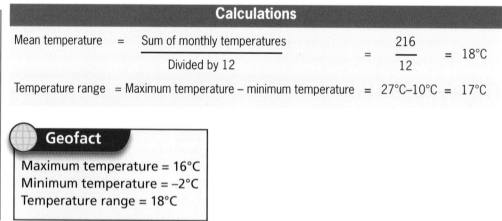

**Calculations**

Mean temperature $=\dfrac{\text{Sum of monthly temperatures}}{\text{Divided by 12}} = \dfrac{216}{12} = 18°C$

Temperature range = Maximum temperature – minimum temperature = 27°C–10°C = 17°C

**Geofact**

Maximum temperature = 16°C
Minimum temperature = –2°C
Temperature range = 18°C

## Measuring atmospheric pressure

Atmospheric pressure is the weight of the atmosphere as it presses down on Earth.

◎ Atmospheric pressure is measured with a **barometer**. A **barograph** connects a barometer to a chart to record the atmospheric pressure.

◎ The unit of measurement of atmospheric pressure is **millibars** (mb) or **hectopascals**.

◎ **Isobars** are lines on a weather map that join places of equal pressure.

4 The end of the pointer has an inked nib that records the pressure on the graph paper.

1 The corrugated drum is partially emptied of air. When the pressure of the air increases, the drum contracts slightly. When the pressure of the air falls, the drum expands slightly.

3 A drum slowly rotates, with a page of graph paper attached.

2 The movement of the drum is transferred to a pointer by a series of levers.

Atmospheric pressure is measured and recorded on a barograph

## Measuring relative humidity

Relative humidity refers to the amount of water vapour in the air compared to the amount it would contain if it were saturated.

◎ Relative humidity is measured with a **hygrometer**. The most common type of hygrometer uses wet and dry bulb thermometers.

◎ The measurement is expressed as a **percentage**; the saturated air has a relative humidity of 100 per cent.

◎ The difference in temperature between the two thermometers is used to find the relative humidity. The greater the difference between the temperatures, the lower the relative humidity.

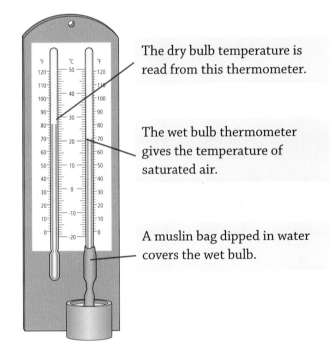

The dry bulb temperature is read from this thermometer.

The wet bulb thermometer gives the temperature of saturated air.

A muslin bag dipped in water covers the wet bulb.

Fig 4.27 Wet and dry bulb thermometers are used to measure relative humidity

## Measuring wind speed and direction

The lower layer of the atmosphere is always in motion. This moving air is called wind.

◎ The speed of the wind is measured with an **anemometer**.
◎ The unit of measurement is either miles or **kilometres per hour** (kph).
◎ The direction of the wind is indicated by a **weather vane**.
◎ Wind direction is described by the direction **from** which the wind is blowing.

Wind strength can also be described by observing the damage it causes to the landscape. The wind strength is divided into 12 forces.

Wind strength is judged by the damage that it causes. This is known as the **Beaufort scale**, after the Irishman who devised it.

The three cups spin in the wind. They rotate more quickly when the wind is strong.

The speed of the wind is read from a dial on a meter.

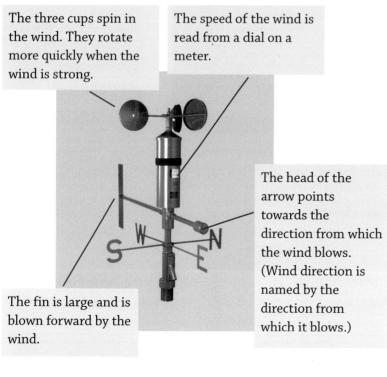

The head of the arrow points towards the direction from which the wind blows. (Wind direction is named by the direction from which it blows.)

The fin is large and is blown forward by the wind.

Fig 4.28 Anemometer and wind vane

## Measuring precipitation

Moisture that results from the condensation of water vapour in the atmosphere returns to Earth as precipitation. It occurs in a variety of forms, including rain, hail, sleet and snow.

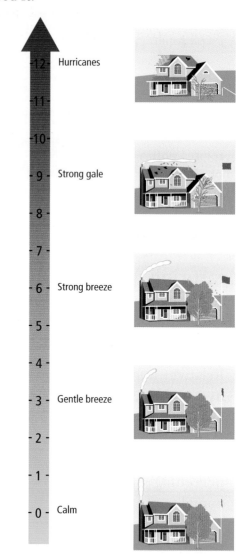

Fig 4.28 The Beaufort scale

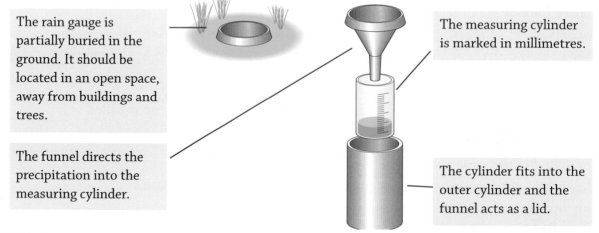

The rain gauge is partially buried in the ground. It should be located in an open space, away from buildings and trees.

The measuring cylinder is marked in millimetres.

The funnel directs the precipitation into the measuring cylinder.

The cylinder fits into the outer cylinder and the funnel acts as a lid.

Fig 4.29 A rain gauge

◎ Precipitation is measured with a **rain gauge**.
◎ The unit of measurement is **millimetres** (mm).

## Measuring sunshine

◎ Sunshine is measured with a **Campbell-Stokes sunshine recorder**.
◎ The unit of measurement is **hours per day**.

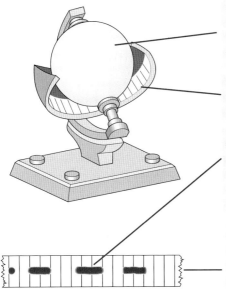

A glass sphere concentrates the rays of the sun onto a spot on the strip of paper.

The paper is marked off in hourly intervals.

If the sun is shining, it burns a mark on the paper. If the sun does not shine, the paper is unmarked.

As the sun moves across the sky, its rays concentrate on a different section of paper.

 **Question**

For how many hours did the sun shine on the strip of paper in Fig 4.30?

Fig 4.30 Campbell-Stokes sunshine recorder

---

### SUMMARY

◎ Weather is the state of the atmosphere at any particular time and place.
◎ Weather instruments are used to measure characteristics of weather.
◎ Accurate weather forecasts are important for some occupations and activities.

---

### QUESTIONS

1  (a) What is meant by the term 'weather'?
   (b) What is a Stevenson screen?
2  Name four instruments used to measure the elements of weather and state what each is used to measure. (JC)
3  Select the weather element of your choice and
   (a) Name the weather instrument used to measure it.
   (b) With the aid of a labelled diagram, explain how the instrument works.
   (c) Name the unit of measurement. (JC)
4  Explain the difference between the following pairs of terms:
   ◎ Thermometer – Isotherm
   ◎ Anemometer – Wind vane
   ◎ Isobar – Isotherm
   ◎ Maximum and minimum thermometers – Wet and dry bulb thermometers

# 4.8 The Greenhouse Effect and Global Warming

Earth is heated by solar energy. The atmosphere, the land and the oceans absorb this energy.

Some of the energy is lost back into space, but the gases of the atmosphere trap much of it. The gases act like the glass on a greenhouse, letting heat in but preventing most of it from getting out. This is nature's way of keeping Earth warm. It is known as the natural **greenhouse effect**.

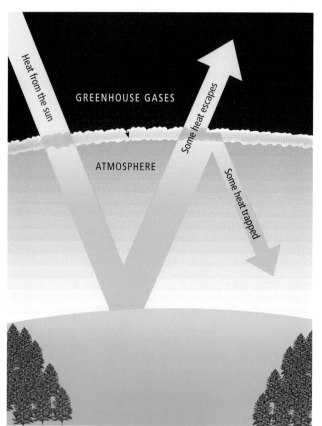

Carbon dioxide, methane, chlorofluorocarbons (CFCs) and nitrous oxide are the most effective gases at trapping heat. As a result, they are known as the **greenhouse gases**.

The greenhouse effect is important because, without it, the temperatures on Earth would be more than 30°C colder than they are today and Earth would not be warm enough to support life.

## Global warming

Over the years there was a balance between the incoming energy and the outgoing energy. As a result, Earth's temperatures remained more or less constant.

Earth is now warmer than it has been for thousands of years. Scientists believe that global temperatures will continue to rise. The heating up of planet Earth is called **global warming**.

Fig 4.31 The natural greenhouse effect

**Geofact**

Fourteen of the warmest years on record have occurred since 1990.

## Causes of global warming

Global warming is thought to be due to the greenhouse effect. The amount of greenhouse gases in the atmosphere has increased enormously in recent years and this is upsetting the balance.

Greenhouse gases trap more heat and the world's temperatures are gradually increasing.

Most of the increase in greenhouse gases is as a direct result of human activity.

- The **burning of fossil fuels** (including oil, coal and natural gas) in homes, factories and power stations raises the level of **carbon dioxide** in the atmosphere.

- **Deforestation** also contributes to the increase in **carbon dioxide**. Trees absorb carbon dioxide and give off oxygen in its place. As more forests are cut down, there are fewer trees to perform this function.

- Paddy fields (where rice is grown) are the main source of **methane**. Cattle produce it as they digest their food. Methane is also released into the atmosphere from decaying organic matter in landfill sites.

- The **burning of fuels** (transport and power stations) and the production of goods such as nylon produces **nitrous oxide**. The use of nitrates as a fertiliser also adds to the increase of the gas in the atmosphere.

- **CFCs** are the most damaging of all the greenhouse gases. Their use in fridges, aerosols and foams has been reduced – not because of the greenhouse effect – but because they damage the ozone layer.

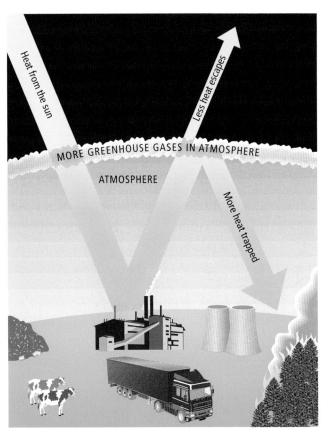

Fig 4.32 Global warming as a result of the increase in greenhouse gases

### Geofacts

- CFCs are 10,000 times more effective at trapping heat than carbon dioxide.
- Nitrous oxide is also known as laughing gas.

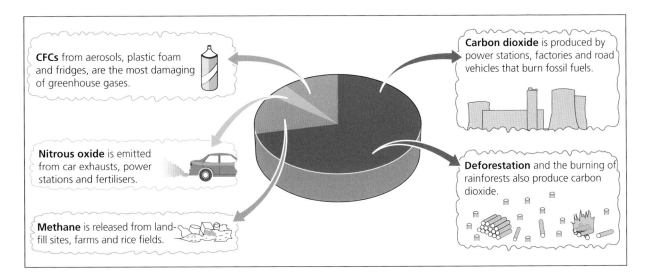

**CFCs** from aerosols, plastic foam and fridges, are the most damaging of greenhouse gases.

**Nitrous oxide** is emitted from car exhausts, power stations and fertilisers.

**Methane** is released from land-fill sites, farms and rice fields.

**Carbon dioxide** is produced by power stations, factories and road vehicles that burn fossil fuels.

**Deforestation** and the burning of rainforests also produce carbon dioxide.

Fig 4.33 Greenhouse gases and global warming

## Impacts of global warming

Nobody knows exactly what the full impact of global warming will be. Scientists are in agreement about some of them, including:

◎ **A rise in sea levels**: As global temperatures increase, the polar ice caps will melt. Sea temperatures will increase and the water in them will expand. Overall, sea levels will rise by up to 60 cm over the next century.

◎ **Climate change**: Tropical storms and hurricanes will become more frequent and stronger. The hurricane season may also become longer. Rainfall patterns will change, some areas will get wetter and others will suffer increased drought. Weather forecasting will become unpredictable.

1 Ireland's soft rains will become strong downpours in the north and west. This will lead to increased flooding and bog bursts.

2 Summers in the south and the interior will become warmer and drier. This may lead to water shortages. It will also lead to a change in agriculture as crops replace grass. This will impact on livestock farming.

3 Should the North Atlantic Drift slow down, it will have less of a warming effect on our shores.

4 Low lying areas will be open to flooding from both rising sea levels and increased storm strength and frequency. Soft coastlines will be open to erosion. Land will be lost as sea defences are too expensive.

5 While drier summers will have a negative impact on growing crops such as potatoes, Mediterranean crops may be grown instead.

6 Storm activity will become more frequent and more severe.

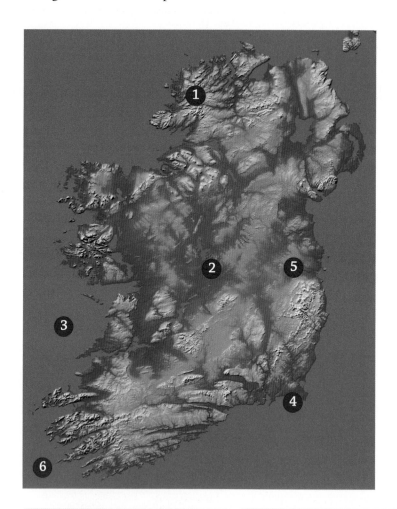

Fig 4.34 Some likely impacts of global warming on Ireland

## Solutions to global warming

It is difficult to get governments to agree to reduce the amount of greenhouse gases being produced. The **Kyoto Protocol** is an agreement on climate change. Thirty-seven industrialised countries and the EU, agreed to reduce greenhouse gas emissions to below their 1990 levels. Ireland's emissions are currently 30 per cent above their 1990 level.

 **Question**

Find out what is meant by your 'carbon footprint'.

There are many ways in which the impact of global warming can be reduced:

◎ **Clean energy**: Reduce dependence on fossil fuels. Use cleaner and renewable energy sources such as solar, wind, wave and hydropower.
◎ **Reduce deforestation**: This should be accompanied by reafforestation (replanting trees), especially in tropical regions.
◎ **Reduce, reuse and recycle**: Reduce the need for manufactured goods and their transport over long distances.
◎ **Use energy-efficient appliances**: These include lights, fridges and heaters.

### SUMMARY

◎ Solar energy trapped by the atmosphere is called the greenhouse effect.
◎ Greenhouse gases include carbon dioxide, methane and CFCs.
◎ The increase in greenhouse gases has led to global warming.
◎ The increase in greenhouse gases is a result of human activity.
◎ Global warming has resulted in climate change and rising sea levels.
◎ Solutions to global warming are difficult to impose on countries.

### QUESTIONS

1 Explain what the following terms mean:
 ◎ Global warming
 ◎ The greenhouse effect
2 (a) Name three greenhouse gases.
 (b) How do they lead to global warming?
3 (a) Explain how human activity has contributed to global warming.
 (b) Describe two of the effects of global warming. (JC)
4 Suggest two ways by which global warming might be reduced. (JC)

# CLIMATES AND NATURAL REGIONS

## 5.1 Introducing Climate

Climate is the average condition of the weather over a long period of time – usually thirty-five years – across a large area of the world's surface.

### Factors that influence world climates

There are several different climates across the world, each with its own characteristics of temperature and precipitation. The way that different climates develop is influenced by the following factors:

◉ Latitude
◉ Distance from the sea
◉ Prevailing wind and ocean currents

### Latitude

Latitude is the angular distance north or south of the equator. Areas near the equator receive more sunlight than anywhere else on Earth. The sun is high in the sky and its rays are concentrated on a smaller area of Earth's surface, giving greater heat.

Further from the equator, the sun's rays are more slanted. Its heat is spread over a wider area, so it is cooler.

**Question**

Explain the term 'prevailing wind'. What is Ireland's prevailing wind?

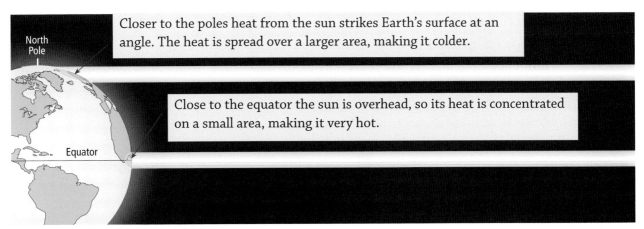

Fig 5.1 The influence of latitude on temperature

## Distance from the sea

The sea heats much more slowly than the land during summer. The sea also takes longer to lose heat during winter. As a result, coastal areas have cooler summers and milder winters than inland areas. Coastal areas also have a smaller temperature range than inland areas.

Land heats and cools faster than the sea. As a result, the further away from the sea that you are, summers are warmer and winters colder. This means that these areas have a larger temperature range. This type of climate is often described as **continental**.

**Question**

What is the annual temperature range at:
(a) Shannon?
(b) Berlin?

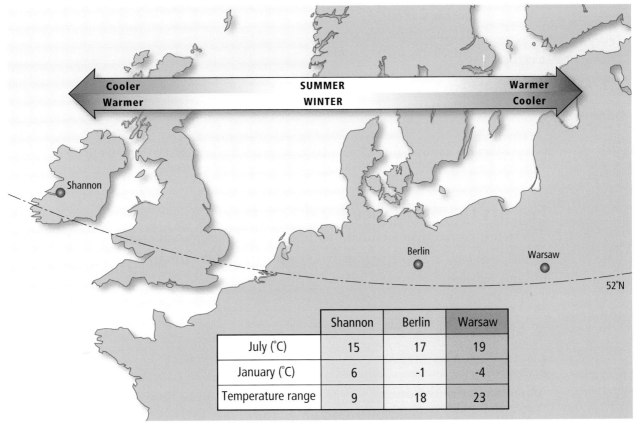

| | Shannon | Berlin | Warsaw |
|---|---|---|---|
| July (°C) | 15 | 17 | 19 |
| January (°C) | 6 | -1 | -4 |
| Temperature range | 9 | 18 | 23 |

Fig 5.2 Temperature variations between coastal areas and inland areas

## Prevailing wind

Winds influence the temperature and precipitation that an area receives. This influence depends on the direction from which the winds blow and whether they pass over land or sea.

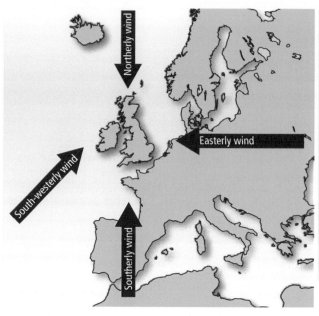

**Northerly winds**
◎ Northerly winds are cold because they come from cold, high latitudes.
◎ They bring snow in winter.

**South-westerly winds**
◎ South-westerly winds are cool in summer because the sea takes longer to heat than the land.
◎ They are mild in winter because the sea cools more slowly than the land.
◎ They are rain-bearing because they absorb moisture as they pass over the ocean.

**Southerly winds**
◎ Southerly winds are warm because they come from the lower latitudes.
◎ They may bring some rainfall because they cool as they move towards the higher latitudes.

**Easterly winds**
◎ Easterly winds are warm in summer because the land has absorbed heat quickly.
◎ They are cold in winter because the land loses heat quickly.
◎ They are usually dry because there is little moisture to absorb over the land.

Fig 5.3 How different wind directions can influence climate. Ireland's prevailing wind is the south-westerly

# Factors that influence local climates

There are variations of climate within the larger regional climates. The climate experienced by a small region is known as a **local climate**. Local climates are influenced by:

◎ Aspect
◎ Altitude

## Aspect

**Aspect** refers to the direction a slope faces in relation to the sun's rays.

In the northern hemisphere, south-facing slopes are warmer because the sun's rays strike the ground at a more direct angle. These slopes are also influenced by warm, southerly winds.

In the northern hemisphere, north-facing slopes are colder because they do not get the direct rays of the sun and may be in the shade. These slopes may also be in the path of cold, northerly winds.

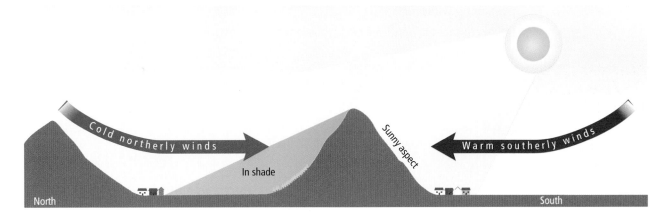

Fig 5.4 In the northern hemisphere, south-facing slopes are warmer and sunnier. North-facing slopes are often in the shade

## Altitude

**Altitude** refers to height above sea level. The higher the place is above sea level the colder it is. This is because, as altitude increases, air becomes thinner and is less able to absorb and hold heat. Temperatures drop by about 7°C for every 1,000-metre increase in altitude.

Upland areas are more exposed to wind than sheltered lowland areas. This reduces temperatures even further.

Upland areas also receive more precipitation because, as the air is cooled, it holds less water vapour.

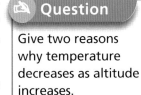

**Question**

Give two reasons why temperature decreases as altitude increases.

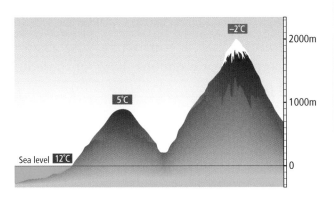

Fig 5.5 The influence of altitude on temperature

Even though it lies close to the equator, the summit of Mount Kilimanjaro is snow-capped

---

📄 **SUMMARY**

◎ Climate is the average weather conditions in an area over a long period of time.
◎ Global climates are influenced by latitude, distance from the sea and the prevailing wind.
◎ Local climates are influenced by aspect and altitude.

---

**QUESTIONS**

1 (a) What is climate?
  (b) List three factors that can influence the climate of a region.
2 (a) Explain the term 'local climate'.
  (b) How are local climates influenced by aspect and altitude?

---

## 5.2   Natural Regions and World Climates

A natural region is an area of the world that has its own unique characteristics that make it different to other areas. These characteristics include:

☝ **Definition**

**Natural vegetation:** The cover of plants and trees that grow in an area before it is changed by human interference.

◎ Climate
◎ Natural vegetation
◎ Wildlife
◎ Human activities

Climate is the most important of these characteristics. The climate of a region influences what vegetation grows there, what animals inhabit it and the way of life of the people who live there.

 **Geofact**

Most of the world's people inhabit regions with a temperate climate because they are the most comfortable regions to live in.

### World climates

Earth can be divided into different climatic regions. Each of these has its own **temperature** and **rainfall pattern**.

There are three broad climate zones:

◎ Hot climates
◎ Temperate climates
◎ Cold climates

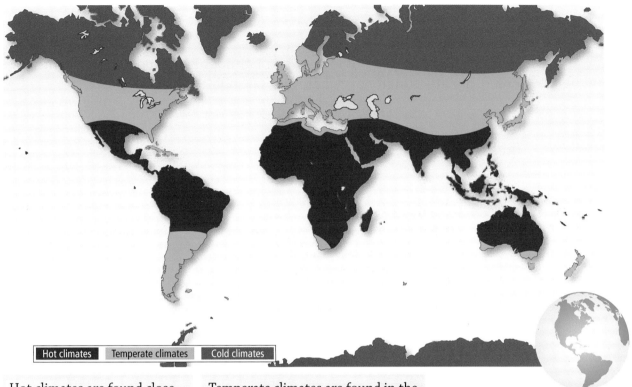

Hot climates | Temperate climates | Cold climates

Hot climates are found close to the equator. They include:
- Equatorial climate
- Hot desert climate
- Savanna climate

Temperate climates are found in the mid-latitudes. They include:
- Cool temperate oceanic climate
- Warm temperate oceanic climate (also called Mediterranean climate)

Cold climates are found close to the poles. They include:
- Tundra climate
- Boreal climate

Fig 5.6 There are three broad climate zones: hot, temperate and cold

## SUMMARY

- A natural region had a set of characteristics that include climate, vegetation and wildlife.
- Climate influences the vegetation and wildlife of a region.
- There are three broad climate zones: hot, temperate and cold.

## QUESTIONS

1. (a) What is a natural region?
   (b) List three characteristics of a natural region.
2. (a) Name the three broad climate zones.
   (b) Name one climate type in each zone.
3. Use your atlas to identify the climate zones in which the following countries are located: Ireland, Iceland, Sudan, Spain, Canada and Mexico.

# 5.3 | Hot Climates of the World

Most hot climates are found between latitudes 30°N and 30°S. They include hot desert climate, equatorial climate and savanna climate.

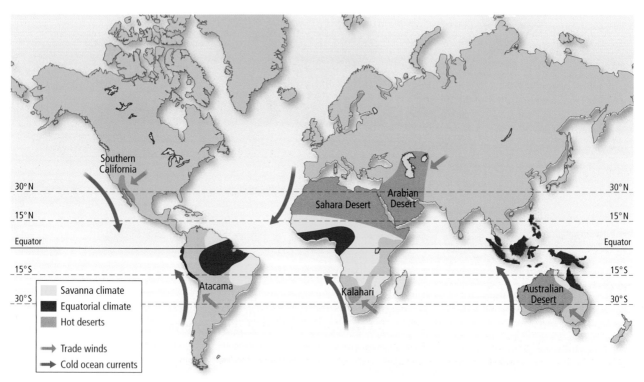

Fig 5.7 Almost all areas with hot climates are found between 30°N and 30°S

| Characteristics of other hot climates | | |
|---|---|---|
| | **Equatorial climate** | **Savanna climate** |
| **Temperature** | ◎ Hot all year round (averaging 32°C)<br>◎ One-season climate | ◎ Hot all year round (averaging 25°C to 35°C)<br>◎ Two-season climate |
| **Rainfall** | ◎ Rainfall every afternoon<br>◎ Annual total: over 2,000 mm<br>◎ High level of humidity | ◎ Annual total: over 800 mm<br>◎ Summers wet<br>◎ Winters dry |
| **Natural vegetation** | ◎ Rain forest (jungle)<br>◎ Hardwoods (mahogany, teak, cherry) | ◎ Scattered trees<br>◎ Grassland (green and brown, depending on the season) |
| **Wildlife** | ◎ Exotic birds (parrots etc.)<br>◎ Snakes, monkeys, butterflies | ◎ Herds of cattle<br>◎ Lions, cheetahs, giraffes |

# Focus on hot desert climate

## Location

The hot deserts of the world are found between 15° and 30° north and south of the equator and lie along the western sides of the landmasses.

## Characteristics of a hot desert climate

### Temperature

Daytime temperatures are high, varying between 30°C to 50°C.

◎ Hot deserts are located in the tropics, where the sun is always high in the sky.
◎ Cloudless skies allow for long hours of sunshine.

Night-time temperatures are as low as 5°C.

◎ The absence of cloud cover and vegetation mean that there is a rapid loss of heat at night.
◎ Night is said to be the 'winter of the desert'.

There is a large daily temperature range.

### Rainfall

Rainfall is rare. The annual total can be less than 100 mm. There are long periods of drought, broken by sudden downpours.

◎ The hot deserts are in the path of the trade winds. These blow overland towards the equator. Thus, they become warmer and hold their moisture. As a result, they are dry winds.
◎ Some deserts are in the path of winds that blow over cold currents. As they do so, they are cooled and lose their moisture over the ocean.

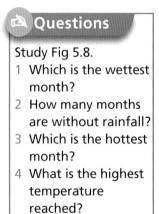

**Questions**

Study Fig 5.8.
1 Which is the wettest month?
2 How many months are without rainfall?
3 Which is the hottest month?
4 What is the highest temperature reached?

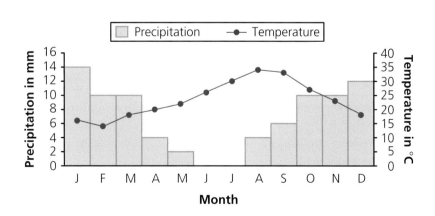

Fig 5.8 Temperature and precipitation chart of a hot desert climate

## Vegetation in hot deserts

There is very little vegetation (flora) in deserts due to the shortage of moisture. Plants are almost all ground-hugging shrubs and short woody trees. The plants are able to survive because they have adapted to desert conditions.

◉ Plants, such as the cactus, have a thick waxy skin and needles. This reduces the loss of moisture.
◉ Plants, such as the date palm, have taproots that grow deep into the ground to find moisture.
◉ Plants, such as the Joshua tree, have juicy flesh that stores water.

## Animals in hot deserts

Animals (fauna) that live in deserts have adapted to the harsh climatic conditions of intense heat and lack of water.

◉ Animals, such as the desert fox, stay in cool underground burrows by day and come out in the cool of the night.
◉ Animals have changed their body form. The jack-rabbit has long ears that help it lose body heat.
◉ Rattlesnakes get moisture from the small creatures that they eat.

The saguaro cactus can reach 18 metres in height.

The saguaro cactus has:
◉ Needles that offer protection against animals.
◉ Thick, waxy bark that prevents moisture loss.
◉ Juicy flesh that is able to store water.
◉ Roots that spread out to gather moisture, as there are few other plants.

A camel rests at an **oasis**.

◉ Camels store fat in their hump for times when water and food are scarce.
◉ They have long eyelashes and nostrils that open and close, giving protection in sandstorms.
◉ They have wide hooves that enable them to walk on dry sand.
◉ They have thick lips, enabling them to eat prickly plants.

 **Definition**

**Oasis:** A fertile area in a desert where water is found close to the surface.

# Desertification

Desertification means **turning land into desert**. It occurs when desert conditions spread into areas that were once fertile.

The areas most affected by desertification are those at the edge of existing deserts. This is especially true in the case of the **Sahel**, a region at the southern edge of the Sahara Desert.

# Causes of desertification

Desertification is caused by a combination of **climate change** and **human factors**. This has affected many groups of people including the **Tuareg** who live in a number of countries in the Sahel region.

## Climate change

The climate of the Sahel has changed over the last thirty years.

- ◎ Rainfall in the region is unreliable. Rains may come late or not come at all.
- ◎ Higher temperatures, as a result of global warming, lead to increased evaporation and less condensation.
- ◎ As a result, several **droughts** have occurred.
- ◎ Rivers and water holes have dried up.

## Human factors

The countries of the Sahel have a high birth rate, leading to rapid population growth and an increased demand for food.

- ◎ People keep large herds of cattle and goats, leading to overgrazing of the land.
- ◎ Farmers change their way of farming. They change from grazing to growing food crops. Without fertilisers, the soil soon loses its nutrients and the crops fail.
- ◎ Trees and shrubs are cut down for cooking and heating. As a result, soil erosion is speeded up.

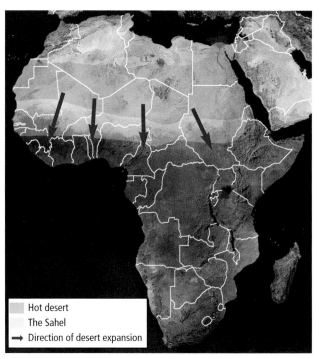

Hot desert
The Sahel
➡ Direction of desert expansion

Fig 5.9 The Sahel lies to the south of the Sahara Desert

> ### ✍ Question
> With the aid of your atlas, identify four countries that make up part of the Sahel.

In the Sahel region, cattle ownership was seen as a sign of wealth. Large herds of poor quality cattle destroyed the vegetation

## Results of desertification

Desertification has had very serious results for the people of the Sahel.

Refugee campsites lie at the edge of Timbuktu, a Tuareg town in Mali in the Sahel region

- Hundreds of thousands of people have died as a result of famine. The countries that have suffered most are Sudan and Ethiopia.
- Millions of people were forced to migrate in search of food or aid. Many of these still live in refugee camps. Refugee camps also grew because of wars.
- Many people moved into urban areas, leading to the growth of slums.
- Millions of animals have died.
- Vast areas of land are now unable to support agriculture.
- Towns and villages have been swallowed up by the advancing sands.

### Solutions to desertification

Most solutions to desertification are taken at local level rather than in the region as a whole.

- Slow down soil erosion by planting trees as shelter belts.
- Bind the soil particles by planting grasses that are resistant to drought.
- Dig deeper wells to find water for irrigation.
- Introduce new breeds of animals to produce more milk, but with smaller herds.

### SUMMARY

- Hot deserts of the world are found at the western margins of continents and lie between 15° and 30° north and south of the equator.
- Hot desert climates are very hot and dry, with cloudless skies. There is a large daily temperature range.
- The scant vegetation has adapted to the hot dry climate by having deep roots, thick bark, spongy flesh and being widely spaced.
- Desertification is caused by climate change, rapid population growth and poor farming practices.
- Millions of people have been displaced or suffered from famines in Africa.
- Much of the land has lost its fertility and the topsoil has been blown away.

## QUESTIONS

1 Examine the graph below and answer the questions that follow:

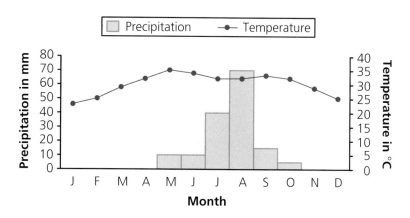

Fig 5.10

   (a)  What is the hottest month?
   (b)  In how many months of the year does the average daily temperature reach 30°C or higher?
   (c)  Which of these is the annual temperature range: 15°C, 20°C or 25°C?
   (d)  What is the wettest month? How much precipitation falls during it?
   (e)  What is the total precipitation for May, June and July?
   (f)  How many months are without precipitation? (JC)

2  (a)  Describe the general location of hot deserts.
   (b)  Explain the climate conditions found in hot deserts. Refer to:
        (i)  daytime temperature,
        (ii)  night-time temperatures and
        (iii)  rainfall.
   (c)  Explain how the climate affects vegetation. (JC)

3  Name one desert animal and one desert plant. Describe how each has adapted to desert conditions. (JC)

4  (a)  Explain why desertification occurs.
   (b)  Describe the impact of desertification on people.
   (c)  Suggest ways by which desertification may be slowed down. (JC)

5  Describe three effects which a severe drought might have on the development of a country in the Sahel. (JC)

# 5.4 Temperate Climates of the World

Most temperate climates are found in the mid-latitudes. They include warm temperate oceanic climate and cool temperate oceanic climate.

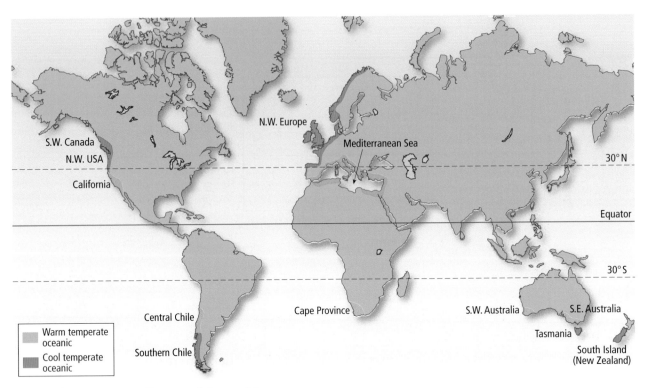

Fig 5.11 The temperate climates of the world

Ireland has a cool temperate oceanic climate.

| Characteristics of a cool temperate oceanic climate | |
| --- | --- |
| **Temperature** | ◎ Summers are warm, with temperatures averaging 15°C to 17°C.<br>◎ Winters are mild, with temperatures averaging 4°C to 6°C.<br>◎ Annual temperature range is about 11°C, making it a moderate climate. |
| **Rainfall** | ◎ Rain falls throughout the year, but there is a winter maximum.<br>◎ Annual total varies between 800 mm and 2,000 mm.<br>◎ The weather conditions are cloudy and changeable. |
| **Natural vegetation** | ◎ Deciduous forest.<br>◎ Tree species include oak, ash, elm and willow.<br>◎ Most of it has been removed for farming, transport and settlement. |

# Focus on warm temperate oceanic climate

Regions that have a warm temperate oceanic climate are found along the western edges of the continents and lie between 30° and 40° north and south of the equator.

Warm temperate oceanic climate is also known as **Mediterranean climate** because the area surrounding the Mediterranean Sea is the largest region that experiences this climate.

Fig 5.12 Regions in Europe and North Africa that experience a Mediterranean climate

## Characteristics of a warm temperate climate

**Summer**

Summers are hot with temperatures averaging 30°C.

◎ These regions are reasonably close to the equator and the sun is still high in the sky, especially in summer.
◎ Cloudless skies allow for long hours of sunshine.

Summers are generally dry, with some drought.

◎ High-pressure belts dominate these regions.
◎ They are under the influence of the trade winds that blow over dry land masses.

**Winter**

Winters are mild, with temperatures averaging between 4°C and 6°C.

◎ The sun is still high enough in the sky to give warm conditions.
◎ The prevailing wind in winter is the south-westerly. As it blows from lower latitudes, it is a warm wind.

Winters are moist, with rainfall between 400 mm and 700 mm.

◎ The prevailing winds blow in over the Atlantic Ocean, bringing moist air.
◎ Depressions form over the Mediterranean Sea.
◎ Rain falls in heavy showers.

## Questions

Study Fig 5.13.

1  What is the highest temperature?
2  What is the lowest temperature?
3  What is the temperature range?
4  In how many months does precipitation exceed 50 mm?
5  What is the driest month?

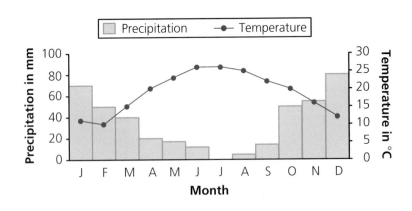

Fig 5.13 Climate graph showing temperature and precipitation in a warm Mediterranean climate

Lavender and olives are grown in the South of France

# Vegetation in Mediterranean regions

The natural vegetation of the Mediterranean region is evergreen woodland. Trees include the cork oak, cypress, cedar and olive. These adapted to their hot, dry environment because:

◎  They absorb and store moisture during winter.
◎  They have very thick bark and waxy leaves to prevent moisture loss.
◎  They are widely spaced to avoid competition for moisture.

As the woods were cleared, a new type of natural vegetation took over. It consisted of low-lying heathers and herbs. These include thyme, lavender and rosemary.

Rows of fruit are irrigated in southern Spain

# The changing Mediterranean landscape

Human activity has changed the Mediterranean landscape over thousands of years and most of the woodland had been cleared for agriculture.

◎  Sheep and goats are the animals most commonly reared.
◎  Overgrazing has damaged the scant vegetation and the soil has been exposed to erosion by sudden downpours of rain.
◎  Fruit and vegetable farming takes place throughout the year.
◎  Irrigation schemes have been introduced to overcome the problems of summer drought.

◎ The main crops grown are citrus fruits (oranges, lemons and grapefruit), tomatoes and vines.

◎ Other crops that are produced include wheat, maize and sunflowers.

Torremolinos on Spain's Costa del Sol has apartment blocks and a motorway fronting the beach

The hot, dry, sunny weather of the Mediterranean climate is very attractive to holidaymakers. As a result, **tourism** is the most important industry in many coastal areas, including the Costa del Sol, Riviera and Majorca. While it has brought wealth and jobs to these regions, it has also led to worries because of pollution, water shortages and badly planned developments.

## SUMMARY

◎ Warm temperate oceanic climates occur on the western edge of the continents, between 30° and 40° north and south of the equator.

◎ Summers are hot and dry. Winters are mild and moist.

◎ The natural vegetation is evergreen woodland, shrubs and heathers.

◎ Most of the natural cover has been removed for agriculture.

◎ Drought is overcome by irrigation.

◎ The attractive climate conditions have led to the development of a huge tourism industry.

## Geofact

Spain attracted almost 60 million tourists in 2007. The majority came from France, Germany and Britain.

## QUESTIONS

1  (a) Give another name for warm temperate oceanic climate.
   (b) In what regions of the world is it found?
   (c) In your copybook complete each of the following sentences:
      ◎ Summers are warm because …
      ◎ Summers are dry because …
      ◎ Winters are mild because …
      ◎ Winters are moist because …

2  'The Mediterranean area has hot, dry summers and mild, moist winters.' Explain why weather conditions are so different in summer and winter in Mediterranean areas. (JC)

3  (a) Describe the natural vegetation of a warm temperate climate region.
   (b) Explain how human activity has changed the natural vegetation.
   (c) What aspects of Mediterranean climate are attractive to tourists? (JC)

## 5.5 Cold Climates of the World

The cold climates of the world are found mainly in the northern hemisphere because, apart from Antarctica, there is no matching landmass in the southern hemisphere.

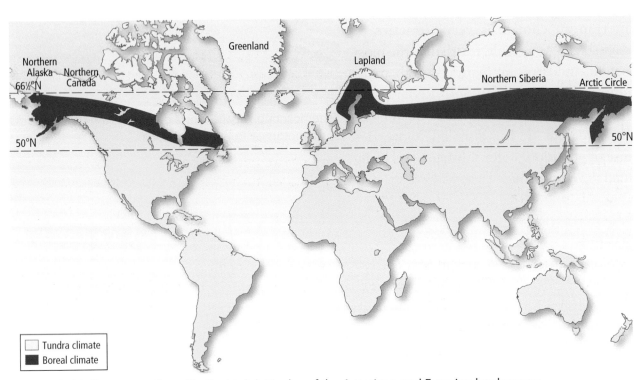

Fig 5.14 Cold climates are found in the high latitudes of the American and Eurasian landmasses

| Geofact | Characteristics of a tundra climate | |
|---|---|---|
| The word tundra means 'without trees'. Why don't trees grow there? | **Temperature** | ◎ Summers are short and cool, with temperatures averaging about 5°C.<br>◎ Winters are long and cold, with temperatures dropping to −35°C.<br>◎ There is a large annual temperature range. |
| | **Precipitation** | ◎ Precipitation is low, usually less than 250 mm per annum.<br>◎ The main form of precipitation is snow. |
| | **Natural vegetation** | ◎ There is very little vegetation due to the extreme cold.<br>◎ The main types are heathers, mosses and lichens. |
| | **Wildlife** | ◎ Animal and birdlife can survive in the region during the summer.<br>◎ Most of them migrate south for the winter. |

# Focus on boreal climate

## Location

The word **boreal** means 'northern'. Boreal climate is found in a belt that runs across America and Eurasia between 55°N and the Arctic Circle.

## Characteristics of a boreal climate

### Temperature

Summers are short and have long hours of daylight. Coastal areas are cool (about 10°C). Inland areas are warmer (about 15°C).

◎ The northern hemisphere is tilted towards the sun.
◎ The long hours of sunshine allows the land to gradually absorb some of the heat.

Winters are cold and have long hours of darkness. Temperatures can reach as low as –25°C.

◎ The northern hemisphere is tilted away from the sun.
◎ The sun is low in the sky, so its rays have to cover a large area of ground, giving little heat.

### Precipitation

Precipitation is generally less than 400 mm per annum. It is mainly in the form of snow. Maximum precipitation occurs in summer.

◎ Polar winds are too cold to hold much moisture.
◎ Many boreal regions are very far from the sea, so the winds that blow over them are dry.

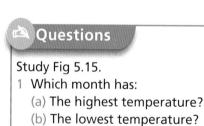

**Questions**

Study Fig 5.15.
1 Which month has:
   (a) The highest temperature?
   (b) The lowest temperature?
2 Calculate:
   (a) Annual temperature range.
   (b) Total precipitation for January to April inclusive.

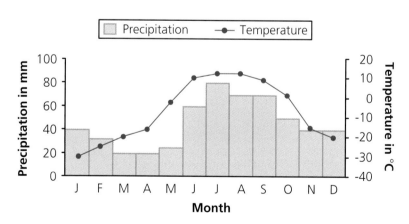

Fig 5.15 Temperature and precipitation in the boreal climate

## Vegetation in a boreal climate

The natural vegetation of the boreal climate is an evergreen forest called **taiga**. Some trees in the taiga are **coniferous**. Trees in the taiga use a lot of energy to grow their needles. They keep their needles all year round and, when the sun comes out again in the spring, these trees are already gathering much needed sunlight instead of wasting more energy to grow new needles.

Since the climate is too harsh for agriculture, the forests have survived largely intact. The taiga accounts for over 20 per cent of the world's forested area.

> ☞ **Definition**
>
> **Coniferous:** Trees that are cone-bearing.

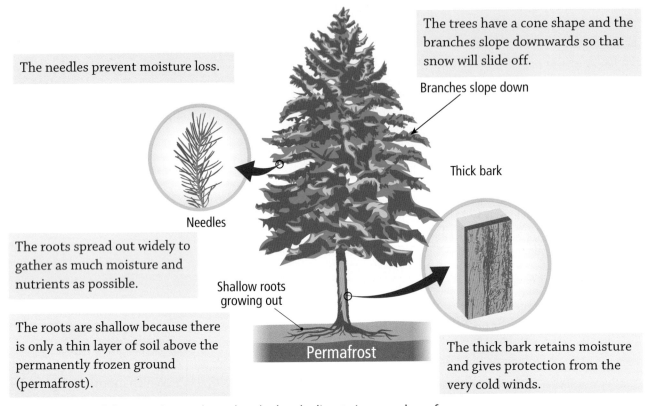

The trees have a cone shape and the branches slope downwards so that snow will slide off.

Branches slope down

The needles prevent moisture loss.

Thick bark

Needles

The roots spread out widely to gather as much moisture and nutrients as possible.

Shallow roots growing out

The roots are shallow because there is only a thin layer of soil above the permanently frozen ground (permafrost).

Permafrost

The thick bark retains moisture and gives protection from the very cold winds.

Fig 5.16 The trees of the taiga have adapted to the harsh climate in a number of ways

> ☞ **Question**
>
> How have the trees of the taiga adapted to the severe climate?

Winter in the boreal forest

## Wildlife in the boreal

The taiga is home to a rich variety of wildlife, including the mink, bear, wolf and eagle. They have adapted to their environment in a number of ways:

◎ Some animals, such as the grizzly bear, avoid the stresses of winter by spending the cold season in **hibernation**.
◎ Fur acts as an insulating layer, keeping an animal's body warm in winter and cool in summer.
◎ Some animals have hooves that spread out to act as snowshoes.
◎ Birds migrate to the south during winter.

Brown bear cubs in the taiga in Finland

**Definition**

**Hibernation**: Animals passing all or part of the winter in a deep sleep.

## People in the boreal

Very few people live in the boreal forest because of the harsh climate. Miners, foresters and small groups of native peoples populate this remote landscape.

There are more than 50,000 Sami people living in Lapland, which stretches across the northern reaches of Norway, Sweden, Finland and part of Russia. The Sami are Europe's last tribe. In the past, they were herders and their lifestyle was based on the migration of reindeer herds. Today, many have become urban dwellers, working in the forestry industry.

A Sami herding reindeer in North Norway

For many years the boreal forest was untouched by human interference. Today, the boreal forests of Russia and Canada are at risk from logging companies, many of which clear the forests of all trees. The wood is in huge demand for paper and chipboard. The forest areas are also at risk from mining and oil exploration companies.

**SUMMARY**

- The boreal climate is found between 55°N and the Arctic Circle.
- Summers are short and warm. Winters are long and cold.
- The natural vegetation is evergreen forest (taiga).
- Trees have shallow roots, thick bark and needles.
- Animals have adapted to their environment by hibernating, migrating and growing thick fur.
- Very few people live in the taiga. Most nomadic tribes have now settled.

 **QUESTIONS**

1 Examine the climate table for Siberia below and answer the questions that follow:

| Temperature table | | | | | | | | | | | |
|---|---|---|---|---|---|---|---|---|---|---|---|
| **Month** | Jan | Feb | Mar | Apr | May | Jun | Jul | Aug | Sept | Oct | Nov | Dec |
| **Temperature (°C)** | –30 | –25 | –20 | –17 | –7 | 2 | 3 | 2 | –2 | –7 | –18 | –28 |
| **Precipitation (mm)** | 10 | 15 | 10 | 15 | 15 | 16 | 25 | 25 | 16 | 25 | 10 | 15 |

   (a) Name and give the temperature of the coldest month.
   (b) For how many months is the temperature above freezing point (0°C)?
   (c) What is the annual temperature range?
   (d) For how many months is precipitation below 15 mm?
   (e) What is the total precipitation for the twelve months? (JC)

2 Explain why each of the following occur in the boreal climate:
   (a) Winters are very cold.
   (b) There are long hours of darkness in winter.
   (c) Precipitation is mainly in the form of snow.

3 (a) What is the natural vegetation of the boreal climate?
   (b) Explain how the natural vegetation of the boreal climate has adapted to its environment. (JC)

4 Explain how climate has slowed down the development of a country of your choice. (JC)

# 6 SOILS

## Learning Outcomes

In this chapter you will learn that:

◎ Soil is made up of five main ingredients.
◎ Soil is formed by a number of factors.
◎ A soil profile consists of three horizons.

◎ Ireland has four main soil types.
◎ Soil and vegetation influence each other.

## 6.1 What Is Soil?

Soil is the thin layer of loose material on Earth's surface. It is one of the world's most important natural resources. Plants are rooted in soil and obtain their minerals there. Thus, without soil there would be no food for animals or people.

Soil has five main ingredients, both living and non-living. They are:

◎ Mineral matter
◎ Air
◎ Water
◎ Living organisms
◎ Humus

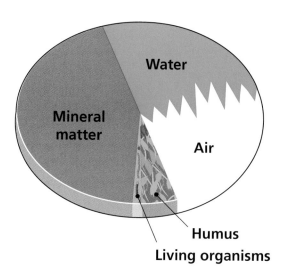

Fig 6.1 The amount of water and air in soil varies, depending on the weather and how well the soil can hold water

## Mineral matter

Mineral matter is the biggest ingredient in soil. It consists of the remains of rocks that have been broken down into smaller particles by weathering and erosion. It includes stones, sand, silt and clay.

**Question**

Explain the terms:
◎ Weathering
◎ Erosion

## Air

Air fills the pores or spaces between the mineral particles in the soil. Air contains oxygen and nitrogen. These are vital for the growth of plants. Air also allows living organisms to survive in the soil.

## Water

Water helps to bind the soil particles together. Water is important for plant growth because it contains dissolved minerals. Plants absorb these minerals through their roots.

## Living organisms

**Geofact**

There are more micro-organisms in one handful of soil than there are people on Earth.

Soil is home to creatures such as earthworms, woodlice and slugs. It is also home to millions of tiny creatures, too small to be seen by the naked eye, called micro-organisms. They include bacteria and fungi.

When worms burrow through the soil, they mix it and also make it easier for water and air to pass through. Micro-organisms help to break down dead plants into humus.

## Humus

Humus is the dark, partly decayed organic matter found in soil. It is produced from the remains of dead creatures and plants. These are broken down and mixed in the soil by the living organisms.

Humus provides nutrients that make the soil fertile. It also helps to bind the soil particles together.

Earthworms break up soil and help the passage of air and water through it

# How soils are formed

A number of factors work together over a period of time to form soil. They are:

◎ Climate
◎ Parent material
◎ Vegetation
◎ Living organisms
◎ Landscape
◎ Time

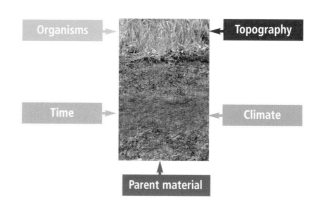

Organisms → ← Topography
Time → ← Climate
↑ Parent material

Fig 6.2 The factors that influence how soil is formed

## Climate

Temperature and rainfall influence the rate at which the parent rock is broken down by weathering. Hot climates experience **chemical weathering**, while cold climates experience **freeze-thaw**.

## Parent material

The type of rock in an area also affects soil formation. Granite is slow to break down by weathering, while sandstone breaks down easily and forms soil quickly.

Soils that develop from limestone are more fertile than those that develop from granite or sandstone.

## Vegetation

When vegetation dies, it is broken down and decays to add humus and nutrients to the soil. Deciduous vegetation provides more leaf fall than coniferous vegetation.

## Living organisms

Micro-organisms such as bacteria and fungi help to break down the dead plant and animal life in the soil, turning it into humus.

As animals such as earthworms dig through the soil, they break it up and mix it, allowing more water and air to enter the soil. When these creatures die, their remains add nutrients to the soil.

## Landscape

Upland areas are cold and wet, so soils are often waterlogged. There is little plant and animal life, so there is less humus.

Lowland soils are generally deeper and well-drained. They have more humus as there is plentiful plant and animal life.

## Time

Time is one of the most important factors in soil formation. The longer a rock is exposed to the forces of weathering, the more it is broken down. It may take up to 400 years for 1 cm of soil to form.

> ### 🌐 Geofact
>
> People can also influence the make-up of soil.
>
> ◎ They can make it more fertile by drainage, adding fertiliser, ploughing and irrigation.
> ◎ They can make it less fertile by overusing it or by removing vegetation.

# Soil profiles

If you dig down into the ground as far as the bedrock, you will find a number of different layers. Each layer is called a **horizon**. They are usually seen along road cuttings and other areas where the soil is exposed.

Apart from the surface layer of **plant litter**, there are usually three horizons in a soil profile. They differ from one another in colour, content and texture (particle size).

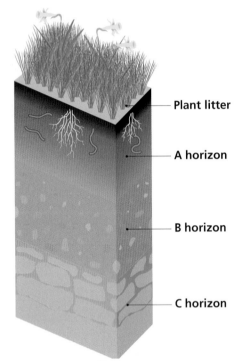

Fig 6.3 A typical soil profile

Plant litter

A horizon

B horizon

C horizon

**A horizon**
The upper layer of soil is called the **topsoil**. It is usually darker than lower layers as it has a high humus content. It is loose and crumbly. Most of the organisms live in this layer. It is generally the most productive layer of soil.

**B horizon**
Found beneath the A horizon, this is called the **subsoil**. It is usually lighter in colour because it has less humus. It has more stones than the A horizon because it is closer to the parent material and is protected from weathering.

**C horizon**
This consists of the parent rock of the soil. The upper section may be broken down into rock particles, but the lower section consists of solid bedrock.

A soil profile

# Leaching

In wet climates, such as in Ireland, excess water moves down through the soil profile. As it does so, it washes minerals, humus and nutrients down into the B horizon. This process is known as **leaching**.

Leaching can cause the A horizon to lose its fertility. It also interferes with the growth of some plants, as it washes the nutrients down beyond the reach of their roots.

If leaching is very severe, minerals such as clay and iron oxide (rust) build up at the bottom of the A horizon. They are cemented together to form a crust called **hardpan**. Since hardpan is impermeable, it causes the soil above it to become waterlogged.

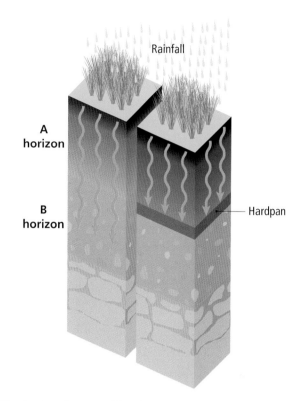

Flg 6.4 Leaching and hardpan

## SUMMARY

◎ Soil is a natural resource.
◎ Soil consists of mineral matter, humus, organisms, water and air.
◎ Soil formation is influenced by climate, parent rock, living organisms, vegetation and time.
◎ A soil profile consists of a number of horizons.
◎ Soil fertility is influenced by leaching and human activity.

## QUESTIONS

1   (a)  What is soil?
    (b)  List the five ingredients of soil.
    (c)  Which two ingredients vary according to the weather?
2   Explain the following terms:
    ◎ Micro-organism
    ◎ Plant litter
    ◎ Soil profile
    ◎ Leaching
    ◎ Hardpan
3   Draw a labelled diagram of a typical soil profile.
4   Soil is a mixture of (a) minerals, (b) plant remains, (c) living things, (d) air and water. Select any two of the above soil components and describe how they affect soil quality. (JC)

The grey colour at the bottom of the soil horizon is a result of leaching

# 6.2 Irish Soils

There are four main soil types in Ireland:

◎ Brown earth soils
◎ Podzol soils
◎ Peaty soils
◎ Gley soils

## Brown earth soils

Brown earth soils developed on the boulder clays deposited after the last Ice Age. These areas were formerly covered by **deciduous forest**. They are currently under grassland or crops.

There was a plentiful supply of plant litter available. This decayed rapidly to form **humus**, giving the soil its dark brown colour. Rainfall is limited so there is **very little leaching** of minerals.

Brown earth soils are **fertile** and are suited to a wide range of farming types, including arable and pastoral farming.

Brown earth soils are the most common soil in Ireland and are found in the drier lowlands of the south, Midlands and east.

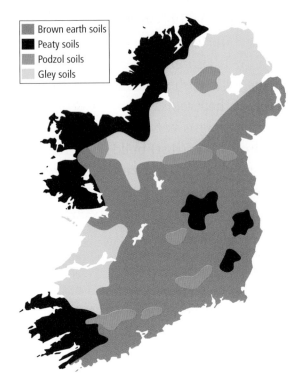

| | |
|---|---|
| ▮ | Brown earth soils |
| ▮ | Peaty soils |
| ▮ | Podzol soils |
| ▮ | Gley soils |

Fig 6.5 The main soil types in Ireland

Brown earth soil covers much of the Irish landscape. It is fertile and suited to arable and pastoral farming

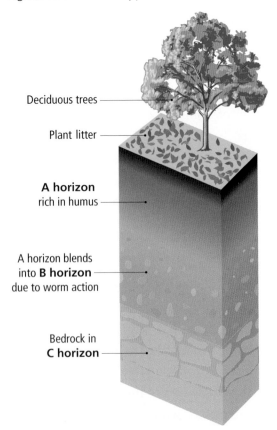

Deciduous trees

Plant litter

**A horizon** rich in humus

A horizon blends into **B horizon** due to worm action

Bedrock in **C horizon**

Fig 6.6 Brown earth soil profile

## Podzol soils

Podzol soils developed in cold and wet areas that were covered by **coniferous forest**. The forest provided only limited amounts of plant litter in the form of pine leaves.

The plant litter decayed very slowly in the colder temperatures, to form only **small amounts of humus**. The cold also limits earthworm activity.

The heavier rainfall causes **leaching** and hardpan may develop. This leaves the A horizon with a grey colour.

Podzol soils are **relatively infertile** and are also slightly acidic.

They are found in the damp, poorly-drained upland areas of Cork, Galway and Tipperary.

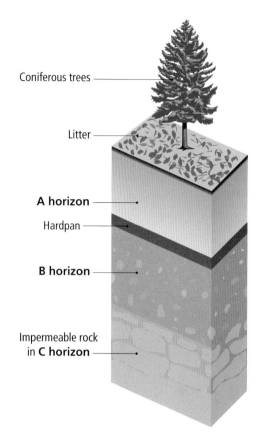

Fig 6.7 Podzol soil profile

The plant litter on the floor of a coniferous forest leads to limited amounts of humus in podzol soils

**Peaty soils** (above) develop in cold, upland areas that have very high rainfall. These soils are heavily leached and are easily waterlogged

**Gley soils** (left) develop in areas where the bedrock or the clay above it is impermeable. This interferes with the drainage as rain is unable to drain away. These soils are easily waterlogged and are suitable only for pastoral farming

📄 **SUMMARY**

◎ Brown earth soils are the most common soils in Ireland.
◎ They developed in lowland areas that were once covered by deciduous forests.
◎ Rich in humus, brown earth soils are well-drained and fertile.
◎ Podzol soils developed in wet, upland areas that were once covered by deciduous forests. They have a limited amount of humus and are relatively infertile.

📝 **QUESTIONS**

1 Examine Fig 6.5, on page 128, and answer the following questions:
   (a) Which is the most common soil type in Ireland?
   (b) What is the main soil type in your county?
   (c) Name one soil type found in lowland areas.
   (d) Name one soil associated with upland areas.
2 Describe fully one Irish soil type that you have studied. Draw a labelled diagram to show the soil profile of the soil type that you selected. (JC)

## 6.3 | Tropical Red Soils

Tropical red soils are found in areas that have a tropical or equatorial climate. Their formation is influenced mainly by the hot, wet, climatic conditions. As a result, chemical weathering is very active. This causes the rock to decompose very rapidly, forming soil that is several metres deep.

**Geofact**

The soils of the humid tropical and equatorial zones are called **latosols**.

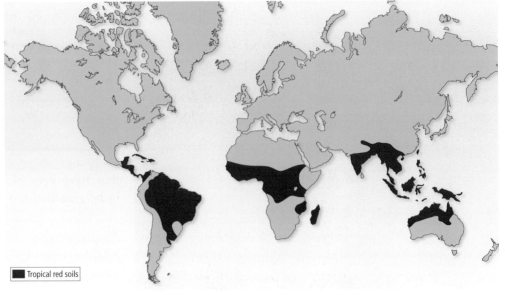

■ Tropical red soils

Fig 6.8 Tropical red soils are found in tropical and equatorial regions

◎ There is continuous leaf fall in the forest throughout the year, giving a thick layer of plant litter. This is rapidly broken down, partly by organisms and partly due to the humid conditions.

◎ The acids from the decaying humus speed up the weathering of the bedrock. The high temperatures encourage chemical action, again causing the bedrock to break down.

◎ Weathering breaks down the iron in the soil into iron oxide (rust), giving the soil its reddish colour.

◎ The soil is heavily leached due to the very heavy rainfall.

Under normal conditions, tropical red soils are very fertile. When the forests are cut down, the soils lose their source of humus. The heavy rains quickly leach any remaining nutrients from the now bare soil. The soil loses its fertility and is eventually washed away by surface water.

Latosol or tropical red soil in the rain forest of Brazil

### ✎ Question

Examine the picture on the left. Apart from its colour, what evidence suggests that this is a tropical red soil?

### 📄 SUMMARY

◎ The development of latosols, or tropical red soils, is influenced by the hot, wet and humid climatic conditions.

◎ The soils are deep because chemical weathering breaks down the bedrock.

◎ Latosols have a reddish colour and are heavily leached.

### ✎ QUESTIONS

1  (a)  What are tropical red soils?
   (b)  In what parts of the world are tropical red soils found?
   (c)  Why do tropical red soils have a red colour?
   (d)  What happens to tropical red soils when the vegetation cover is removed?

2  Describe the influence of climate in the development of tropical red soils. (JC)

## 6.4 Natural Vegetation and Soil

Soil conditions can influence vegetation while vegetation, in turn, can influence soil conditions.

### Soil influences vegetation

◎ Soil influences vegetation by its ability to retain water. Sandy soils are free-draining and support a wide range of vegetation. Clay soils become waterlogged easily and are only able to support a limited range of vegetation.

◎ Fertile soils have many nutrients, including nitrogen, calcium and potash. They support a wide variety of vegetation. Infertile soils support a limited range of vegetation, including coniferous forests.

◎ Acid soils lack lime. This limits the range of vegetation that they can support, although plants such as azaleas and rhododendrons flourish.

◎ Deep soils support vegetation with long roots, such as ash, oak and beech. Coniferous trees, including pine and spruce have roots that spread outwards, so they can survive in shallow soils.

### Vegetation influences soil

◎ Vegetation provides the plant litter to form humus. Deciduous trees provide a plentiful supply of humus, leading to brown earth soils. Coniferous trees provide a limited supply of needles, leading to podzol soils.

◎ Vegetation reduces the effects of leaching. A plentiful supply of plant litter ensures a supply of humus. If some leaching occurs, deep roots can bring the leached minerals back to the surface.

Deep, fertile soils support a variety of lush vegetation

◎ Vegetation cover slows down or prevents soil erosion. It reduces the impact of heavy rain on the soil. The roots help to bind the soil particles together. When soil cover is lost, soil erosion occurs.

Soil erosion occurs when vegetation dies following overgrazing

📄 **SUMMARY**

◎ Vegetation is influenced by the depth of the soil, by its ability to retain moisture and by the amount of humus and minerals that are present in it.
◎ Soil is influenced by the type of vegetation, the amount of plant litter present and by the ability of the roots to prevent soil erosion.

✏️ **QUESTIONS**

1 (a) List two ways by which vegetation is affected by the quality of the soil.
　(b) List two ways by which vegetation can change the quality of the soil.
2　Describe one way in which soil influences vegetation and one way in which vegetation influences soil. (JC)

# MAPS AND PHOTOGRAPHS

In this chapter you will learn:

◎ How symbols and colour are used in Ordnance Survey (OS) maps.

◎ Skills in measurement and drawing.

◎ To interpret the physical landscape in maps and photographs.

◎ To interpret the human landscape in maps and photographs.

## 7.1 | Ordnance Survey

A map is a drawing or plan of part or all of Earth's surface.

Maps:

◎ Are drawn to scale.

◎ Use colours, symbols, and labels to represent features found on the landscape.

### Scale

Scale is the ratio or relationship between a distance on the map and the corresponding distance on the ground.

Maps are drawn to different scales, depending on the amount of information that is required and the area of ground that the map must cover.

Fig 7.1 Small-scale maps show a large area but with little detail. This map, showing the Limerick region, is drawn to a scale of 1:450,000

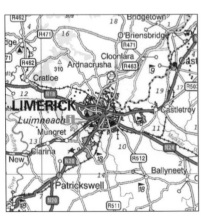

Fig 7.2 Large-scale maps show a smaller area but with greater detail. This map, showing Limerick city centre, is drawn to a scale of 1:20,000

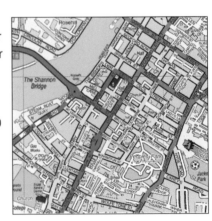

# Discovery Series of maps

The Ordnance Survey of Ireland (OSI) publishes a series of maps, called the Discovery Series. These maps are drawn at a scale of 1:50,000. This means that each centimetre on the map represents 50,000 centimetres (or 500 metres) on the ground.

Fig 7.3 The Discovery Series of maps are designed for tourists and leisure activities. They are drawn to a scale of 1:50,000

## Scale on a map

Scale on a map may be shown in three ways:

1. Representative fraction (RF)
2. Linear scale
3. Statement of scale

**1 Representative fraction** (RF)
The scale is written as a ratio. In this case, the scale is 1:50,000.

**2 Linear scale**
The scale is shown along a ruled line that is divided into kilometres and miles. One section of the linear scale divides miles and kilometres into tenths.

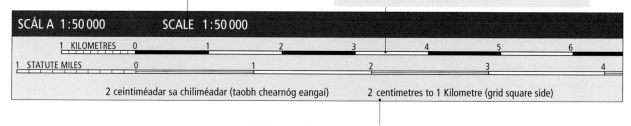

SCÁL A 1:50 000   SCALE 1:50 000

KILOMETRES 0 1 2 3 4 5 6

STATUTE MILES 0 1 2 3 4

2 ceintiméadar sa chiliméadar (taobh chearnóg eangaí)

2 centimetres to 1 Kilometre (grid square side)

**3 Statement of scale**
The map gives a written description of the scale. In this case, 2 centimetres on the map represent 1 kilometre on the ground.

Fig 7.4 The three methods of showing scale on a map say the same thing in different ways

# OS map legend

Maps are crammed full of information. Writing it all onto a map would be impractical as the map would become cluttered. Instead, we use symbols to represent the information, e.g. natural features (such as beaches and rivers) and man-made features (such as roads, buildings and woodland). The symbols vary from map to map, depending on the scale.

Fig 7.57, on page 183, shows the legend that is associated with the 1:50,000 Discovery Series of OS maps.

## Measuring distance

Scale is the same for all parts of a map. This is important because it enables us to measure distances on the map.

### Straight-line distance

Straight-line distance is the shortest distance between any two points. It is often called 'as the crow flies'.

To measure a straight-line distance between two points on a map:

1 Place a strip of paper on the map so that its edge passes through the two points.
2 Mark the edge of the paper where it touches the two points on the map.
3 Place the paper against the linear scale on the map and read the distance in kilometres (km).

**Question**

What is the straight-line distances between the top of Lugnaquilla Mountain and (a) Slievemaan and (b) Corrigaste?

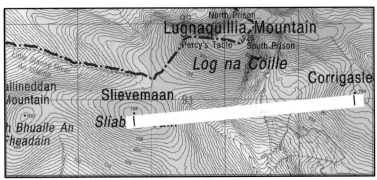

Fig 7.5 Measuring straight-line distance (as the crow flies) on a map. Measure the distance from the top of Slievemaan to the top of Corrigaste.

The distance is 3 km.

### Curved-line distance

Curved-line distance is used to measure a distance along any line that is not straight, e.g. roads, railways and rivers.

To measure a curved-line distance between two points on a map:

1 Place the edge of your paper strip at the start point and put a pencil mark on both the map and paper (A).
2 Hold the edge of the paper along the line until you reach the first bend or turn. Put a pencil mark on both map and paper (B).
3 Keep the marks at (B) in line with one another. Move the paper strip so that it is in line with the next section of the line. Put a pencil mark on both map and paper (C).

4   Repeat this process until you have measured the required distance.
5   Place the paper strip on the linear scale and read the distance in kilometres.

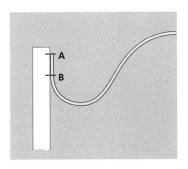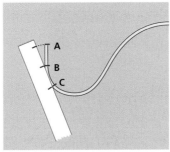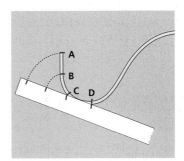

Fig 7.6 Measuring a curved-line distance on a map

# Calculating area

Two types of area can be measured on an OS map:

◎   A regular-shaped area such as the actual map extract.
◎   An irregular-shaped area such as an island, lake or mountain.

**Geofact**

Each square on a 1:50,000 scale OS map has an area of 1 kilometre squared (km²).

## To calculate the area of a map extract
1   Measure the distance along the base of the map.
2   Measure the distance along the vertical side of the map.
3   Multiply the two totals. This gives you the area of the map extract in kilometres squared (km²).

**Example**

**Calculate the area of the map extract shown in Fig 7.7.**
1   Length along base of map = 5 km
2   Length up side of map = 3 km
3   Area of map = 5 x 3 = 15 km²

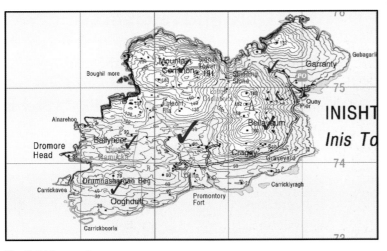

Fig 7.7 Measuring area

**Example**

**Calculate the area of the island in the map extract shown in Fig 7.7.**
1   Number of complete squares = 1
2   Number of areas that take up half or more of a square = 5
3   Area of island = 6 km²

## To calculate the area of an irregular shape
1   Count all the complete squares.
2   Count each square where the shape covers half or more of its area. Ignore those squares where the shape takes up less than half its area.
3   Add the totals from steps 1 and 2 to find the total area in kilometres squared (km²).

**Question**

Calculate the sea area in the map extract shown in Fig 7.7.

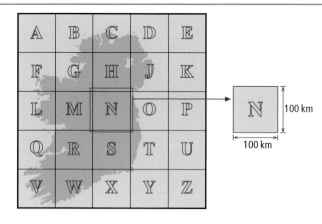

Fig 7.8 The National Grid

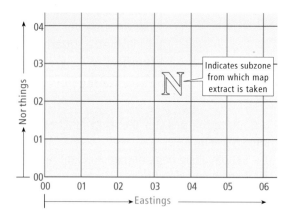

Fig 7.9 A grid reference consists of a sub-zone letter, an Easting and a Northing

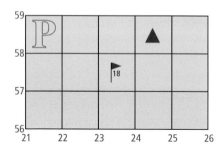

Fig 7.10
The Golf Course is at P 23 57
The Youth Hostel is at P 24 58

# The National Grid

The **National Grid** covers Ireland and some of its sea areas. It consists of twenty-five squares called **sub-zones**, each named by a letter of the alphabet. Each sub-zone is 100 km in width and 100 km in height.

## Finding location with grid references

The sides of each sub-zone are divided into 100 equal parts by a series of lines. These lines are called **co-ordinates** and are numbered from 00 to 99.

We use these co-ordinates together with the sub-zone letter to find a location on a map. This location is called a **grid reference**.

Grid references are made up of three parts (call them **LEN**).

◎ **L** refers to the sub-zone letter.
◎ **E** refers to the Easting. This is the vertical co-ordinate. Its value is read from left to right along either the base or top of the map.
◎ **N** refers to the Northing. It is the horizontal co-ordinate. Its value is read from bottom to top along the sides of the map.

## Four-figure grid references

A four-figure grid reference will give you the location of any single square on the map.

The following are examples of four-figure grid references from the map extract in Fig 7.11 on the opposite page.

**Castlemaine Public Telephone**
Sub-zone letter: Q
Easting: 83
Northing: 03
This gives a four-figure grid reference of Q 83 03

Mass Rock: Q 84 01
Cillín: Q 82 02
Milltown PO: Q 82 00

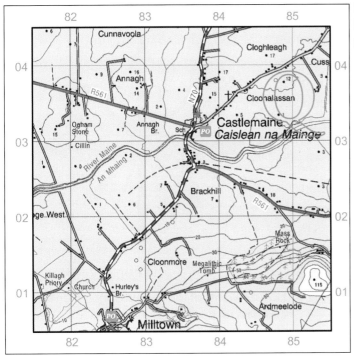

Fig 7.11 Castlemaine: four-figure grid references

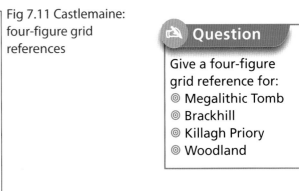

**Question**

Give a four-figure grid reference for:
◎ Megalithic Tomb
◎ Brackhill
◎ Killagh Priory
◎ Woodland

## Six-figure grid references

A **six-figure grid reference** gives a more exact location than a four-figure grid reference. It refers to a definite point within a grid square.

Imagine that each side of the grid square is divided into ten equal parts, as in decimal measurement. This will then give a third figure for both the Easting and the Northing.

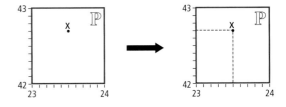

The sub-zone letter is **P**
The Easting is **23.5**
The Northing is **42.7**
Ignore the decimal point when writing the grid reference.
The six-figure grid reference for **X** is **P 235 427**.

Fig 7.12 Point X is at P 235 427

The following are six-figure grid references from the Blarney map extract.

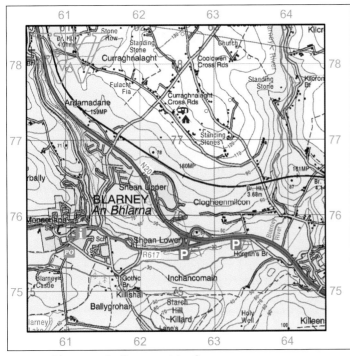

Fig 7.13 Blarney: six-figure grid references

**Camping site**
Sub-zone letter: W
Easting: 62.6
Northing: 77.2
This gives a grid reference of
W 62.6 77.2 and it is written as W 626 772.
Coolowen Crossroad:
W 627 781
Post Office: W 610 755
Stone Row: W 617 785
Holy Well: W 634 746

**Question**

Give a six-figure grid reference for:
◎ Caravan Park
◎ Church
◎ Fulacht Fia
◎ Tourist Information
◎ Blarney Castle

139

## Directions

Directions on a map are described by using compass points. The four main points of the compass – north, east, south and west – are called the cardinal points.

If the spaces between the cardinal points are divided, four more compass points are created. These are NE, SE, SW and NW.

A further division creates eight more minor compass points.

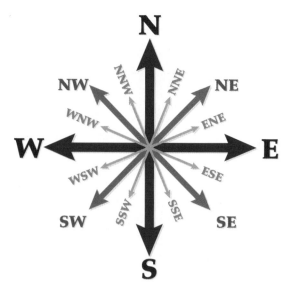

Fig 7.14 Points of the compass shown on a compass rose

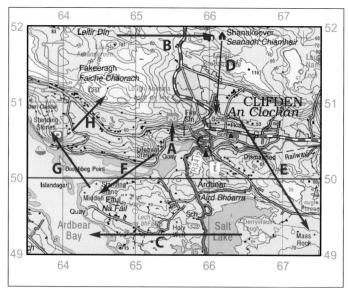

Fig 7.15 Finding direction on a map

A: The PO is to the **north** of the Quay.
B: The Caravan Park is to the **east** of Leitir Din.
E: The Mass Rock is to the **south-east** of the Hospital.
F: The Midden is to the **south-west** of the Lifeboat Station.

## Height

Height on an Ordnance Survey map is expressed in metres above sea level.

Height is shown on a map in four ways:

1 Colour
2 Contours
3 Triangulation pillars
4 Spot heights

**Colour** gives a general picture of height. Green indicates lowland areas up to 200 metres in height. Brown represents higher areas, with the shade of brown becoming darker as height increases.

**Triangulation pillars** can be found at the top of a hill or mountain. They are shown on a map by a black triangle with the exact height of the ground at that point written next to them.

**Contours** are lines on a map that join places of equal height. They are usually drawn at intervals of 10 metres. The height is written next to the contours.

**Spot heights** give the exact height of a point. They are shown on a map by a small black dot with the height of the ground at that point written next to it.

Fig 7.16 Showing height on an OS map

# Slope

Slope is also called **gradient**. Changes in slope are identified by the spacing of the contours.

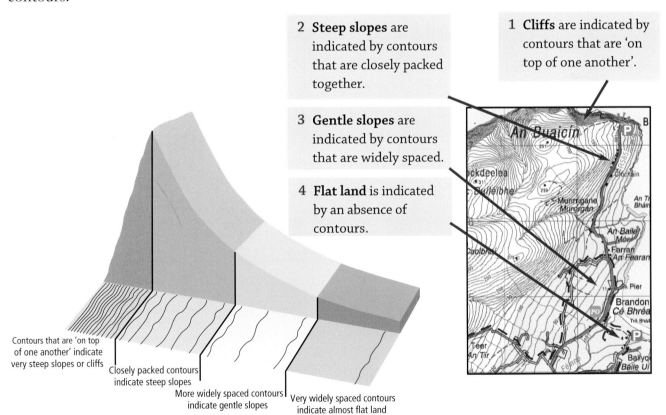

2 **Steep slopes** are indicated by contours that are closely packed together.

3 **Gentle slopes** are indicated by contours that are widely spaced.

4 **Flat land** is indicated by an absence of contours.

1 **Cliffs** are indicated by contours that are 'on top of one another'.

Contours that are 'on top of one another' indicate very steep slopes or cliffs

Closely packed contours indicate steep slopes

More widely spaced contours indicate gentle slopes

Very widely spaced contours indicate almost flat land

Fig 7.17 The spacing of contours gives an indication of how steep or gentle a slope is

Fig 7.18 Different slopes on an OS map

## Types of slope

There are three types of slope. They can be identified by the pattern of the contours.

**Even slope**: The contour pattern shows evenly spaced contours.

**Convex slope**: This slope is steep at the bottom (closely packed contours) and gentle at the top (widely spaced contours).

**Concave slope**: This slope is gentle at the bottom (widely spaced contours) and steep at the top (closely packed contours).

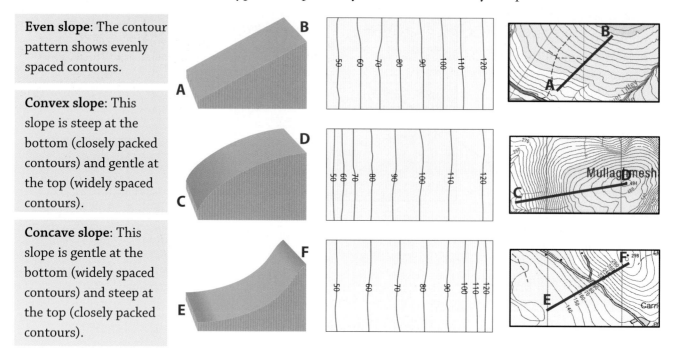

Fig 7.19 We can identify the type of slope from the pattern of the contours

## Calculating gradient

We can give a more accurate description of the slope by expressing it as a ratio. It is calculated as follows:

$$\frac{\text{The difference in height between any two points}}{\text{The distance between the points}}$$

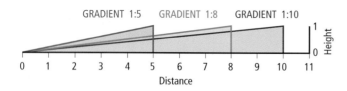

Fig 7.20 A gradient of 1:8 (1 in 8) means that the slope rises or falls 1 unit for every 8 units travelled along the ground

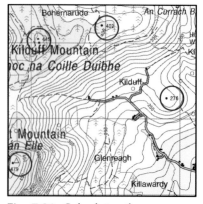

Fig 7.21 Calculate the average gradient between .445 and Δ479

**Question**

What is the average gradient between the spot heights .402 and .276?

| Difference in height | = 479–445m | = 34m | = 34 | = 1 |
|---|---|---|---|---|
| Distance between points | 1.7 km | 1,700m | 1,700 | 50 |

This can be written as 1:50 (there is a gradient of 1 in 50).

# Cross-sections

A cross-section is a slice across and through a landscape to show its shape or profile.

Cross-sections are drawn on graph paper. The horizontal scale (along the ground) remains true. The vertical scale is exaggerated so that relief (the shape of the land) stands out clearly.

Fig 7.22 A cross-section of a city skyline

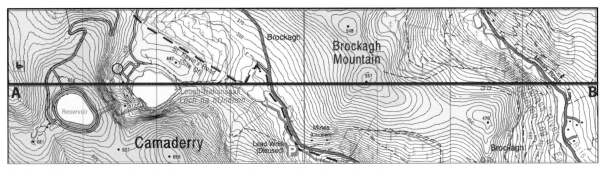

Fig 7.23 The cross-section below is drawn along the line from A to B

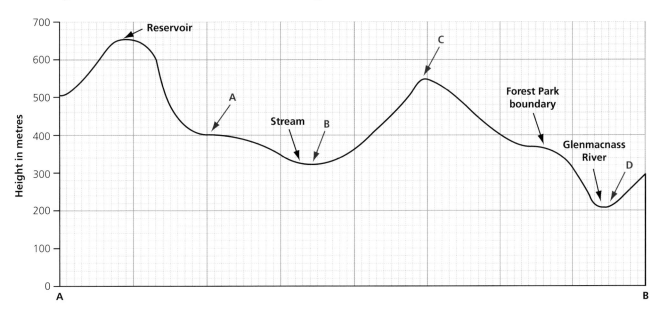

Fig 7.24 A cross-section drawn from A to B on the map extract above (Fig 7.23). Some of the features on the landscape have been named

 **Question**

Examine the map and cross-section. Can you name the features marked A, B, C and D?

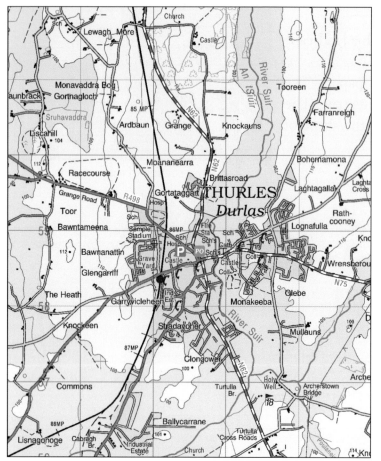

Fig 7.25 Map extract of the Thurles area

# Drawing a sketch map

To draw an Ordnance Survey map extract follow these steps:

1  Draw a frame that is the same shape as the map extract. It may be smaller than the map extract.
2  Give the sketch a title and indicate north with a direction arrow.
3  Draw the coastline (if there is one on the map extract). Insert the features that you were asked for. Do not insert any extra features.
4  Identify each feature by name or by a legend or key.

### Hint

In order to help you to position the features correctly, draw the sketch map on graph paper. Each square on the graph paper will correspond to a square on the map.

A sketch map of the Thurles area showing the following features:

◎ Built-up area
◎ N62
◎ River Suir
◎ Racecourse
◎ Railway station
◎ An area of woodland
◎ A castle
◎ A third-class road

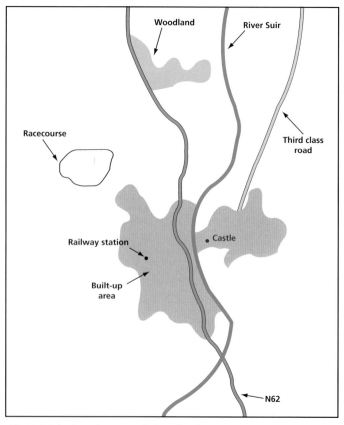

Fig 7.26 A sketch map of the Thurles area

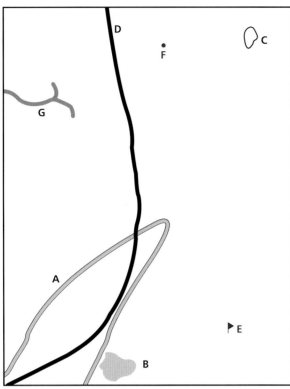

Fig 7.27 A sketch map of the Thurles area

## SUMMARY

◎ Maps are drawn to various scales.
◎ Many features on maps are identified by symbols (seen in the legend).
◎ Direction is described using compass points.
◎ Location is described by four-figure and six-figure grid references.
◎ Height is indicated by colour, contours, spot heights and triangulation pillars.
◎ Slopes (even, convex or concave) are indicated by the closeness of the contours.

## QUESTIONS

Draw a sketch map of the Thurles area. On it show and name the following features:
◎ Railway line
◎ N75
◎ R498
◎ Industrial estate
◎ Post Office
◎ Semple Stadium

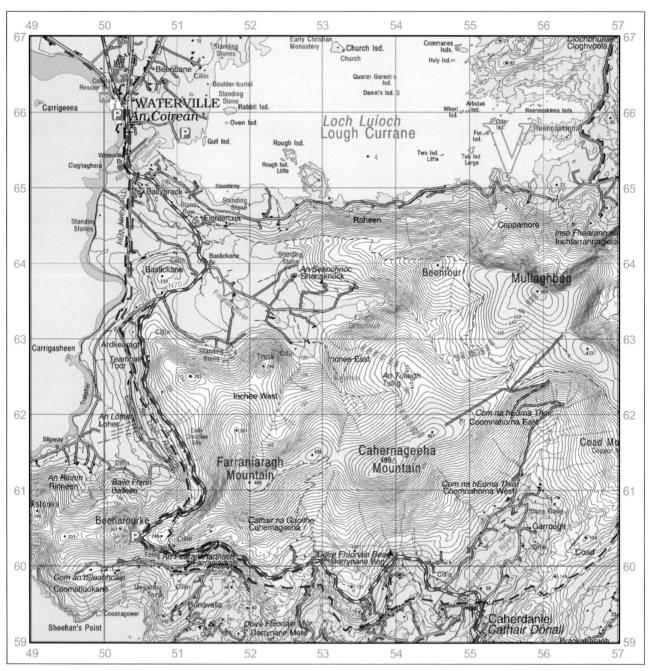

Fig 7.28 Waterville OS map extract

## QUESTIONS

1  Calculate the following distances:
   (a) The straight-line distance between the tops of Cahernageeha Mountain and Mullaghbeg.
   (b) The straight-line distance between the Parking Area in Waterville and the Parking Area at Beenarourke.
   (c) The distance along the N70 between the same two Parking Areas.

2  Calculate the area of each of the following:
   (a) The full map extract
   (b) Lough Currane

3  Identify one feature at each of the following four-figure grid references:
   (a) V 53 63
   (b) V 51 62
   (c) V 50 59
   (d) V 49 64

4  Give a four-figure grid reference for each of the following:
   (a) Post Office in Waterville
   (b) Church Island
   (c) Parking Area at Beenarourke
   (d) Lough Dreenaun

5  Identify the feature at each of the following six-figure grid references:
   (a) V 504 604
   (b) V 491 661
   (c) V 549 660
   (d) V 499 646
   (e) V 525 639
   (f) V 550 660

6  Give a six-figure grid reference for each of the following:
   (a) Church Island
   (b) Parking Area at Waterville
   (c) Caherdaniel Post Office
   (d) Top of Cahernageeha Mountain
   (e) Lough Dreenaun
   (f) Sheehan's Point

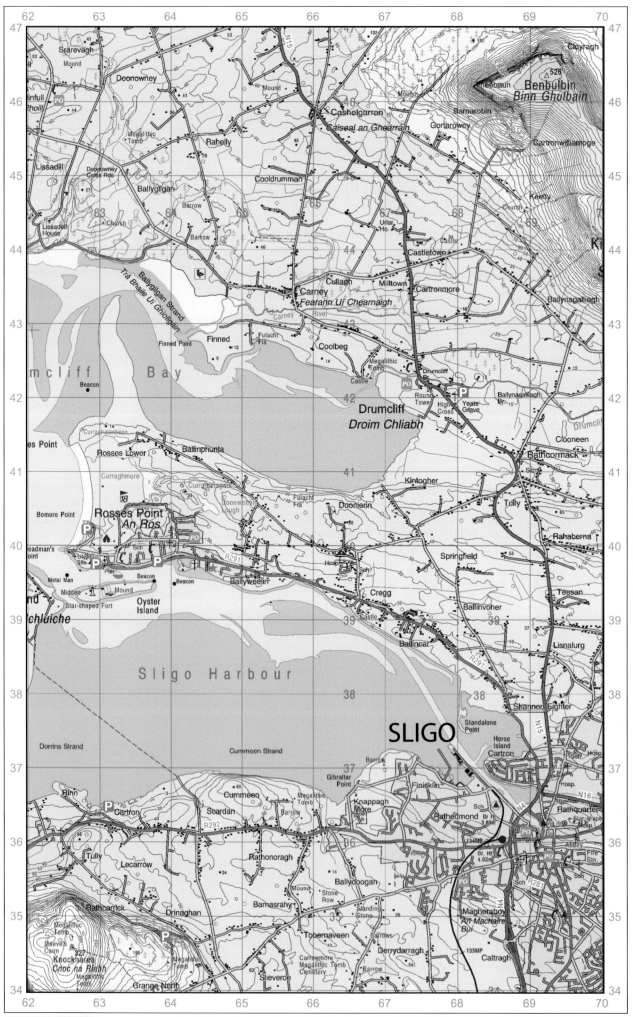

Fig 7.29 Sligo OS map extract

## QUESTIONS

1 Draw a sketch map of the area shown on the map. On it show and name:
   (a) the coastline
   (b) Drumcliff river
   (c) a regional road
   (d) a beach
   (e) an isolated hill
   (f) an antiquity
   (g) an area of forest
   (h) railway station.

2 (a) Calculate the straight line distance (in kilometres) from the Parking Area at Drumcliff to the parking Area at Rosses Point.
   (b) Calculate the straight line distance from the Post Office at Rosses Point to the Post Office at Drumcliff.
   (c) Calculate the distance (in kilometres) of the R291. (JC)

3 (a) Calculate the area of the full map extract.
   (b) Calculate the area of Sligo Harbour. (JC)

4 Give a six-figure grid reference for each of the following:
   (a) Benbulbin
   (b) Golf course
   (c) Railway station
   (d) Caravan park
   (e) Nature Reserve
   (f) Tourist Information Office. (JC)

5 Identify the feature located at each of the following grid references:
   (a) G 626 346
   (b) G 623 444
   (c) G 681 420
   (d) G 629 440
   (e) G 670 370
   (f) G 674 340. (JC)

6 Identify each of the following directions:
   (a) Sligo lies to the _____ of Benbulbin.
   (b) Rosses Point lies to the _____ of Benbulbin.
   (c) The Nature Reserve lies to the _____ of Sligo.
   (d) Drumcliff lies to the _____ of Rosses Point.
   (e) The Carney River flows in a _____ direction.
   (f) The R292 comes into Sligo from the _____. (JC)

7 (a) What is the name and height of the second highest peak on the map?
   (b) By how many metres is Benbulbin higher than Knocknarea?
   (c) List three ways by which height is shown in grid square G 64 36.
   (d) What is the height above sea level of the water in Lough Curraghmore? (JC)

8 Select the correct answer from the brackets:
   (a) The northern side of Benbulbin has a (convex/even) slope.
   (b) The slopes of Knocknarea are (steep/gentle).
   (c) The slope in grid square G 68 45 is (even/concave). (JC)

# 7.2 Reading the Physical Landscape

By understanding colour, contours and gradient on OS maps, it is possible to identify different features of the physical landscape. These relate to relief and drainage.

## Relief

Relief refers to the shape of the physical landscape. It includes references to:

◎ Height and slope (see pages 141 and 142)
◎ Landforms or shapes in the landscape

If you refer back to these maps, you will find that we have already identified some landforms on OS maps:

◎ Map showing fluvial (river) landforms (see page 43).
◎ Map showing coastal landforms (see page 56).
◎ Map showing glacial landforms (see page 63).

We can also identify a number of other relief features on an OS map.

**Lowland:** An area of land that is below 200m in height (shown in green on map).

**Mountain:** A landform, often with steep sides, that is above 400m in height.

**Hill:** An area of land that is above 200m but below 400m in height.

**Gap:** A low area between two areas of upland. Roads often follow gaps.

**Plateau:** An upland area with steep sides and a fairly flat top.

**Ridge:** A long narrow area of upland, with steep sides falling away from it.

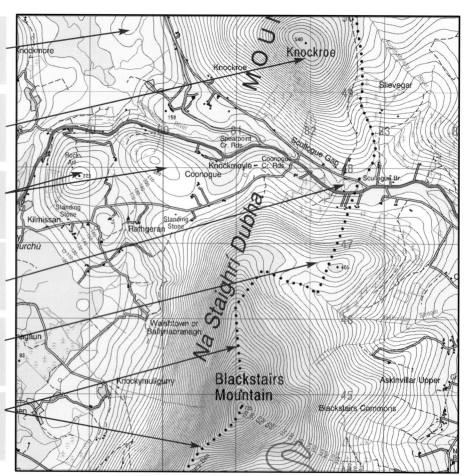

Fig 7.30 Some relief features on an OS map

# Drainage

Drainage refers to the ways that water flows in the landscape. It includes rivers, lakes and marshy areas.

We can identify areas that are well drained or badly drained by the following characteristics.

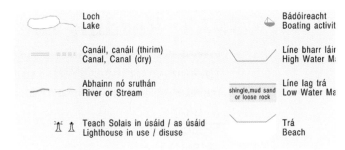

Fig 7.31 Water symbols on an OS map

| Lots of settlement (houses and villages) | Lots of roads, including minor roads | Little surface water. Few rivers |
|---|---|---|

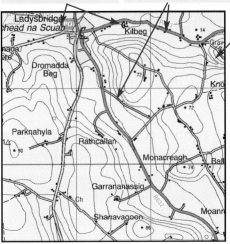

Fig 7.32 Evidence of a well-drained landscape

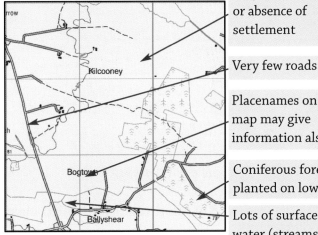

Fig 7.33 Evidence of a badly-drained landscape

Very little settlement or absence of settlement

Very few roads

Placenames on the map may give information also

Coniferous forests planted on lowlands

Lots of surface water (streams or small lakes)

---

### SUMMARY

◎ Relief refers to the shape of the landscape and includes height, gradient and landforms.

◎ Drainage refers to water in the landscape.

---

### QUESTIONS

1 Examine the OS map of Waterville, Fig 7.28, on page 146. Link each grid reference to one of these features: bridge, lake, beach, island.
   (a) V 499 623
   (b) V 518 660
   (c) V 503 653
   (d) V 535 634

2 Examine the OS map of Sligo, Fig 7.29, on page 148. Link each grid reference to one of these landforms: cliff, sand spit, meander, hill.
   (a) G 625 345
   (b) G 633 420
   (c) G 648 369
   (d) G 653 432

# 7.3 Reading the Human Landscape

The human landscape refers to the changes that humans have made to the natural landscape. In particular it refers to:

◎ Communications
◎ Settlement
◎ Urban functions
◎ Land use

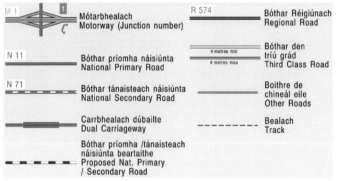

Fig 7.34 Symbols for the different classes of road

## Communications

Communications on an OS map refer to **roads**, **railways**, **canals**, **ferries** and **airports**.

The road network is by far the most important of these. The different classes of road include:

◎ **Motorways and national routes (primary and secondary)**: These link cities and large towns. The motorways are relatively new and by-pass towns rather than pass through them.

◎ **Regional roads and third class roads**: These link small towns and villages as well as connecting them to the national routes.

◎ **Third class roads and other roads**: These serve rural areas and link them to the more important routes listed above.

### Influences on communications

1 **Few roads are built in upland areas.**
   ◎ Very few people live in these areas so there is no need for roads.
   ◎ The steep gradients make road building both difficult and expensive.

2 **Most roads are built in low-lying areas.**
   ◎ Roads are built to serve people and most people live in low-lying areas.
   ◎ The gentler gradients make road building easier.
   ◎ Roads are often built to follow the contours at the foot of a hill, giving them a level course.

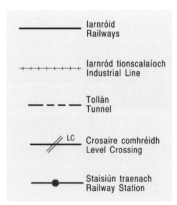

Fig 7.35 Other types of communications are identified by the symbols above

3 **Roads cut through mountains at their lowest point.**
   ◎ Roads take the easiest and lowest route through mountains. This is along a valley floor or through a gap, again following the contours where possible.

4 **Roads are influenced by rivers.**
   ◎ When roads follow a river valley, they are built at the edge of the floodplain, well back from the river, where possible. This is to avoid the risk of flooding.
   ◎ Bridges are built where there is a need for a road to cross a river. These locations are called **bridging points**.

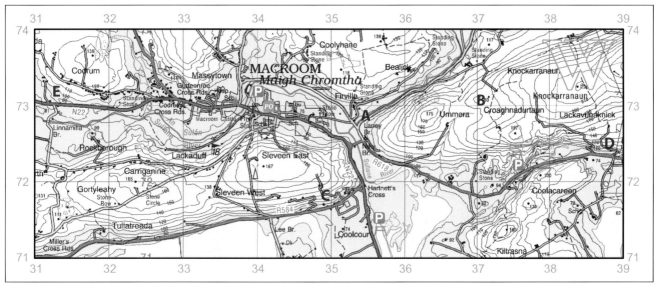

Fig 7.36 Roads in and around Macroom

## Settlement

A **settlement** is a place where people live. It can vary in size from a single house to a large city.

   The study of settlement can be divided into three sections:

◎ Ancient settlement
◎ Rural settlement
◎ Urban settlement

## Ancient settlement

Ancient settlement refers to a place that is no longer occupied. It includes historical sites and antiquities. These are **shown** and **named in red** on Ordnance Survey maps. Many are identified by a **symbol**, also in red.

> **Question**
>
> Which of the factors, numbered 1 to 4 above, influenced the building of roads at the locations lettered A, B, C, D and E?

· Séadchomhartha
  Ainmnithe
  Named Antiquities

o Clós, m.sh. Ráth nó Lios
  Enclosure, e.g. Ringfort

⚔ Láthair Chatha (le dáta)
  Battlefield (with date)

Fig 7.37 Symbols for antiquities on OS maps

Examples of ancient settlement include the following shown in the table below. They are grouped according to the function that they served.

| Burial sites | Defence | Worship/Religion | Everyday life |
|---|---|---|---|
| ◎ Megalithic tomb | ◎ Ring fort | ◎ Stone circle/Row | ◎ Midden |
| ◎ Dolmen | ◎ Crannóg | ◎ Bullaun stone | ◎ Fulacht fia |
| ◎ Cairn | ◎ Lios | ◎ Holy well | ◎ Togher |
| ◎ Mound (barrow) | ◎ Dún/Fort | ◎ Cill/Cillín | |
| ◎ Graveyard | ◎ Round tower | ◎ Church | |
| ◎ Ogham stone | ◎ Motte and bailey | ◎ Friary/Abbey | |
| ◎ Standing stone | ◎ Castle | ◎ High cross | |

**✍ Question**

Examine the map on the right. Identify one example of each of the following:
◎ Burial site
◎ Defence
◎ Religion
◎ Everyday life

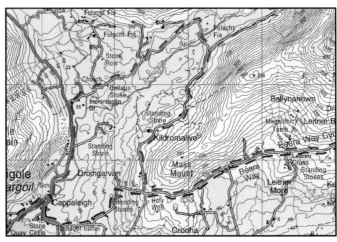

Fig 7.38 Antiquities in an OS map

**✍ Question**

Examine the photograph. List three pieces of evidence that indicate that Clonmacnoise is an ancient religious settlement.

Clonmacnoise is an ancient religious settlement

# Rural settlement

The location (or distribution) of rural settlement is influenced by a number of factors. When people first decided where to settle, they were attracted by some factors and put off by others.

## Altitude

Most people live on land that is below 200 metres in Ireland (green on an OS map). Above 200 metres, the weather can be too cold, too wet and too windy.

## Aspect

The direction in which a settlement faces is called its **aspect**. South-facing slopes attract settlement because they get more sunshine and are warmer than north-facing slopes.

## Shelter

Valley floors provide a sheltered location for settlement. Settlements that are located at the foot of a hill or mountain are sheltered also.

## Slope

People are attracted to flat or gently sloping land because there is better soil for farming and it is easier to build houses and roads.

## Drainage

People prefer to settle in areas that are well drained. Poorly drained land is likely to flood and may not be suitable for agriculture.

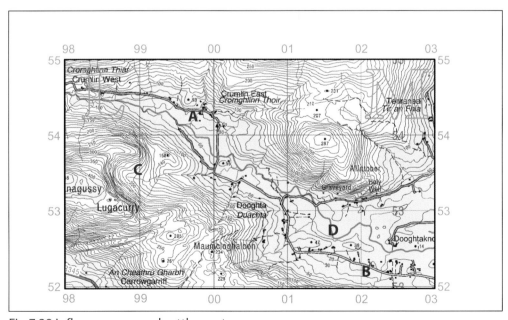

Fig 7.39 Influences on rural settlement

### Questions

1 What factors have attracted settlement to A and B?
2 Why is there an absence of settlement at C and D?

## Patterns of rural settlement

There are three patterns of rural settlement:

◎ Nucleated settlement
◎ Linear settlement
◎ Dispersed settlement

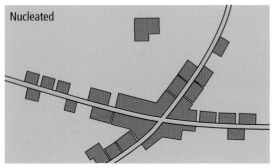

Fig 7.40a

Fig 7.40b Nucleated (or clustered) settlement pattern

## Nucleated settlement

In nucleated settlements houses are clustered together in groups. This generally happens at a small village or at a point where roads meet.

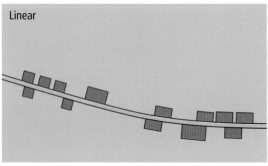

Fig 7.41a

Fig 7.41b Linear settlement pattern

## Linear settlement

Linear settlement can also be called **ribboned** settlement. Houses are built in a line along a road. This pattern is usually found along a coastline, at the foot of a mountain or at the edge of a village or town.

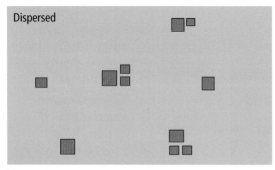

Fig 7.42a

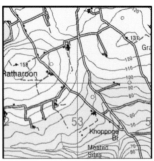

Fig 7.42b Dispersed settlement pattern

## Dispersed settlement

In dispersed settlement individual houses are scattered around the countryside in a random pattern. Many are farmhouses, each on their own farm and with their outbuildings. Others are one-off houses.

## Urban settlement

Urban settlement refers to cities, towns and large villages. These are built-up areas where the buildings are grouped closely together. Built-up areas are identified on an OS map by the grey-coloured symbol in Fig 7.43.

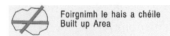

Fig 7.43 OS symbol for a built-up (urban) area

## Location of urban settlements

Location refers to the place where a town developed and its surrounding area. The three main factors that influenced the development of towns are:

◎ Relief
◎ Drainage
◎ Communications

| Urban settlement was influenced by relief |
| --- |

Most towns developed on flat or gently sloping lowland areas.
◎ The construction of roads and buildings was easier and cheaper.
◎ The surrounding area was more likely to have fertile agricultural land to supply food.

| Urban settlement is influenced by rivers |
| --- |

Most towns developed near rivers.
◎ In times past, rivers were used for water supply and transport.
◎ Rivers provided defence from attack.
◎ Towns developed at places where bridges could be built (bridging points).

| Good transport links allowed trade to develop |
| --- |

Towns developed where:
◎ A number of roads met (**route focus**).
◎ The town was on a rail route (with a railway station).
◎ The town had a canal link (look for locks).
◎ The town developed as a port (trade and fishing).

| Hint |
| --- |

When explaining something on an OS map, always use some evidence (names etc.) taken directly from the map. See the Case Study below.

> ☞ **Definition**
>
> **Route focus:** Occurs where several roads meet, e.g. at a bridging point.

## Case Study

## Location of Navan

### Describe the location of Navan

◎ Navan is built on gently sloping land, just below the 50-metre contour.
◎ Navan is a **route focus**, built at the meeting point of several roads. The N3, N51, R161, R153 and R162 meet there.
◎ Navan is built at two bridging points. These are at the confluence (meeting point) of two rivers, one of which is the River Boyne.
◎ Navan is surrounded by fertile farmland that is both low-lying (below 70 metres) and well drained.

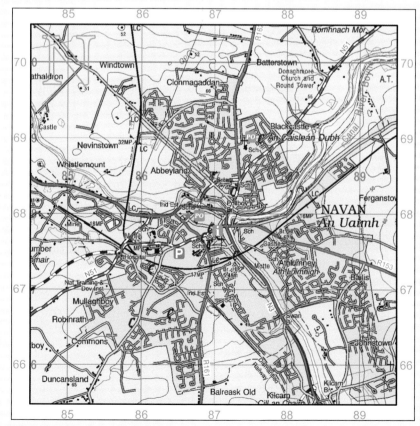

Fig 7.44 Location of Navan

## Urban functions on OS maps

The term **function** refers to the services and activities that the town provides for the people who live or work there or in the surrounding area.

Most Irish towns have several functions. Some can be identified by the symbols on the OS map. Others, such as retail and administrative can be suggested. A wide range of functions attracts people and helps the town to develop.

Present-day functions of urban areas include the following:

| Function | Map evidence |
|---|---|
| **Industrial** | ◎ Is there an industrial estate in or near the town? <br> ◎ Are any raw material available locally? |
| **Transport** | ◎ What roads meet in the town? <br> ◎ Is there a railway and railway station? <br> ◎ Are there car parks in the town? |
| **Port** | ◎ Is the harbour deep and sheltered? <br> ◎ Are there piers, quays or lighthouses? |
| **Tourist** | ◎ What attractions in or around the town would encourage people to visit and stay? <br> ◎ For more details, see pages 161 and 162. |
| **Educational** | ◎ Is there a range of schools and colleges? <br> ◎ Is there a university? |
| **Religious** | ◎ Is there a cathedral as well as a number of churches? |
| **Medical** | ◎ Is there a hospital in or near the town? |
| **Residential** | ◎ Are there residential suburbs on the outskirts of the town? |

## Functions change over time

The importance of some functions **change over time**. Defence and monastic functions were important in the past but may not be so today. However, some evidence of these functions still remains today.

Evidence of a former **defence** function includes castles, towers, mottes and bailies, town walls and town gates.

**Monastic** centres also offered services such as education and healthcare. Evidence of past monastic settlement includes round towers, abbeys, priories and friaries.

# Case Study

## Urban functions of Drogheda

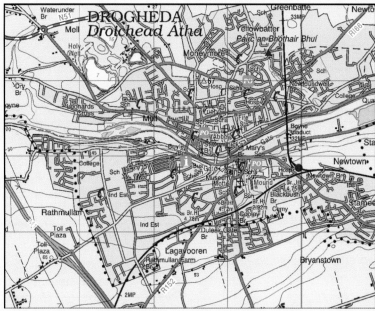

Fig 7.45 Urban functions of Drogheda

### Question

Can you identify two functions of Drogheda that have not been listed in the Case Study? What evidence from the map supports your answer?

Some present-day functions of Drogheda include the following:

| Function | Map evidence |
|---|---|
| **Industrial** | ◎ Two industrial estates |
| **Transport** | ◎ Motorway (M1), national roads (N51)<br>◎ Railway junction and station<br>◎ Bus station |
| **Tourist** | ◎ Tourist Information Office<br>◎ Wide range of antiquities (motte, gate etc.)<br>◎ Youth hostel<br>◎ Museum |
| **Educational** | ◎ Several schools and colleges |
| **Residential** | ◎ Residential estates (Newtown, Yellowbatter etc.) |

Some past functions of Drogheda include:

| Function | Map evidence |
|---|---|
| **Defence** | ◎ Motte, gates |
| **Monastic** | ◎ Priory, abbey |

## Land use

Land use refers to the way in which land is used. We have already studied two land uses: settlement and communications. We can identify or interpret a number of other land uses, including:

◉ Forestry
◉ Agriculture
◉ Bogs
◉ Industry
◉ Tourism and leisure

## Forestry

Forestry is rarely the preferred land use. Forests are usually planted on land that is not suited to agriculture.

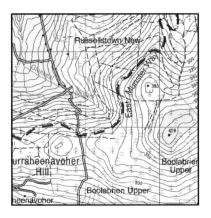

**Coniferous forests** are planted on upland slopes. These areas are unsuited to agriculture because the gradient is too steep and the soil quality is poor. The trees also help to prevent soil erosion.

**Coniferous forests** are planted on lowland areas where the land is poorly drained. The marshy land is also likely to flood and is unsuited to agriculture. The trees also absorb much of the excess moisture.

**Natural woodland** (deciduous trees) and **mixed woodland** are mainly associated with country estates and demesnes. They were often planted for privacy and to enhance the scenery. Many date back to the time of the plantations.

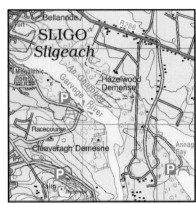

Fig 7.46 Forested areas as shown on OS maps

## Agriculture

Agriculture is the main land use in Ireland. It is not shown on OS maps, but we can argue for its presence.

Most agriculture takes place in lowland areas that are well drained. Dispersed rural settlement, especially when the houses are set back from main roads, are usually farmhouses with their outbuildings. See Figures 7.42(a) and (b) on page 156.

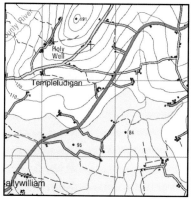

Fig 7.47 Agricultural land as shown on OS maps

## Bogs

Raised bogs are deep, level bogs that are found in the Midlands of Ireland. They contain peat up to a depth of about 7 metres.

The area is very flat (absence of contours). Much of the area does not have any settlement. Part of the area may be planted with coniferous forests. Some placenames also give information.

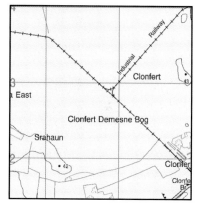

Fig 7.48 Bogland as shown on OS maps

Fig 7.49 Industry on an OS map

## Industry

Many towns have industrial estates. These are usually located at the edge of the town. They are nearly always located next to good transport links. (See also Factory location, on page 330.)

> **Question**
>
> Apart from the industrial estates, is there any other evidence on the map in Fig 7.49 to indicate that the town has an industrial function?

## Tourism and leisure

A wide range of tourist attractions and leisure facilities can be seen on Ordnance Survey maps. Many of them are identified on the legend by symbols.

| | |
|---|---|
| Láithreán carbhán (idirthurais) Caravan site (transit) | Ionad eolais turasóireachta (ar oscailt ar feadh na bliana) Tourist Information centre (regular opening) |
| Brú de chuid An Óige Youth Hostel (An Óige) | Ionad eolais turasóireachta (ar oscailt le linn an tséasúir) Tourist Information centre (restricted opening) |
| Brú saoire Neamhspleách Independent Holiday Hostel | Ionad dearctha Viewpoint |
| Ionad pairceála Parking | An Taisce National Trust |
| Láithreán picnicí Picnic site | Tearmann Dúlra Nature Reserve |
| Teilefón Poiblí Public Telephone | |
| Láithreán campála Camping site | Galfchúrsa, machaire gailf Golf Course or Links |

Fig 7.50 Tourist information shown on an OS map

| Feature | Activities/Attraction |
|---|---|
| Mountains | Scenery, hill walking, rock climbing |
| Rivers and lakes | Cruising, canoeing, fishing, scenery |
| Coast/beaches/harbours | Boating, swimming, fishing, windsurfing, sunbathing, playing on beach |
| Forests | Forest parks, nature trails, picnic sites, orienteering |
| Nature reserves | Wildlife, plants, scenery, bird-watching |
| Historic attractions | Antiquities (castles, ring forts etc.) demesnes, interest in history |
| Recreation | Golf courses, racecourses, sports grounds |
| Accommodation | Youth hostels, caravan parks, camping sites |

## Describing tourist attractions

When describing a tourist attraction or leisure facility:

1 Name the attraction or facility.
2 Locate it using a grid reference.
3 Explain why it is attractive to tourists and what activities it could be used for.

## Question

Can you name and locate, using six-figure grid references, any five tourist attractions in the Waterville area?

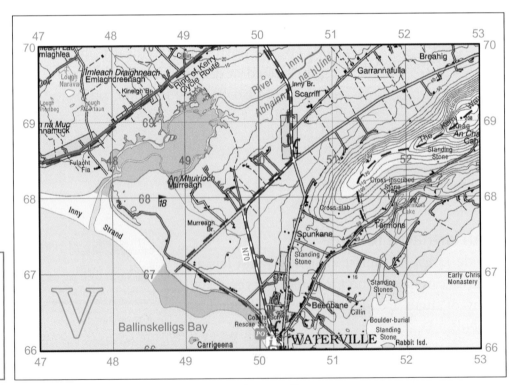

Fig 7.51 Tourist attractions in and around Waterville

# Placenames

Placenames on an OS map can give information about the physical or the human landscape.

While most placenames were originally Gaelic, some have English, Norman or Viking origins. When we know the meaning of the original root word, we can understand the origin of many placenames.

| Root word | Meaning | Examples |
|---|---|---|
| Áth | Crossing point of a river | Athlone, Athy, Baile Átha Cliath |
| Cnoc | Hill | Knock, Knockree |
| Carriag | Rock | Carrick-on-Suir, Carrigaline |
| Gleann | Glen/valley | Glendalough, Glenmore, Glencar |
| Loch | Lake | Loughrea, Lochbeg |
| Port | Harbour/landing place | Portmarnock, Portlaw, Portumna |
| Trá | Beach | Tramore, Tralee |
| Baile | Small town/townland | Ballybunion, Ballyshannon |
| Cill | Church | Kilkenny, Killarney |
| Dún | Fort | Dunmore, Dungarvan |
| Lios | Fort | Lismore, Liscannor |
| Rath | Fort | Rathgar, Rathmore |

## Some placenames with non-gaelic root words

| Root word | Meaning | Examples |
|---|---|---|
| Castle– | Defensive site | Castlebar, Castlecomer |
| –town | Plantation town/estate | Rochestown, Grantstown |
| –land | Land given during plantations | Archersland, Butlersland |
| –ford | Inlet | Waterford, Wexford |

### SUMMARY

- The human landscape refers to communications, settlement and land use.
- Communications include road, rail, ports and these are influenced by relief and drainage.
- Rural settlement is influenced by the physical landscape.
- Rural settlement can be found in a dispersed, linear or nucleated pattern.
- Rural land uses include forestry, agriculture and tourism.
- Urban settlement is influenced by relief, drainage and communications.
- Urban functions refer to the services and activities provided in the area.

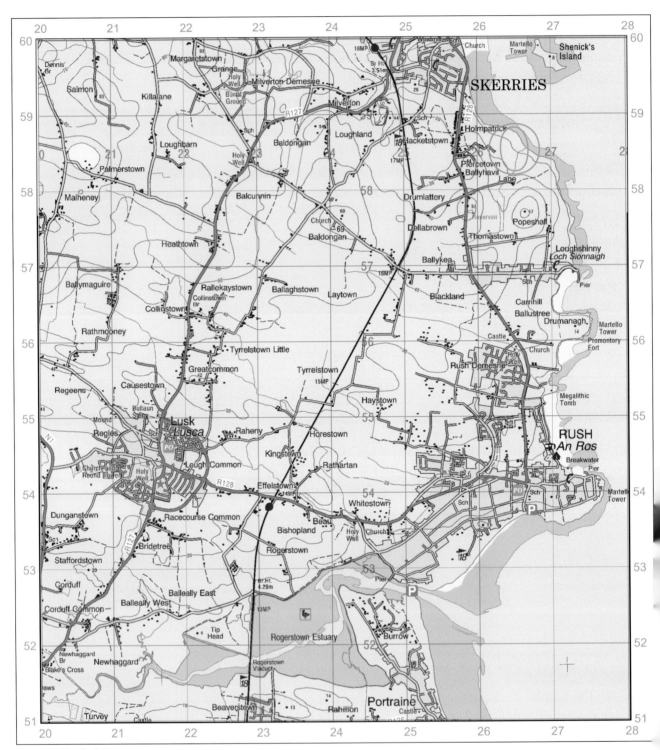

Fig 7.52 Rush OS map extract

## QUESTIONS

1   Identify and locate by six-figure grid reference any three landforms that are
    the result of coastal erosion or deposition. (JC)

2   Identify and give a brief description of the main pattern of rural settlement
    at each of the following locations:
    (a)  O 24 57
    (b)  O 25 55
    (c)  O 210 565. (JC)

3   Using map evidence to support your answer, explain two reasons why Lusk
    developed at this location. (JC)

4   'It is clear that settlement has existed in this area for a long time.'
    With reference to the OS map, identify three pieces of evidence to
    support this statement. (JC)

5   The area has a wide variety of leisure attractions for both locals and tourists.
    Describe any three of these attractions. (JC)

6   'The sea plays an important part in the life of Rush'.
    Examine this statement, using map evidence to support your answer.

7   Briefly describe the transport network in the area shown on the map.

8   It is proposed to build a group of holiday cottages at O 270 559.
    (a)  Describe one advantage and one disadvantage of the site chosen.
    (b)  Give one reason why locals might object to the proposal. (JC)

9   Identify the land use at each of the following grid references:
    (a)  O 233 538
    (b)  O 204 511
    (c)  O 225 522

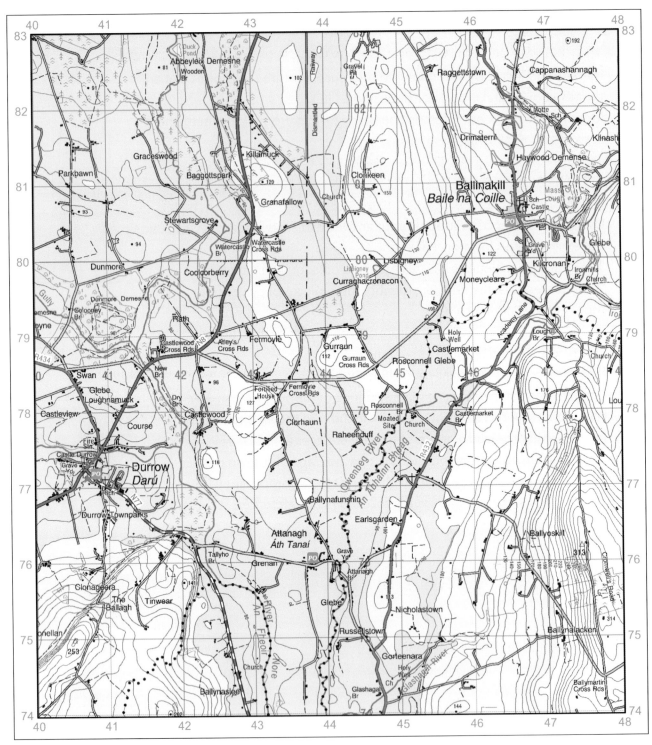

Fig 7.53 Durrow OS map extract

## QUESTIONS

1 With the aid of grid references, identify one example of each of the following from the map:
   (a) confluence
   (b) meander
   (c) floodplain
   (d) Identify one location where an oxbow lake might form.

2 Describe three reasons why Durrow developed at that location. (JC)

3 The presence of antiquities on the map suggests that defence was an important function in times past. Discuss this statement, referring to two pieces of evidence from the map. (JC)

4 Draw a sketch map and show and name the following on it:
   (a) One example of each of four types of road.
   (b) One example of each of the three patterns of settlement.
   (c) One example of each of mixed woodland, lowland coniferous forest, upland coniferous forest. (JC)

5 With reference to the OS map, identify and describe any two tourist attractions in the region. (JC)

6 Explain why there is little or no settlement at each of the following places on the OS map:
   (a) S 47 74
   (b) S 41 81. (JC)

7 Suggest an explanation for each of the following placenames:
   (a) Kilcronan (S 473 800)
   (b) Dunmore (S 413 799)
   (c) Attanagh (S 441 760)

8 With reference to the OS map, describe any two functions of the town of Durrow. (JC)

9 It is proposed to build a sawmill at S 410 780. Describe two advantages and one disadvantage of the site chosen.

# 7.4 Aerial Photographs

An aerial photograph is a view of the land surface taken from the air.

Aerial photographs provide a great deal of information, especially when they are used with Ordnance Survey maps. As is the case with maps, when a small area of ground is covered, more detail is shown.

There are two types of aerial photograph:

◎ Vertical aerial photograph
◎ Oblique aerial photograph

## Vertical aerial photograph

A vertical aerial photograph is taken with the camera pointed as straight down as possible.

It shows a view taken from directly above the landscape. The dominant feature is the roofline of buildings. It does not show the horizon.

The photograph shows the exact shape of the area covered by the camera.

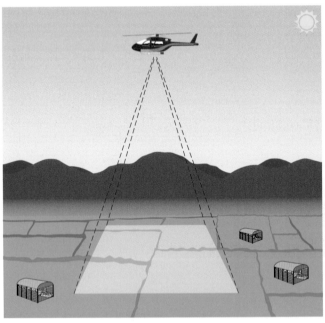

Fig 7.54 Taking a vertical aerial photograph

Vertical aerial photograph of Wexford

## Oblique aerial photograph

An oblique aerial photograph is taken with the camera pointing downwards at an angle.

It shows a view that is similar to viewing the landscape from the top of a high hill or a tall building. It may show the horizon.

The area covered by the camera is not the same shape as the photograph.

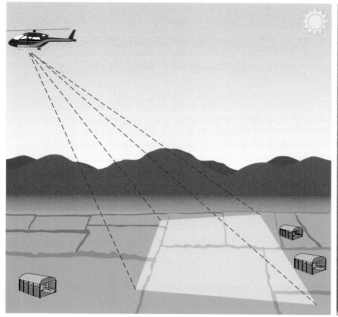

Fig 7.55 Taking an oblique aerial photograph

Oblique aerial photograph of Wexford

# Locating features on photographs

Divide the photograph into nine equally sized sections. These areas are then named according to the type of photograph used.

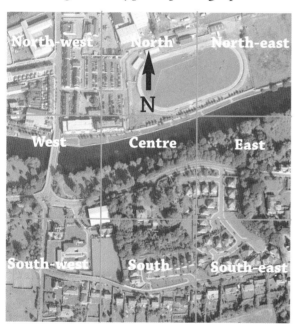

A vertical aerial photograph will have an arrow that points to the north. Use compass directions to describe the location of features

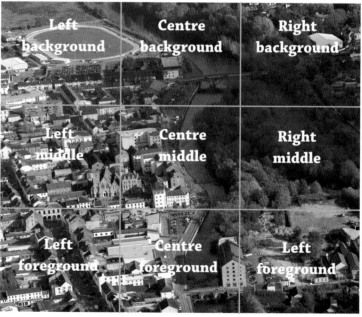

To describe location on an oblique aerial photograph, use the names of the nine divisions as shown in the picture

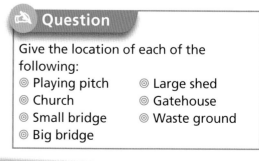

**Question**

Give the location of each of the following:
◎ Playing pitch ◎ Large shed
◎ Church ◎ Gatehouse
◎ Small bridge ◎ Waste ground
◎ Big bridge

## Scale in aerial photographs

| Vertical photographs | Oblique photographs |
|---|---|
| ◎ Scale remains true at all times.<br>◎ Features keep the same proportion to one another in the photograph as they do on the ground. | ◎ Features that are located in the foreground of the photograph appear larger.<br>◎ Features that are located in the background of the photograph appear smaller.<br>◎ The background of an oblique photograph covers a much larger area of ground than the foreground. |

# Identifying the season

It is possible to identify the season when an aerial photograph was taken by using the following pointers:

| Summer | Winter |
|---|---|
| ◎ Deciduous trees have full foliage cover.<br>◎ High summer sun casts short shadows.<br>◎ Cattle are seen grazing in the fields.<br>◎ Ripening crops are identified by bright colours.<br>◎ Hay bales may be seen in the fields. | ◎ Deciduous trees have lost their foliage cover.<br>◎ Low summer sun casts long shadows.<br>◎ Cattle have been moved indoors.<br>◎ Fields have been freshly ploughed.<br>◎ Chimney smoke from houses indicates cold weather. |

An Irish landscape viewed in the summer

# Drawing a sketch map

To draw a sketch map of an aerial photograph, follow these steps:

1 Always use a pencil (or coloured pencils).
2 Draw a frame that is the same shape as the photograph. It may be smaller than the photograph.
3 Give the sketch map a title.
4 Draw the coastline (if there is one on the map).
5 Draw the outline of the required features in a shape similar to the original.
6 Identify each feature either by name or by using a labelled key.

**Remember**: Do not trace the photograph. Do not include features that you were not asked for.

## Question

What evidence indicates that this photograph was taken in the summer?

**Question**

Draw a sketch map of the area shown on the photograph. On it show and name the following:

◎ A stream
◎ The main street
◎ A sports ground
◎ A church ruin
◎ A castle
◎ A car park
◎ A factory

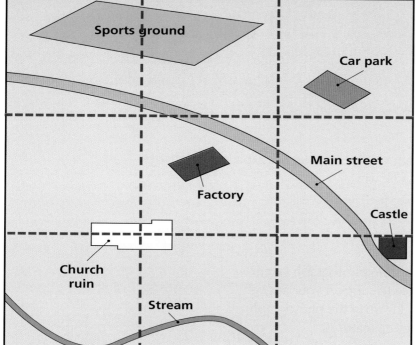

**Hint**

Draw light lines to divide the photograph frame into nine sections. This makes it easier to locate features on the sketch.

Fig 7.56 Sketch map of Kilmallock drawn from the aerial photograph above

---

**SUMMARY**

◎ Aerial photographs can be vertical or oblique.

◎ Location on oblique photographs is described by a grid system.

◎ Most photographs are taken in the summer, when skies are clear.

**QUESTIONS**

Cavan

1  What type of photograph is this: vertical or oblique? Explain your answer.
2  Give a location for each of the following:
   (a) a lake
   (b) a church
   (c) a large clump of trees
   (d) a sports ground
3  (a) At what time of the year was the photograph taken?
   (b) Give two pieces of evidence to support your answer.
4  Draw a sketch map of the area shown in the photograph.
   On it show and name the following features:
   (a) a church
   (b) a lake
   (c) two streets
   (d) a car park
   (e) a sports' field
   (f) a clump of trees
   (g) a detached house

# 7.5 Rural Settlement and Land Use

It is possible to identify evidence of rural settlement (historic and present-day) as well as land use on aerial photographs.

## Historic settlement

Historic rural settlement includes the following:

| Defensive settlements | Burial sites | Religious settlements |
|---|---|---|
| ◎ Castles | ◎ Graveyards | ◎ Monasteries/abbeys |
| ◎ Stone forts | ◎ Standing stones | ◎ Church ruins |
| ◎ Round towers | ◎ Dolmens | ◎ Crosses |

## Present-day settlement

Most present-day settlement in rural areas consists of individual houses. Some are farmhouses. They can be identified by their farm buildings and the farmland that surrounds them. They form a **dispersed** settlement pattern (see page 156).

Some houses are built along the sides of rural roads, where they form a **linear** pattern (see page 156).

## Land use

Some rural land uses can also be identified in aerial photographs.

- ◎ **Pastoral farming**: Identified by green fields in which grass is growing and animals are grazing.
- ◎ **Arable farming**: Identified by ploughed fields or by fields where crops are ripening or have been harvested.
- ◎ **Woodland**: Identified by areas of coniferous or deciduous trees.
- ◎ **Market gardening**: Identified by areas of polythene tunnels or glasshouses.
- ◎ **Mining or quarrying**: Identified where large areas have been excavated.

Historic rural settlement

> **Question**
>
> Examine the photograph.
> (a) Identify two different examples of historic rural settlement.
> (b) Identify two rural land uses.

◎ Dispersed and linear rural settlement patterns may be identified on photographs.
◎ Rural land uses that can be identified on photographs include pastoral farming, arable farming and forestry.

🪨 QUESTIONS

Present-day rural settlement and land use

1  (a)  Identify two patterns of rural settlement in the photograph.
   (b)  Select one of these patterns and explain how it developed. (JC)
2  (a)  Identify two land uses in the photograph.
   (b)  Describe any one of them.
3  Draw a sketch map of the area shown on the photograph. On it show and name the following:
   (a)  two roads
   (b)  linear settlement
   (c)  farm outbuildings
   (d)  pastureland
   (e)  fields with cereals growing
   (f)  rough pasture. (JC)

## 7.6 Urban Settlement

Many of the aspects discussed here are similar to those that apply to Ordnance Survey maps (see pages 134–45).

## Location of urban settlement

The location and growth of urban settlement is influenced by a combination of the following factors:

### Relief

◎ The construction of roads and buildings is easier on flat or gently sloping lowlands.

### Transport

◎ A number of roads may meet there (route focus).
◎ A railway may pass through the town.
◎ The town may be built next to a canal.

 **Question**

Describe three reasons why the town of Drogheda developed at this location.

### Rivers

◎ In times past, rivers were used for water supply.
◎ Towns developed at points where the river could be crossed (bridging point).
◎ Large rivers were used for trade and transport.
◎ Rivers are important for tourism and leisure.

### Coast

◎ The town may develop as a fishing port.
◎ The town may develop as a tourist resort.
◎ The town may develop as a commercial port.

Drogheda: the camera is pointing towards the mouth of the river

## Urban functions

The term **function** refers to those services and activities that a town provides for people who work or live in the town or surrounding areas. (See also Urban functions on OS maps, page 159.)

Some urban functions that can be identified on aerial photographs include the following:

◎ **Residential** (houses, apartments etc.)
◎ **Transport** (roads, rail, car parks, port, canal)
◎ **Retail** (shops, shopping centres etc.)
◎ **Commercial** (office blocks etc.)
◎ **Religious** (churches, abbeys, convents etc.)
◎ **Port** (docks, cranes, containers, ships etc.)
◎ **Industrial** (factories, industrial estates)
◎ **Educational** (schools and colleges)
◎ **Recreational** (playing fields, tennis courts, golf course)

◎ **Tourist** (marinas, beaches, golf course, historic buildings)
◎ **Health** (hospitals)

It is also possible to identify past functions of a town. These include:

◎ **Defensive** (town walls, castle, towers, mottes)
◎ **Industrial** (mill-races or wheels, weirs, old mill buildings)
◎ **Market** (market squares, market houses, warehouses near the river or canal)

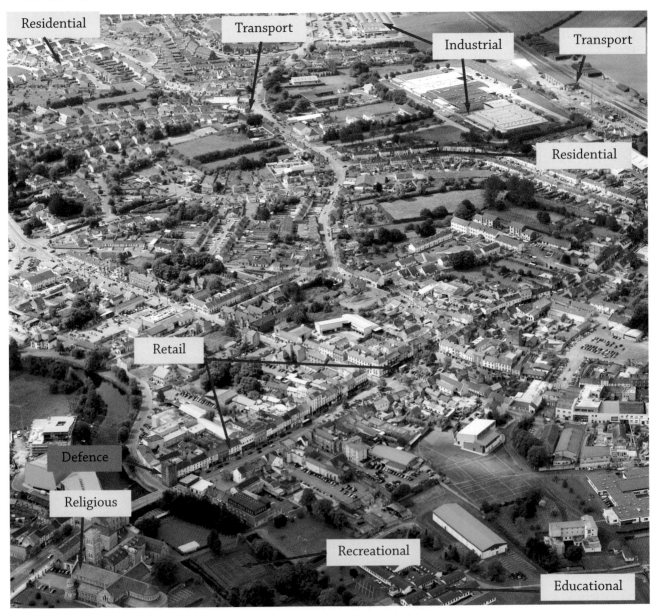

Some of the functions of Thurles

# Identifying tourism and recreational attractions

Photographs also provide details on some of the tourist and leisure attractions that may be available in the town and surrounding area.

| Feature | Activities/Attraction |
| --- | --- |
| Recreation | Golf courses, racecourses, sports grounds, tennis courts |
| Rivers and lakes | Cruising, canoeing, fishing, scenery |
| Coast/beaches/ harbours | Boating, swimming, fishing, windsurfing, sunbathing, playing on beach |
| Forests | Nature trails, picnic sites, walking |
| Historic attractions | Antiquities (castles, towers, walls etc.) demesnes, architecture |
| Accommodation | Caravan parks, camping sites, holiday homes |
| Shopping | Shopping centres, shops |

**Question**

Name and locate four examples of tourist or leisure facilities on the photograph of Lahinch, Co. Clare.

Lahinch, Co. Clare

Managing traffic near the North Gate Bridge in Cork

## Question

Identify four ways by which the Local Authority has attempted to manage traffic flow in this part of Cork.

## Managing traffic

The increase in the number of cars on Irish roads has led to an increase in traffic congestion in urban areas. It is possible to pinpoint where this congestion is likely to occur. These include:

◎ The main shopping streets.
◎ Places where several streets meet.
◎ Points where streets become narrow.
◎ Points close to schools and shopping centres.

Measures that have been taken to reduce traffic congestion include the following:

◎ Controlling traffic flow with traffic lights.
◎ Yellow boxes to ease congestion where roads intersect.
◎ Double yellow lines to prevent on-street parking.
◎ One-way streets to regulate the flow of traffic.
◎ Pedestrianising some streets.
◎ Roundabouts to reduce delays at intersections.
◎ Bypasses and ring roads to reduce the amount of traffic passing through a town.
◎ Off-street car parking and multi-storey car parks.

## Identifying house types

A number of different housing types can be identified on aerial photographs, including:

◎ Terraced houses
◎ Semi-detached houses
◎ Detached houses
◎ Apartment blocks

We can give more information on the houses by referring to some of the following points:

| Gardens | Front garden, back garden, no garden |
|---------|--------------------------------------|
| Location | In the town centre, on an outlying street, in the suburbs |
| Density | High density (apartments and terraces), low density (detached and semi-detached houses) |
| Pattern | In a set or planned pattern (suburban estates), one-off housing |
| Open space | Green or open space (suburban estates), fronting directly on to streets (terraces) |

Different housing types in Swords

# Urban planning

Urban areas are rapidly expanding. Most of this is accounted for by the growth in residential areas and industrial estates. Other facilities, including shopping centres and schools, are also part of urban growth.

This expansion needs to be properly planned and controlled.

## Locating a factory

◎ **Site**: Large greenfield site to allow for factory buildings, storage, parking and future expansion.

◎ **Transport**: Access to major roads, a railway or a port is required for transporting raw materials and finished products as well as ease of access for workers.

◎ **Environment**: The location should be at a reasonable distance from residential areas, schools and hospitals, because of noise and traffic considerations.

**Questions**

1 Identify one example of each of the housing types listed above in the photograph of Swords?

2 Select any two housing types and give a brief description of each.

## Locating a residential area

◎ **Site**: Level sites are preferred for ease of construction. Space for the provision of recreational facilities is required.

◎ **Transport**: Access to main roads for car owners and the availability of public transport are essential.

◎ **Environment**: The location should be at a reasonable distance from industrial areas because of noise and traffic considerations.

## Locating a school

◎ **Site**: A large site is required for school buildings, sports facilities and parking.

◎ **Transport**: Schools should be distant from main routeways because of traffic danger, noise and air pollution. They should be located close to residential areas to reduce the need for transport.

◎ **Environment**: The location should be at a reasonable distance from industrial areas because of noise and traffic considerations.

## Locating a shopping centre

◎ **Site**: A large site is required for the shopping centre, customer car park and delivery trucks.

◎ **Transport**: Access to major roads for delivery trucks as well as customers' cars is essential.

◎ **Environment**: Many shopping centres are built close to residential areas, reducing the need for transport.

### Questions

1 Identify and describe any three housing types in the photograph of Claremorris.

2 Describe two reasons why a shopping centre was built at this location.

A shopping centre and residential areas at Claremorris

## SUMMARY

◎ Urban settlement is influenced by relief, drainage and communications.

◎ Urban functions include residential, transport, retail, religious, educational, recreational and tourist.

◎ Past urban functions include defensive and market.

◎ Local authorities have introduced measures to manage traffic flow.

◎ Housing types include detached, semi-detached, terraced and apartments.

◎ Proper planning is important when locating factories, schools and residential areas.

## QUESTIONS

Trim

1 Give a location for each of the following features:
the big bridge, the castle, a ruined tower, a building site. (JC)

2 Draw a sketch map of the area shown on the photograph. On it show and name one piece of evidence for each of the following: tourism, shopping, agriculture, and transport, residential, construction.

3 Describe two pieces of evidence in the photograph to suggest that the functions of Trim have changed over time. (JC)

4 It is proposed to develop the land in the left foreground of the photograph.
(a) Suggest a suitable use for this land.
(b) Explain two reasons for your choice. (JC)

5 Describe any two reasons why Trim developed at this location. (JC)

Westport

1   Draw a sketch map of the aerial photograph. On it show and name the following:
     two streets, a factory, a church, a car park, a clump of trees, a canal. (JC)
2   The buildings in the left middleground and the right background differ greatly.
     Describe any three differences between these buildings. (JC)
3   The Local Authority has made efforts to reduce traffic congestion in Westport.
     Using the photograph only, describe two such methods. (JC)
4   In what season was this photograph taken? Describe two pieces of evidence
     that support your answer. (JC)
5   Identify and locate any three functions of Westport. Describe any two of them.

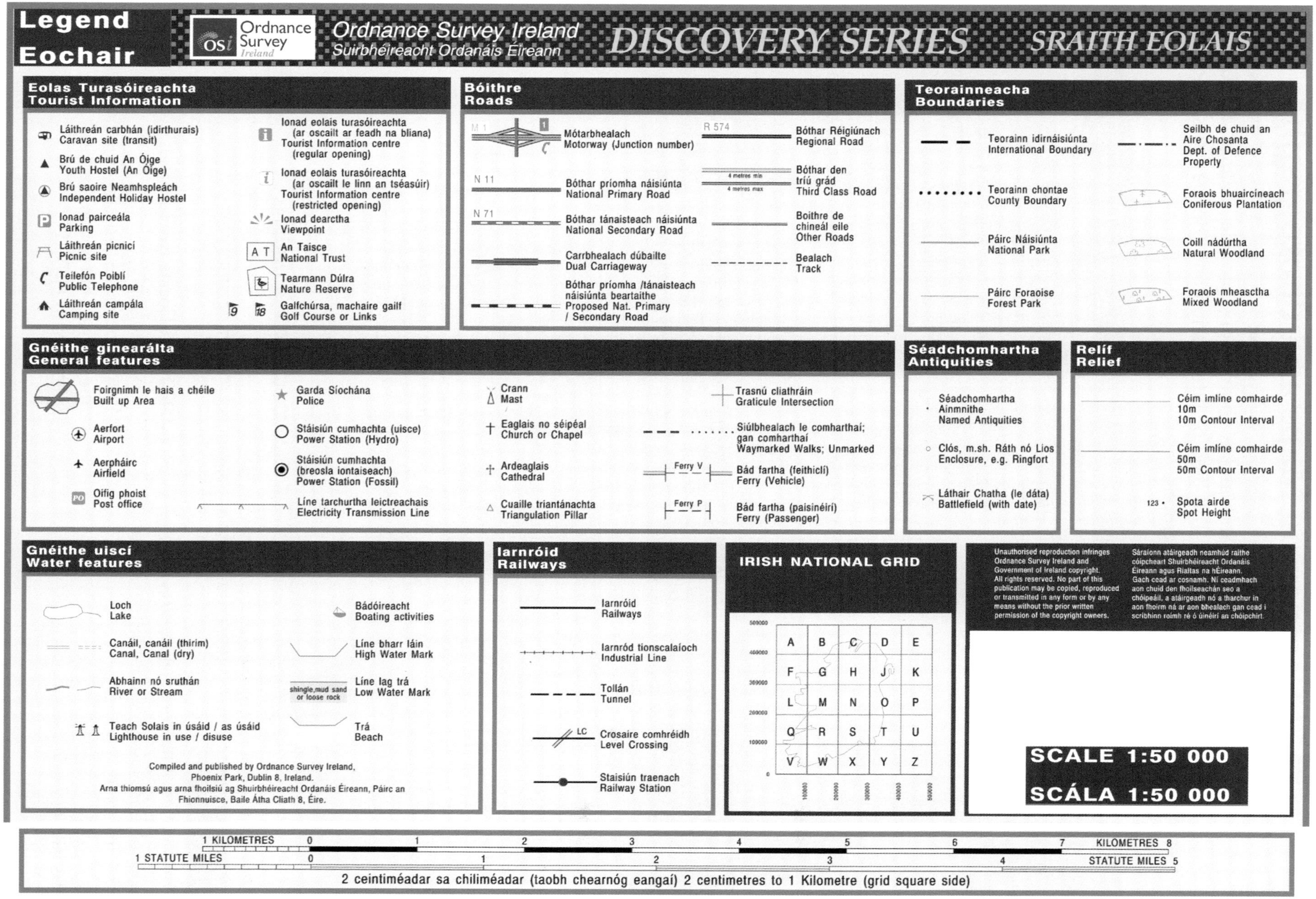

# Legend
# Eochair

**Ordnance Survey Ireland**
*Suirbhéireacht Ordanáis Éireann*

## DISCOVERY SERIES
## SRAITH EOLAIS

### Eolas Turasóireachta
### Tourist Information

- Láithreán carbhán (idirthurais)
  Caravan site (transit)
- Brú de chuid An Óige
  Youth Hostel (An Óige)
- Brú saoire Neamhspleách
  Independent Holiday Hostel
- Ionad páirceála
  Parking
- Láithreán picnici
  Picnic site
- Teileafón Poiblí
  Public Telephone
- Láithreán campála
  Camping site

- Ionad eolais turasóireachta
  (ar oscailt ar feadh na bliana)
  Tourist Information centre
  (regular opening)
- Ionad eolais turasóireachta
  (ar oscailt le linn an tséasúir)
  Tourist Information centre
  (restricted opening)
- Ionad dearctha
  Viewpoint
- An Taisce
  National Trust
- Tearmann Dúlra
  Nature Reserve
- Galfchúrsa, machaire gailf
  Golf Course or Links

### Bóithre
### Roads

- Mótarbhealach
  Motorway (Junction number)
- Bóthar príomha náisiúnta
  National Primary Road
- Bóthar tánaisteach náisiúnta
  National Secondary Road
- Carrbhealach dúbailte
  Dual Carriageway
- Bóthar príomha /tánaisteach náisiúnta beartaithe
  Proposed Nat. Primary / Secondary Road

- Bóthar Réigiúnach
  Regional Road
- Bóthar den tríú grád
  Third Class Road
- Bóithre de chineál eile
  Other Roads
- Bealach
  Track

### Gnéithe ginearálta
### General features

- Foirgnimh le hais a chéile
  Built up Area
- Aerfort
  Airport
- Aerpháirc
  Airfield
- Oifig phoist
  Post office

- Garda Síochána
  Police
- Stáisiún cumhachta (uisce)
  Power Station (Hydro)
- Stáisiún cumhachta
  (breosla iontaiseach)
  Power Station (Fossil)
- Líne Iarchurtha leictreachais
  Electricity Transmission Line

- Crann
  Mast
- Eaglais nó séipéal
  Church or Chapel
- Ardeaglais
  Cathedral
- Cuaille triantánachta
  Triangulation Pillar

### Gnéithe uisci
### Water features

- Loch
  Lake
- Canáil, canáil (thirim)
  Canal, Canal (dry)
- Abhainn nó sruthán
  River or Stream
- Teach Solais in úsáid / as úsáid
  Lighthouse in use / disuse

- Bádóireacht
  Boating activities
- Líne bharr láin
  High Water Mark
- Líne íag trá
  Low Water Mark
  shingle,mud sand or loose rock
- Trá
  Beach

### Teorainneacha
### Boundaries

- Teorainn idirnáisiúnta
  International Boundary
- Teorainn chontae
  County Boundary
- Páirc Náisiúnta
  National Park
- Páirc Foraoise
  Forest Park

- Seilbh de chuid an Aire Chosanta
  Dept. of Defence Property
- Foraois bhuaircíneach
  Coniferous Plantation
- Coill nádúrtha
  Natural Woodland
- Foraois mheasctha
  Mixed Woodland

### Séadchomhartha
### Antiquities

- Séadchomhartha Ainmnithe
  Named Antiquities
- Clós, m.sh. Ráth nó Lios
  Enclosure, e.g. Ringfort
- Láthair Chatha (le dáta)
  Battlefield (with date)

### Relif
### Relief

- Céim imlíne comhairde 10m
  10m Contour Interval
- Céim imlíne comhairde 50m
  50m Contour Interval
- Spota airde
  Spot Height

**IRISH NATIONAL GRID**

| | | | | |
|A|B|C|D|E|
|F|G|H|J|K|
|L|M|N|O|P|
|Q|R|S|T|U|
|V|W|X|Y|Z|

## SCALE 1:50 000
## SCÁLA 1:50 000

Fig 7.57 Map legend for the 1:50,000 series of OS maps

# 7.7 Comparing Maps and Photographs

Ordnance Survey maps and aerial photographs provide a large amount of information for the user. The type of information and the way it is used vary between maps and photographs.

| Ordnance Survey map | Factor | Aerial photograph |
|---|---|---|
| ◎ Shown exactly by grid reference. | **Location** | ◎ General location can be described. |
| ◎ National and regional roads and some services are named. | **Names** | ◎ Features are not named. |
| ◎ Map is true to scale at all times. | **Scale** | ◎ Vertical photographs are true to scale. <br> ◎ Scale varies in oblique photographs from foreground to background. |
| ◎ Easy to calculate accurately. | **Distance** | ◎ Can only be estimated. |
| ◎ Map shows a larger area of land. | **Area** | ◎ Photograph shows a smaller area of land. |
| ◎ Important buildings are named. <br> ◎ Individual buildings in built-up areas are not shown. | **Buildings** | ◎ Shape and size of individual buildings are shown. <br> ◎ Height in storeys can be seen. |
| ◎ Some are shown, but only by symbol. | **Land use** | ◎ Clearly shown or can be guessed. |
| ◎ Altitude is clearly shown. <br> ◎ Gradient can be calculated accurately. | **Altitude and gradient** | ◎ Altitude is not shown. <br> ◎ Gradient is not clear, especially in vertical aerial photographs. |

Fig 7.58 Bandon

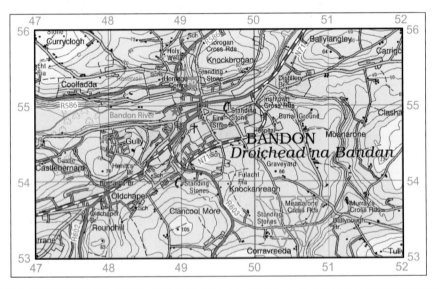

---

### QUESTIONS

1  Describe one difference in the way in which each of the following is shown in the OS map and in the aerial photograph:
   (a) roads
   (b) land use
   (c) buildings

2  (a) Name and locate two land uses shown in the photograph.
   (b) Name and locate two land uses shown in the OS map, but not on the aerial photograph. (JC)

Aerial photograph of Bandon

## QUESTIONS

3 (a) In what direction was the camera facing when the photograph was taken?

   (b) Give a six-figure grid reference on the map for the large church in the foreground of the photograph.

4 Identify one specific place on the aerial photograph where traffic congestion might occur in Bandon. Use both the map and the photograph to explain your choice of location. (JC)

5 Referring to both the map and the aerial photograph, describe any three services available in Bandon.

6 Using both the map and the photograph, explain three reasons why the town of Bandon developed at this location. (JC)

7 Describe two differences in the way roads are shown on the map and on the photograph.

8 List three pieces of information about the built-up area of Bandon that we can tell from the photograph but not from the map.

9 List three pieces of information about the built-up area of Bandon that we can tell from the map but not from the photograph.

Aerial photograph of Kilkenny

## QUESTIONS

**Photograph only**

1   Draw a sketch map of the area shown on the aerial photograph, showing and labelling each of the following:
    (a)  the river
    (b)  the castle
    (c)  two streets
    (d)  a car park
    (e)  a school
    (f)  a building site. (JC)

2   Identify and locate a location where traffic congestion is likely to occur. Explain two reasons why you selected that location. (JC)

3   The functions of Kilkenny have changed over time. Examine this statement, referring to one past function and one present function of Kilkenny. (JC)

4   It is proposed to build a new school in the castle grounds in the right foreground. With reference to the photograph only, give one advantage and one disadvantage of the location. (JC)

5   (a)  Identify and locate four functions or services provided in the town.
    (b)  Write a brief description of two of them. (JC)

**Map and photograph**

6   Using both the map and the photograph, explain three reasons why the town of Kilkenny grew up at this location. (JC)

7   The town of Kilkenny offers a wide variety of attractions to tourists. Identify and describe any three of these attractions, referring to both the OS map and the aerial photograph. (JC)

Fig 7.59 Kilkenny

## QUESTIONS

**Map only**

8 (a) Calculate the area, in kilometres squared, of the built-up area of the town.

   (b) Calculate the length, in kilometres, of that section of the N10 shown on the map. (JC)

9 Locate each of the following by a six-figure grid reference: (a) golf course (b) crannóg (c) railway station (d) hospital (e) Fulacht fia (f) a roundabout on the N10. (JC)

10 The area shown on the map has a long history of settlement.

(a) Name and locate any two different examples of historic settlement.

(b) Briefly describe each of them. (JC)

11 Identify and describe the pattern of rural settlement at each of the following locations:

(a) S 474 563

(b) S 52 58. (JC)

12 Kilkenny is an important route focus. Using three pieces of map evidence, examine this statement.

Aerial photograph of Clonmel

### QUESTIONS

**Photograph only**

1 Draw a sketch map of the area shown on the aerial photograph, showing and labelling each of the following:
   (a) the river (b) a bridge
   (c) two streets (d) a church
   (e) a school (f) a sports ground. (JC)

2 It is proposed to build an apartment block in the field in the right foreground. With reference to the photograph only, give one advantage and one disadvantage of the location. (JC)

3 Briefly explain one advantage and one disadvantage of living along the main street of a town like Clonmel. (JC)

4 Name and locate three different land uses shown in the photograph.(JC)

**Map and photograph**

5 With reference to both the OS map and the aerial photograph, describe three reasons why Clonmel developed at this location. (JC)

6 Identify one place on the aerial photograph where traffic congestion might occur in Clonmel. Use both the map and the photograph to explain your choice of location.

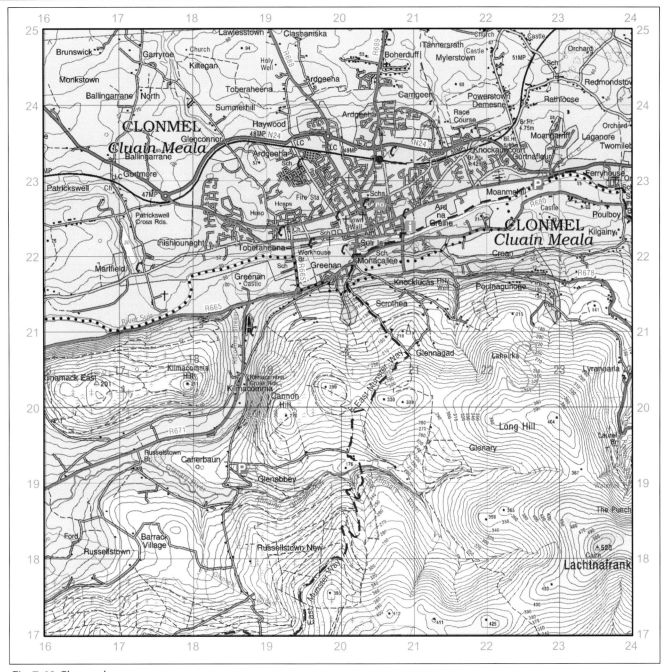

Fig 7.60 Clonmel

### QUESTIONS

**Map only**

7 The town of Clonmel provides a variety of services. With reference to the OS map only, describe three of these services. (JC)

8 Draw a sketch map of the area shown on the OS map. Mark and identify the following features:
   (a) the River Suir  (b) the N24
   (c) a regional road  (d) the railway
   (e) an area above 400 metres. (JC)

9 (a) Calculate the area of the map to the south of Northing 21.
   (b) What is the height of the highest point on the map?
   (c) How is height shown at S 167 203? (JC)

10 Identify and describe any two rural land uses in the area shown on the map.

11 Identify and describe the pattern of settlement at the following locations:
   (a) S 20 24  (b) S 17 24. (JC)

189

Aerial photograph of Ardee

### 📖 QUESTIONS

**Photograph only**

1   At what time of the year was the photograph taken? Suggest two pieces of evidence from the photograph to support your answer. (JC)

2   Using the photograph only, draw a sketch map of Ardee town. Show and identify the following:
   (a)  two connecting roads
   (b)  a historic building
   (c)  grain silos
   (d)  a church and graveyard
   (e)  a building site
   (f)  a clump of trees. (JC)

3   Briefly explain one advantage and one disadvantage of living along the main street of a town like Ardee. (JC)

4   (a)  Identify Ardee's main street.
   (b)  With reference to the photograph, give two pieces of evidence to suggest why this is Ardee's main street. (JC)

5   Locate and describe three different land uses shown on the aerial photograph. (JC)

**Map and photograph**

6   (a)  Identify a site on the photograph where you would locate a new shopping centre.
   (b)  With reference to the photograph and the map, give one advantage and one disadvantage of this location. (JC)

7   Describe three differences in the way that information about Ardee is shown on the OS map and on the aerial photograph.

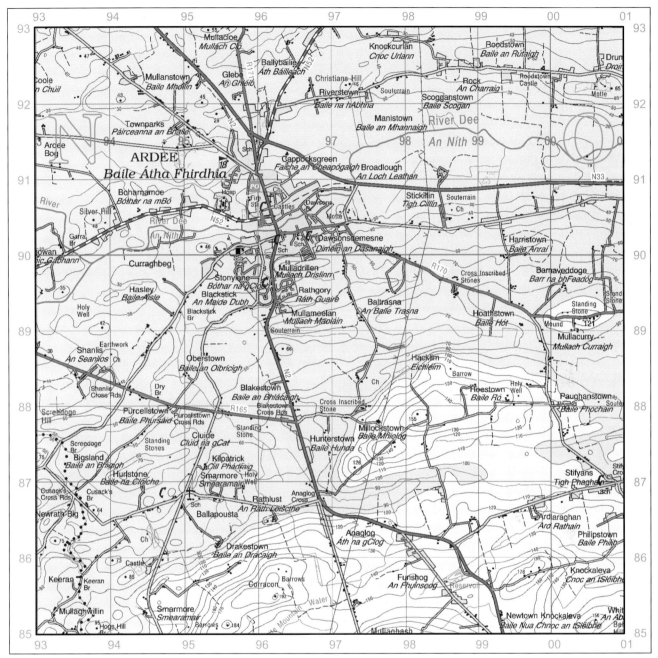

Fig 7.61 Ardee

---

📖 **QUESTIONS**

**Map only**

8 What is the length, in kilometres, of each of the following?

  (a) The section of the R165 shown in the photograph.

  (b) The section of the R170 shown in the photograph. (JC)

9 Draw a sketch map of the area shown on the OS map. On it show and name the following:

  (a) the built up area of Ardee

  (b) two national roads

  (c) a named river  (d) an antiquity

  (e) a coniferous plantation. (JC)

10 Using evidence from the map only, explain three reasons why Ardee developed at that location. In your answer, refer to both the past and present. (JC)

11 Explain why there is an absence of settlement at each of the following locations:

  (a) N 96 85  (b) N 97 91. (JC)

Aerial photograph of Macroom

## QUESTIONS

**Photograph only**

1 Identify one place on the aerial photograph where traffic congestion might occur in Macroom. Explain two reasons why you selected that location. (JC)

2 Draw a sketch map of the area shown on the photograph. On your sketch map show and label each of the following features:
   (a) two streets  (b) a church
   (c) a school  (d) a sports ground
   (e) a car park  (f) a castle. (JC)

3 Identify and locate the main shopping area in Macroom. Give two pieces of information to support your selection. (JC)

4 In your opinion, is the town of Macroom a planned settlement? Give two pieces of information to support your answer.

**Map and photograph**

5 Outline three reasons for the development of Macroom at this location. Use evidence from the OS map and aerial photograph to support your answer. (JC)

6 Using both the map and the photograph, describe two reasons why the castle was built at that site.

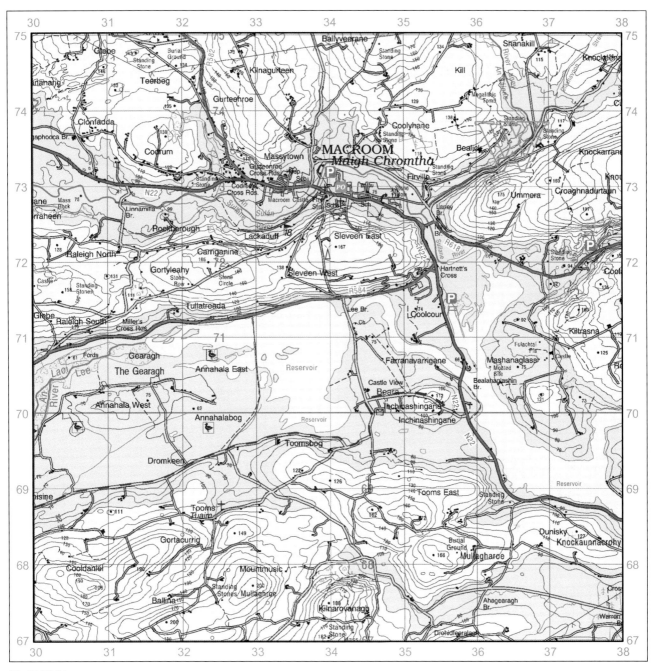

Fig 7.62 Macroom

---

### QUESTIONS

**Map only**

7  Explain two different reasons why the countryside surrounding Macroom is attractive to tourists. (JC)

8  (a)  Explain why there is an absence of settlement at W 31 69.
   (b)  Identify and describe the patterns of rural settlement at (i) W 319 732 (ii) W 31 67. (JC)

9  (a)  Identify the antiquity at each of the following grid references: (i) W 358 682 (ii) W 303 727 (iii) W370 736.
   (b)  What evidence is there to suggest that there has been settlement at Macroom for a long period of time? (JC)

10  What evidence suggests the section of the River Lee shown in the map is in its old stage? (JC)

11  Describe one influence of each of the following on the road system:
    (a) relief  (b) drainage.

Aerial photograph of Dublin

### QUESTIONS

**Photograph only**

1  Using evidence from the photograph only, describe three commercial activities in the area covered by the photograph. (JC)

2  There is evidence that the area shown in the photograph is undergoing change. Identify and describe any two such changes. (JC)

3  Draw a sketch map of the area shown on the photograph. On it show and name:
   (a) a railway station  (b) a river and 2 bridges
   (c) a building site  (d) a marina
   (e) a warehouse  (f) a park. (JC)

4  Identify two pieces of evidence to suggest that port activity has declined in the area shown on the photograph. (JC)

**Map and photograph**

5  River crossings are major focal points of transport routes in a city centre. Explain how the aerial photograph and OS map illustrate the above statement. (JC)

6  A developer has proposed to build a hotel in the green area marked A in the photograph (O 163 340 on the map). Explain two reasons why city planners would refuse to grant planning permission for the development.

Fig 7.63 Dublin

---

### 📖 QUESTIONS

**Map only**

7  Identify the feature found at each of the following grid references:
   (a)  O 138 343
   (b)  O 193 358
   (c)  O 164 376. (JC)

8  Give the direction of each of the following from Trinity College (O 162 340):
   (a)  Whitehall (O 162 384)
   (b)  Artane (O 193 380)
   (c)  Sandymount (O 187 325). (JC)

9  Name and identify, by grid reference, four different facilities or services for tourists. In the case of each, say how it can be used by tourists. (JC)

10  The area on the map shows evidence of a variety of transport modes. Describe three of these, using map evidence to support your answer.

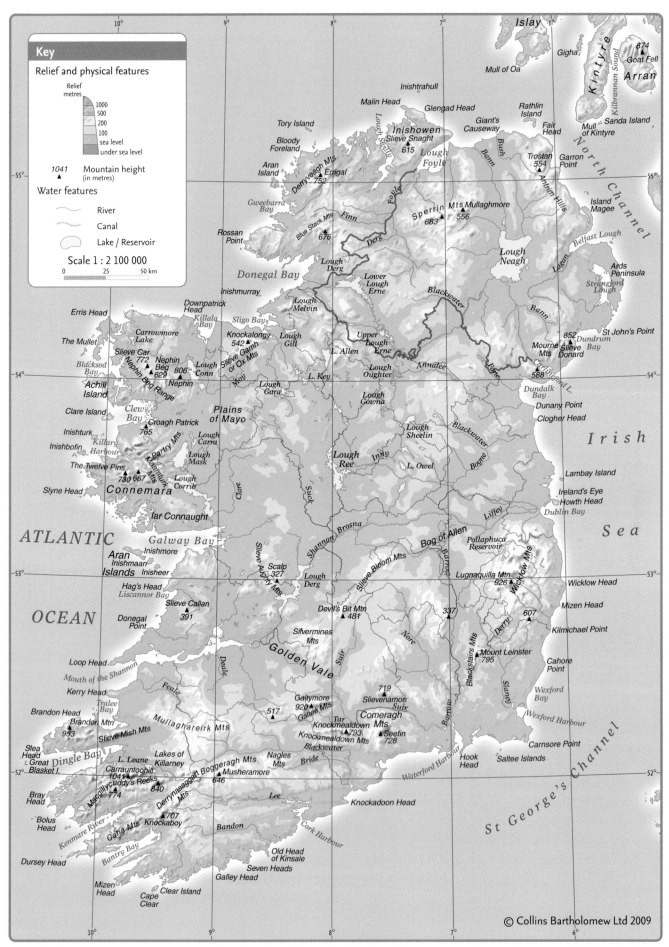

**Key**

Relief and physical features

Relief metres
1000
500
200
100
sea level
under sea level

1041 ▲ Mountain height (in metres)

Water features

~~~ River

~~~ Canal

Lake / Reservoir

Scale 1 : 2 100 000

0    25    50 km

## Ireland Relief

© Collins Bartholomew Ltd 2009

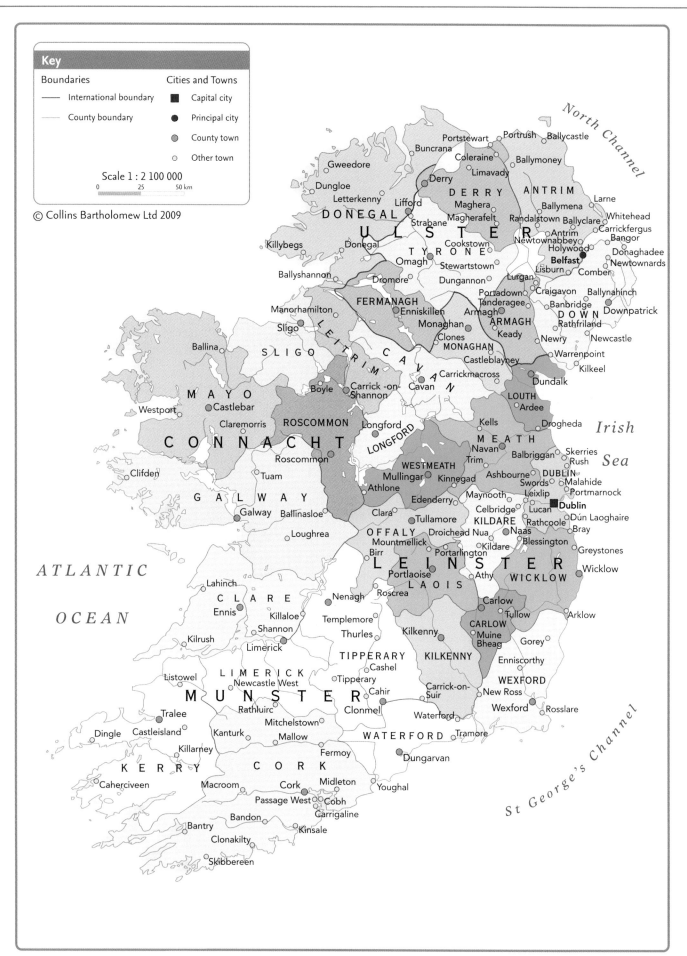

**Key**

Boundaries

—— International boundary

—— County boundary

Cities and Towns

■ Capital city

● Principal city

● County town

○ Other town

Scale 1 : 2 100 000

0      25      50 km

© Collins Bartholomew Ltd 2009

*North Channel*

Portstewart    Portrush    Ballycastle
Buncrana    Coleraine    Ballymoney
Gweedore    Limavady
Dungloe    Derry    **D E R R Y**    **A N T R I M**
Letterkenny    Maghera    Larne
**D O N E G A L**    Lifford    Magherafelt    Ballymena    Whitehead
**U L S T E R**    Strabane    Randalstown    Ballyclare    Carrickfergus
Killybegs    Cookstown    Antrim    Bangor
Donegal    **T Y R O N E**    Newtownabbey    Donaghadee
Omagh    Stewartstown    Holywood    Newtownards
Ballyshannon    Dungannon    **Belfast**
Dromore    Lurgan    Lisburn    Comber
**F E R M A N A G H**    Portadown    Craigavon    Ballynahinch
Manorhamilton    Enniskillen    Tanderagee    Banbridge    **D O W N**    Downpatrick
Sligo    Monaghan    Armagh    **A R M A G H**    Rathfriland
Ballina    **L E I T R I M**    Clones    Keady    Newry    Newcastle
**S L I G O**    **C A V A N**    **M O N A G H A N**    Warrenpoint
Boyle    Castleblayney    Kilkeel
**M A Y O**    Carrick -on-    Carrickmacross    Dundalk
Westport    Castlebar    Shannon    Cavan    **L O U T H**
Claremorris    Longford    Ardee    *Irish*
**C O N N A C H T**    **R O S C O M M O N**    Kells    Drogheda    *Sea*
Roscommon    **L O N G F O R D**    **M E A T H**    Skerries
Clifden    Tuam    **W E S T M E A T H**    Navan    Balbriggan    Rush
**G A L W A Y**    Mullingar    Trim    Ashbourne    **DUBLIN**    Malahide
Galway    Ballinasloe    Athlone    Kinnegad    Swords    Portmarnock
Loughrea    Edenderry    Maynooth    Leixlip
Clara    Celbridge    Lucan    **Dublin**
Tullamore    **KILDARE**    Rathcoole    Dún Laoghaire
**O F F A L Y**    Droichead Nua    Naas    Bray
Mountmellick    Kildare    Blessington
Birr    Portarlington    Athy    Greystones
Portlaoise    **L E I N S T E R**    **W I C K L O W**    Wicklow
Lahinch    **L A O I S**    Arklow
**C L A R E**    Nenagh    Roscrea    Carlow
Ennis    Killaloe    Templemore    Tullow
Shannon    Thurles    Kilkenny    **CARLOW**    Gorey
Kilrush    Limerick    Muine    Enniscorthy
Listowel    **L I M E R I C K**    **T I P P E R A R Y**    **KILKENNY**    Bheag
Newcastle West    Cashel    Carrick-on-    **W E X F O R D**
**M U N S T E R**    Tipperary    Suir    New Ross
Rathluirc    Cahir    Waterford    Wexford    Rosslare
Tralee    Mitchelstown    Clonmel    Tramore
Dingle    Castleisland    Kanturk    Mallow    **W A T E R F O R D**
Killarney    Fermoy    Dungarvan
**K E R R Y**    **C O R K**
Caherciveen    Macroom    Midleton
Cork    Youghal
Passage West    Cobh
Bandon    Carrigaline
Bantry    Kinsale
Clonakilty
Skibbereen

*ATLANTIC*

*OCEAN*

*St George's Channel*

## Ireland Political

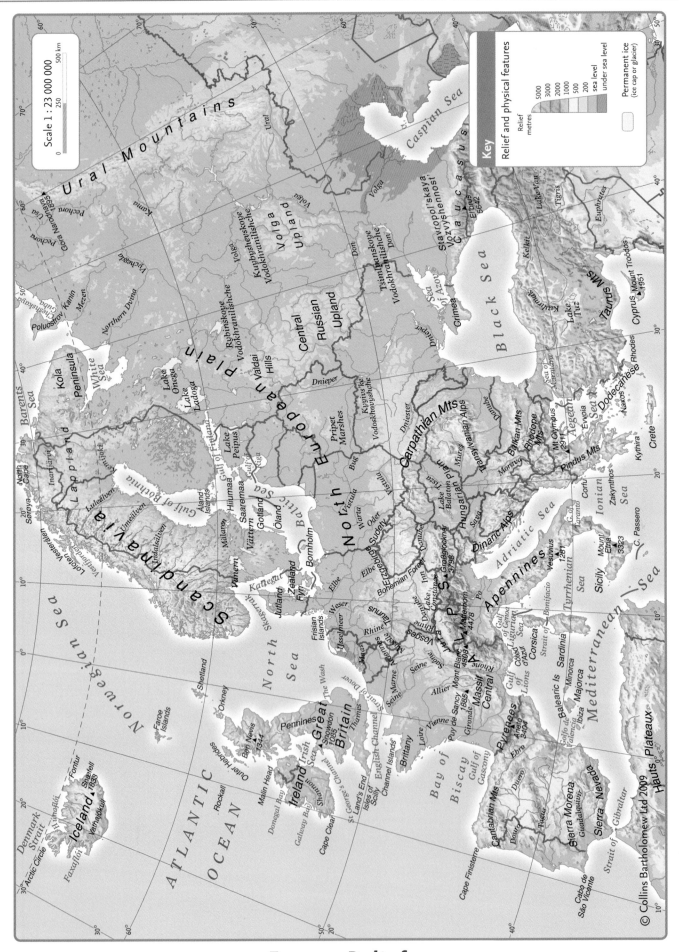

Europe Relief

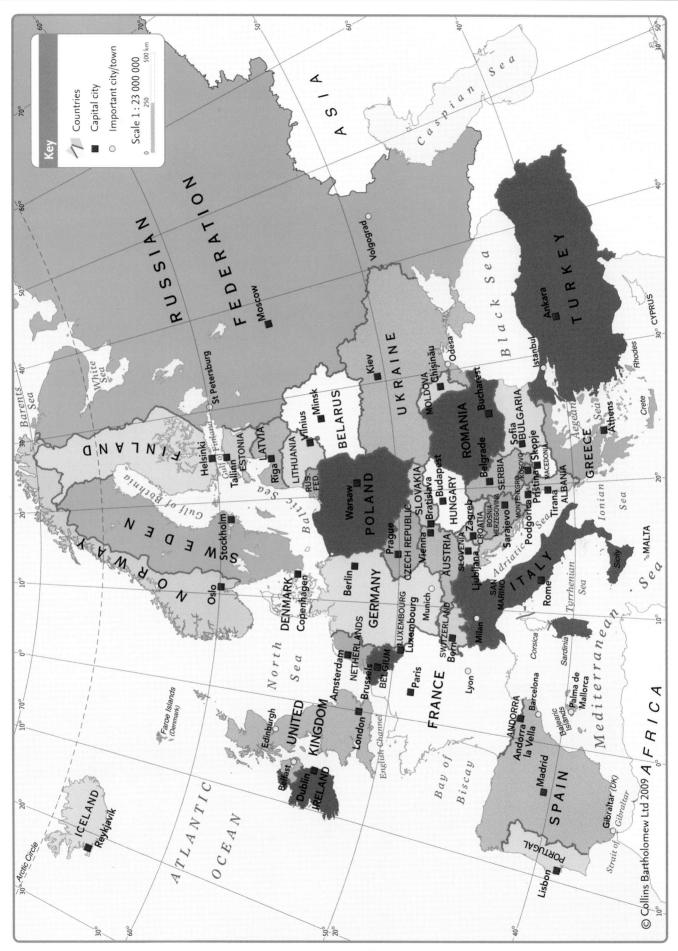

# Europe Political

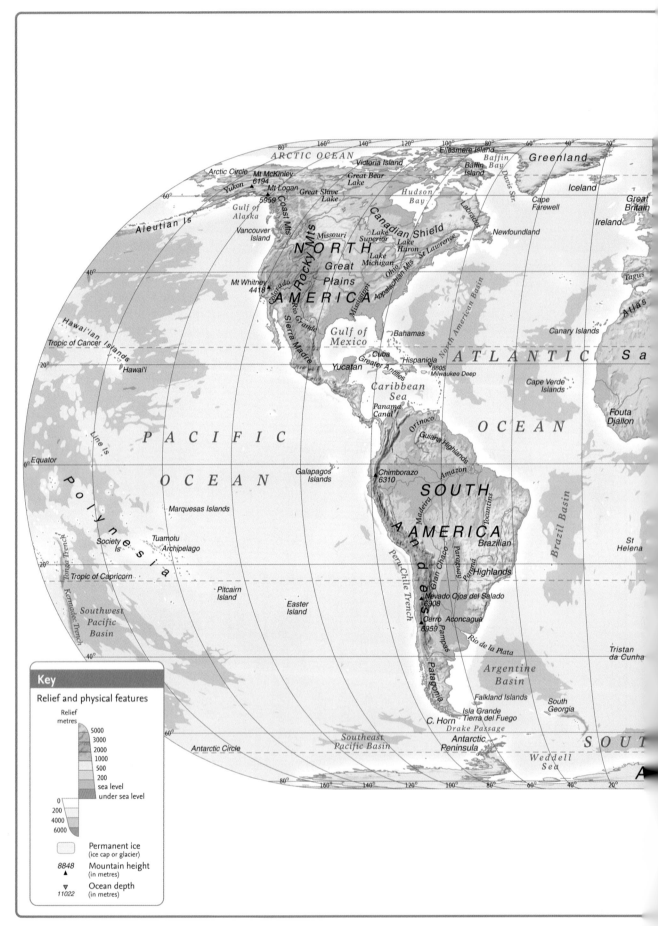

ARCTIC OCEAN
Ellesmere Island
Baffin Bay
Greenland
Victoria Island
Baffin Island
Arctic Circle
Iceland
Mt McKinley 6194
Great Bear Lake
Hudson Bay
Cape Farewell
Great Britain
Yukon
Mt Logan 5959
Great Slave Lake
Ireland
Gulf of Alaska
Coast Mts
Aleutian Is
Vancouver Island
Canadian Shield
Labrador
Davis Str.
Missouri
Lake Superior
Lake Huron
Newfoundland
NORTH
Rocky Mts
Great Plains
Lake Michigan
St Lawrence
Tagus
Mt Whitney 4418
Colorado
Appalachian Mts
AMERICA
Ohio
Mississippi
North American Basin
Atlas
Rio Grande
Hawai'ian Islands
Sierra Madre
Gulf of Mexico
Bahamas
Canary Islands
Tropic of Cancer
Yucatan
Cuba
Hispaniola
ATLANTIC
Sa
Hawai'i
Greater Antilles
8605
Milwaukee Deep
Caribbean Sea
Cape Verde Islands
Fouta Djallon
Panama Canal
OCEAN
PACIFIC
Orinoco
Galapagos Islands
Guiana Highlands
Equator
Chimborazo 6310
Amazon
OCEAN
SOUTH
Brazil Basin
Line Is
Marquesas Islands
Madeira
Tocantins
AMERICA
St Helena
Polynesia
Society Is
Tuamotu Archipelago
Brazilian
Paraná
Highlands
Peru-Chile Trench
Andes
Paraguay
Tonga Trench
Gran Chaco
Tropic of Capricorn
Pitcairn Island
Nevado Ojos del Salado 6908
Kermadec Trench
Easter Island
Cerro Aconcagua 6959
Pampas
Southwest Pacific Basin
Rio de la Plata
Tristan da Cunha
Argentine Basin
Patagonia
Falkland Islands
South Georgia
Isla Grande
Tierra del Fuego
C. Horn
Drake Passage
Antarctic Circle
Southeast Pacific Basin
Antarctic Peninsula
SOUT
Weddell Sea
A

**Key**

Relief and physical features

Relief metres

5000
3000
2000
1000
500
200
sea level
under sea level

0
200
4000
6000

Permanent ice
(ice cap or glacier)

8848 ▲ Mountain height
(in metres)

▼
11022 Ocean depth
(in metres)

# World Relief

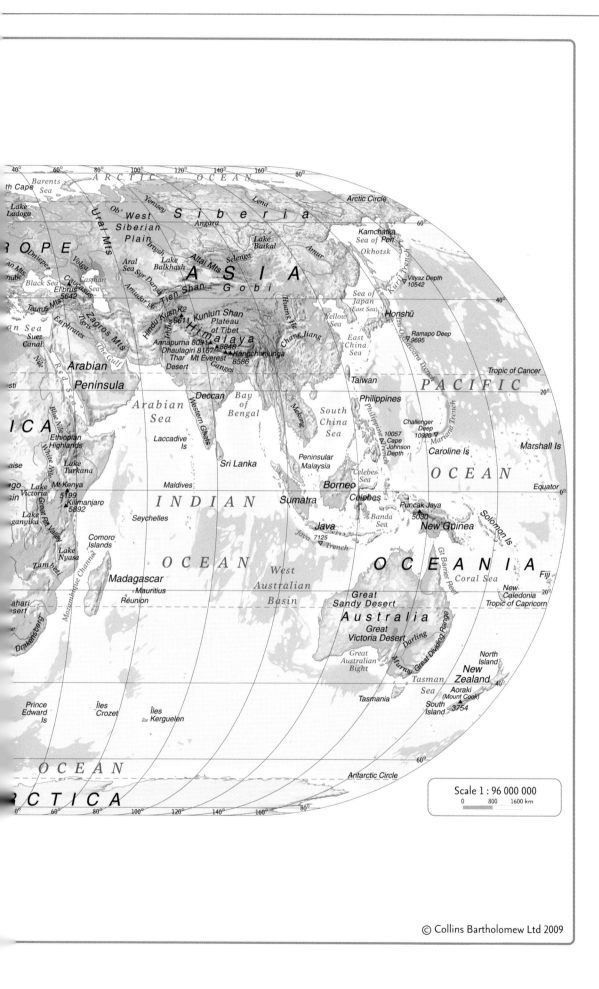

Scale 1 : 96 000 000

0    800    1600 km

© Collins Bartholomew Ltd 2009

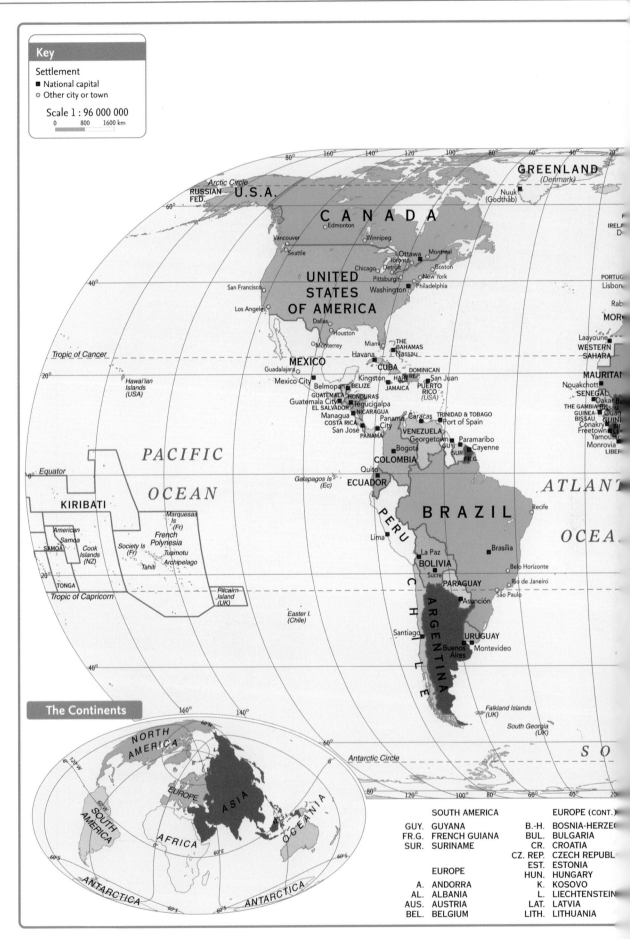

**Key**

Settlement
- ■ National capital
- ○ Other city or town

Scale 1 : 96 000 000

0    800    1600 km

**The Continents**

| SOUTH AMERICA | | EUROPE (CONT.) | |
|---|---|---|---|
| GUY. | GUYANA | B.-H. | BOSNIA-HERZEG |
| FR.G. | FRENCH GUIANA | BUL. | BULGARIA |
| SUR. | SURINAME | CR. | CROATIA |
| | | CZ. REP. | CZECH REPUBL |
| | | EST. | ESTONIA |
| | | HUN. | HUNGARY |
| EUROPE | | K. | KOSOVO |
| A. | ANDORRA | L. | LIECHTENSTEIN |
| AL. | ALBANIA | LAT. | LATVIA |
| AUS. | AUSTRIA | LITH. | LITHUANIA |
| BEL. | BELGIUM | | |

# World Political

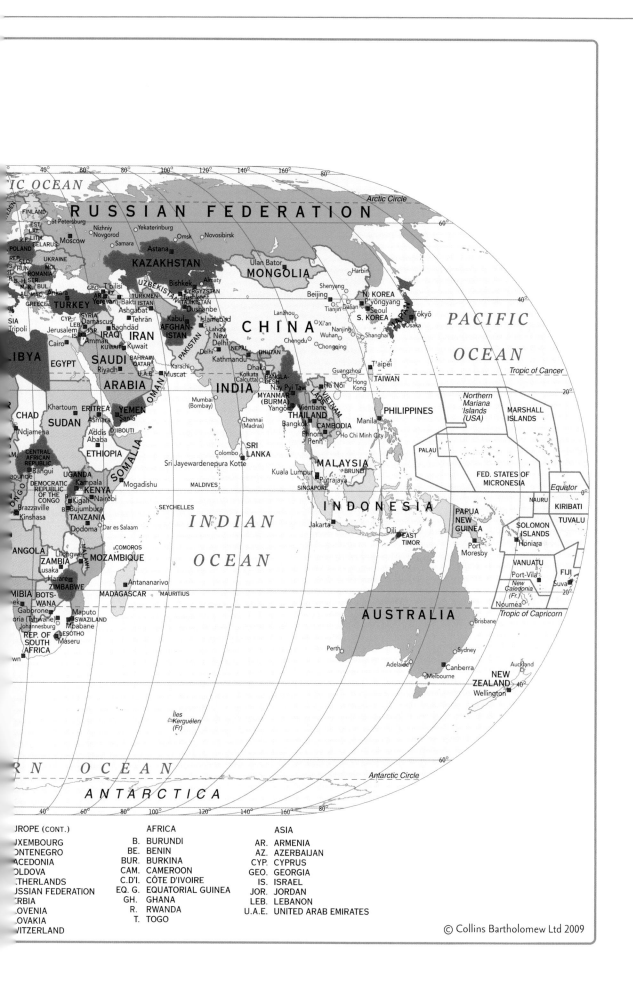

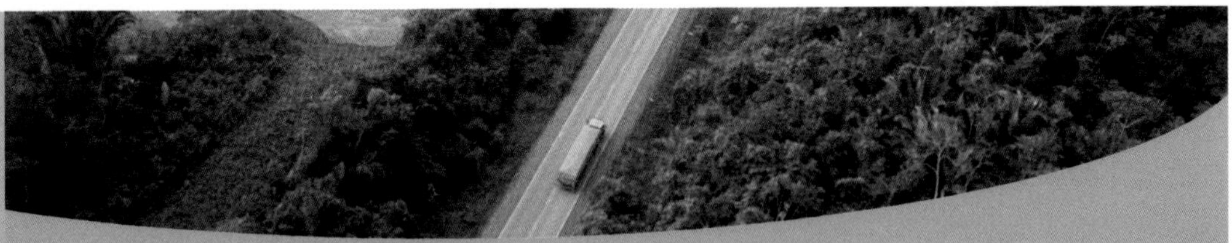

# 8 Population: Distribution, Diversity and Change

**Learning Outcomes**

In this chapter you will learn that:

- The population cycle explains how birth and death rates change over time.
- Population density varies from place to place.
- A country's population structure is shown with a population pyramid.
- High densities and low densities of population have different social and economic effects.
- Death rates are higher in poor countries than in rich countries.
- Migration can be individual or organised.

## 8.1 Population Growth

World population has increased throughout time at a fluctuating and uneven rate.

The population of the world had reached 6.7 billion people by 2009. Presently, the population is increasing by about 77 million every year or about 1.5 million people every week.

However, the population did not increase at this rate in earlier centuries. This was because almost as many people died as were born. Famine, wars and plagues such as the Black Death caused the deaths of many people. In fact, the Black Death was so severe that it caused the population of Europe to **fluctuate**.

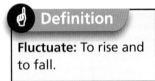

**Definition**

**Fluctuate:** To rise and to fall.

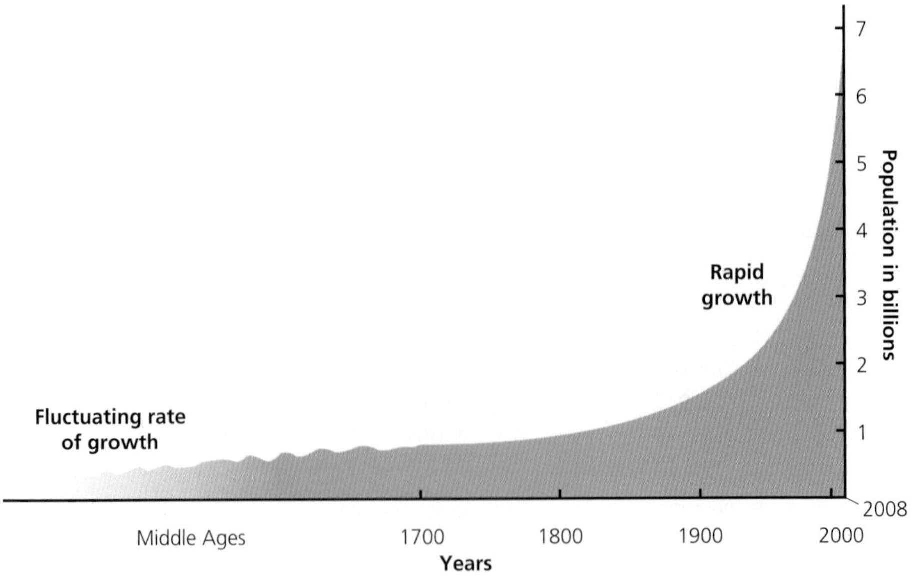

Fig 8.1 Population increase from the Middle Ages to the present

However, since about 1900, the world's population has dramatically increased. This is because most babies who are born survive to become adults and to have children of their own. This population growth is called the **population explosion**.

## Where is population growth greatest today?

Today, almost all population growth is in poorer countries, also known as the **developing world**. The populations of many countries in South and South-west Asia and in Africa are growing rapidly.

On the other hand, the populations of Europe, North America and Japan are growing very slowly, because parents are having very few children. In some countries, the population is in decline.

A crowded shopping street in Guangzhou, China. China has more than 20 per cent of the world's people

## The population cycle

People who study population growth have drawn up a model to help us to understand how a population increases over time. This is called the **population cycle** or **demographic transition model**.

The demographic transition model shows the changes in the **birth rates** and **death rates** of a country over time.

> **Definitions**
>
> **Birth rate:** The number of births per 1,000 people in one year.
>
> **Death rate:** The number of deaths per 1,000 people in one year.

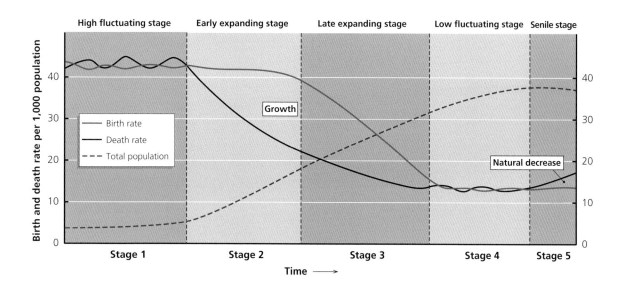

Fig 8.2 The The demographic transition model (population cycle)

## The stages of the population cycle

◎ In **stage 1** of the population cycle, birth rates and death rates are high. The population does not grow in this stage because high death rates cancel out the high birth rates (e.g. isolated tribal groups are at this stage). Famine, disease and natural disasters cause high death rates. This was the case in medieval Europe.

◎ In **stage 2** countries have started to develop their economies. Governments begin to provide clean water and health services. The birth rate remains high but the death rates declines, therefore the population grows (e.g. in Mali).

◎ In **stage 3** economic development is more advanced. People are more educated than in stage 2. Parents begin to plan family size. Families have fewer children because they survive due to good health services. Population growth is less than in stage 2 (e.g. in Brazil).

◎ In **stage 4** countries are wealthy. Parents plan their families. Birth and death rates are very low. Most people survive to old age. Population growth is very low (e.g. in Ireland).

◎ In **stage 5** the death rate is greater than the birth rate. This is because mothers have very few children and more of the population is elderly. The population begins to decline in this stage (e.g. in Germany).

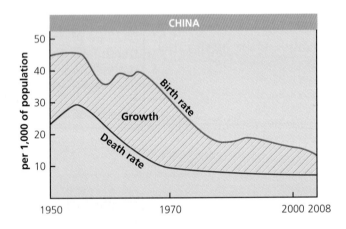

Fig 8.3 Population cycle of China over time

A typical family in a developed country today

### How to calculate natural increase

If the birth rate is higher than the death rate, natural increase occurs.

◎ Example: In a country at stage 2, the birth rate may be 40 and the death rate may be 15.

Growth = 40–15 = 25 per 1,000

$$\frac{25}{1,000} = 2.5\%$$

The natural increase is 2.5% per year.

### Question

What is the percentage increase in a country with the following rates?

Birth rate per 1,000 = 20
Death rate per 1,000 = 10

## SUMMARY

◎ Population growth has been very rapid since 1900.
◎ Growth is very strong in poor countries, especially in Africa.
◎ All countries go through the population cycle.
◎ As countries develop, birth rates decline and population growth slows.

## QUESTIONS

1 Why is the term population explosion used to describe population growth since 1900?
2 Look at the demographic transition model in Fig 8.2, page 205, and answer the following questions:
   (a) Why does the death rate decline sharply in stage 2?
   (b) Why does the birth rate decline sharply in stage 3?
   (c) Why is population growth very low in stage 4?

# 8.2 Factors Influencing the Rate of Population Change

**Geofact**

One hectare = 10,000 metres square, or half the size of Croke Park.

A number of factors influence the rate of population change:
1 Food supply          2 Improved technology
3 Health               4 War
5 The status of women  6 Education

## 1 Food supply

Extra food helps a population to grow. Modern farmers use better seeds than before. They use **crop rotation** to stop the soil from losing minerals. Fertilisers greatly increase food output per **hectare**. Farmers have learned to store grain in silos so that it is not spoiled by rain or eaten by pests.

With additional food supplies, the population of Europe and North America increased rapidly in the nineteenth and early twentieth centuries. **Colonisation** by Europeans brought modern agricultural advances to Africa, South America and Asia.

**Definitions**

**Crop rotation:**
Growing a different crop in the same field each year in order to reduce the risk of pests and to prevent soil exhaustion.

**Colonisation:**
One country takes political control over another country.

A Canadian wheat region with grain silos used for storage; grain can be stored safely in silos for many years

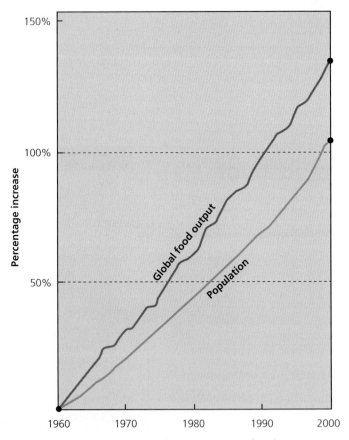

Fig 8.4 From 1960 to 2000 the increase in food output was greater than the increase in population in the world as a whole

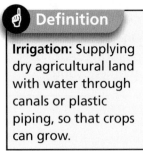

**Definition**

Irrigation: Supplying dry agricultural land with water through canals or plastic piping, so that crops can grow.

## The dependence on the potato in nineteenth-century Ireland

The population of Ireland grew from 4.5 million in 1800 to more than 8 million in 1845. This was because a hectare of land could produce enough potatoes and vegetables to support a family.

However, when the potato crop failed during the Great Famine of 1845–48, food supply declined. As a result, almost one million people died.

## Increased food supply in Brazil

The population of Brazil grew from 17 million in 1900 to 192 million in 2007. This was due to high inward migration from Europe and because of a high birth rate. Brazilian farmers cleared land for agriculture. Farmers could then increase food supplies of rice, maize, vegetables and fruit to feed the rapidly growing population.

## 2 Improved technology

Technology has been developed over time to increase food supply. Tractors, better ploughs, combine harvesters and other equipment have made farming more efficient.

In **Germany**, cereals such as wheat are grown using modern technology and chemical fertilisers. Output of wheat per hectare is very high.

In dry lands, vast areas are now under **irrigation**. Dams and plastic piping provide water for crops. Irrigation greatly increases food supply.

## 3 Health

The health of a population affects death rates. People's health is affected by several factors including:

◎ The quality of drinking water
◎ Proper sanitation
◎ Childhood vaccinations
◎ A good health service

## Rich countries

In wealthy countries, treated water, safe for domestic use, has been available since the end of the nineteenth century.

In Ireland, Germany and other developed countries, treated domestic water supplies and modern sanitation are available to almost all of the population.

Tuberculosis (TB) caused the deaths of more than 3,000 adults in Ireland annually until the middle of the twentieth century. However, after 1948 it was stamped out in a major campaign using new drugs.

Farm workers using modern technology plant cabbages in a field in Germany. In the spring, farm workers plant 80 million cabbages

## Poor countries

In Brazil, filtered water is widely available in cities, but not in many rural areas. People who live in the countryside depend on a well. This water may be unsafe if it is contaminated by animals.

Millions of Brazilians also live in shantytowns outside the large cities. In shantytowns, safe drinking water is often unavailable. This can lead to outbreaks of disease such as cholera.

Mothers await care and advice at a health centre in Brazil

# 4 War

War has a major impact on people's lives. It disrupts farming, health services, water supplies and sanitation systems. People's health is therefore affected.

Modern weapons and bombing campaigns can also lead to death on a terrible scale for soldiers and civilians alike.

Germany took part in the First and Second World Wars in the twentieth century. Over 5 million Germans died during the Second World War. These included soldiers at the front and civilians who died from the Allied bombing of German cities. These deaths reduced the German population during the 1940s.

War is a common occurrence in the developing world today, especially in Africa. Nearly 4 million people died in a recent civil war in the Democratic Republic of the Congo.

A boy drinks from a filtered water supply in Brazil. Filtered water helps people to stay healthy

# 5 The status of women

Women in developed countries today have a far higher status in society than their grandmothers had. The **feminist movement** that began in the 1960s together with high levels of female education brought about this change.

Two generations ago in Ireland and Germany, most women were confined to the roles of mothers and full-time homemakers. In 1970, Irish mothers had an average of four children each.

**Question**

Study the bar chart. Explain the connection between female literacy and the number of children per mother.

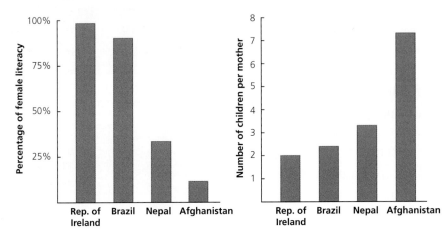

Fig 8.5 Female literacy and the number of children per mother in selected countries

German mothers have small families

However, today women have many options. Many mothers pursue a career. They plan their families. In 2007, Irish mothers had an average of two children each.

In Germany, the average number of children per mother is 1.4. This means that ten mothers have fourteen children between them. The German figure is well below the replacement level of 2.1 children per mother. The Irish and German populations would decline without inward migration, which is taking place in both countries. There are now 7.3 million non-nationals living in Germany.

In developing countries, mothers have much more traditional roles. Women in many of these countries have low status. In many African countries mothers have more than five children each. Many women do not have access to family planning. This is leading to a sharp increase in the overall population in Africa.

# 6 Education

The more educated the population, especially women, the smaller the family and the lower the population growth. When mothers are educated, they are more likely to make personal decisions about family size.

Educated mothers are more likely to practise family planning and to raise healthy children. Educated mothers learn about children's diet, personal hygiene and the importance of clean water in raising healthy children.

When parents see that their children are surviving to adulthood, they have fewer children. Birth rates are low in Ireland and Germany because mothers are educated and raising a large family is more expensive than a small one.

In some developing countries in Africa and Asia, many young women have less education than boys. Therefore, many are unaware of family planning services.

In Brazil, great strides have been made in girls' education in recent decades. In 2006, 98 per cent of girls aged 15–24 were literate, while 50 per cent of girls attended secondary school. This helps to explain why the number of children per mother in Brazil today has declined to 2.2.

> **Geofact**
>
> In Chad, only 23 per cent of young women are literate. The birth rate per mother is 6.2 children.

Fig 8.6 Annual rates of population growth today in selected countries

Fig 8.7 Parents in poor countries have large families because children look after their parents when they are old

---

### SUMMARY

◎ An increased food supply – helped by technology – allows a population to grow.
◎ Safe drinking water and good sanitation reduce a country's death rate.
◎ War causes many deaths.
◎ Educated women with high social status have fewer children.

### QUESTIONS

1 Explain why the population of Ireland declined during the Great Famine.
2 Explain how the following factors have helped to increase food supply: farm machinery, chemical fertilisers, crop irrigation.
3 Explain one way in which infant vaccinations reduce deaths among children.
4 Why are birth rates low in countries where women have high status?
5 Give two reasons why mothers in poor countries have large families.

# 8.3 Future Rates of Population Increase

Opinion is divided as to future rates of population increase.

| Population increase per annum | |
|---|---|
| Year | Additional population |
| 1990 | 87 million |
| 2002 | 79 million |
| 2006 | 77 million |

The rate of increase is slowing down

The population of the world has grown from 1.6 billion in 1900 to 6.7 billion in 2009. Will that rate of increase continue into the future? If it does, the population will reach the 10 billion mark by the middle of the twenty-first century.

However, the signs are that the population growth is slowing. Many countries are actually moving through the population cycle quickly today. Latin America, China, Indonesia and many other countries are on the threshold of stage 4 of the population cycle.

However, many Arab states, Africa and the poorest Asian countries – Bangladesh, Nepal, Afghanistan – and parts of India have high birth rates. Parents have large families in these countries because many children – especially sons – provide security for them in their old age.

It is in the poorest countries that parents will continue to have large families. That situation will continue until all girls in those countries are educated. Then, women can choose to have fewer children.

**What happens to the number of humans...**

World population is expected to reach somewhere between 7.3 billion and 10.7 billion by 2050

**...depends on how fast fertility rates fall**

(babies born per woman)

Fig 8.8 UN projections for future population growth

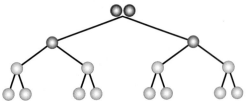

**Three-child families**

**Two-child families**

Fig 8.9 In three generations, three-child families produce more than three times the number of people that two-child families produce

Fig 8.10 The world may reach a limit as to the population it can hold during this century

**SUMMARY**

◎ It is difficult to forecast the future population of the world.
◎ Future population growth partly depends on whether girls in poor countries will be educated or not.

**QUESTIONS**

1 Population growth in the world in the next ten years is likely to be close to which of the following?
   (a) 700 million    (b) 1,500 million    (c) Zero

   Give one reason for your answer.

# 8.4 Population Pyramids

Any population grouping displays a characteristic structure, for example in sex/age composition. The structure of a rapidly increasing population differs in recognisable ways from that of a slowly growing or static population.

Population pyramids are a useful way to study the structure of a country's population.

◎ Age groups are arranged in four-year cycles.
◎ The male column is on the left and the female column is on the right.

| Birth rates per mother | Life expectancy |
| --- | --- |
| Brazil: 2.2 | 72 years |
| Ireland: 2.0 | 79 years |
| Germany: 1.4 | 79 years |

We can see at a glance whether the population of a country is young or elderly. We can also calculate the percentage of elderly people over 65 and the percentage of children of 14 and younger in a country. These groups are called the dependent population.

### The population pyramid of Brazil

◎ The population of Brazil has the widest base of the three pyramids. This is because the birth rate per mother is higher in Brazil than in either Ireland or Germany.
◎ Mothers in Brazil today have fewer children than mothers had some years ago. This is why the percentages of children in Brazil are narrower than those of teenagers and people in their twenties.
◎ The pyramid of Brazil is very narrow at the top due to the lower life expectancy of Brazilians. Therefore, the percentage of Brazilians over 60 is low.

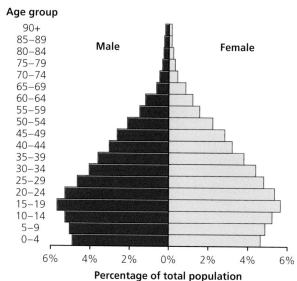

Fig 8.11 Population pyramid of Brazil

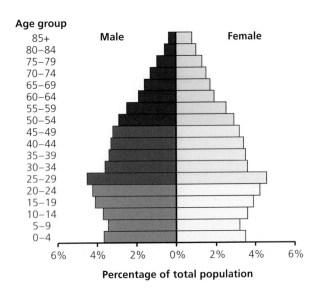

Fig 8.12 Population pyramid of Ireland

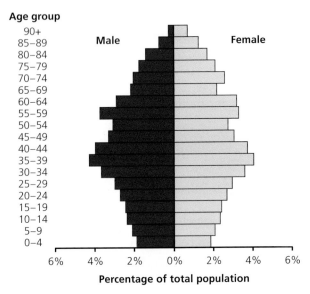

Fig 8.13 Population pyramid of Germany

Germany has an ageing population

## The population pyramid of Ireland

◎ The population pyramid of Ireland has the widest percentages among young adults, as mothers a generation ago had more children than today.

◎ Inward migration of young East European adults also helps to explain the high percentages in the young adult population in Ireland.

◎ The percentages of children and teenagers are less than the percentages of people in their twenties. This is because the birth rate in Ireland is less now than it was more than thirty years ago. Two reasons for that are better family planning and high numbers of working mothers.

◎ Older age groups have quite high percentages. This is because life expectancy is many years higher in Ireland than in Brazil. Women live longer than men.

## The population pyramid of Germany

◎ The base of Germany's population pyramid is narrow. Because of family planning, mothers had very few children during the last decades.

◎ The percentages of older people are high. This is because of the high life expectancy in Germany.

◎ Women live longer than men in Germany. Many women live into their eighties.

## Who studies population pyramids?

Population pyramids are used by people who plan for the future needs of a population.

Brazil has a high percentage of young people. Government planners can see that schools have to be built for them and teachers trained to teach Brazil's young people.

In Germany, many people are elderly. The government has to plan for their health and transport needs.

## An ageing population

Ireland has a lower percentage of young people and a higher percentage of elderly people than Brazil. Germany has the highest percentage of elderly people of the three pyramids.

◎ The cost of pensions for the elderly in Ireland and Germany is likely to grow as the population ages.

◎ Caring for the elderly will also be a challenge for health services.

◎ Elderly people spend less and need a lot more medical care than young people. The population of Ireland and Germany is **greying**.

### SUMMARY

◎ Population pyramids give us the percentages of people in each age bracket in a country.

◎ Population pyramids help the government to see the needs of a population in areas such as education and jobs.

### QUESTIONS

1 Look at the information in the table and answer the following questions:

(a) In the table which are the two developed countries?

(b) Which is the least developed country? (JC)

| Country | Birth rates per 1,000 population | Death rate per 1,000 population | % population under 15 years |
|---------|-------|-------|-------|
| A | 13 | 12 | 19 |
| B | 42 | 16 | 39 |
| C | 32 | 8 | 41 |
| D | 16 | 9 | 22 |
| E | 44 | 19 | 42 |

2 Study the population pyramids Fig 8.14 and Fig 8.15 below and answer the following questions.

(a) Which country is a developed country ?

(b) Calculate the percentage of the population which is aged 4 and under in each country.

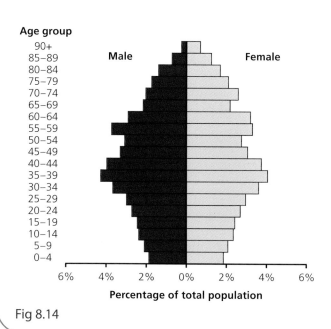

Fig 8.14

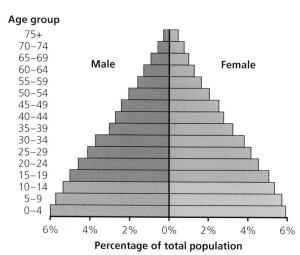

Fig 8.15

215

## 8.5 Variations in Population Distribution and Density

The population of the world is unevenly distributed across Earth's surface. Within most regions, population density varies throughout time and space.

Some of the factors that cause this variation are:

◎ Social and historical
◎ Related to resources and terrain

> **Definitions**
>
> **Population distribution:** The dispersal of people in the world. It is very uneven.
>
> **Population density:** The average number of people living in a square kilometre.

The world's population is unevenly distributed. People avoid regions that are very high, very wet and humid or very dry. For example, Greenland has very few people because most of it is covered by an ice cap. The Sahara and other deserts are too dry for agriculture.

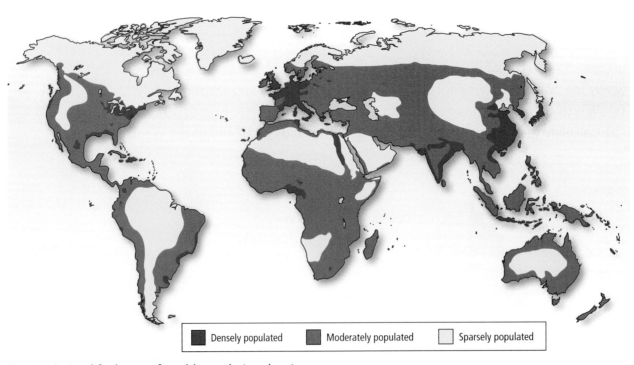

■ Densely populated   ■ Moderately populated   □ Sparsely populated

Fig 8.16 A simplified map of world population density

On the other hand, very high densities of people exist in many of the great floodplains of the world. These include the Ganges Basin in India and the Nile Valley in Egypt.

Western Europe has high population densities. This is due to its moderate climate, many excellent soils and large industrial cities.

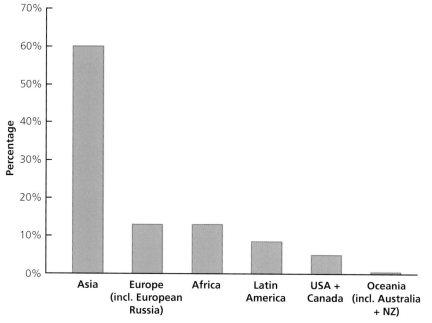

Fig 8.17 Percentage share of the world's population by continent

> **Question**
>
> What percentage of the world's people is found in:
> (a) Africa?
> (b) USA and Canada?

# 1 Social and historical factors: West of Ireland

The population density of the West of Ireland has changed dramatically over the last two centuries.

## Population growth before the Famine

After 1800, the population of the West of Ireland grew very rapidly. This was because of:

◎ Early marriage and large families
◎ The subdivision of farms into small plots
◎ The dependence of people on the potato

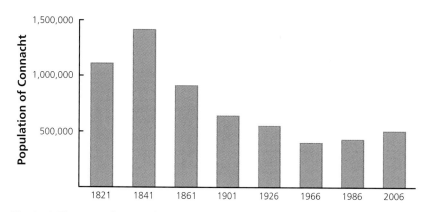

Fig 8.18 The population change of Connacht over time.
People emigrated because of the lack of resources in the West

## The impact of the Famine

The Great Famine of the 1840s halted population growth. Thousands of people died of hunger and famine fever in the West of Ireland and many more emigrated.

After the Famine, farmers no longer subdivided their land among their sons. The eldest son inherited the family farm. The eldest son married only after the younger family members had emigrated. Therefore, family size was reduced.

As a result of emigration, the population of the West of Ireland declined steadily from after the Famine until the 1960s.

## Population growth in recent decades

Population decline was halted and reversed after the 1960s. The government under Séan Lemass encouraged multinational corporations to invest in Ireland. Ireland joined the EEC (later the EU) in 1973. These two factors helped job creation in the West of Ireland.

The Celtic Tiger years that began in 1995 also helped to create jobs in the West of Ireland. Many companies, both Irish and foreign, invested in the west, particularly in Galway City. The population of urban centres such as Letterkenny, Sligo, Galway and Ennis grew very rapidly.

However, some rural areas in the West of Ireland continued to lose people to nearby towns and to the Dublin region where many jobs were available.

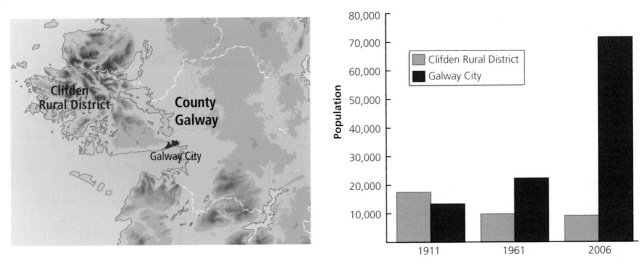

Fig 8.19 Population change in Clifden Rural District and Galway City

Scattery Island is located in the Shannon Estuary. This picture was taken about 100 years ago. The island is now uninhabited. What did the people in this village do for a living?

# 2 Social and historical factors: Brazil

Population densities vary across Brazil and have also varied over time.

**Geofact**

In 1492 Christopher Columbus reached the island in the Caribbean that he called San Salvador.

| Brazil's population in figures | |
| --- | --- |
| Population 2007 | 192 million |
| Population density | 22.5 per km² (Rep. of Ireland: 60) |

## Original inhabitants

The first people to live in Brazil crossed the Bering Straits from Asia and spread down through the American continents. It is estimated that 5 million inhabitants lived in Brazil before the European discovery of the Americas. They were mainly hunters and food gatherers. Brazil had a very low population density.

## European settlers

After the European discovery of the Americas, waves of Portuguese colonists arrived and settled along the east coast of Brazil.

The coastal climate was suitable for the growing of coffee, cotton and sugar cane. Ports such as Rio de Janeiro were built so that sugar, coffee and other produce could be exported to Europe.

Population densities rose sharply on the east coast because of the high birth rate and also because people continued to migrate from Europe into the twentieth century. Many migrants from Germany, Italy and Switzerland settled on the cooler coast of Southern Brazil.

## Migration into the interior

In the 1960s, the Brazilian government began to encourage settlement into the interior of the country. A new capital, Brasilia, was built 1,000 km inland. New roads were opened up and settlers were offered free land. Vast mineral resources, such as iron ore and precious metals were also discovered.

**Population density**
people per km²

| | |
| --- | --- |
| | >100 |
| | 50–100 |
| | 10–50 |
| | 1–10 |
| | <1 |

**Urban areas**
in millions of inhabitants

1  2  5  <10

Fig 8.20 Population density in Brazil; 84 per cent of the population live in urban centres in Brazil

Roads have been built through the Amazon rainforest to encourage migration into the interior

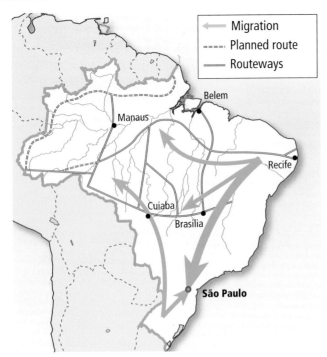

Fig 8.21 Internal migration in Brazil

Settlement in the interior is not easy for the following reasons:

◎ Much of the land is infertile as heavy rains leach away the minerals from the soil.
◎ The climate is very extreme, with high temperatures and humidity.

For those reasons, the Amazon Basin has been called a **green hell**. The result is that many new settlers have sold their farms in the interior to large companies and ranchers. Vast estates now raise cattle or grow soya beans and crops for **biofuels**. A small number of workers use machines to work these estates.

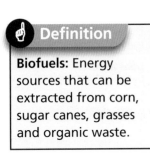

**Definition**

**Biofuels:** Energy sources that can be extracted from corn, sugar canes, grasses and organic waste.

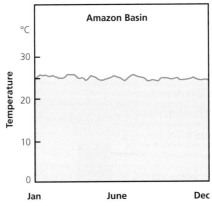

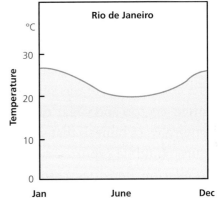

Fig 8.22 Temperatures in the Amazon Basin are hot all year round. Temperatures along the coast of Brazil are varied, e.g. in Rio de Janeiro

A heavily populated district in Sao Paulo; the population of Sao Paulo is 18.3 million

## The fate of native tribes

Native tribes of the interior have fared very badly. Over the centuries their population has fallen to 200,000 – a fraction of what it was 500 years ago.

Native people have low immunity to European diseases such as measles, which has resulted in thousands dying.

Therefore, almost fifty years after the modern settlement of the interior began in earnest, population densities in the interior remain low. East coast cities continue to expand.

# 1 Resources and terrain: Dublin region

Dublin City and County contained 1.2 million people in 2006. This is more than twice the population of Connacht. In the Dublin region, population density is just over 1,000 people per km².

Fig 8.23 The magnetic pull of Dublin is due to the many jobs in the region

Market gardens in North Co. Dublin provide fresh vegetables for Dubliners. Population density is low in this area

The expanding city of Dublin; new towns have grown around Dublin in recent decades

However, population density in the Dublin region varies from place to place and has changed over time. The population of the city has grown dramatically since 1960 as the economy of the country has grown.

Coastal towns, such as Malahide, are expanding as the population of the region grows.

North Dublin has a low population density for two reasons:
◎ Because of the airport, the city cannot expand to the north.
◎ Much of the farmland of North Co. Dublin is used for market gardening, which supplies the city with fresh vegetables.

The city has expanded to the west because **the terrain** is flat. Towns such as Tallaght and Clondalkin have grown rapidly in recent years. Many people in these new towns commute to the city for work.

The city of Dublin has a high population density. Many people live in multi-storey apartments close to the city centre. The city also contains high density terraced houses and estates of semi-detached houses. The city centre has very high densities during the day because of the large number of office workers.

The city cannot expand to the south because of the mountains. Settlement is almost completely absent in the Dublin Mountains because the **terrain** is too steep. The area is also exposed to strong winds and winter frosts.

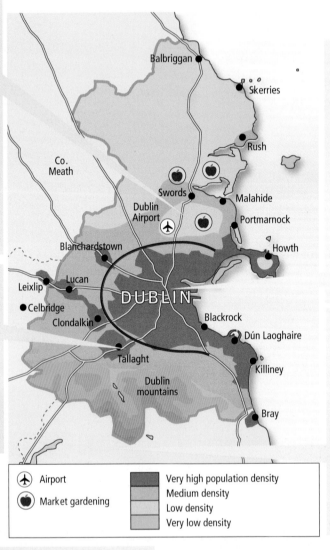

| | |
|---|---|
| ✈ Airport | Very high population density |
| ◉ Market gardening | Medium density |
| | Low density |
| | Very low density |

The Dublin region has many **resources**. It is Ireland's largest port. The city provides thousands of jobs in the civil service, media, shops and in transport.

Fig 8.24 Dublin City and County: varying population densities

## 2 Resources and terrain: Sweden

Sweden is a big country – more than six times the size of the Republic of Ireland. Sweden has a population of 9.1 million. The average population density is only 20.3 per km² – one-third of that in the Republic of Ireland. However, population distribution is uneven. Natural conditions such as climate, resources and terrain play a role in where people live.

> **Geofact**
>
> Sweden stretches from latitude 56° in the south to latitude 69° in the north.

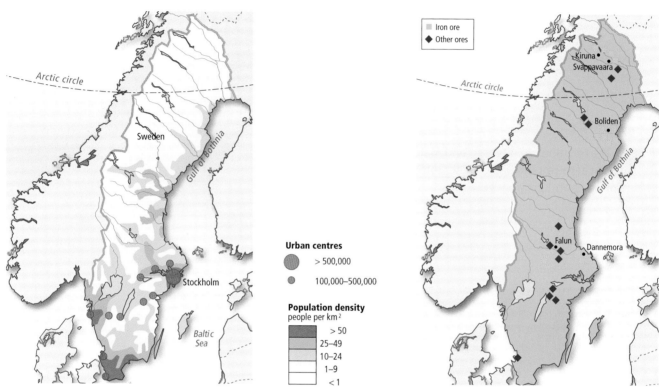

Fig 8.25 Population density in Sweden. The South is more densely populated than the North

Fig 8.26 Mineral deposits in Sweden

### Central and Southern Sweden

Population density in the centre and south of Sweden is much higher than it is in Northern Sweden. This is because of **climate**, **resources** and **terrain**.

Almost all of Southern Sweden has a **flat or rolling terrain**. This makes it easy to build roads, rail and urban centres.

The extreme south of the country – known as Scania – has a climate warm enough to grow wheat and other cereals. Hardier cereals such as rye, oats and barley are grown in Central Sweden.

Central Sweden is very rich in **mineral resources** such as iron ore. High quality steel is smelted in Central Sweden. The steel is used to manufacture ships, cars, trucks and other engineering products in the centre and south.

Swedish companies including Volvo, Saab, Husqvarna, Electrolux and Swedish Match are located in Southern and Central Sweden where they are closer to the EU and other foreign markets.

Fig 8.27 The location of Göteborg and Malmö in the Kattegat at the mouth of the Baltic. Both cities are major ports and provide many jobs

The coastal cities of the south such as Göteburg and Malmö have grown because they have benefited from their position as gateways to the Baltic. They have been important port cities since the Middle Ages. They are also ice-free.

Flat agricultural plain in Southern Sweden

Mountains in Northern Sweden

## Northern Sweden

Population density is much lower in Northern Sweden. The far north is above the Arctic Circle. Here, it is dark around the clock for six weeks in winter. Northern Sweden has up to 200 days of snow annually. The **extreme cold** and the cost of living make the north a less attractive place to live than the south.

The **terrain**, snow covered for many months, is difficult for road maintenance and driving. Apart from the coast, roads are few. Most people live along the coast of the Gulf of Bothnia where the land is level. The interior is remote, forested and mountainous.

Northern Sweden's many **resources** include timber, hydroelectricity, iron ore and other minerals. However, the rough terrain, the long cold winters and the distance from EU markets make the working of these resources difficult and expensive. Towns in the north are small and are located beside mines and saw mills.

The Gulf of Bothnia freezes over for five months each winter. Ores from the far north have to be exported westwards through Norwegian ports. The ports are ice-free because of the North Atlantic Drift.

The nomadic **Sami** people live in the far north. Some Sami continue to herd reindeer, but many have become foresters, miners and moved to towns.

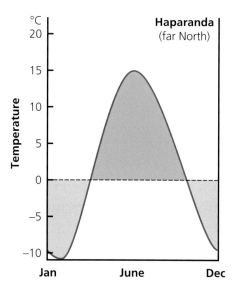
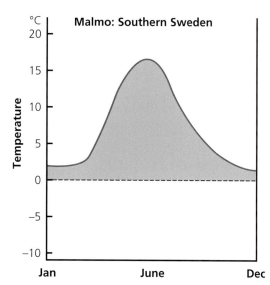

Fig 8.28 Temperature variation in Sweden

## SUMMARY

◎ Population densities differ widely from place to place.
◎ Emigration reduced population densities in the West of Ireland until recent times.
◎ For historic reasons, Brazil's population densities have been highest on the coast.

## QUESTIONS

1  Study Fig 8.17 on page 217. Draw a labelled pie chart with the same information.
2  How was the Great Famine a turning point in the population density of the West of Ireland?
3  Explain why the population of the West of Ireland began to grow in recent times.
4  Draw a map of Brazil. Mark in and name:
   ◎ Sao Paolo and Brasilia
   ◎ The River Amazon
   ◎ Write H in an area of high population density.
   ◎ Write L in an area of low population density.
5  Explain two reasons why people are migrating to the interior of Brazil.
6  Study Fig 8.28 above. How does the temperature in Malmö differ from the temperature in Haparanda? Give two differences.
7  With reference to a country that you have studied:
   (a) Name one region with a high population density.
   (b) Name one region with a low population density.
   (c) Describe and explain one reason for the high population density.
   (d) Describe and explain one reason for the low population density. (JC)

## 8.6 Low Population Densities

Very low populations densities can lead to:

◎ Low marriage rates
◎ Abandonment of agricultural land
◎ Political and economic isolation

## 1 The West of Ireland

The population density of the West of Ireland is very low in comparison to that of the east coast counties of Ireland. This has had important consequences for the West of Ireland.

### Low marriage rates in rural areas

Before the 1930s a matchmaker arranged marriages as if they were a business deal. It guaranteed a wife for the eldest son on the farm. But, matchmaking had little to do with romance.

*'A match was made when a farm needed a woman.'*
*Traditional saying*

However, with the decline in matchmaking, it was up to a young farmer to seek a wife. Many girls from the West of Ireland emigrated to Britain. Girls with secondary education moved to Dublin to find jobs in the civil service, teaching or nursing. A young farmer finished his education at age 13 and stayed at home. He eventually inherited the family farm.

He was very unlikely to persuade a young female teacher, civil servant or nurse back from Dublin to live in a small house on a poor, remote farm. As a result, large numbers of bachelor farmers in the West lived lonely lives with their ageing parents.

The introduction of mass secondary education in the late 1960s meant that young men were better educated and gained confidence. As a result, the number of bachelors fell significantly. In recent decades, young people have become more mobile, because many of them own cars. This makes it easier to find a partner in the West.

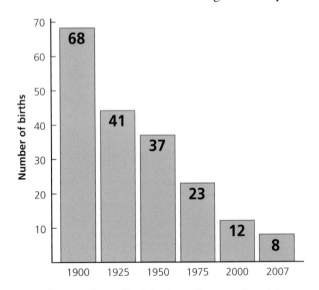

Fig 8.29 The number of babies born in a rural parish in the West of Ireland in selected years

An abandoned farmhouse in the West of Ireland

## Abandonment of agricultural land

Many farms in the West are very small. It has become impossible to make a living from the income of these farms alone. Many farmers' children now go on to third level education. The economic opportunities in the manufacturing and service industries in urban centres, such as Letterkenny, Sligo and Ennis, allow many young people the opportunity to work in jobs other than agriculture.

The result is that many small farms in the West are now being used for forestry. Near the western seaboard, some land is being turned over to tourism, e.g. caravan parks and golf courses.

Students at college in NUI, Galway

A disco in the West of Ireland

## Political and economic isolation

The West of Ireland is distant from Dublin – the economic centre of the state. Because of its low population, the West has only a small number of TDs and Senators in the Dáil. Therefore, the West lacks the political influence of the Dublin region.

Communications in the West are not as modern as those in the east of Ireland:

◎ In 2008, there was no motorway in any of the western seaboard counties.
◎ Many parts of the West still did not have broadband in 2008, which is vital to business today.

The West's position on the edge of Ireland and Europe means that companies are less likely to locate there, because of the distance from markets at home and abroad.

> **Geofacts**
>
> 46: The number of TDs representing Dublin City and County.
> 19: The number of TDs representing all of Connacht.

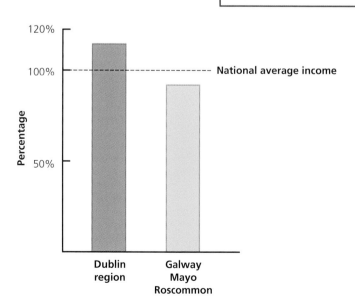
Fig 8.30 The income of people in western counties is much less than that of people in Dublin

## 2 Mali: a country with low population density

Mali is located in West Africa and is a landlocked state. Southern Mali is part of the Sahel, see page 111. Northern Mali forms part of the Sahara desert. Mali is one of the world's poorest countries. Mali, a very large country, is more than twelve times the size of the island of Ireland, but its population density is very low.

| Mali | |
| --- | --- |
| Area | 1,240,100 km² |
| Estimated population 2007 | 12,337,000 |
| Population density | 9.9 per km² |
| Urban population | 30% |
| Annual population growth | 3% |
| Babies per mother (average) | 6.5 |

Mali's population is composed of many cultural groups. Most people live in the south because of the higher rainfall.

In the south, farmers live along the River Niger where they grow food with the help of irrigation canals. They also raise cattle. Cotton is grown as an export crop.

Nomadic herders live in the desert and semi-desert regions of the north. Their animals include camels, donkeys, sheep and goats.

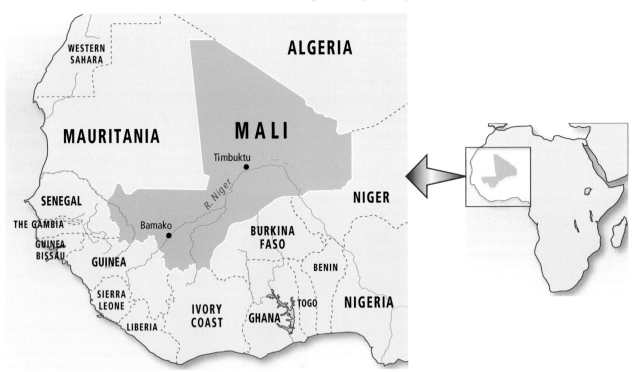

Fig 8.31 Mali and surrounding countries

### Drought

Mali suffers from frequent droughts. When drought occurs, the already sparse scrub is quickly stripped bare by grazing animals. People cut the already scarce timber for firewood. Long periods of drought, overgrazing and cutting of firewood lead to **desertification** in the Sahel.

When animals die in times of drought, herders are forced to abandon agricultural land on the desert edges and to head for the towns and cities in the south. This disrupts family life.

## Political and economic isolation

Mali has very poor road and rail links with its neighbours. Therefore, foreign trade is very low. It has no known reserves of oil or gas and therefore, is of little interest to the outside world. However, gold mines in the south of the country have created employment and led to an increase in exports.

The government of Mali has attempted to reduce its political and economic isolation in recent years with the following steps:

◎ Mali is now a member of the African Union, an organisation of states. This has helped to reduce its isolation from its neighbours.
◎ Mali joined the World Trade Organisation (WTO) to help it to increase foreign trade.
◎ The Mali government has established good relations with the USA.

Nomads living in a temporary camp in Mali

During a drought, a sandstorm hovers over a town in Mali

### SUMMARY

◎ The low densities of regions such as the West of Ireland and Mali can lead to problems such as economic and political isolation.

### QUESTIONS

1 Why did some men in the West of Ireland find it difficult to marry after the tradition of matchmaking ended?
2 Explain how the West of Ireland suffers from political and economic isolation.
3 Draw a map of West Africa. Mark in and name:
  ◎ Mali
  ◎ The River Niger
  ◎ One city in Mali
  ◎ Two neighbouring countries
4 Explain two problems caused by low population density that the people of Mali face. (JC)

# 8.7 High Population Densities

The density of population in an area has significant effects on the social and economic geography of that area.

Very high densities can lead to:

◎ Overcrowding
◎ Shortage of clean water
◎ Pollution
◎ Lack of open space

Higher level students must study Kolkata **and** Hong Kong. Ordinary level students study Kolkata **or** Hong Kong.

> **Geofact**
>
> Calcutta was renamed **Kolkata** in 2001.

We will examine high population densities in **Kolkata** and Hong Kong.

## 1 Kolkata (Calcutta)

Kolkata (Calcutta) has one of the world's largest populations. It is a great manufacturing city and a major port. It has a famous university and modern hospitals. However, wealth and poverty exist side by side in the city. Kolkata has many problems.

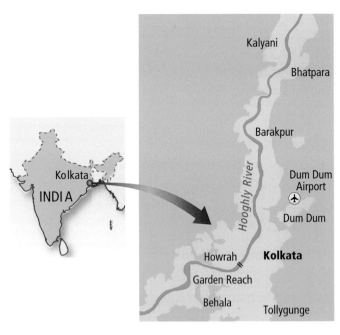

Fig 8.32 Kolkata stretches for 64 km along the River Hooghly

## Overcrowding

Many areas of the city have a density of more than 32,000 people per km². A large number of people from the countryside migrate to Kolkata because of evictions, famine, floods, violence and poverty.

In residential districts, three generations of one family live in a very small home. When weather permits, many people sleep on the street or on the roof.

Newly-arrived, poor migrants to the city live in makeshift dwellings made of plastic and waste timber in the shantytowns. These are found near railway stations and in open ground at the edge of the city. Some families also live on pavements where pollution from diesel fumes is a serious health threat.

| Population growth in Kolkata | | | |
|---|---|---|---|
| **Year** 1820 | 1931 | 1961 | 2008 |
| 250,000 | 1.2m | 4.4m | 15.7m |

As well as refugees, Kolkata's high birth rate has contributed to the rapid growth of the population.

The smells from refuse heaps waiting to be collected, smoke from the cooking stalls that line many streets, and monsoon rains that flood the streets, are other challenges that people in the city face.

## Shortage of clean water

Providing a clean water supply for a rapidly growing population has been a major challenge for the city. Middle-class homes and hotels have water on tap. However, most people who can afford it use an electrically powered water filter.

Kolkata has many slums or shantytowns

Poor districts do not have water piped to homes. Instead, water pipes, located on the pavement, provide drinking water for short periods several times a day. People collect their daily water supply in plastic containers.

People in poor districts wash clothes and take showers in washing areas located on pavements using water that has been pumped from the River Hooghly. Shantytown residents have to travel to nearby streets for drinking water.

Pollution from traffic is a major problem in Kolkata. People who live on pavements face seriously polluted air every day.

## Lack of open space

The centre of Kolkata has a large park, most of which is open to the public. It is located on the banks of the River Hooghly and also contains a racetrack and sports grounds.

Open space is in short supply in Kolkata because of population pressure. Front and back gardens are non-existent. Children play on the side streets beside their homes.

Much of city life is lived on the pavements. Thousands of people sleep on them; craftspeople conduct their business on them. Many people cook and sell food to passing trade on the pavements.

Kolkata is one of the world's most polluted cities

Kolkata people are very proud of their city and of its tolerance for different cultures. They do not welcome the image of poverty that Kolkata has in many countries and think that it is undeserved.

The city has an excellent and cheap underground railway line. The Internet is widely available in Internet centres.

Kolkata people are friendly, cheerful and extremely hard working. Most people make great sacrifices to send their children to school, which they see as an escape route from poverty.

## 2 Hong Kong

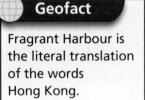

**Geofact**

Fragrant Harbour is the literal translation of the words Hong Kong.

Hong Kong had a population of 7.2 million people in 2007 in an area the size of Co. Dublin. It has very high population density because most of its population is crowded into two districts, Kowloon and Victoria. These two districts make up a mere 10 per cent of the land area of the New Territories. Therefore, overcrowding is severe.

However, Hong Kong is a wealthy city in comparison to Kolkata. The figures below indicate that the standard of living in Hong Kong is quite high. However, Irish people, accustomed to low-rise dwellings, would consider Hong Kong to be extremely overcrowded.

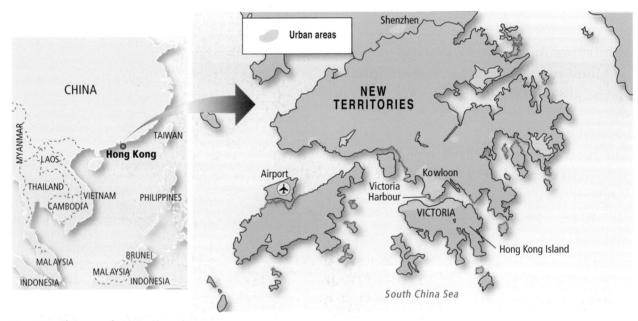

Fig 8.33 China and Hong Kong

**Geofact**

14 million tourists visited Hong Kong in 2005.

| Hong Kong in figures – 2007 | |
|---|---|
| Life expectancy in years | 82 |
| Number of children per mother | 1 |
| Infant mortality rate per thousand live births | 3.7 |
| Income per head in US$ | $26,668 |
| Percentage of Internet users | 53% |

## High-rise apartment living

Hong Kong grew rapidly in the twentieth century, from 500,000 people in 1920 to 7.2 million in 2007. For much of the twentieth century, the city had a high birth rate. The population also grew because of a large influx of refugees mainly from Communist China.

Most of the population live in high-rise apartment blocks. Each apartment block houses hundreds of families. With births averaging one child per mother, most apartments have just two small bedrooms.

People have always lived in houseboats along the coast and that tradition continues today. In the city centre, thousands of old people without a family sleep in overcrowded dormitories in bunks that may be three tiers high.

## Water supply

Providing the 7.2 million people with adequate and safe water has been achieved in the following ways:

Hong Kong has many high-rise buildings and suffers badly from pollution

- ◎ A bay on the coast known as Plover Cove was dammed to store fresh water from streams and became a huge reservoir of fresh water.
- ◎ China agreed to provide water from a nearby river. Modern filter systems make the water supply safe.
- ◎ Seawater is used for flushing toilets using separate mains and piping. This accounts for 15 per cent of water use.

## Pollution

Hong Kong is a hive of economic activity. The city is teeming with factories and workshops. Air pollution is a major problem. The source of this pollution is from power plants, sea traffic in the bay, city traffic and factories in nearby industrial areas of China.

Smog and haze reduce visibility in the harbour area and affect people's health. At street level, traffic emissions along with the summer heat and humidity can be very difficult for residents.

Many beaches and bays around Hong Kong are heavily polluted from industrial effluents. Several beaches have algae known as a **red tide**. These algae are a health hazard for bathers.

People wear masks in Hong Kong to protect themselves from pollution

### Lack of open space

Hong Kong is so built up that sunlight rarely reaches street level because of the height of buildings. In the bay area, new industrial zones have been created on land reclaimed from the sea. The only place to locate the new international airport was an artificial island in the bay, from where passengers are transported by fast ferry to the city.

However, residents throng to the racecourse for a day out. The hills outside the city are too steep for buildings and are covered in trees. These areas have forest tracks, which provide a peaceful area for people to escape the bustle of the city.

 **SUMMARY**

◎ Some cities such as Kolkata and Hong Kong have very high population densities.

 **QUESTIONS**

1 Explain two reasons for the inward migration of people from the countryside to Kolkata.
2 Describe two problems that exist in Kolkata.
3 Give three facts that show that Hong Kong is a wealthy city.
4 Outline two problems that the people of Hong Kong experience.

## 8.8 Global Patterns: The North/South Divide

In the world as a whole, sharp social inequalities exist among regions, related in part to population characteristics.

 **Definitions**

**The North:**
The developed world or the First World.

**The South:**
The developing world or the Third World.

## An unequal world

There are two major economic regions in the world: the developed world (**the North**) and the developing world (**the South**).

In the developed world, almost all babies survive infancy and most people have long lives. People have clean water, plenty of food and a good quality of life.

In the **developing world**, most children are born to poor parents. Many babies die in infancy and many children, especially girls, do not attend school.

Therefore, it is an unequal world. We will examine how unequal it is in relation to:

◎ Child mortality
◎ Life expectancy

# Child mortality in the developed world

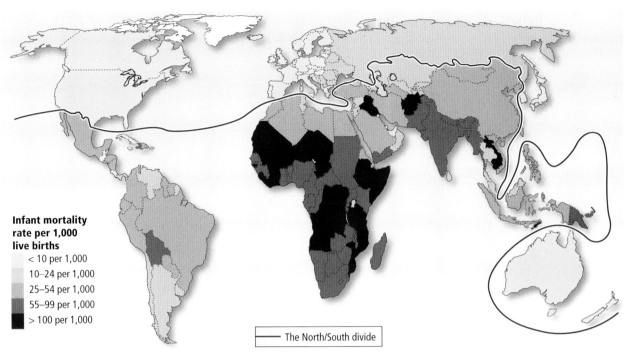

Fig 8.34 World map of infant mortality (deaths of children under the age of one)

**Infant mortality rate per 1,000 live births**
- < 10 per 1,000
- 10–24 per 1,000
- 25–54 per 1,000
- 55–99 per 1,000
- > 100 per 1,000

—— The North/South divide

Child mortality is very low in the developed world (the North) because children's health is a priority. There are several reasons for this:

- Healthy mothers have healthy babies.
- Mothers receive excellent care during pregnancy.
- Most women have their babies in maternity hospitals where the health of mothers and babies can be monitored around the clock.
- Young children receive many vaccinations that include the 3 in 1, MMR and vaccinations against polio and meningitis.
- Safe water – free of harmful bacteria – is available on tap. Sanitation systems keep cities free of health hazards.
- Mothers – educated and aware – generally provide their children with a balanced and a healthy diet.

A healthy baby in the North

**Geofacts**

- The **3 in 1** vaccination protects children against diphtheria, whooping cough and tetanus.

- The **MMR** vaccination protects children against measles, mumps and rubella.

235

# Child mortality in the developing world

Why do so many babies and children die in the developing world (the South)? There are several reasons for this, many of them related to poverty:

Open sewers in an Ethiopian slum

◎ Many mothers give birth at home in villages where medical care is unavailable. Therefore, many babies die if there is a birth complication.

◎ The poorer the family, the more likely it is that a mother's health is poor. Unhealthy mothers are more likely to have babies who are underweight. These babies are at risk from measles, whooping cough and other infections.

In many countries, mothers are uneducated. They may be unaware of the importance of hygiene. Therefore, they often use unboiled water to feed babies and young children. This can cause stomach infections, which can lead to diarrhoea, dehydration and the death of a young child in a short time.

Major efforts are being made to vaccinate babies and young children against killer infections even in the poorest countries. However, malaria and measles still cause many young children to die in the developing world, especially in Africa. The best way to prevent malaria is to sleep under a treated mosquito net. However, in Sub-Saharan Africa, only 5 per cent of children under 5 years of age sleep under them. This leads to many deaths.

### Geofact

10.1 million children under the age of 5 died in 2005. Almost all of them were in the South.

### Question

The Millennium Goal is to reduce by two-thirds, between 1990 and 2015, the under-five mortality rate. This is a major challenge. Can you think of any three suggestions that would help to achieve that goal?

A school dormitory in Tanzania that has mosquito nets for every bed

# Life expectancy in the developed world

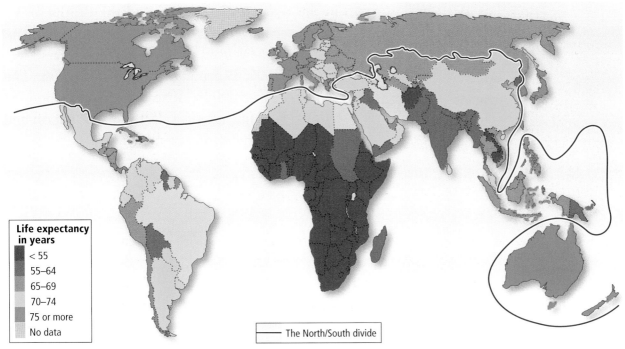

Fig 8.35 World map of life expectancy

The age at which people die depends on where in the world they live. People live much longer in rich countries than in poor countries. Life expectancy in developed countries (the North) is high for many reasons:

◎ Infant mortality is very low, because of vaccinations against childhood infections.
◎ People have a balanced diet that helps to keep them healthy.
◎ Safe water supplies and sanitation systems are available to all.
◎ Excellent medical services help people to live longer.
◎ Smoking bans in workplaces are reducing the health risks that are linked to smoking in many countries.

**Geofact**

Ireland's infant mortality rate is 4.9 per thousand live births.

# Life expectancy in the developing world

Life expectancy varies greatly between countries in the developing world (the South). This is because countries in the developing world are at different stages of development. However, countries where life expectancy is low have some common characteristics:

◎ Infant mortality is high.
◎ Malnutrition affects the poor in developing countries. Malnourished people are more likely to die of malaria, TB and other diseases.
◎ Tens of millions of people drink water that is unsafe and contains bacteria. This leads to continuous infections that can shorten people's lives.
◎ Over 500,000 women die in childbirth each year, most live in poor countries.

Many children in the South die as a result of malnutrition

Many countries in the developing world experience terrible wars. The civil war in the Democratic Republic of Congo in the years 1997–2006 caused the deaths of 3.5 million people. Many other countries including Sudan, Liberia and Iraq experienced conflicts in recent years.

By the end of 2006, 39.5 million people had AIDS. The majority are in Sub-Saharan Africa, the world's poorest region. AIDS is a major cause of death in that region and has reduced life expectancy in several countries.

Orphans collect water In Swaziland

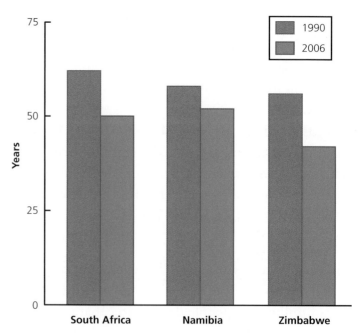

Fig 8.36 The reduced life expectancy 1990–2006 for three countries due to death caused by AIDS

## Improvements in life expectancy

Outside of many countries in Sub-Saharan Africa, almost all other developing countries have seen increased life expectancy in recent decades. This is because of the efforts made by governments, the World Health Organisation, and other organisations to improve life expectancy. China and India are examples of countries that have longer life expectancy today.

| Life expectancy | | |
|---|---|---|
| **Country** | **1990** | **2006** |
| China | 68 | 73 |
| India | 59 | 64 |

### SUMMARY

◎ Great social inequalities exist in the world.
◎ Child mortality is much higher in the South than in the North.
◎ Life expectancy is many years lower in the South than in the North.

### QUESTIONS

1 Explain three reasons why many babies and young children die in poor countries.
2 Give two reasons why life expectancy is higher in countries of the First World (the North) than it is in countries of the Third World (the South). (JC)

## 8.9 People on the Move

Movement of people has occurred throughout history and continues today. People migrate between regions for a variety of reasons, both repellent and attractive. Migration may be individual or organised.

### Individual migration

People migrate from one place to another because some things about where they live are repellent to them. Repellent reasons **push** them away. **Push factors** include overcrowding, unemployment, poverty and a dull social scene.

People migrate because the places to which they move are attractive in some way. Attractive reasons **pull** migrants to a particular place or region. **Pull factors** include better job opportunities, a lively social scene and because friends and family members have already migrated to that place.

> **Definition**
>
> **Individual migration:** When people either as individuals or families choose to move. They may leave the city for the suburbs or they may move from rural areas to towns because of economic opportunities.

239

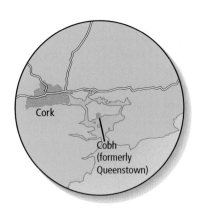

Fig 8.37 From 1848–1950 over 6 million adults and children emigrated from Ireland. Of these 2.5 million left from Cobh in Cork harbour

 **Question**

Explain the terms migrant, emigrant and immigrant.

 **Geofact**

In the 1960s, 6,000 Irish priests, nuns and brothers worked abroad in mission fields in every continent.

Migrants also experience barriers when migrating, e.g. travel costs and visa requirements.

Many individuals have emigrated to Britain and the USA, especially since the Famine. At the present time, many immigrants from Eastern Europe now live in Ireland.

## Migration from the west to the east of Ireland

People have migrated from the west to the east of Ireland for generations. This was because of the poor job prospects that existed in the west and the better job prospects that existed in the east, especially in Dublin.

From the 1940s to the 1960s, few people sat the Leaving Certificate and career choices were limited. Jobs that were available included:

◎ Civil service jobs in Dublin
◎ Teaching
◎ Nursing
◎ Life as a priest, nun or missionary

Ireland was a poor country for most of the twentieth century. Many parents from the West of Ireland encouraged their children to take up secure public sector jobs. Primary teaching was an example.

Achill Island lost many people to emigration

The landscape near Louisburgh, Co. Mayo; few jobs were available there

## Primary teaching

Primary teaching was a career that led to migration from the west to the east of Ireland. Firstly, two teacher-training colleges were in Dublin. Secondly, there were relatively few teaching posts in the west. This was because the population in the west was declining rapidly due to outward migration.

## The pull of Dublin

On the other hand, Dublin's population was growing and schools were expanding since the foundation of the state in 1922. Therefore, young teachers from the west began their teaching careers in Dublin and many remained there all their lives. With the rapid increase in the population of Dublin City and County since the 1960s, this trend has continued to the present time.

## Case Study

# A teacher's story

John was born into a West of Ireland rural community in the late 1940s. Education was very important to his parents because they saw that it was the key to better job prospects for children.

John was the eldest of seven children. At 13 years old he was enrolled in a secondary school 10 km from his home. Free transport did not exist, so John and others cycled to and from school for five years – on roads that had almost no traffic. His parents paid an annual fee to the school, as this was before the days of free post-primary education.

John was academically very bright and chose teacher training after he completed his Leaving Certificate. He attended St Patrick's Training College in Drumcondra, Dublin for two years and became a teacher.

He took up an appointment in an inner-city Dublin school where he taught for two decades. He then became principal of a new, large school on the outskirts of the city.

John is married to a civil servant from the West of Ireland and they have two children, both living in the Dublin area.

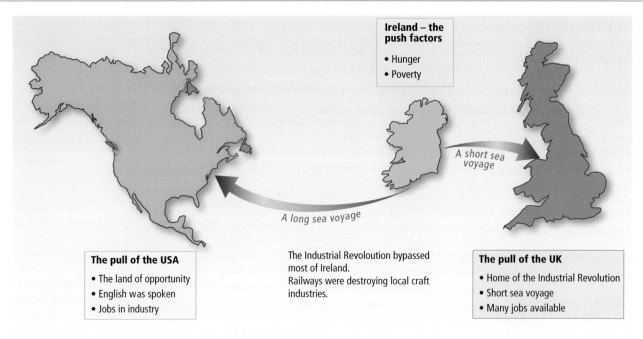

Ireland – the push factors

• Hunger
• Poverty

*A short sea voyage*

*A long sea voyage*

**The pull of the USA**

• The land of opportunity
• English was spoken
• Jobs in industry

The Industrial Revolution bypassed most of Ireland.
Railways were destroying local craft industries.

**The pull of the UK**

• Home of the Industrial Revolution
• Short sea voyage
• Many jobs available

Fig 8.38 Outward migration of Irish people to the UK and the USA in the nineteenth century

## Emigration from Ireland to the UK and the USA

People with Irish blood are found in many countries abroad from Britain to the USA, Canada and Australia. This is because many Irish people have emigrated especially since the Famine of the 1840s. The push of poverty and overcrowding at home, and the pull of economic opportunities abroad, were the reasons for this mass outward migration.

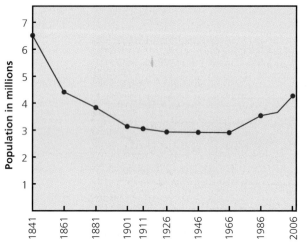

Fig 8.39 The population of the twenty-six counties that became the Republic of Ireland. After the Famine, emigration caused the population to decline

Irish emigrants are economic migrants. Recession at home leads to outward migration. An economic boom at home leads to inward migration.

Ellis Island in New York harbour was the entry point for immigrants to the USA from 1892–1954

## Ireland: Migration from 1950s onwards

| 1950s | 1960s | 1970s | 1980s | 1990s | 2000 and beyond |
|---|---|---|---|---|---|
| Loss of population. | Population began to grow for the first time since the Great Famine. | Population continued to grow. | Outward migration began again. | Population began to grow again. | Population growth continued with inward migration. |
| Migrants left by boat for the UK and USA. A disastrous decade for Ireland's people. 411,000 emigrated because of the lack of jobs. Governments failed to provide jobs. | During the Lemass era (1958–66), a golden age dawned. Programmes for economic expansion led to jobs at home. Emigration was greatly reduced. | Inward migration exceeded outward migration by 104,000. Ireland joined the EEC. EEC funds helped the economy to grow. This was a decade of optimism. | A recession at home, with job numbers down to 1.1 million, led to outward migration of more than 200,000. Emigrants were now well-educated and moved into well-paid jobs abroad. | The Celtic Tiger provided at least 50,000 new jobs every year. Migrants returned. People from the EU and other countries also came to work in Ireland. | The economy grew to more than 2 million workers. By 2008, people from many nations, such as Poland, were living and working in Ireland. The population was at its highest figure since 1871. |

Irish people migrated to London to find work

# Organised migration

In the past, migration was frequently organised by governments in order to colonise distant lands. By doing this, a government could extend its territory and its power. Two such organised migrations were:

1  The Plantation of Ulster
2  The Spanish colonisation of part of South America

 **Definition**

**Organised migration:** When a government undertook the settlement or colonisation of territory abroad, e.g. the Plantations by English and Scottish settlers in Ireland.

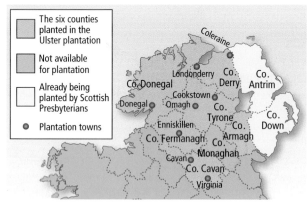

Fig 8.40 The Plantation of Ulster, 1609

Map legend:
- The six counties planted in the Ulster plantation
- Not available for plantation
- Already being planted by Scottish Presbyterians
- ● Plantation towns

# 1 The Plantation of Ulster

In order to extend their rule over Ireland, English monarchs took over parts of Ireland that had belonged to rebellious Irish chiefs. They gave this land to English and Scottish settlers who were loyal to the Crown. This transfer of land was known as a **plantation**. The purpose of plantation was to extend the Crown's control over Ireland.

Many plantations took place in the sixteenth and seventeenth centuries. These included the Plantation of Laois/Offaly and the Plantation of Munster. One of the best organised was the Ulster Plantation.

## Flight of the Earls

After an unsuccessful rebellion, Gaelic chieftains from Ulster left Ireland for Rome. This event is known as the **Flight of the Earls**.

The counties of Donegal, Derry, Tyrone, Fermanagh, Armagh and Cavan were now available for plantation.

## Land survey

Mapmakers appointed by the Crown surveyed the land. Estates were given to English and Scottish settlers known as **undertakers** and **servitors**. These groups were given estates. They had to build fortified dwellings and enclosures with roofs of slate to protect themselves against attacks from the native Irish. The first planters arrived in 1609 with tools, seeds and animals to cultivate the land.

## Scottish settlers

At the same time, Scottish settlers were settling in the Glens of Antrim and in the Lagan valley in counties Antrim and Down.

Therefore, all counties of Ulster, except Monaghan, received an influx of English and Scottish settlers.

## The reaction of the native Irish

The native Irish who had lost their lands often attacked the new planters in the decades that followed the plantation. Fortified and planned towns such as Londonderry, Donegal town, Belfast and Enniskillen were built.

## Results of the plantation

◎ Despite attacks from the native Irish, the planters prospered and the Crown tightened its grip on Ulster.

◎ The ownership of much of the land of Ulster was transferred to English and Scottish settlers. The native Irish became tenants on land they had previously regarded as their own.

A march by members of the Orange Order in Northern Ireland

From left to right: Martin McGuinness, Gordon Brown and Peter Robinson, political leaders involved in the affairs of Northern Ireland

◎ Planters brought the English language and Protestant religion to Ulster.
◎ The Irish language, together with Gaelic laws and customs declined.
◎ The relationship between the two cultures remained very hostile. This hostility led to much conflict and bloodshed, which has continued up until recent times.

## 2 European colonisation of South America

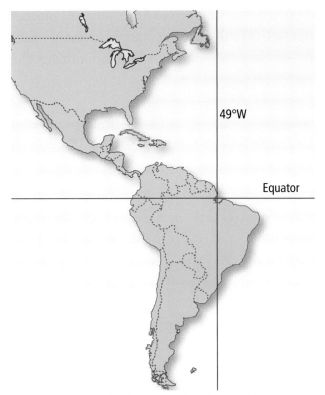

Fig 8.41 In 1494 the Pope divided the world between Spain and Portugal east and west of the line of longitude 49° west

The New World, already settled by native Americans, was 'discovered' by Christopher Columbus in 1492. In the years that followed, the Spanish and Portuguese set their sights on creating new empires in the New World. At this time, the Incas had a vast empire in Peru. The Spanish conquistador Francisco Pizarro destroyed the Inca Empire and claimed its territory for Spain. The Portuguese colonised Brazil. (See also 2 Social and historical factors: Brazil, page 219.)

> **Question**
>
> How did it come about that Portugal seized Brazil and that Spain conquered the rest of South America?

## The results of colonisation

◎ Native empires were no match for the superior weaponry and cavalry of the invaders. The native people, known collectively as **Amerindians** became subject people to the conquering Spaniards. They were little better than slaves. Great numbers of native people died because they had no immunity against infections brought by the conquerors.

◎ Spain and Portugal ruled separate portions of South America for 300 years. Spanish and Portuguese became the languages of rule of the South American continent.

◎ The **cross followed the sword**. Soldiers defeated local resistance, often with much bloodshed. Spanish and Portuguese missionaries followed with the Catholic religion. European architecture was used in the building of cathedrals all over South America.

Many of the colonists were adventurers. They migrated to South America to claim the mineral wealth, such as gold and silver. South America became a source of cheap foodstuffs and raw material for Spain and Portugal. These included coffee, sugar cane and bananas that were grown on large estates.

To provide the labour for these estates, many African slaves were forcibly brought from West Africa to Brazil and the Caribbean. This was **involuntary** or **forced migration**. The descendants of those slaves live in Brazil and in other regions today.

The Spanish and Portuguese brought European animals such as horses and cattle to South America for the first time. Ships returning to Europe carried new foods to Europe such as potatoes and tomatoes. The potato became a very important food in Europe, especially in Ireland during the nineteenth century.

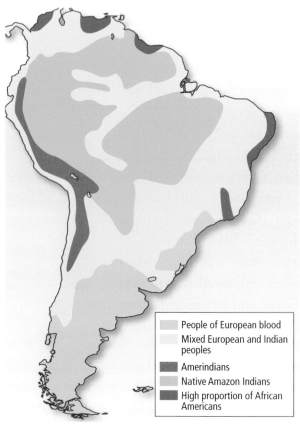

People of European blood

Mixed European and Indian peoples

Amerindians

Native Amazon Indians

High proportion of African Americans

Fig 8.42 The racial composition of South America

Many Brazilians are of mixed race as can be seen in the women's soccer team

## SUMMARY

◎ People migrate because of push and pull factors.

◎ Outward and inward migration in modern Ireland is an example of individual migration.

◎ The Plantation of Ulster and the colonisation of South America are examples of organised migration.

## QUESTIONS

1 Explain the meaning of each of the following terms which relate to human migration:
   ◎ Push factors of migration
   ◎ Pull factors of migration
   ◎ Barriers to migration. (JC)

2 How have push and pull factors caused many young people to migrate from the West of Ireland to the Dublin region for decades?

3 Can you suggest one push and one pull factor that brought East European migrants to Ireland in recent years?

4 Name three counties that were planted during the Ulster plantation.

5 Name three Ulster towns that were founded during the Ulster plantation.

6 Explain two effects of the Ulster Plantation.

7 What effects did European colonisation have on South America? Refer in your answer to the following:
   ◎ The spread of European languages and religion
   ◎ The destruction of native cultures
   ◎ The slave trade from Africa

8 'Movement of people has led to both emigration and immigration.'
   Describe one example of migration of peoples you have studied. In your answer refer to the push and/or pull factors. (JC)

9 'The Plantations of Ulster and European colonisation of South America are examples of organised migration.'
   Choose one of the above migrations and explain three effects the migrations had on the area to which the people moved. (JC)

# 9 SETTLEMENT

## 9.1 Early Settlers in Ireland

Students must study an example of settlement from one of the following eras:
• Pre-Christian
• Viking
• Norman
• Plantation

We will study Pre-Christian settlement.

The landscape today shows evidence of human settlement, past and present. The location of initial settlement in an area is related to:

◎ Where people were coming from.

◎ Their need for water, food, defence and communication.

### Pre-Christian settlement

#### Where did early settlers come from?

Waves of settlers originally came to Ireland at intervals from 7000 BC onwards. These settlers came on foot to Ireland via land bridges that connected Ireland with Britain after the Ice Age. Sea level was much lower at that time.

We know that many very early settlers remained near the north-east coast because of excavations at **Mount Sandel** on the River Bann in Co. Derry.

#### Where did early settlers live?

Archaeologists have uncovered many sites of early settlements.

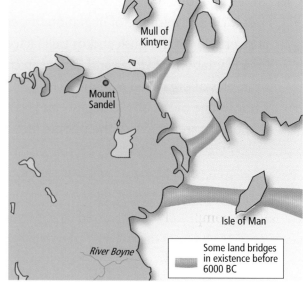

Fig 9.1 Land bridges connected Ireland to Britain during the Ice Age

Many of these settlements are found along river valleys and lakes where water was available, e.g. Mount Sandel and Lough Gur in Co. Limerick.

## What did early settlers eat?

Early settlers were hunters and food-gatherers. They gathered food from the sea shore. They hunted wild pigs, caught salmon and collected hazelnuts. They used primitive stone weapons to kill and skin animals.

Archaeologists have also found bones of small birds, hares and deer at early sites. Early people threw the discarded bones of animals into rubbish heaps that are called **middens**.

## Early farmers

New Stone Age farmers came to Ireland after 5000 BC. These farmers brought seed and domesticated animals with them. They cooked meat in **fulachtaí fia**. They built large stone graves known as **megalithic tombs** that still exist. These are older than the pyramids of Egypt.

Many of these tombs are found on the Burren, Co. Clare and along the River Boyne. The valley of the Boyne had alluvial soil that was excellent for growing crops.

## The Celts and defence

After 800 BC, the Celts came to Ireland. These Iron Age people built defensive settlements. They built hill forts on elevated sites and promontory forts on small headlands on the coast. They built **crannógs** on small islands in lakes.

The Celts introduced the Irish language to Ireland. Today, we still use placenames that have their origins in the Celtic era, for example:

Fig 9.2 Early settlers built crannógs on islands for their own protection

◎ **Dún** (fort), e.g. Dún Aengus, Dunmore
◎ **Inis** (island), e.g. Inishmore, Inishfree

## Communications

Pre-Christian Ireland was densely forested. Therefore, settlers lived along the coast and along river valleys. They used flimsy boats to travel from place to place. Vast areas remained completely untouched. However, over time, some forests were cut down and tracks became established.

The Celts used oak timbers to make paths through short sections of bogland in the Midlands. These were known as **toghers**.

Dún Aengus, an ancient Celtic fort, sits high on the cliffs of Inishmore, Aran Islands

People travelled along **eskers** in the centre of Ireland. These were ridges – left by glaciers – that enabled people to cross the boglands of the Midlands and the floodplain of the Shannon. Esker Riada was the name given by the Celts to describe an ancient east-west route through the Midlands. In Christian times, this route became An Slí Mór (the Great Highway).

## SUMMARY

◎ Ireland's first people were hunters and food-gatherers.
◎ Early settlement sites leave clues about people's need for water, food and defence.
◎ Communication in early times was along rivers, eskers and the coast.

## QUESTIONS

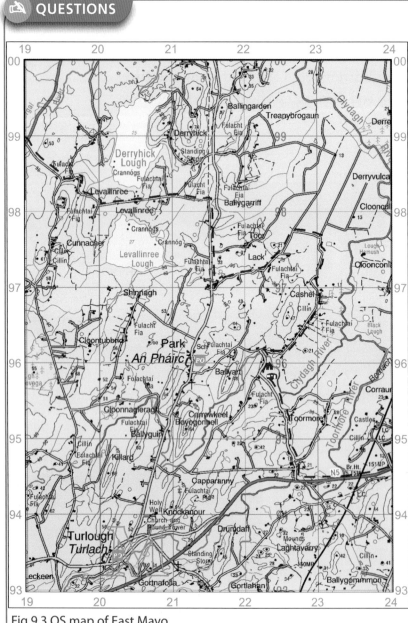

Fig 9.3 OS map of East Mayo

1 Study the ancient Pre-Christian sites marked in red on the OS map and answer the following questions:
   (a) Name two lakes in which crannógs were built.
   (b) Using evidence from the map, explain why water was widely available for early settlers in this area.

2 Can you explain why fulachtaí fia were close to streams and lakes?

3 Look at the ring fort at Boyogonnell, M 212 952.
   (a) At what altitude is the ring fort located?
   (b) Can you suggest one reason why it was built at that location?
   (c) Give a grid reference for another ring fort built on a similar site.

4 Write a paragraph describing settlement in Pre-Christian Ireland referring to the following points:
   ◎ Where the settlers came from.
   ◎ Two locations in which they settled.
   ◎ How those locations met their needs.

# 9.2 Nucleated Settlements

Patterns in the distribution of nucleated settlements in Ireland are related to a number of factors, which include:

◎ Social and historical – past patterns and processes
◎ The primacy of Dublin
◎ Resources and terrain – altitude, drainage patterns, land quality

◎ **Nucleated** or **clustered settlements** are houses and buildings that are grouped together in a cluster (nucleus). People chose to locate a settlement because it possessed a distinctive advantage, e.g. a spring, a dry point or an easily defended site. These nuclei (plural) grow over time to form villages and towns.
◎ **Dispersed settlements** occur when houses are scattered across the countryside and people are isolated from each other.
◎ **Linear settlements** occur when houses are built in a line along a road. This type of settlement is very evident in the countryside of Ireland today.

Fig 9.4 Patterns of settlement

## Social and historic influences

Over a long period of time, many different groups of settlers came to Ireland from abroad. Most of these groups built settlements that grew into towns over a long period.

Each wave of settlers chose particular locations in which they established settlements.

## Viking settlements

The Vikings arrived in Ireland at the end of the eighth century. They were a sea-faring people with settlements on the coast of Britain, the Faroe Islands and Iceland. They were plunderers of monasteries at first. Later, they established settlements along the coast in bays, and in harbours at the mouths of rivers. This meant that they could maintain contact with Vikings abroad.

Fig 9.5 Settlements of Viking origin are located along the coast and on estuaries

The placenames of many coastal towns today indicate their Viking origin. Many of their settlement names ended with the Norwegian word **fjord**, meaning an inlet. This later became **ford**, e.g. Carlingford, Wexford and Waterford.

The **low** used at the end of Wicklow and Arklow was the Viking word for low-lying land.

Dublin was also a Viking settlement because of its good harbour at the mouth of the River Liffey.

## Monastic settlements

The ruins of early monasteries are found all over Ireland. Many of these monasteries were established by Irish monks in remote areas, e.g. Scattery Island, Glendalough and Clonmacnoise.

The Franciscans came to Ireland shortly after the Normans. Their function was to serve the people of the towns that were now growing. They built monasteries that grew into settlements. This is how Ennis, in Co. Clare began.

The names of many towns indicate that they were once associated with monasteries. These include Monasterevin, **Mainistir** na Buaille, (Boyle), Mainistir na Corann (Midleton) and Mainistir Fhearmaí (Fermoy).

Boyle Abbey, Co. Roscommon

## Norman settlements

The Normans invaded Ireland in the twelfth century. Unlike the Vikings, they were interested in fertile land.

They brought with them a tradition of castle-building. They built many castles with

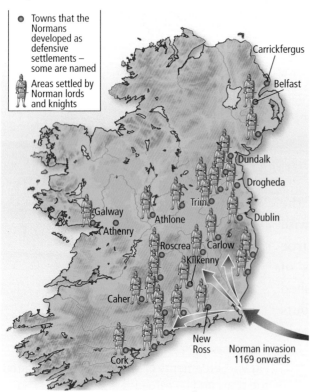

Fig 9.6 Some of the towns that were developed by the Normans

Trim Castle, Co. Meath, sits on the bank of the River Boyle and dates from Norman times

a keep and bailey. A town developed around the castle. The Normans also developed towns that the Vikings had established, e.g. Dublin.

Towns that were founded or developed by the Normans include Trim, Carrickfergus, Kilkenny and Athenry.

The Normans were Christians and introduced European monastic orders.

## Plantation settlement

Plantations by English settlers took place in the sixteenth and seventeenth centuries. Examples include the plantations of Laois-Offaly, Munster and Ulster (see page 244).

Where plantations occurred, towns were built to provide protection for settlers. These settlements have grown into modern towns.

| Some plantation towns | |
|---|---|
| **Plantation** | **Town** |
| Laois-Offaly | Portarlington, Daingean |
| Munster | Youghal, Mallow |
| Ulster | (London)Derry, Strabane, Virginia, Co. Cavan |

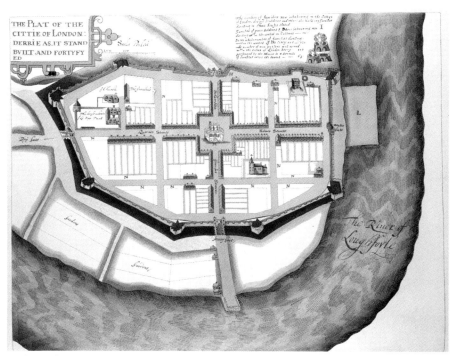

A plan of Londonderry; the city was built after the Ulster Plantation of 1609

## Landlords' towns

After the Cromwellian Plantation of the seventeenth century, landlords became the most important people in Irish society. Several landlords built towns on their estates. These towns were planned, with straight streets, town squares and English architecture, e.g. Abbeyleix, Birr, Kilrush and Strokestown.

Strokestown, Co. Roscommon; the straight streets from the original plan remain

## The primacy of Dublin

Dublin is a **primate city**. A primate city is at least twice as big as the next city in the same state. Paris and Copenhagen are European examples of primate cities.

Dublin is the economic heart of the state. Dublin is a capital with many functions:

◎ It is the seat of government. The Dáil, Seanad and most of the civil service are in Dublin.
◎ Dublin is Ireland's chief port. It has the largest airport in the state, with thousands of employees.
◎ Dublin is at the centre of Ireland's road and rail network. The transport system radiates outward to the provinces from Dublin.
◎ Dublin is Ireland's most important financial centre. Large companies such as banks, and insurance companies have their headquarters there.
◎ Dublin is the most important centre for shopping, tourism, education and health in the state.

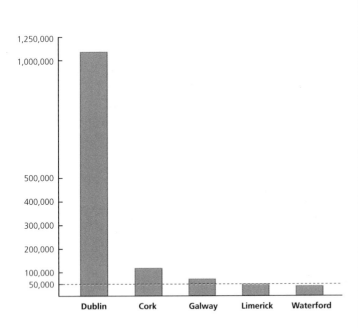

Fig 9.7 The population of Dublin and other cities

Dublin from the air; St Stephen's Green can be seen clearly in the centre

Therefore, Dublin is multi-functional. It is growing very rapidly. From 1981–2006, the population of Dublin City and County grew by 184,000. During the Celtic Tiger years that began in 1995, many major companies from abroad chose Dublin as the location of their European headquarters. More than 28 per cent of the population of the Republic now live in the Dublin region.

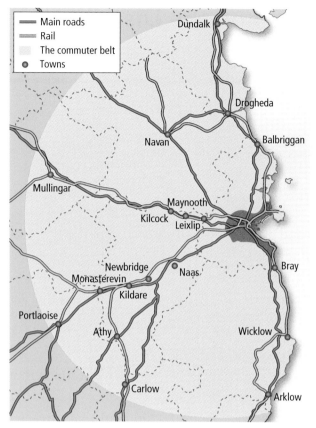

Fig 9.8 Dublin draws workers from the surrounding areas, which results in the commuter belt

Leinster House, Dublin, is the seat of government in the Republic of Ireland

> **Definition**
>
> **Decentralisation:** Moving some economic activities from Dublin to other parts of the country in order to promote economic activity nationwide.

## Is decentralisation a solution to Dublin's growth?

The government has tried to halt Dublin's growth by a policy of **decentralisation**. Some government offices have been relocated in provincial towns. For example, the Examinations branch of the Department of Education and Science has been in Athlone for many years. However, in 2008, the government decided to halt funding for decentralisation because of the economic downturn.

### SUMMARY

◎ Waves of settlers who migrated to Ireland each chose specific locations for their towns.
◎ Dublin – Ireland's primate city – has been the country's key administrative centre for centuries.

### QUESTIONS

1 Describe one characteristic of Celtic, Viking and Norman settlement in Ireland.
2 Examine the picture of Trim Castle on page 252. What evidence is there to show that defence was important for the Normans?
3 Explain three reasons for the primacy of Dublin.

## 9.3 Resources, Terrain and the Distribution of Settlements

The following factors influence the distribution of towns and cities:

◎ Altitude
◎ Drainage patterns
◎ Land quality

### Altitude

Nucleated settlements in Ireland avoid high altitudes. Mountains and hills are exposed to high winds. They also attract relief rain. Temperatures are lower than at sea level.

Nucleated settlements are confined to the coast and to valleys that cut through mountains.

### Drainage patterns

Rivers and river valleys have attracted settlement in Ireland since ancient times.

River valleys contain fertile land that attracted farming settlement and provided food for towns located by the river.

Many towns are located at **bridge points** on rivers. That is because bridge points become a route focus. Towns grow to provide services for people at these crossing points.

Many towns in Ireland contain the Irish word **áth**, e.g. Baile Átha Luain – Athlone; Baile Átha Cliath – Dublin; Béal an Átha – Ballina. **Áth** means **ford**. This indicates that these settlements are located at crossing points.

The largest urban centres on the island of Ireland are located at river mouths or on the banks of river estuaries. These include Dublin, Belfast, Sligo, Galway, Limerick, Cork and Waterford. These centres are on the lowest crossing point of the river on which they are located.

### Land quality

Poor land that may be marshy, infertile or subject to flooding repels settlement. Fertile land attracts settlement. Much of the best land in the country is in the eastern half of Ireland.

Carlingford, Co. Louth is located on coastal lowlands with sheltering uplands in the background

Drogheda – Droichead Átha – grew into a town at a bridge point located at the mouth of the River Boyne

Towns that were located in the centre of rich agricultural land thrived. This was because they became market centres for the produce from the surrounding area. They also provided services for the local population.

The Normans settled mainly in Leinster and East Munster in rich agricultural valleys. Maynooth is surrounded by the fertile plains of Kildare. Kilkenny, on the River Nore, became a market centre for the farmers of the rich agricultural region.

The fertile lands of the Lagan Valley and the Glens of Antrim attracted settlers from Scotland in the seventeenth century. Towns such as Belfast and Lisburn grew as market centres in the Lagan Valley.

## Coastal settlements

Some settlements are located on the coast. They may be fishing ports, such as Killybegs, Co. Donegal, or coastal resorts such as Tramore, Co. Waterford.

## Marshlands

Marshy land that contains large peat bogs repels settlement. Therefore, people have avoided the large peat bogs that are located in the centre of Ireland. Nucleated settlements developed on the boundaries of the peatlands. They have grown because Bord na Móna provides employment in nearby peatlands. These settlements include Shannonbridge and Tyrellspass.

Galbally, Co. Limerick is located in the fertile farmlands of the Glen of Aherlow

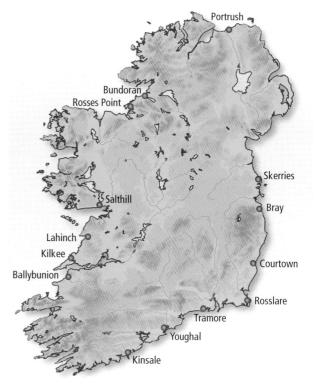

Fig 9.9 Some of Ireland's coastal resorts

Shannonbridge is located at an important bridge point on the River Shannon. Today, it is a resource-based settlement. The peat resources in the background are exploited for the power station. The power station is located in the foreground

## SUMMARY

◎ Nucleated settlements generally avoid upland regions in Ireland.

◎ Many towns are found in river valleys and at crossing points.

◎ Fertile lands attract nucleated settlements.

## QUESTIONS

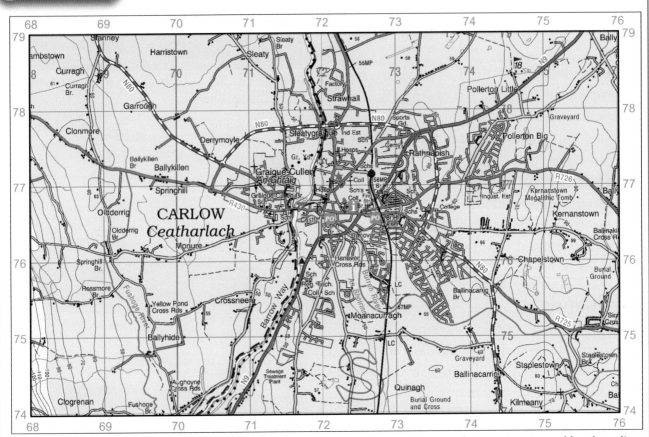

Fig 9.10 The OS map of Carlow and its surroundings illustrates the importance of rivers, terrain and land quality in the location of a nucleated settlement

1 Draw an outline of the OS map above (not a tracing) and include the following features:
   ◎ The River Barrow and the River Burren
   ◎ The area of Carlow town
   ◎ Two spot heights that are evident in the OS map
   ◎ A national primary and a national secondary routeway

2 What evidence in the OS map indicates that Carlow is a route focus?

3 Do you think that the land around Carlow is well drained? Explain your answer.

4 The ruins of a castle are located within the town at S 717 766. What does that suggest about the possible origins of the town of Carlow?

5 Why are many towns located at river crossing points? Refer to two examples in your answer.

6 Explain two reasons why some settlements develop on the coast. Give one example in each case.

# 9.4 Settlement in the New Polders of the Netherlands

In recent times, the creation of new settlement has continued on land newly reclaimed from the sea.

## The Netherlands

The Netherlands is the most densely populated country in the western hemisphere. Much of the country is below high-tide level. For hundreds of years, the Dutch have built dykes – called **polders** – to create new land below sea level.

## The Zuyder Zee project

Until the 1930s, the Zuyder Zee was open to the sea. Disastrous storms and loss of life over the years led the Dutch to enclose the Zuyder Zee with a barrier dam. They were then able to create new land for farming and turn Lake Ijssel into a freshwater lake for domestic use.

'God made the world but people made Holland.'

> **Geofact**
>
> Population density in the Netherlands is 395 per km² (Republic of Ireland: 60 per km²).

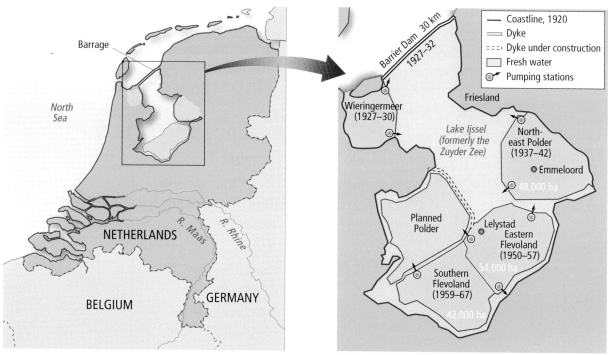

Fig 9.11a The Netherlands has reclaimed polders from the sea by building a barrage across the former Zuyder Zee, now Lake Ijssel

Fig 9.11b The new polders have added significantly to the land mass of the Netherlands

> **Geofact**
>
> One-third of the Netherlands lies below sea level at high tide.

### How were the new polders of the Ijsselmeer formed?

1 A barrier dam enclosed the newly named Lake Ijssel from the sea.
2 Salt water was pumped out using oil-powered pumps.
3 New polders were created by building dykes of mud and stone around large areas.
4 Roads were laid out. Drainage channels were excavated. Diesel and electrically powered pumps controlled ground water levels.
5 Roads, farms and villages were planned and laid out. New settlements grew throughout the twentieth century in each of the new polders.

The barrier dam enclosing Lake Ijssel

Settlement on the polders. Much of the land is used to grow crops

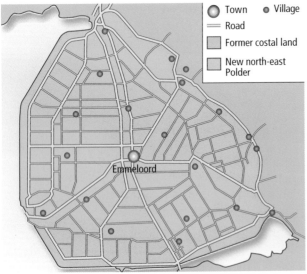

Fig 9.12 The North-east Polder

## Settlement patterns in the North-east Polder

In the North-east Polder, farmers live on family-run farms where the fields are laid out in a chessboard pattern. Farm houses are built in a linear pattern along a rural road.

The locations of nucleated settlements were carefully chosen. Emmelourd is the main urban centre to provide important services for the entire population of the polder. Villages were built in a radial pattern around Emmelourd to provide for the local population's day-to-day needs.

## Settlement in Eastern and Southern Flevoland

The new polders of Eastern and Southern Flevoland are very near the **Randstad**, a ring of cities that are very overcrowded. The Dutch, therefore, decided that Flevoland would be used to relieve some of the population pressure in the Netherlands. Lelystad and Almere are now large urban centres. Almere has a population of 183,000.

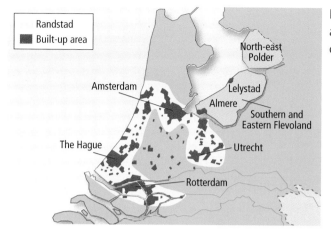

Fig 9.13 The Randstad contains almost 40 per cent of the population of the Netherlands

## SUMMARY

◎ The Dutch created new land from the sea called polders.
◎ New settlements patterns were laid out in each polder.

## QUESTIONS

1 Explain the meaning of the word polder.
2 Explain one reason why the Dutch built a barrier dam at the mouth of the former Zuyder Zee.
3 What is a polder? Describe one way in which settletment on polders is different from other areas. (JC)

## 9.5 Functions of Nucleated Settlement

Nucleated settlement may be classified by function:

◎ The village
◎ The market settlement
◎ The defensive settlement
◎ The resource-based settlement

◎ The port settlement
◎ The residential/dormitory settlement
◎ The recreational settlement
◎ The ecclesiastical settlement

All urban centres have functions. Usually, urban settlements have more than one function. When we classify a settlement according to its function, we use its most important function.

For example, Killarney has a residential function because people live there. However, its most important function is recreational. It also has schools, shops, medical and personal services. Therefore, Killarney is multi-functional.

Explain why people with families might like to holiday in Duncannon.

Duncannon, Co. Wexford, is a recreational settlement

## Settlement classification

| Settlement type | Functions | Examples |
| --- | --- | --- |
| Village | Provides a small range of services to the people of the surrounding parish, e.g. primary school, church, shop, post office. | Ballinalee, Co. Longord; Doonbeg, Co. Clare |
| Market settlement | Provides a wide range of services, e.g.<br>◎ Supermarkets and other retail outlets<br>◎ Hotels and restaurants<br>◎ Dental and medical services<br>◎ Financial services – banks and building societies | Mullingar, Co. Westmeath; Ennis, Co. Clare; Castlebar, Co. Mayo |
| Defensive settlement | Many settlements began with the building of a castle on a defensive site. The ruins of the castle are part of the heritage of the town today. | Trim, Co. Meath; Carrickfergus, Co. Antrim; Bunratty, Co. Clare |
| Resource-based settlement | Resource-based settlements grow because a resource such as an important mineral ore or peat exists nearby. | Navan, Co. Meath; Silvermines, Co. Tipperary |
| Port settlement | Ports are equipped to handle ships and their cargos. They contain docks and cranes to load and unload ships. Ports provide a lot of employment. Ports also often have other functions. | Dublin, Co. Dublin; Waterford, Co. Waterford; Foynes, Co. Limerick |
| Residential/ dormitory function | People live in a dormitory town, but they commute to work daily in a nearby town or city. | Sixmilebridge, Co. Clare – dormitory town for Shannon and Limerick<br>Towns surrounding Dublin, e.g. Malahide, Blanchardstown |
| Recreational settlement | People go on holidays to these settlements, because of particular attractions such as beautiful scenery, beach facilities or golfing facilities. | Lahinch, Co. Clare; Bundoran, Co. Donegal; Killarney, Co. Kerry |
| Ecclesiastical settlement | Ecclesiastical settlements have a religious function. They provide for people's spiritual needs. | Knock, Co. Mayo; Maynooth, Co. Kildare |

# Settlement in an Irish river basin: the Shannon Basin

The Shannon is the longest river in Ireland and Britain. The Shannon has many urban centres throughout its length. Limerick is the largest centre by far, with Athlone taking second place in terms of population.

**Shannonbridge**
A defensive settlement where the British built fortifications to stop a French invasion.
It is a resource-based settlement with a large electricity station that uses a local resource – peat.

**Clonmacnoise**
A major ecclesiastical centre in early Christian Ireland.
It is an important stop for many tourists in the Midlands.

**Athlone**
A major crossing point and route focus; it is an important market centre in the Midlands.
It has a recreational function for tourists on the Shannon.
It is an educational centre.

**Portumna**
A recreational settlement that has holiday homes and boating facilities for nearby Lough Derg.

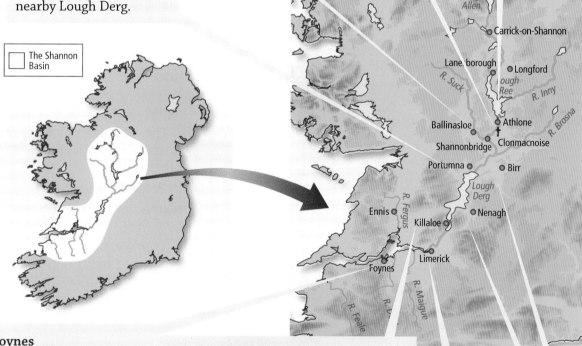

**Foynes**
A port settlement located on the south bank of the estuary. The estuary's waters are more than 21 metres deep at low tide, enough to take large ships.

**Killaloe/Ballina**
A residential centre for people who work in Limerick and an important recreational centre for leisure craft on the Shannon.
The location of St Flannan's Cathedral makes it an ecclesiastical centre for the Church of Ireland community.

**Limerick**
see Case Study

**Nenagh and Birr**
Important market towns located in the Shannon Basin.

Fig 9.14 The Shannon Basin

## Case Study

# Limerick City: A multi-functional urban centre

St John's Castle lies on the banks of the River Shannon in Limerick and dates from the twelfth century

### 1 Defensive function

The Vikings settled in Limerick in 822. The Normans developed the city in later centuries. King John's Castle was built at the beginning of the thirteenth century. Massive city walls were built over time.

The city played a central role in the Williamite Wars, 1689–91. King William's siege of the city ended with the Treaty of Limerick. Limerick's defensive function ended with that treaty.

### 2 Market function

Limerick is located on the lowest bridge point of the River Shannon. The city became a route focus in North Munster.

Therefore, the city grew as a market centre over time. Limerick's port function also helped the city to grow.

Today, Limerick is a major shopping centre for the mid-west of Ireland. The city has major department stores and suburban shopping centres.

### 3 Residential function

Limerick has a population of more than 52,000. Many people who work at Shannon Airport and at Shannon's industrial estates live in Limerick. The city has expanded as an educational centre with the University of Limerick. It also has many hospitals and industrial estates.

Lecturers, medical staff and manufacturing workers required residential accommodation.

Therefore, the city has expanded by building many new residential areas to house its growing population.

New residential apartments overlook the Shannon in Limerick

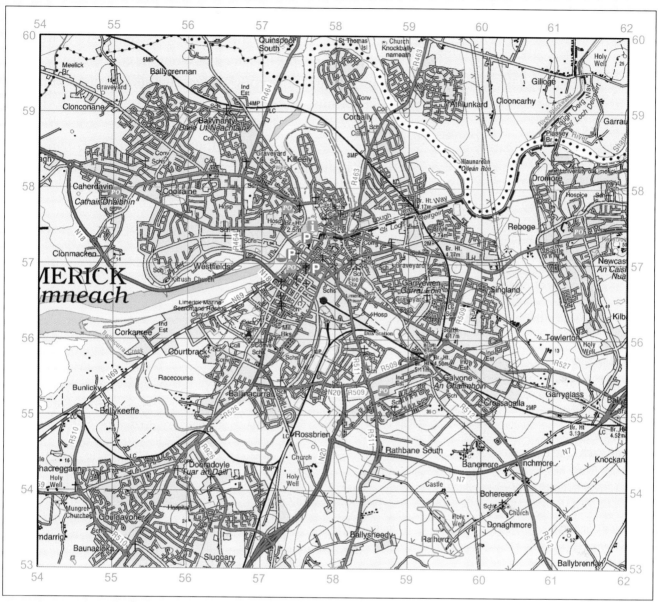

Fig 9.15 OS map of Limerick City

## QUESTIONS

1   Draw a sketch map of the area shown in Fig 9.15 above. Include the following:
   - The River Shannon
   - The railway station and railways
   - The national primary routeways shown in the OS map
   - A hospital
   - The castle (at R 577 578)

2   What evidence does the OS map above provide of the following?
   (a) Limerick's function as a recreational settlement
   (b) Limerick as a bridge point
   (c) Limerick's residential function today

Fig 9.16a The River Rhine in Europe

# Settlement in the River Rhine Basin

The Rhine is one of the great rivers of Western Europe. Millions of people live in cities along its course. Its cities are home to some of Europe's largest manufacturing industries.

The Rhine waterway is a great artery of trade. Barges carrying coal, sand, timber and mineral ores are a frequent sight on the Rhine and its tributaries. Therefore, many cities on the Rhine have a port function, as well as other functions.

## Rotterdam

Rotterdam is Europe's largest port and among the largest in the world. Docks, warehouses and oil terminals line each side of the river from Rotterdam to the mouth of the Rhine, a distance of 27 km. Cargoes are distributed by train, barge and pipeline to Rhineland cities.

## Cities of the Ruhr

The Ruhr is a group of cities that developed on the Ruhr coalfield. Therefore, these cities grew as resource-based settlements.

Ruhr cities were home to coalminers who worked the coal pits every day until the 1950s. By then, the best coal seams were exhausted. Thousands of workers became redundant.

Today, the Ruhr is a great manufacturing region.

## Recreational settlements

The Rhine supports a great tourist industry. Cruise boats carry tourists through the Rhinelands every day.

Rudesheim is a recreational settlement on the Rhine with craft shops and art galleries.

Heidelburg has a famous castle that is very popular with tourists.

## Basel

Basel, Switzerland's port, is located hundreds of kilometres from the sea. Barges unload imports for the Swiss economy, including minerals, timber and oil.

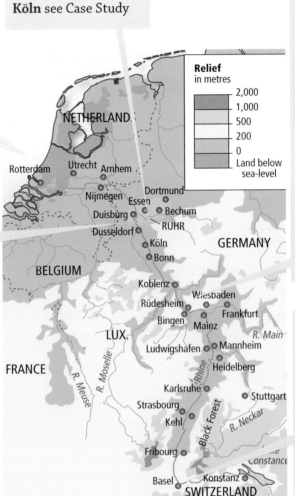

Fig 9.16b The River Rhine Basin

# Case Study

## Köln (Cologne)

### 1 Market function

Köln (Cologne) is one of the most important bridge points on the River Rhine in Germany. The city is a major route focus for rail and road transport routes. Its port is one of the most important on the Rhine. As a **nodal point**, it has become a modern market centre. The city has shopping, banking and business facilities.

### 2 Port function

Köln is one of the most important inland ports on the Rhine. The docks are large enough to handle ocean-going vessels.

As Köln is a route focus, cargo from barges is easily distributed to its hinterland.

Köln is also an important port of call for river cruises. Cruise vessels carry passengers upstream where the Rhine passes through beautiful countryside and towns.

### 3 Recreational function

Köln has an important recreational function. It is one of Germany's most beautiful cities with belfries, cathedral spires and bridges.

Köln has the largest historic town centre in Germany and has interesting medieval architecture.

Much of the historic centre near the city's famous cathedral has been pedestrianised. The area is lined with bookshops, art galleries, coffee shops and boutiques.

**Definition**

**Nodal point:** A city or town where natural routeways meet.

Köln cathedral dominates the city centre. The cathedral survived the bombing campaign of WWII

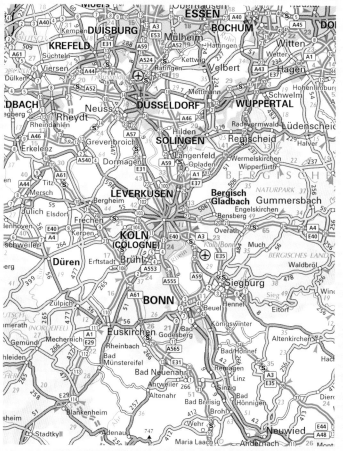
Fig 9.17 Köln is located at a major transport junction on the banks of the Rhine

### SUMMARY

◎ Nucleated settlements can be classified according to function.
◎ The Shannon has many urban centres on its banks each with an important function or functions.
◎ Limerick has many functions and is the largest settlement on the Shannon.
◎ The River Rhine Basin has major urban centres such as Köln.

### QUESTIONS

1 (a) Name the urban settlement in which you live or where you attend school.
  (b) Name three functions of that settlement.
  (c) Name any past function of that settlement that no longer exists today.
2 (a) Draw a map of the River Shannon.
  (b) Mark in and name four towns on the River Shannon and two towns in the Shannon Basin.
3 Name four urban centres on the River Rhine. Give one example of an important function of each centre.

## 9.6 Change in the Function of Settlements

Settlements may change in function over time where mining has become important.

### 1 Navan: where mining has become important

Navan is the county town of Co. Meath. It is a route centre and therefore, it has a market function for people of Co. Meath.

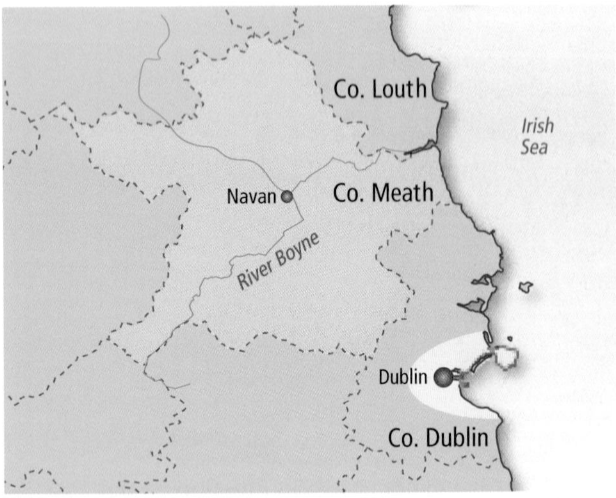

The town has also been an important manufacturing town, with furniture and carpet manufacturers. Navan Carpets exported its products to many countries. However, in 2004 foreign competition brought an end to Navan Carpets .

### Navan: a mining town today

In 1970 a large lead and zinc deposit was discovered within 3 km of Navan. In 1977, Tara Mines began to mine the deposit. Since its opening, lead and zinc ores have been exported via Dublin port to smelters mainly in Norway and Finland.

Fig 9.18 The location of Navan, the county town of Co. Meath

## Impact of mining on Navan's economy

◎ Tara Mines employed about 670 people in 2008.

◎ The mine is a major boost to the town's economy. Housing sales, car sales, restaurants and shops have benefited from the presence of the mine since 1977.

◎ Suppliers of equipment, to run the mine, both in Navan and further afield, also benefit. Explosives, drilling equipment and transport are major requirements.

Boliden mine is located on the outskirts of Navan

## Navan: a dormitory town

Navan has also become a dormitory town for Dublin in recent years. After 1995, when the Celtic Tiger economy began, Dublin house prices soared. Many people bought cheaper homes in Navan and towns surrounding Dublin. These workers commute to the capital every day. Because of this, Navan's population doubled between the years 1991–2006. Navan has a good quality of life with a wide range of services.

Fig 9.19 Navan's population inceased sharply during the years 1991–2006

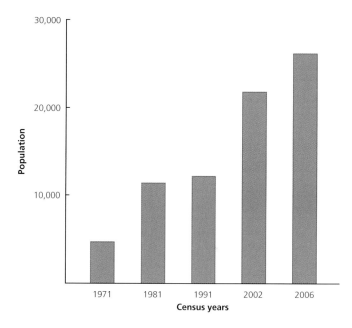

Navan, Co. Meath, on the River Boyne. Name two urban functions that are evident in the picture

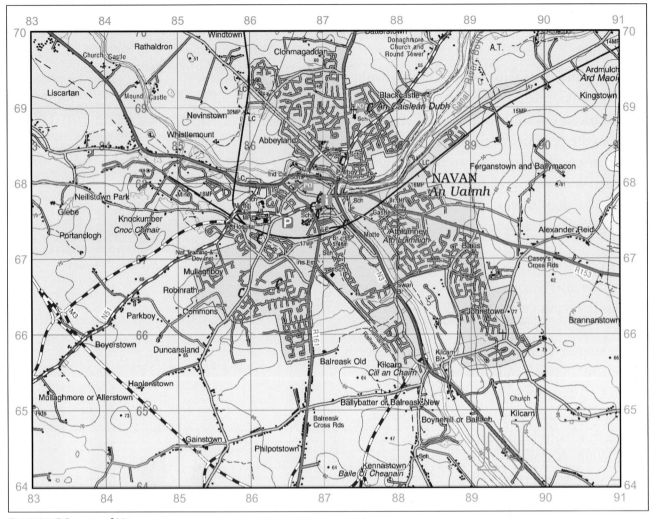

Fig 9.20 OS map of Navan

---

📄 **SUMMARY**

◎ Early functions of settlements may be replaced by modern functions.

◎ Navan gained a mining function with its nearby lead and zinc mine.

---

📖 **QUESTIONS**

1  Draw a sketch of the area in Fig 9.20 above, with the following features:
   ◎ A castle and motte
   ◎ The main road routes
   ◎ The railway
   ◎ An industrial estate
   ◎ The mine at N 851 678

2  How did the discovery of lead and zinc deposits change the function of Navan?

3  What evidence in the OS map above suggests that Navan has a market function?

4  Study Fig 9.20 and name one residential part of Navan. Explain your answer.

# 9.7 Large-scale Industrial Development

Settlements may change in function over time where large-scale development takes place.

Since the 1960s, Irish governments have invited multinational companies from abroad to locate in Ireland. They were offered tax incentives to establish in Ireland and to create jobs. Companies set up factories in towns across the Republic. Clarecastle, near Ennis in Co. Clare is one such location.

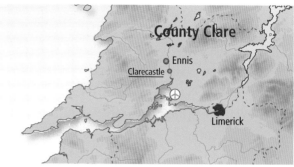

Fig 9.21 The location of Clarecastle in Co. Clare

## Clarecastle: changing functions over time

◎ Clarecastle began as a crossing point or ford on the River Fergus.

◎ When the Normans came to Ireland, an Anglo-Norman knight built a castle beside the bridge on a dry point of the floodplain of the Fergus. Clarecastle acquired a **defensive function** for a time.

◎ Clarecastle was chosen as a garrison village in later centuries. British soldiers lived in a large barracks. Therefore, Clarecastle had a **garrison function** until Ireland won its independence in 1922.

◎ Clarecastle had a **port function** in the nineteenth century, as ships unloaded grain for Ennis.

◎ Clarecastle has had a **dormitory function** for many decades as many people from Clarecastle work in Shannon and Limerick.

◎ In the 1970s, Clarecastle became the **location of a large pharmaceutical plant** – Syntex Ireland. The plant is now owned by Roche.

Roche makes pharmaceuticals for the healthcare industry. The factory is located on a large site beside Clarecastle. It employed about 230 people in 2008.

The pharmaceutical plant has been the most important economic activity in Clarecastle over the past thirty years.

The Roche plant is located in Clarecastle

📄 **SUMMARY**

◎ Clarecastle gained an industrial function with the establishment of Syntex – now Roche.

✏️ **QUESTIONS**

1  Using one piece of evidence from the OS map, suggest how Clarecastle may have got its name.

2  On the OS map what evidence suggests that Clarecastle had a port function?

3  On the OS map the site of the Roche plant is marked with an R. Suggest one possible reason why this site was chosen for the factory.

4  Suggest one reason for the absence of settlement in the area of Lissan East? The grid reference for Lissan East is R 350 728.

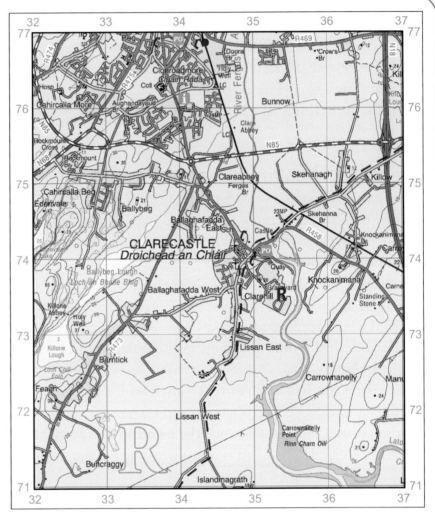

Fig 9.22 OS map of Clarecastle

All students must study the Irish road network. Higher level students must study EU airports and transport on the Rhine. Ordinary level students must study one of the topics.

## 9.8 Communication links

Movements of people, goods and information (including electronic telecommunications) between settlements leads to the development of communications links. The existence of such links aids the development of settlements. In this section, we examine these important communication links:

◎ The Irish road network
◎ EU airports
◎ Transport on the River Rhine

# Case Study

## The Irish road network

The road network that exists in Ireland today was laid out when Ireland was a colony of Britain. Dublin became the political centre of the colony. Ireland supplied Britain with cheap raw materials and Dublin grew to become the main port for the export of goods. Therefore, Ireland's road network is radial. Major roads radiate outwards from Dublin to the provinces.

### Roads aid the development of settlements

◎ Manufacturing towns and industrial estates need good access for trucks that bring raw materials to factories. Shannon New Town and industrial estate is served by the N18 and the N19. This has helped the town to grow.

◎ Market towns grow when they have good access to their hinterlands. People use access roads to go to town to do the shopping and for other personal and financial services, e.g. county towns such as Navan (see page 270).

◎ Towns grow as dormitory towns especially around Dublin. Naas, Navan, Drogheda, Wicklow and many others are dormitory towns for people who work in Dublin. These commuter towns are all connected by road and increasingly, by motorway (see page 255).

◎ An urban centre that is located at an important river crossing point becomes the focus of several routes. This brings traffic and business to the urban centre and helps it to grow, e.g. Limerick (see page 265).

◎ Tourist towns need good road access, so that visitors can travel to these towns easily, e.g. the tourist centres of the south coast.

**National Road Network
By Carriageway Type
Dec. 2007**

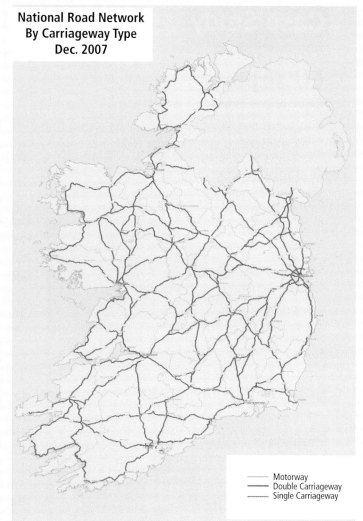

Motorway
Double Carriageway
Single Carriageway

Fig 9.23 The Republic of Ireland's main roads

Motorways bypass local towns and are safer than two-lane roads

# Case Study

# EU airports

Busy air routes link urban centres. Air routes make urban centres very accessible to each other.

Air transport is very popular today because:

◎ The population of Western Europe is wealthy.

◎ Low-cost airlines and competitive prices have greatly reduced air fares.

Fig 9.24 The location of major airports in the EU

Europe's busiest airports include London (Heathrow), Paris, Frankfurt, Barcelona and Schiphol Airport in Amsterdam. Stansted Airport near London has grown because it is a Ryanair hub.

Many EU airports such as London Heathrow and Charles de Gaulle Airport in Paris have connections with international airports in every continent.

Tourism accounts for most of the passenger traffic in Mediterranean airports.

| Airport passengers per year | |
| --- | --- |
| Heathrow | 68 million |
| Charles de Gaulle | 57 million |
| Frankfurt | 52 million |
| Schiphol | 46 million |
| Barcelona | 32 million |
| Dublin | 22 million |

## How do air links help to develop settlements?

To answer that question, we will briefly examine London and Shannon.

## Airports serving London

London's five airports: Heathrow, Gatwick, Stansted, London City Airport and Luton employ great numbers of people. This employment has helped London and its surrounding towns to grow.

Heathrow has 70,000 employees in the airport itself. About forty flights an hour touch down at London Heathrow during peak hours.

London is home to the headquarters of some of the most important companies in Europe and indeed in the world.

Fig 9.25 The locations of London's airports

Airlines bring passengers and passengers bring business. Many people travel to London for business reasons. It is a major centre for international conferences because it is so accessible by air. London is a great tourist destination for the same reason and because of its cultural attractions. Therefore, London is a major hotel centre.

While visitors are in London, they stay in hotels, use taxis, eat out, do some shopping and take in a show. In other words, they spend money. This creates employment in London.

Heathrow Airport is located to the west of London and covers an enormous area

## Shannon Airport

Shannon Airport is very important to nearby urban centres. Many people working in the airport live in Limerick, Ennis, Newmarket-on-Fergus, Clarecastle and Sixmilebridge. These centres have a dormitory function for people working in Shannon.

> ### Geofact
> London Heathrow handles more than 1,000 flights a day and has direct flights to 200 international airports.

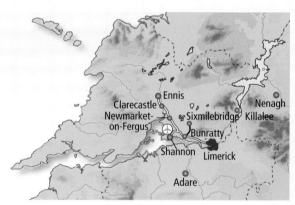

Fig 9.26 Shannon Airport and nearby urban centres

Part of Shannon Airport; Shannon Town and industrial estate can be seen to the right

## A new town

In 1962, a new town was begun near the airport called Shannon Town. People, living in the town, work in the airport and nearby industrial estates. Aviation industries such as Shannon Aerospace are located beside the airport. This has led to further growth in Shannon Town. The population of Shannon Town had almost 10,000 people in the 2006 census.

>
> ### Geofact
> Shannon Airport served 3.6 million passengers in 2007.

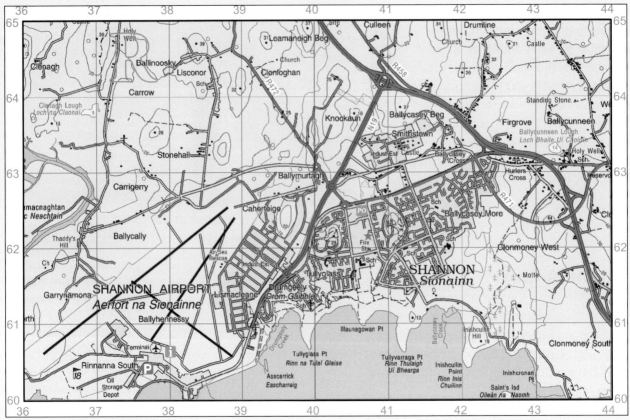

Fig 9.27 OS map of Shannon Airport and Shannon Town

---

### QUESTIONS

1   Study the OS map of Shannon Airport above and name the features found at the following locations:
    ◎ R 407 622
    ◎ R 380 606
    ◎ R 409 632
    ◎ R 367 604

2   Study the site on which the airport is built. State two geographic advantages that the site has for an airport.

3   Study the area of Shannon on the map. Name two pieces of evidence on the map that show that Shannon has a residential function.

# Case Study

## Transport on the River Rhine

Many large urban centres are located on the banks of the River Rhine and its tributaries. The Rhine is a **navigable river.** It reaches into the heart of Western Europe as far as Switzerland.

**Definition**

**Navigable river:** A river that has been deepened and possibly straightened a little so that barges can use it.

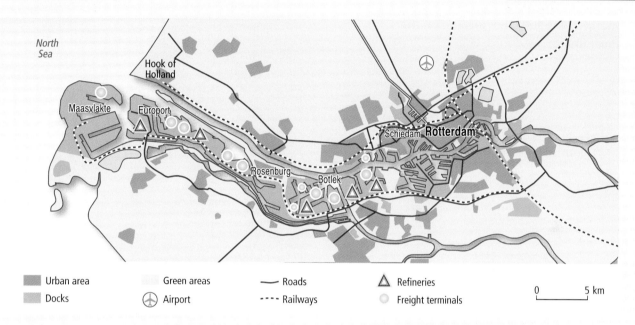

| | | | |
|---|---|---|---|
| ▨ Urban area | Green areas | — Roads | △ Refineries |
| ▨ Docks | ✈ Airport | ---- Railways | ○ Freight terminals |

0      5 km

Fig 9.28 The location of the port of Rotterdam

### Rotterdam-Europoort

Rotterdam-Europoort is located at the mouth of the Rhine. As one of the world's largest ports, Rotterdam imports raw material such as crude oil, metal ores, timber, chemical raw materials and much more. This material is then transported by barge to manufacturing centres as far as Switzerland. (See also Settlement in the River Rhine Basin, page 266.)

### Manufacturing cities on the banks of the Rhine

The Rhine waterway has aided the growth of manufacturing cities that are located on its banks. The Rhine gives industries access to raw materials. Therefore, heavy industries are located on the Rhine in cities such as Duisburg, Köln and Ludwigshafen.

### Advantages of water transport

Water transport is a cheap mode of transport for bulky imperishable cargo, e.g. mineral ores, timber, sand and coal. Even though river transport is slow, barges can carry enormous loads. Barges last a long time and, apart from the engine, need very little maintenance.

Barge transport on the River Rhine

## A waterway network

Barges also travel on many of the tributaries of the Rhine that are navigable. The Rhine is connected to other inland waterways in Western Europe. Therefore, the Rhine is the central artery in a great river and canal network in Western Europe.

Tourists travel on cruise boats to many towns and cities located on the River Rhine.

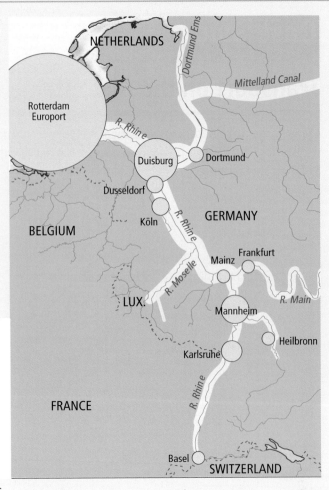

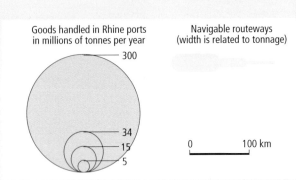

Goods handled in Rhine ports in millions of tonnes per year

300

34
15
5

Navigable routeways (width is related to tonnage)

0    100 km

Fig 9.29 Traffic on the Rhine and adjoining waterways

---

📄 **SUMMARY**

◎  The Irish road network connects settlements with each other.
◎  Good communication links help urban centres to grow.
◎  Airports in the EU link urban centres to each other.
◎  Employment in Shannon Airport has helped local towns to grow.
◎  The River Rhine is a very busy waterway.

---

✍ **QUESTIONS**

1  (a)  Explain one way in which the Irish road network has aided the development of your town or city.
   (b)  Name three urban centres that are linked to your town or city by the road network.
2  How has Shannon Airport helped nearby urban settlements to grow?
3  Name three cargoes that are carried on Rhine barges.
4  Give two reasons why the River Rhine is a very important navigable waterway.
5  'The functions of many towns have changed over time.'
   In the case of one named Irish town or city that you have studied, describe how its functions have changed. In your answer refer to three different functions. (JC)

## 10.1 Changing Patterns in Where We Live: Cities

**The growth of towns and cities has occurred over time through the development of economic, administrative and social activities.**

Towns and cities have existed for thousands of years. Over time towns and cities became centres of **economic activities**. They developed as market centres where people bought and sold goods.

Towns and cities also became centres of **administrative activities**. Cities became the places from which rulers governed their territory by using law courts and civil servants.

Towns and cities became centres of **social activities**. People came to see plays and sporting activities, to meet friends and to enjoy themselves.

## Dublin's development over time

### Viking Dublin

The Vikings built a fortified settlement on the south bank of the River Liffey in the early ninth century. The Vikings used wood as a building material. Viking Dublin continued as a trading post after the Vikings were defeated at the Battle of Clontarf in 1014.

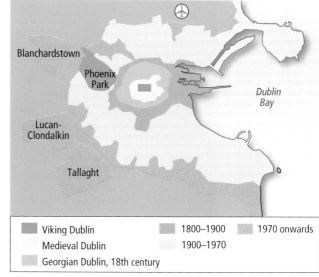

| Viking Dublin | 1800–1900 | 1970 onwards |
| Medieval Dublin | 1900–1970 |
| Georgian Dublin, 18th century |

Fig 10.1 Since Viking times, Dublin has grown outwards from the centre

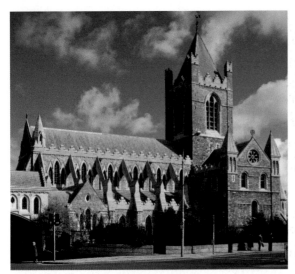
Christchurch Cathedral in Dublin

An aerial view of St Stephen's Green and surrounding streets in Dublin

## The Anglo-Normans

After the Normans invaded Ireland in 1169, Norman knights occupied Dublin. As stone builders, they built city walls.

Dublin became a medieval city of narrow streets and unhealthy conditions. The Black Death caused the death of many of its citizens in the fourteenth century.

Dublin Castle was built and extended over time. Dublin became the **administrative centre** of English power in Ireland. St Patrick's Cathedral and Christchurch were added over the years.

## The sixteenth to the eighteenth centuries

Queen Elizabeth extended English rule over large parts of Ireland. Therefore, Dublin became more important as an administrative centre. Trinity College was also built, adding to the city's importance.

Throughout the eighteenth century, Dublin was extended. Streets and squares were built on the north and south sides. St Stephen's Green and Merrion Square were laid out and surrounded by **Georgian houses**. These large houses were occupied by wealthy Irish gentry who came to Dublin from the provinces to attend parliament.

Wealthy Dubliners had an excellent **social life**, they enjoyed plays and concerts.

Poor housing in Dublin around 1900

## The nineteenth century

The Act of Union abolished the Irish Parliament in Dublin. Members of parliament moved to London and sold their Dublin homes to landlords. Dublin's social life collapsed. Dublin became a city of tenements, it had terrible overcrowding. **Tenements** often housed one family per room.

**Economic activity** centred around the port. Canals and later railways connected Dublin to the provinces. Goods from the port were distributed by canal and rail to urban centres all over Ireland.

> **Geofact**
>
> In 1885, one nine-roomed house was home to nine families, which consisted of sixty-three people.

## The capital of the Irish state

Dublin has grown very rapidly since independence in 1922. The reasons for this include the following:

- The city had high birth rates for several decades after independence.
- Inward migration from the provinces increased the population.
- During the Celtic Tiger years, Dublin became the most important economic region in the country. Many companies from abroad, such as Google and Microsoft, brought more jobs and people to the city.

## Urban growth in the twentieth century

New suburbs have extended outwards into the countryside to house the growing population. From the 1970s onwards, satellite towns such as Tallaght were built.

The city of Dublin, its suburbs and surrounding dormitory towns now have close to 1.2 million people. (See also The primacy of Dublin, page 254.)

---

### SUMMARY

- Dublin, a Viking settlement, was developed by the Normans.
- Georgian houses are an attractive feature of Dublin's architecture.
- Dublin developed as the country's main port.
- Dublin is now a multi-functional city.

---

### QUESTIONS

1  Describe the growth of Dublin with reference to four of the following:
   - Viking origins
   - Medieval buildings
   - Georgian architecture
   - The importance of the port
2  Explain three reasons why Dublin grew in the decades after Ireland became independent in 1922.

## 10.2 Cities: Functional Zones

Within each city, a generalised pattern of functional zoning can be identified:

◎ The CBD (Central Business District)
◎ A core area of shopping activity
◎ Smaller shopping areas
◎ Shopping centres
◎ Industrial areas
◎ Residential areas
◎ Open space for recreation

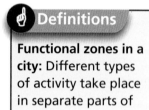 **Definitions**

**Functional zones in a city:** Different types of activity take place in separate parts of the city.

**CBD:** The Central Business District.

Many different activities take place in cities. These include business, shopping, manufacturing and leisure activities. People live in cities in residential areas. We will now examine these different activities.

### The CBD

The centre of every city has a CBD (Central Business District). This is where banks, building societies, large department stores and company headquarters are found. Great numbers of people work in office blocks in the CBD. Land in the CBD is very expensive.

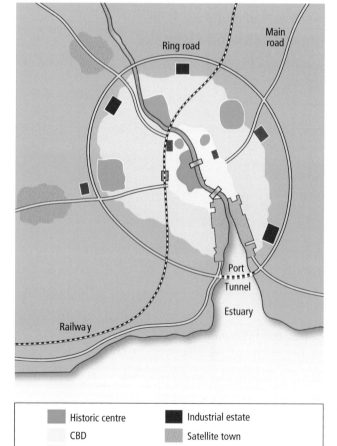

Legend:
- Historic centre
- CBD
- Industrial area
- Residential area
- Industrial estate
- Satellite town
- Shopping centre
- Open spaces for recreation

Fig 10.2 Urban functional zones

Describe in detail what you see in the picture of Chicago's CBD

## Small shopping areas

Most people who live in cities do not go into the CBD every day to do their shopping. They shop in smaller shopping areas in the residential district where they live. These shopping areas have parking spaces and have a neighbourly atmosphere. People often meet their friends there.

## Large shopping centres

Large shopping centres exist in the suburbs of Irish cities. They are built close to ring roads so that shoppers have good access by car. Therefore, fewer people shop in the city centre.

A shopping centre, located in Dooradoyle, Limerick

## Industrial areas

Cities are also manufacturing centres. Seaport cities have industries in the port area, e.g. oil refining, ship manufacturing and flour milling. **Heavy industries**, such as the manufacturing of train carriages and engines, are located near railway lines and canals.

### Industrial estates

Modern industrial estates with light industry are located on the outskirts of towns and cities. There are many reasons for this:

◎ Land is cheaper on the outskirts than in the city centre and therefore more space is available.
◎ Workers live in nearby suburbs.
◎ A ring road around the city makes factories very accessible to heavy lorries. Materials can enter and leave the factories easily.

## Open space for recreation

Cities need green spaces where children can play and people can escape from the hustle and bustle of traffic. Green spaces bring the countryside into the city. **Phoenix Park**, in Dublin, is one of Europe's finest city parks.

Doughcloyne Industrial Estate, Cork

# Case Study

## Paris

Paris is the capital of France and is also a **primate city**. The population of Greater Paris is more than 11 million people. Lyon, the second city of France, has 2.5 million people.

### A world city

Paris is a **world city**, ranking in importance with New York, Tokyo and London. Paris has a world influence in fashion and culture.

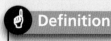

> **Definition**
>
> **World city:** A city that has a global influence in a certain field, e.g. finance or fashion.

### Functional zones in Paris

#### The CBD

The CBD in Paris is a core area of business and shopping activity. It contains:

- The headquarters of many French banking and commercial companies.
- The stock exchange, known as the **Paris Bourse**.
- The political and administrative offices of the government of France.

The CBD is served by the underground rail system – the Paris Metro. Therefore, the area is very accessible. The CBD now reaches as far as **La Défense**, a new high-rise office district.

### Shopping activity

Paris is a shoppers' paradise. As a world centre of fashion, both for men and women, the CBD has large shopping areas. Big department stores such as **Galerie Lafayette** and Printemps are found in many locations in central Paris. The streets around the **Champs Elysées** and Boulevard Hausmann are major shopping areas.

### Smaller shopping areas

Paris grew outwards from its centre over time. Therefore, it absorbed nearby villages. These villages became suburbs of Paris. Each of those suburbs has a smaller shopping area where locals do their shopping. Branches of supermarket chains such as Champion and Carrefour are found in many residential districts in Paris.

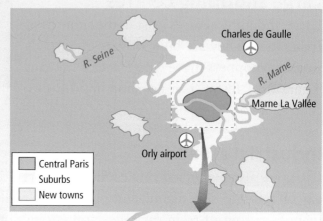

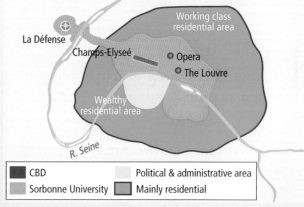

Fig 10.3 Functional zones in Paris

Part of central Paris

## Where do Parisians live?

The greater portion of Paris is made up of residential districts. Most people live in apartment blocks that are up to ten storeys high. The city has high population densities.

Many apartment blocks have a **concierge**, who acts as door person and checks on the comings and goings in the building. The city has affluent areas, middle-class areas and working-class areas.

## Satellite towns

Many people now live in the new towns that have been built around Paris. The new towns have a variety of housing types, ranging from apartment blocks to attached and detached homes. Amenities in these new towns are very good; they have parks, artificial ponds and leisure areas. Disneyland Resort, Paris, is located in one of the new towns called **Marne-la-Valée**.

## Industrial areas

Paris is the most important manufacturing region in France:

◎ The **fashion industry** is located on the banks of the River Seine in central Paris where fashion products are designed and produced. **Jewellery** and **perfumes** are produced in the same parts of Paris.

◎ **Printing** and **publishing** firms are found near the Latin Quarter, where the Sorbonne University is located.

◎ **Modern industries** such as aerospace, defence equipment, healthcare and optical equipment are located in the technological parks on the urban fringe and in the new towns.

◎ The **car assembly industry** has been part of the Paris scene for more than 100 years. However, car assembly factories are now moving to Eastern Europe where labour is cheaper.

British fashion designer Vivienne Westwood acknowledges applause at the end of the presentation of her collection in Paris

## Open spaces in Paris

Paris has a wide variety of parks that are open to the public. The Bois de Boulogne is in the very centre of the city. Famous gardens include the Jardin de Luxembourg and the Jardin de Plantes.

Thousands of people stroll along the tree-lined quays on the banks of the Seine, where artist display their work.

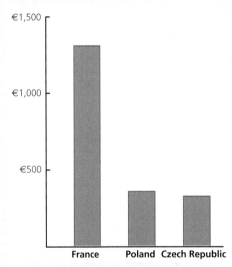

Fig 10.4 The minimum wage per month in France, Poland and the Czech Republic

The Champs de Mars is a large open space in the centre of Paris

> ### Geofact
> In 1980, one worker in four in Paris worked in manufacturing. By 2008 it had declined to one in seven.

**SUMMARY**

◎ Cities have functional zones.
◎ Functional zones include the CBD, shopping areas, residential and industrial areas.
◎ Functional zones are clearly evident in Paris.

**QUESTIONS**

1  Name three functional zones that exist in cities.
2  On a sketch map of Paris, mark in the following functional zones:
   ◎ The CBD, including La Défense
   ◎ One wealthy residential district
   ◎ The political and administrative zone
3  Name two manufacturing industries in Paris, referring to where they are located.

## 10.3 Land Values in Cities

Intensity of land use and land values tend to increase towards the city centre.

**Definition**

Land value: The cost of purchasing or renting land for a particular use.

### The city centre

Land in the city centre is very expensive, whether you rent or buy. This is because roads meet in the city centre, and thus the city centre has access to many customers. Buildings in the city centre tend to be multi-storey, in order to make the greatest use of the available land. Many buildings also include basements.

### Business in city centre locations

Many shops locate in the city centre, e.g. boutiques, jewellers, entertainment retailers and mobile phone shops. Cinemas, banks and some hotels also locate to the centre. The turnover – number of customers – of these companies is so high that they can afford the high cost of a city centre location.

**Office blocks** are also found in the city centre. Companies that are found here include law firms, accountancy firms, newspaper companies and advertising agencies.

Office buildings located along the south bank of the Liffey in Dublin's CBD

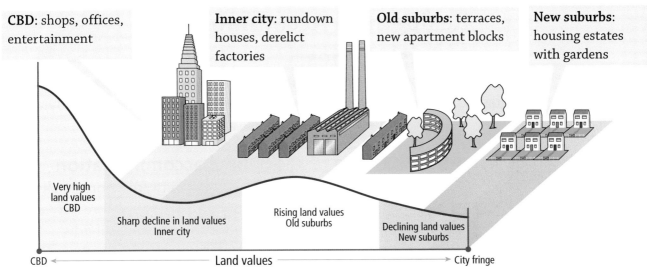

**CBD**: shops, offices, entertainment

**Inner city**: rundown houses, derelict factories

**Old suburbs**: terraces, new apartment blocks

**New suburbs**: housing estates with gardens

Very high land values CBD

Sharp decline in land values Inner city

Rising land values Old suburbs

Declining land values New suburbs

CBD ← Land values → City fringe

Fig 10.5 Land values and land use in cities. Land values are very high in the city centre

## Business in the suburbs

Some business companies need lots of space, e.g. car sales rooms, timber yards, builders' providers and shopping centres. Land in the city centre is too expensive for these companies. They locate in the suburbs where land costs less.

Blanchardstown Shopping Centre is located on a large site, where plenty of space is available

### SUMMARY

◎ City centres have intensive land use and high land values.
◎ A business with a high turnover can afford the cost of a city centre location.

### QUESTIONS

1   Look at Fig 10.5 above and answer the following questions:
   (a)  Why are the highest buildings found in the city centre?
   (b)  Why do land values decrease sharply away from the CBD?
   (c)  Name the part of the city that is least likely to have a leisure park. Explain your answer.
2   Describe land values and buildings within the CBD of any large city in the developed world. (JC)

# 10.4 Residential Accommodation in Irish Cities

The quality, type and age of residential accommodation vary significantly within a city.

Georgian houses in Limerick city centre

Modern apartments in Limerick overlook the River Shannon

## Age of residential accommodation

Ireland's cities have grown outwards from small town centres over hundreds of years. Therefore, city centre residences are older than recently built suburbs.

Many city centre residences have housing styles that belong to earlier centuries. For example, Georgian houses were built more than 200 years ago. They are evident in many cities and towns in Ireland.

## Types of residential accommodation

Many types of residential accommodation exist in cities today.

◎ **Council apartment blocks** have replaced poor quality housing in the inner city. They are four to five storeys high and have a high population density.

◎ **Streets of terraced housing** are close to the city centre. They have very small back yards and do not have front gardens. The front door opens directly onto the pavement.

◎ **Expensive town houses** and high quality apartment blocks exist near the city centre. High earners, who may work in the nearby CBD, live in them.

◎ Large housing estates of **semi-detached homes** are found in the suburbs. They are modern family homes that have front and back gardens. Many front gardens have been paved over as parking spaces for two or three cars.

◎ **Luxury homes** are found in highly desirable locations, e.g. close to the sea or on elevated sites.

◎ Increasingly, high quality **apartment blocks** are being built in suburban centres in Irish cities. This is because land prices everywhere became very expensive during the Celtic Tiger years after 1995.

# Quality of residential accommodation

The quality of residential accommodation has changed greatly over the years in several ways that include:

◎ Home size
◎ Materials used

Semi-detached housing in Limerick

## Home size

Many years ago, in poor times, much of the housing in the centres of towns and cities consisted of brick-built terraced houses. Most were small and called **two up and two down** houses. They had two bedrooms upstairs and a kitchen and sitting room downstairs heated by a coal fire. The toilet was outside in the back yard.

Terraced houses have been modernised over the years.

In recent decades, as Ireland has become wealthy, larger suburban homes that have three to four bedrooms are standard.

## Modern materials

In recent times, fuel has become very expensive which has affected the cost of home heating. Therefore, **home insulation** is very important today. Modern homes – both apartments and houses – have double-glazing, attic and wall insulation, and efficient gas and oil boilers. Some housing estates have been built of **superwarm** materials.

Terraced housing found close to Dublin's city centre

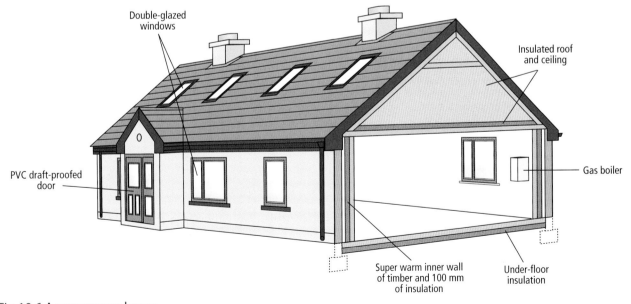

Double-glazed windows

Insulated roof and ceiling

PVC draft-proofed door

Gas boiler

Super warm inner wall of timber and 100 mm of insulation

Under-floor insulation

Fig 10.6 A superwarm home

📄 **SUMMARY**

◎ Cities have grown outwards from the centre.
◎ Cities have a great variety of residential accommodation.
◎ Modern homes are built for today's lifestyles with insulation as a priority.

✏️ **QUESTIONS**

1 Explain the following terms:
   ◎ Town houses
   ◎ Georgian houses
   ◎ Terraced houses
   ◎ Public housing
2 Explain two reasons why small terraced homes were built close to the city centre in previous generations.
3 Explain two ways in which modern homes differ from earlier homes.

# 10.5 Commuting to Work in Cities

The daily movements of people within a city make recognisable patterns in time and space.

## The commuting journey

People commute to the CBD of Irish cities and towns for work every weekday. This can be a very stressful experience for motorists.

## Rush hour

Rush hour traffic is challenging for traffic planners and commuters alike. This is because most offices and schools open around 9 am. As roads get busier, more parents bring their children to school by car. Streets into the city centre are **congested** at rush hours.

## Congestion charges

Many cities abroad use congestion charges to make motorists think twice about using the car during the day.

In London, cars entering the Congestion Zone between **7 am and 6 pm** are charged a fee.

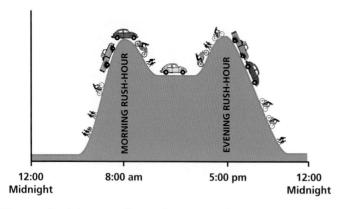

Fig 10.7 Rush hour traffic peaks twice a day

# Public transport

Is public transport the solution to rush-hour traffic congestion? Two cars occupy the same space as a bus. Most cars are occupied by just the driver, while a bus carries seventy-five passengers. Therefore, persuading people to leave the car at home is one solution to rush-hour traffic congestion. However, public transport must be **nearby**, **cheap**, **reliable** and **fast**. Public transport includes buses, suburban rail and light rail.

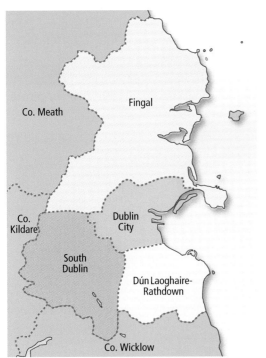

Fig 10.8 Co. Dublin has four council areas

Fig 10.9 The different modes of transport used by commuters in Dublin City, South Dublin and Co. Meath

## Public transport in Dublin

Great sums of money have been spent on public transport in the Dublin area in recent years.

◎ Dublin has a very good **bus network** with 1,600 buses. Quality bus corridors (**QBCs**) on bus lanes have made commuting by bus much faster.

◎ The **DART** (Dublin Area Rapid Transit) brings commuters from coastal towns and suburbs to Dublin's CBD.

◎ **Luas** has two lines and is a major success. Unfortunately, the two lines are not joined in the city centre yet.

◎ A **metro** from the city centre north to the airport and onwards to Swords is likely to be built in a few years time.

QBCs in Dublin help buses to quickly reach their destination

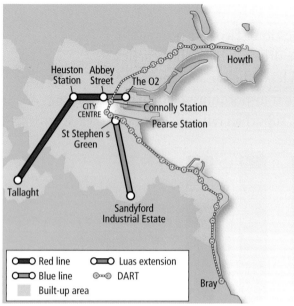

Fig 10.10 The DART and Luas lines in Dublin offer commuters an alternative to the car

The Luas at Tallaght brings passengers into the city centre quickly and in comfort

## Restricting car use

Many measures are now restricting car use in city centres, for example:

◉ Expensive parking charges per hour
◉ Clamping for illegal parking and heavy on-the-spot fines
◉ Pedestrian-only streets

Traffic management includes traffic lights, yellow grids and no parking lines

### SUMMARY

◉ Cities have twice-daily rush hours.
◉ Efficient public transport can relieve pressure on city streets.
◉ Expansion of Dublin's public transport is a work in progress.

### QUESTIONS

1 Explain two reasons why the car is the most popular mode of transport for daily commuters.
2 Explain the terms:
   ◉ Rush hour
   ◉ QBCs
   ◉ DART
3 Give two advantages and two disadvantages of public transport for the daily commuter.

# 10.6 Urban Problems

The rapid pace of social and economic change within western cities in the twentieth century has caused problems for urban dwellers:

◎ Zones of decline and sprawl
◎ Unemployment
◎ Crime
◎ Community disruption
◎ Inadequate infrastructural services

> **Higher level students must select two of the problems listed for study. Ordinary level course students must select one problem.**

## Zones of decline and of sprawl

### The inner city: a zone of decline

Many cities have a zone of decline, known as the **inner city**. The inner city is in the city centre, beside or around the CBD. It is one of the oldest parts of the city. The inner city has several characteristics:

◎ Many people are unemployed because industries that once boomed have closed or moved away.
◎ The population of the inner city declines because people move to the suburbs over the years.
◎ A high proportion of inner-city housing is composed of large blocks of local authority housing.
◎ There are many derelict sites. Some buildings are boarded up and empty.

### Urban sprawl

**Sprawl** is the word used to describe the uncontrolled spread of the city into the countryside around it. This is happening in Irish cities. Large estates of semi-detached homes are built on areas that were once farms. Population densities are low in these estates.

Parents like to have a front and back garden for children to play in. Urban sprawl has many disadvantages:

◎ Sprawl invades the countryside and leads to the cutting of hedges, and a reduction in wild life.
◎ Sprawl leads to long daily commuter journeys to the CBD.
◎ Sprawl causes the spread of the **concrete jungle** over a large area.

We will see in the next section how the problems of inner-city decline and urban sprawl can be addressed.

A scene in Dublin's inner city. Identify two features that make living in this area a challenge

> **Geofact**
>
> More than 60 per cent of Irish people now live in towns and cities.

> **Definition**
>
> **Concrete jungle:** Buildings, pavements and roads that cover the natural world of fields and hedges.

A sprawling housing estate spreading into the countryside

Fig 10.11 Urban sprawl disrupts the natural world

Fig 10.12 Unemployment in the inner city. What is the message in the cartoon?

## Unemployment

Unemployment has been a problem for many decades in the inner city. The reasons for this include the following:

◎ Modern manufacturing companies prefer to locate near ring roads on the city fringe, where larger and cheaper sites are available.

◎ Many jobs in the nearby CBD are skilled office jobs where high levels of education are demanded. Many inner-city students, especially boys, drop out of school before taking the Leaving Certificate. Therefore, jobs in banks and insurance, for example, in the CBD are beyond their reach.

◎ Young people in deprived inner-city communities are less likely to be computer literate. Without this skill, they are less likely to get a job.

◎ Many inner-city people have basic work skills only. When the country enters an economic depression, these are among the first to lose their jobs.

# Crime

Crime is not confined to inner cities. The great majority of inner-city residents do not turn to crime. However, crime in inner cities is much higher than the national average.

## Drug-related crime

Much of the crime in inner cities is drug-related. Many murders in recent years have occurred among rival drug gangs.

Very often, young people feeding a drug habit are unemployed. They need money for their daily supply. Many turn to crime to do so by robbing vulnerable people.

Several community-based projects are helping people with substance addictions in Irish cities today.

## Racist abuse

Some inward migrants have also been the targets of racist abuse in recent years in urban areas.

# Community disruption

What maintains a sense of community? Weddings, funerals, community sports teams and shared memories can all bind a community together.

The **extended family** is one of the most important social units in a community. When grandparents, uncles and aunts, cousins and in-laws are living in the same inner-city neighbourhood, family members are able to offer support to each other.

# Migration to Ballymun

In Dublin, in the 1960s, the inner city faced a housing shortage. Young couples were

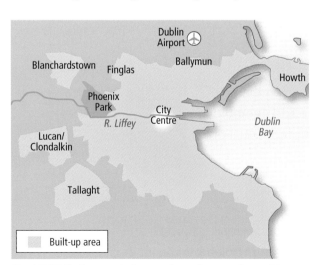

Fig 10.13 Ballymun is located on the northern fringe of Dublin

Fig 10.14 Ballymun was seen as a solution to Dublin's inner-city housing crisis. But, it did not work as it was planned

encouraged by the local authorities to **migrate** to Ballymun, or to satellite towns such as Tallaght on Dublin's urban fringe.

The migration caused **community disruption**. Young parents who moved from the inner city lost the support of the extended family. It took a long time to get to know new neighbours, especially in high-rise flats in Ballymun. These factors and high unemployment in the area led to a social crisis in Ballymun.

Ballymun in the 1960s

New low-rise housing in Ballymun has replaced the tower blocks that were built in the 1960s

### SUMMARY

- ◎ Inner cities have distinct social and economic problems.
- ◎ Urban sprawl invades the countryside on the urban fringe.
- ◎ Some urban areas suffer from crime and unemployment.
- ◎ When urban communities are disrupted, social problems arise.

### QUESTIONS

1 What is the inner city and in which part of a city is it found?
2 Explain why unemployment and crime are problems in the inner city.
3 Explain, with reference to one example, how urban communities can be disrupted.

## 10.7 Urban Improvements

In western cities, attempts by planning authorities to alleviate social and economic problems have led to a number of initiatives:

◎ Inner-city renewal and redevelopment
◎ Planning of new towns

### Inner-city renewal and redevelopment

For many years, urban authorities have been **renewing** and **redeveloping** large areas of the Republic's inner cities.

The Celtic Tiger years made money from private and government funds available for these projects.

**Definitions**

**Urban renewal:**
The demolition of old sub-standard homes in the inner city and the construction of modern houses for the residents in the same location. The area remains residential in function.

**Urban redevelopment:**
The demolition of derelict buildings and homes in the inner city and their replacement with offices, hotels and apartments. The funtion of the area changes.

Urban renewal in Ennis, Co. Clare; the large, grey stone buildings were built as grain stores on the banks of the River Fergus 200 years ago. They have been redeveloped as apartments. Are there any similar projects in your area?

# Case Study

## Urban renewal in Fatima Mansions in Dolphin's Barn, Dublin

**Dolphin's Barn** is located in Dublin's south inner city. The Fatima Mansions community faced many challenges as the twenty-first century dawned:

◎ Lone parents headed 44 per cent of households. Lone parents are at a greater risk of poverty than two-parent families.

◎ Children under 15 made up 38 per cent of the population, which is more than double the national average.

◎ The community was **educationally disadvantaged**: 61 per cent of adults had no formal educational qualifications.

◎ Unemployment was 39 per cent in 2005 – nearly eight times the national average for that year.

◎ The community had high levels of ill health, high school drop-out rates and a serious drugs problem.

These factors indicate **economic and social disadvantage**.

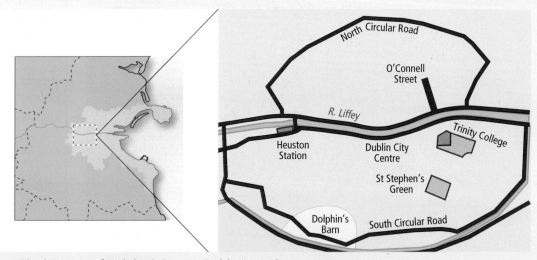

Fig 10.15 The location of Dolphin's Barn in Dublin's south inner city

 **Definition**

**Regeneration:**
Renewal projects in urban communities.

### Renewal of the area

The Fatima **Regeneration** Board began the process of renewing the Fatima community. The local community played a full role in helping to plot the future of the area.

In 2005, demolition and rebuilding began. Fatima Mansions have been replaced with **socially mixed homes**. By 2008, 600 households were living in the newly built area.

**Question**

Describe three social problems that affected the community of Dolphin's Barn.

## Social renewal

The Regeneration Board recognised that bricks and mortar were not enough. The quality of people's lives had to be improved. An eight-part programme has been put in place to achieve this.

**❶** The establishment of a **safe** and **sustainable community** through dialogue between the gardaí and the community.

**❷ Raising education levels in** the community with the appointment of an education officer for both adults and young people.

**❽ Raising environmental awareness** by helping the community to recycle and to take pride in a clean neighbourhood.

**❸ Improving people's health** and wellbeing by raising people's awareness of health issues.

**Social renewal**

**❼ Community facilities** in the neighbourhood.

**❻** The development of **sport** and **recreational facilities** to encourage people of all ages to participate in sport and exercise.

**❺** Emphasis on **arts** and **culture.**

**❹ Providing training** for employment through local training schemes.

Fig 10.16 Social renewal using an eight-part programme

Old housing in Dublin's south inner city

New housing in Dolphin's Barn

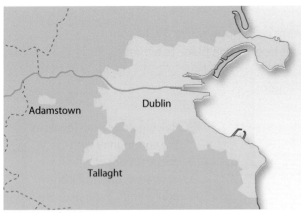

Fig 10.17 The location of Tallaght and Adamstown

| Population of Tallaght | |
| --- | --- |
| 1961 | 1,402 |
| 2006 | 64,281 |

# Planning of new towns

We have seen that urban sprawl has many disadvantages. Planners have created new towns in order to control urban sprawl, e.g. Tallaght, Lucan-Clondalkin and Blanchardstown in the Dublin area. We will examine Tallaght.

## Tallaght

Tallaght is located south west of the city of Dublin. In the 1960s, it was a village surrounded by farmland. Today its population is more than 60,000.

Much of Tallaght was built in the 1970s. The population was composed of people both from Dublin's inner city and of people who came to Dublin from other parts of Ireland.

## Poor services

Housing densities are very low. People without a car have a long walk to the bus stop. For many years, services such as leisure areas, shops and public transport were poor. A high percentage of the population was under 15 years of age. The community had high **unemployment** in the recession of the 1980s. However, much has been done to change Tallaght since then.

Tallaght centre showing recent developments

## Tallaght today

Developments in Tallaght in recent years have brought great advances. New developments include:

◎ The **Square** that is one of Ireland's best-known shopping centres.
◎ A **regional hospital** serving south-west Dublin.
◎ The terminal of the **Luas Red Line** that brings passengers into the city quickly.
◎ **Industrial estates** and business parks that have many international companies.
◎ The **Tallaght Institute of Technology** that caters for third level students.
◎ **Sporting facilities** that comprise the National Basketball Arena, GAA clubs and the home of Shamrock Rovers.
◎ **Cultural projects** that have two theatres.

Because of these investments, thousands of people now work in Tallaght itself.

The lessons learned in the development of Tallaght were applied in the development of the new town of **Adamstown** further west.

# Case Study

## Adamstown: Ireland's first twenty-first century town

Adamstown is a new town 16 km west of Dublin city centre. Work began on the building of Adamstown in 2004.

Adamstown is located beside the Kildare-Heuston railway line. Heuston is on the Luas Red line where there are connections to Dublin's CBD.

Adamstown is a high-density development as most buildings have three floors. Residential density is a minimum of seventy-two houses per hectare. By mid-2008, 1,000 homes were occupied.

Unlike Tallaght in its early years, **services** were provided early. The train station, two QBC corridors, primary schools and crèche facilities were all in place by 2008. Local shopping centres were opened.

In 2008, planning permission was granted for Adamstown District Centre. This centre will include shops, offices, services, leisure facilities and 600 apartments. Up to 2,500 people will work there.

Thirty hectares have been set aside for leisure and sporting areas that include four parks.

### Question

Outline and explain three people-friendly aspects of the new town of Adamstown.

Fig 10.18 The location of Adamstown

A computer model of Adamstown Centre

Adamstown is a new community that is being developed using high-density housing

📄 **SUMMARY**

◎ Inner cities are targets of urban renewal and urban redevelopment.

◎ Dolphin's Barn in Dublin's inner city is one example of urban renewal.

◎ The lessons learned in the development of Tallaght have been applied to Adamstown.

🖐 **QUESTIONS**

1 Describe three steps that are improving the lives of the Dolphin's Barn community.

2 Study the OS map of Tallaght below. Write one leisure activity that is available in the area, using a grid reference.

3 On the OS map below which features are found at the following locations?

◎ O 080 280

◎ O 093 281

◎ O 102 261

4 Which pieces of evidence on the OS map suggest that Kilnamanagh is a residential area?

5 Study Fig 10.19 below and find the light rail line (Luas) that ends in Tallaght at O 086 276. How many stops can you see along the line?

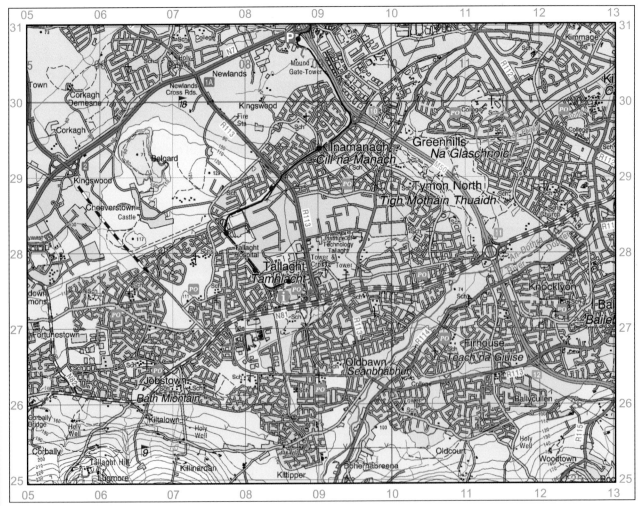

Fig 10.19 OS map of the Tallaght area

# 10.8 Urbanisation in the Developing World

Urbanisation in the developing world has led to patterns and problems of urban growth that differ from those that characterise western cities. These problems are worsening. They include:

Higher level students must study **two** of the problems listed. Ordinary level students must study **one** of the problems.

◎ Sharper social and economic inequalities
◎ Greater degree of unplanned development
◎ Lack of infrastructural services
◎ Faster growth

Westerners, who visit or work in developing world cities, can experience culture shock. They are struck by the contrasts between rich and poor. This is evident in how people dress, the transport they use and the homes in which they live. Many of the poor live under make-shift plastic dwellings.

Wealthy people may choose to live in a new town outside the city, because of the clean air and amenities.

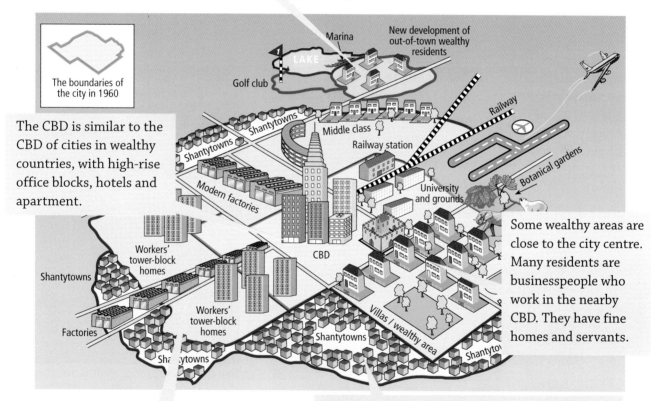

The boundaries of the city in 1960

The CBD is similar to the CBD of cities in wealthy countries, with high-rise office blocks, hotels and apartment.

Some wealthy areas are close to the city centre. Many residents are businesspeople who work in the nearby CBD. They have fine homes and servants.

New industrial estates are located close to working-class districts. Many multinational companies set up factories here. They are attracted by the low wages that workers earn.

Shantytowns are found on the outskirts of the city. These have expanded rapidly in recent decades. The residents are migrants from the countryside. Shantytowns have no sewage and water systems.

Fig 10.20 Developing world cities

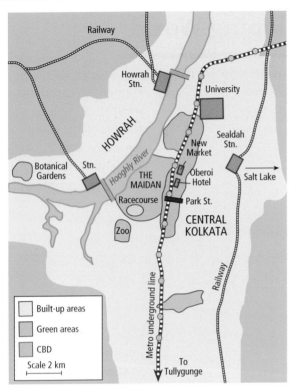

Fig 10.21 Central Kolkata

# Kolkata: a city of contrasts

We have already seen that overcrowding, shortage of clean water and pollution are problems that the people of Kolkata face. (See also High Population Densities in Kolkata, pages 230–2.) We will now examine further aspects of the city:

◎ Social and economic inequalities
◎ Unplanned development
◎ Infrastructural services

## Social and economic inequalities

Sharp social and economic inequalities are very evident in Kolkata. The CBD is in the city centre. It has some luxurious air-conditioned hotels. There are fine shops in the Park Street area that wealthy people visit.

The CBD has nice restaurants. Metered taxis are everywhere and are used by wealthy people. The **New Market** is a huge bazaar area that comes alive in the cool of the evening when locals do their shopping.

### Geofact

Rich and poor share a passion for cricket.

### The lifestyle of the wealthy

Wealthy locals attend race meetings at the Kolkata Turf Club racecourse in the Maidan. The very rich are members of the Tollygunge Club in South Kolkata, a **country club** that offers a wide range of sporting activities.

Salt Lake shopping mall is located in a wealthy suburb of Kolkata

The city centre has several nightclubs and discos, mostly in hotels, for the young who can afford to visit them.

The racecourse in Kolkata

## Poor districts

The greater part of the city is made up of poor neighbourhoods. These have narrow streets and very small, low-rise homes. A family of three generations will live in a tiny home. Some multi-storey rented apartments with basic facilities are being built in these areas now.

## Employment

People in poor districts work as taxi drivers, skilled tradesmen and factory workers. Men provide services such as street-side typists, tailors, and shoe repair and leather workers. If people don't work, they don't eat.

The poorest people live in **squatter settlements** that are examined below.

A tailor at work in Kolkata

## Increase in food prices

Grain prices increased all over the world in 2007. This is evident on the streets of Kolkata where the price of rice increased by 50 per cent over twelve months. The high cost of food particularly affects the lives of the very poor.

> ### Geofact
> Shantytowns and squatter settlements are known as **bustees** in Kolkata.

## Unplanned development: squatter settlements

Kolkata has very high inward migration of rural poor. These people live in squatter settlements or **shantytowns**.

◎ These settlements are found close to railway stations, on rail sidings, on steep banks, on grass road margins, under flyovers, on waste land and on the outskirts of the city. They have no legal right to remain there.

A canal-side squatter settlement in Kolkata. Describe what you see in this settlement

### Health risks

Squatter settlements have **no sanitation or running water**. Infection is a constant hazard. Stomach and chest infections are a threat to children's health.

### Heavy labour

People in squatter settlements are at the bottom of the social ladder.

◎ They work as rickshaw workers, as labourers in construction work and as pullers of heavy loads in two-wheel carts.

◎ Many squatters scrape a living from recycling cardboard, drink cans and waste timber.

◎ Men work as delivery men and carry heavy loads on their heads. Many of the very poor are severely underweight.

## Infrastructural services

The image that some people have of Kolkata is that nothing works. In fact, that is not the case.

◎ The **public telephone infrastructure** is very good. People can phone Ireland cheaply from telephone kiosks that are rented out to the public.

◎ **Email** and **broadband infrastructure** are in place and are widely available in the CBD.

Buses in Kolkata are old, overcrowded and heavy polluters

◎ The city has an excellent underground metro service. The bus service is frequent, but the buses are of poor quality and are heavy polluters. An electrified light rail network also exists.

## Poor services

◎ **The electricity infrastructure:** Electricity power supplies fail, often on a daily basis. When it fails in the evenings the crowded streets are plunged into darkness.

◎ **Waste disposal**: In many districts, **trash** is gathered and stored for several days in rotting heaps, before it is taken away by lorry.

People washing on the side of a street in Kolkata. Individuals make great efforts to keep clean under difficult conditions

## 100 days of work

The city government now guarantees every unemployed labourer 100 days of work on public projects. The result is that the city is now a building site. Streets are constantly dug up to improve sewage systems, to lay water pipes and to upgrade tramlines. Therefore, infrastructure is slowly improving.

---

### 📄 SUMMARY

- ◎ Wealth and extreme poverty exist in developing world cities.
- ◎ Kolkata's wealthy have a good lifestyle.
- ◎ Shantytown residents in Kolkata live in unhealthy conditions.
- ◎ Kolkata's infrastructure is slowly improving.

---

### QUESTIONS

1. Briefly outline the lives of the wealthy in Kolkata. Refer to:
   - ◎ Where they live.
   - ◎ The sources of their incomes.
   - ◎ How they spend some of their leisure hours.
2. Describe the daily lives of people who live in squatter settlements in Kolkata. Refer to:
   - ◎ Where squatter settlements are found.
   - ◎ Their living conditions.
   - ◎ The work that they do.
3. 'The rapid growth of cities in developing countries has led to problems in these cities.' In relation to a named city in the Third World that you have studied, describe two of these problems. (JC)

# 11 PRIMARY ECONOMIC ACTIVITIES

## Learning Outcomes

In this chapter you will learn that:

◎ Primary economic activities involve the production of raw materials.

◎ Resources are either renewable or non-renewable.

◎ Water is vital to people and to agriculture.

◎ Oil is a finite resource and is very important in today's world.

◎ Modern technology can exploit resources very quickly.

◎ Farming is a system of inputs, processes and outputs.

## 11.1 The Earth as a Resource

Primary economic activities are those in which unprocessed raw materials are produced from Earth's rocks, soils and waters.

There are three types of economic activities: **primary**, **secondary** and **tertiary**.

◎ In **primary activities**, raw materials are produced from the earth: farming, fishing and forestry (the three Fs).

◎ In **secondary activities**, workers in factories use raw materials to manufacture goods that people can buy, e.g. the manufacture of cars and computers.

◎ In **tertiary** or **service activities**, people provide **services** that other people require, e.g. teaching and hairdressing.

Fig 11.1 In developing economies most people work in the primary sector. In developed economies most people work in the tertiary sector

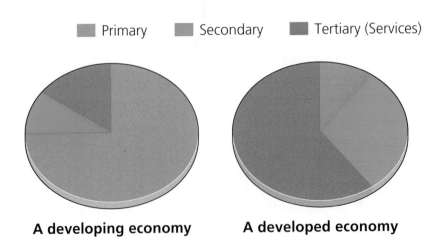

Primary | Secondary | Tertiary (Services)

**A developing economy**     **A developed economy**

| Jobs in each sector | | |
|---|---|---|
| **Primary** | **Secondary** | **Tertiary** |
| Fishermen/women | Bakers | Bank workers |
| Farmers | Tailors | Hotel staff |
| Quarry workers | Furniture makers | Newsreaders |
| Miners | Car assembly workers | DJs |
| Forestry workers | PC assembly workers | Shop assistants |

To which economic sector does each of the above workers belong?

# Economic development

In poor countries, most people are working in the primary sector, as farmers, fishermen/women and miners.

As the wealth of a country grows, more people work in manufacturing and in services. In very wealthy countries, most people work in services.

# Earth's resources

There are two types of natural resources: **renewable** and **non-renewable**.

## Renewable resources

Renewable resources are **non-finite**. They do not run out. If carefully managed, these resources will always exist. Examples of renewable resources include water, fish and timber. If foresters cut down trees, they should replant them. This is called **sustainable exploitation**.

Recycling aluminium cans conserves finite resources

**Definition**

**Sustainable exploitation:** People use a resource for their needs without putting the needs of future generations at risk.

**Question**

What other word describes a renewable resource?

A bauxite mine that produces ore for aluminium.
Minerals are finite

## Non-renewable resources

Non-renewable resources are also known as **finite** resources. Minerals are finite. Oil wells will run dry and coal seams are worked out.

Wealthy people use more resources than poor people. In recent years, we have become aware of the need to recycle our resources so that they will last longer.

### SUMMARY

◎ There are three types of economic activity: primary, secondary and tertiary.
◎ Some resources such as water are renewable (non-finite).
◎ Some resources such as oil are non-renewable (finite).

### QUESTIONS

1 Write the following list of workers into your copybook. Beside each, write down the economic sector to which each worker belongs: violin maker, farm labourer, dressmaker, hairdresser, car salesperson, miner.

2 Study the diagram below and answer the questions that follow.

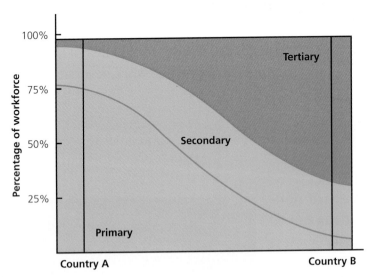

Fig 11.2

(a) Is country A a developed country or a developing country? Explain your answer.
(b) Approximately what percentage of country B's workers are working in services?

## 11.2 Water as a Resource

Water is a basic natural resource, needed to maintain human life and to grow food. It is a renewable resource.

You have already studied the water cycle (see page 87). Water is vital to humans and animals. People die if they are deprived of water for more than four days. Therefore, it is a very precious resource.

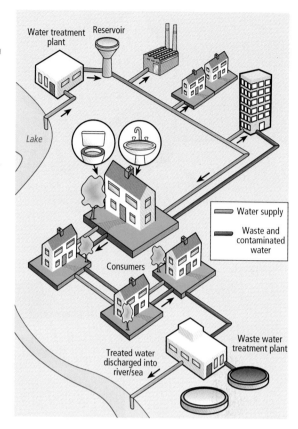

Fig 11.3 Urban water supplies showing water treatment to waste treatment

# Case Study

## Water supply for the Dublin region

The Dublin region has more than one million people, and thus has very high water demands.

Most of Dublin's water supply comes from Co. Wicklow. This is because:

◎ Wicklow has a **high annual rainfall** that is well distributed throughout the year.
◎ The bedrock of the Wicklow Mountains is composed of granite. Water does not seep downwards through **granite** because it is an impermeable rock.
◎ The mountains are **thinly populated.** Farming takes place in the lowlands. Therefore, the region has low levels of pollution.

### Water from the Liffey

Liffey valley waters are collected in Blessington Lakes and in Leixlip Reservoir. Water is treated in modern treatment plants before it is fed into the urban supply system.

Fig 11.4 Dublin's water supply

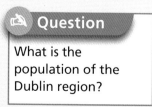

**Question**

What is the population of the Dublin region?

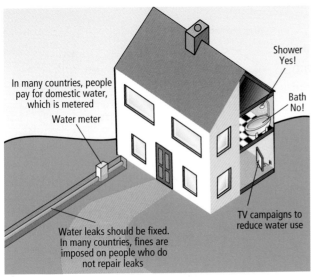

Fig 11.5 Households are becoming aware that water must be conserved

## Water conservation

Water is a precious resource. Ireland has sometimes long periods of low rainfall. Reservoir levels then drop to very low levels. In dry periods, people are encouraged to conserve water. To learn how water can be conserved study Fig 11.5.

## Water pollution

Water is polluted from many sources, including industrial and agricultural wastes. Indeed, the River Rhine has often been called Europe's **open sewer**. It takes much time and money to clean polluted rivers.

> **Question**
>
> Give **two reasons** why Irish people use more water per person today than their grandparents did.

A waste pipe releasing polluted water into a river. Water is polluted in many countries

## Irrigation

Food crops and grass will not grow without water. In many regions of the world, rainfall amounts are low and uncertain. In those regions, farmers have to use irrigation to help crops to grow.

When farmers use irrigation, they apply water to crops, using canals, piping and spraying techniques. Irrigation helps to feed the world's increasing population.

### Irrigation schemes

Large irrigation schemes are found in Australia, the Mediterranean region and in California. In South-east Asia rice is grown in irrigated paddy fields.

# Case Study

## Irrigation in the Nile Valley, Egypt

The Nile is Africa's greatest river. It rises in the highlands of East Africa and its total length is 6,671 km. It flows northwards through the **Sahara** to the Mediterranean. Without the Nile, Egypt and its ancient civilisation would not exist.

## Population distribution

The population of Egypt – 77 million – is found in less than 5 per cent of the the country. People live in the floodplain of the River Nile and in the delta region.

## Annual flooding

Since ancient times, the Nile floodplain in Egypt was under water for several weeks every year because of rains in

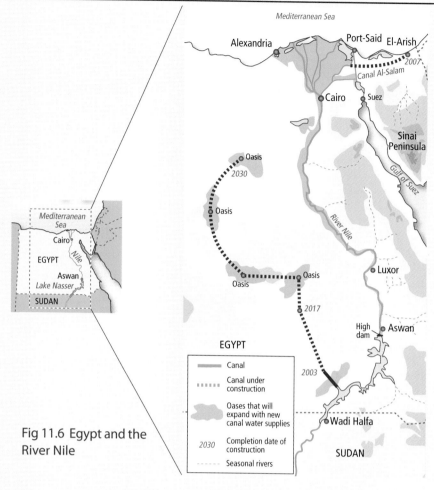

Fig 11.6 Egypt and the River Nile

East Africa. When the waters lowered, people grew crops on the damp soil. The soil was fertilised by sediments carried by the floodwaters. In the 1960s, construction of a dam began in Aswan to control the flooding.

**The Aswan High Dam**

In 1975, the Aswan High Dam was completed. The dam stores millions of tonnes of water in Lake Nasser. Since the dam was built, water can be released throughout the year through **canals** and **plastic piping** along farmland in the Nile Valley. Therefore, farmers can grow **several crops** in succession throughout the year. The farmland provides additional food for Egypt's growing population.

## The disadvantages

There are disadvantages to the irrigation system in Egypt.

◎ The Nile floodplain no longer floods annually because the waters are stored in Lake Nasser. Therefore, fertile sediments that covered the valley floor remain at the bottom of Lake Nasser. Now farmers have to buy expensive fertilisers.

◎ The canals that distribute the irrigation waters in the valley are overrun with a water snail, which carries an infection that affects humans.

◎ Much water is lost because of evaporation from Lake Nasser.

## Future plans

Egypt is developing a major scheme to irrigate parts of the **Western Desert**. A canal will bring water from Lake Nasser to oases in the desert. Some people from the overcrowded Nile Valley have migrated to these areas to begin a new life. (See also Focus on hot desert climate, pages 109–12.)

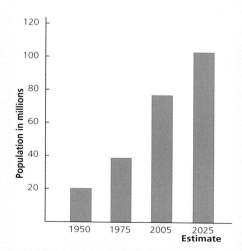

Fig 11.7 Egypt's population growth

### SUMMARY

◎ Water is a renewable resource.
◎ Large urban areas have large water needs.
◎ Irrigation in the Nile Valley is vital to Egypt.
◎ Water must be carefully managed and conserved.

### QUESTIONS

1  Draw a labelled diagram of the water cycle (see page 87).
2  How does the water cycle show that water is a renewable resource?
3  Using the information in Fig 11.4, page 311, briefly describe the water supply network for the Dublin region.
4  Give one example of how people use and abuse water.
5  Give two reasons for the importance of the River Nile to Egypt.
6  'Some countries use large irrigation schemes to help overcome problems associated with water shortages.'
   (a) Name one large scale irrigation scheme that you have studied.
   (b) Describe one advantage and one disadvantage of that irrigation scheme. (JC)

# 11.3  Oil: A Finite Resource

Present-day societies use great quantities of energy. Oil is a very important source of energy. Oil is an example of a finite resource.

In the nineteenth century, coal was a major source of energy. However, oil began to replace coal in the twentieth century.

◎ Oil powers cars and trucks.
◎ Oil is used to generate electricity and to heat homes.

However, like coal, oil is also a source of greenhouse gases (see also pages 98–101).

## A finite resource

Oil will eventually run out, probably within the next 100 years. For that reason, we need to conserve the oil resources of the world.

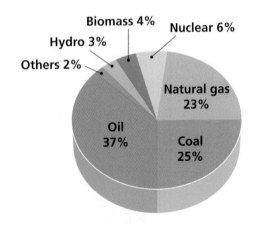

Fig 11.8 Sources of world energy consumption

However, the rich world – the USA, Europe and Japan – has a love affair with cars. This is because cars are very convenient. As long as people can afford petrol, it seems they will use their cars.

A freeway in Los Angeles; Americans own one car for every two people

**Geofact**

There are 2 million cars in the Republic of Ireland, i.e. almost one car for every two people.

**Question**

Suggest two ways in which people can reduce their dependence on cars.

## The location of oil deposits

Oil is found in the USA, Mexico, Venezuela, Russia and other countries. However, the bulk of the world's **oil reserves** are in the Persian Gulf. Oil was found in this area in the 1930s. This region exports oil to the USA, the EU, Japan and other countries. However, it is a region that has seen many wars in recent times.

**Definition**

**Oil reserves:** The known supply of oil underground.

Fig 11.9 The Middle East holds much of the world's oil reserves

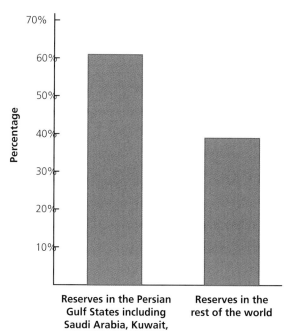

Fig 11.10 World oil reserves

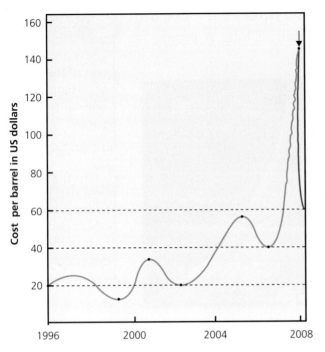

Fig 11.11 Oil prices, 1996–2008, simplified. What happens to the price of goods when demand is greater than supply?

Saudi Arabia is to be studied by Higher level students only.

## The price of oil

Oil prices have risen and fallen for several decades. Oil prices rose sharply in 2007 and early 2008. This was because:

◎ Demand in Europe, USA and Japan remained very high.
◎ Demand increased sharply in China and India.
◎ The market believed that the supply of oil could not meet the extra demand.

The increase in the price of oil was good news for oil producers.

However, the economic recession in 2008 meant that the demand for oil declined. This led to a sharp drop in oil prices in late 2008.

# Case Study

## Saudi Arabia: An oil-producing country

Saudi Arabia is a country that is made up of desert. Until the 1930s, it was a little-known land of nomadic herders. The discovery of oil changed all of that. With the export of oil, vast wealth flowed into Saudi Arabia.

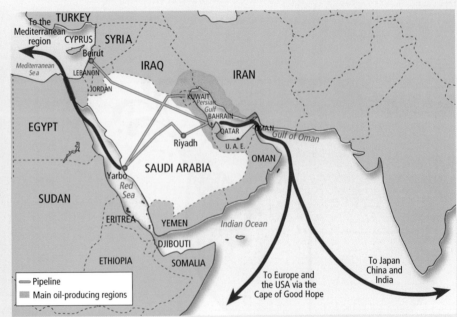

Fig 11.12 Oil regions and oil pipelines in Saudi Arabia and the surrounding regions. Name three oil-producing countries in the Persian Gulf

## Modern lifestyles

Oil production brought with it many jobs. People from the nomadic tribes abandoned the desert and took jobs in the oil industry. Camels were replaced by jeeps and later by SUVs. Desert tents were replaced by urban homes and an urban lifestyle. Shops display expensive consumer goods from all over the world.

## Inward migration

The demand for workers brought many inward migrants to Saudi Arabia. Workers from Egypt, Pakistan, Bangladesh and many other countries work in Saudi Arabia today. Many people from Europe and the USA who work in Saudi Arabia experience **culture shock**. This is because the religion of the country is Islamic.

## Politics

In spite of rapid changes, some aspects of life remain the same. The country is an **absolute monarchy**. The king rules without political parties or elections. Saudi Arabia is not a democracy. There are concerns about human rights, such as the rights of prisoners.

Oil wealth has changed the lifestyle of many people in Saudi Arabia

| Saudi Arabia | |
|---|---|
| Population | 25 million |
| Life expectancy | 73 years |
| Births per mother | 4.1 |
| Urban population | 81% |
| Adult literacy | 79% |

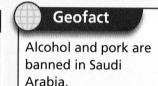

### Geofact

Alcohol and pork are banned in Saudi Arabia.

Saudi women dressed in the chador

## The role of women

The role of women in Saudi Arabia – a strict Islamic country – has not changed in spite of the rapid increase in wealth. It is illegal for a man and a woman who are unmarried to be together in a public place. Women are not allowed to drive and must be completely covered outside the home. Women are banned from participating in athletics. Very few women work outside the home. Many examples show that women are discriminated against in the courts.

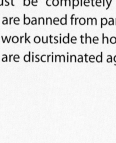

### Question

What, do you think, is the meaning of the words **culture shock**?

# Case Study

## The search for oil in Irish waters

The demand for oil and natural gas in recent decades led many countries to search for oil in offshore waters. This search was successful, especially in the **North Sea**.

### Irish coastal waters

The presence of oil and gas in the North Sea prompted oil companies to look to Irish waters for oil. The government granted licences to oil exploration companies to drill for oil off the Irish coast. Gas was found off the coast of Kinsale and oil was found off the coast of Waterford.

### Waterford oil

The Waterford oil field has not been developed so far. This is because the find is a small one. The cost of bringing the oil ashore would be greater than the value of the oil. However, as oil prices rise in the future, that field may be exploited.

### Natural gas

#### The Kinsale Head Gas Field

The Kinsale Head Gas Field has been providing natural gas for many years. It has supplied natural gas to many Irish towns and cities. However, the Kinsale field will soon be exhausted.

#### The Corrib Gas Field

Natural gas has also been found off the coast of Mayo. This is known as the **Corrib Gas Field**.

#### Safety issues

Bringing the gas ashore from the Corrib Gas Field has been delayed because of a dispute between Shell – the company involved – and some local people. People are concerned about the safety of the gas pipeline and an on-shore refinery. Locals want the refinery to be located at sea. However, in 2008 construction of the onshore pipeline started.

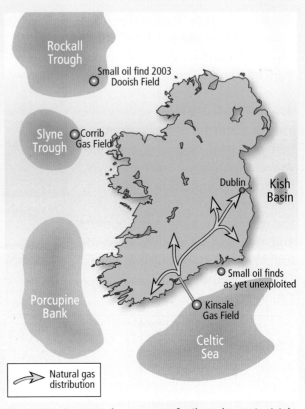

Fig 11.13 Potential sources of oil and gas in Irish territorial waters. Kinsale gas is supplied to many urban centres

Protests in Mayo against the gas pipeline

# Renewable energy

Everyone agrees that the demand for oil and natural gas will be greater than supply in the coming years. Therefore, people must develop other alternative energy sources that are renewable.

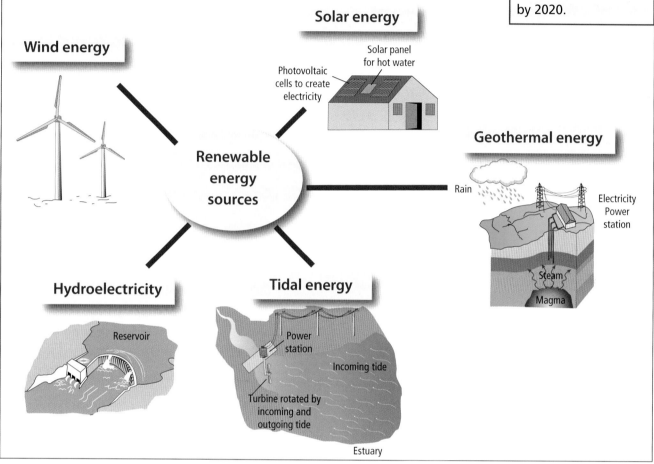

Fig 11.14 Alternative energy sources

## SUMMARY

- Oil is a finite resource that will eventually run out.
- Saudi Arabia has become wealthy because of its oil resources.
- The seas around Ireland have some important supplies of natural gas.
- As oil runs out, alternative energy sources will become more important.

## QUESTIONS

1. Explain two reasons why oil is a very important fuel in many countries today.
2. Name two countries where demand for oil has increased in recent years.
3. Explain two changes that the presence of oil has brought to Saudi Arabia.
4. Explain the term renewable energy and give two examples of renewable energy.
5. Explain one reason why increased use of renewable energy is very important.

# 11.4 The Exploitation of Ireland's Peatlands

The rate of exploitation of a resource is related to technological change.

## Ireland's peat bogs

Bogs in Ireland began to develop 8,000 years ago. There are two types of bogs in Ireland:

◎ **Raised bogs** that are found in shallow depressions in some Midland counties. These bogs can be up to 12 metres deep in their natural state.

◎ **Blanket bogs** are found in upland regions and in lowlands in the western seaboard counties. These bogs are 3 to 4 metres deep.

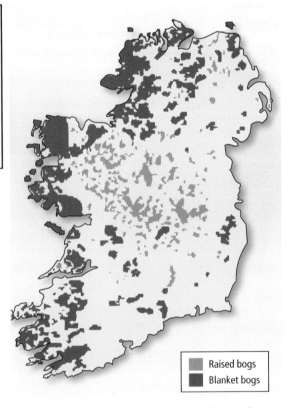

Raised bogs
Blanket bogs

Fig 11.15 The distribution of Ireland's peat bogs

### Definitions

**Meitheal:** A group of neighbours and friends who worked together at a common task in rural Ireland.

**Self-sufficient:** Reliant on a country's own resources.

## Traditional methods of peat cutting

For generations, Irish people harvested turf. **Meitheals** of workers cut turf for kitchen fires using a **sleán** – a type of spade. The sleán was an example of traditional technology. Output per worker was very low. Saved turf was brought home by pony and cart.

## Bord na Móna

In 1946, the Irish government established Bord na Móna to exploit Ireland's bogs and to make the country more **self-sufficient** in energy resources.

## Modern peat production

Bord na Móna developed modern machinery to exploit the bogs of the Midlands. Bogs here covered thousands of hectares and were on level ground. Bogs were drained to allow water to run off allowing the peat to compress. Machinery could then travel over the bogs.

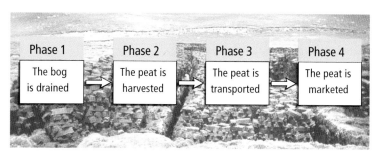

Fig 11.16 The stages in the exploitation of a bog

## The stages in the production of milled peat

◉ A **ditcher** is used to drain the bog.

◉ A **grader** levels the surface of the bog.

◉ A shallow layer of peat is scraped loose by a **miller** on the peat's surface.

◉ This layer is later harrowed using a **harrow** pulled by a tractor to dry it.

◉ Peat is gathered in long ridges using a **ridger** and covered in plastic to protect it from rain.

◉ The ridges of peat are brought to the power station or factory on **light railways**. The peat is either used to generate electricity or manufactured into several products including briquettes and garden compost.

Turf can be cut by hand

A ditcher

A miller

A harrow

A ridger

A train takes peat to the power station

321

### Peat products

Peat products include the following:

- ◎ **Horticultural products** such as moss peat, seed and potting compost are sold to gardeners.
- ◎ **Peat briquettes** are sold to domestic consumers for home heating.
- ◎ **Milled peat** is sold to ESB power stations in the Midlands to generate electricity.

Briquettes and peat products are marketed and sold to consumers.

## The life cycle of a bog

Bogs have developed over thousands of years. However, a bog can be worked out in fifty years. Peatlands are a unique habitat that have rare plants and insect life.

### Conservation

Many people think that at least some bogs should be preserved in their natural state for future generations to enjoy. Bord na Móna is now returning some bogs to wetlands. It is also preserving examples of different bog types.

Bogs that have been exploited in the past may become the location of wind farms in the future.

---

### 📄 SUMMARY

- ◎ There are two types of bogs, raised bogs and blanket bogs.
- ◎ Peat bogs are being rapidly exploited today by modern technology.
- ◎ Peat products are marketed and sold to consumers.
- ◎ Many people think that some bogs should be kept as they are.

---

### QUESTIONS

1 Which bogs are the easiest to exploit: raised bogs or blanket bogs? Explain your answer.
2 Describe the traditional hand methods of turf-cutting.
3 Explain why Ireland's peat reserves have been rapidly exploited in recent decades.
4 Can you suggest one way in which Bord na Móna markets its products to consumers?
5 Why is output per worker in the production of milled peat very high at the present time?

# 11.5 | Fishing

Overexploitation of a resource may lead to its depletion.

Fish is a very important food. It is prized as part of a healthy diet because it is low in fat and contains healthy oils.

## Sustainable fishing

Fish is a renewable resource if it is **sustainably** managed. Fish stocks will eventually disappear when trawlers take more fish than are replaced by breeding.

## Ireland's continental shelf

Irish waters have traditionally been rich in fish. The seas off the Irish coast form a **continental shelf**. This is an area of sea close to land in which large shoals of fish can thrive.

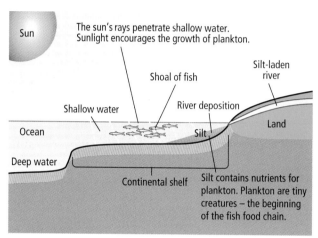

Fig 11.17 The continental shelf: the conditions necessary for the presence of large schools of fish

## The Irish fishing industry

The Irish fishing industry was small in scale until recent decades. Many fishermen fished in-shore for generations in **currachs**. Most trawlers were small and had small nets. Therefore, catches were small. This all changed when Ireland joined the EEC – now the EU – in 1973.

Men carrying a currach. Currachs were incapable of depleting the fish of the seas. Can you explain why?

Fig 11.18 Irish fishing ports

Unloading a pollack catch from the deck of a trawler

## EEC membership

EEC (EU) membership meant that Ireland surrendered control of its fisheries to Brussels. **Ireland had to share its fisheries** with other countries. Therefore, the amount of fish taken from waters around Ireland greatly increased, especially after Spain joined in 1985. The greater portion of the catch in the waters around Ireland today is caught by foreign trawlers.

## Modern fishing technology

The modern trawler is well equipped to catch fish.

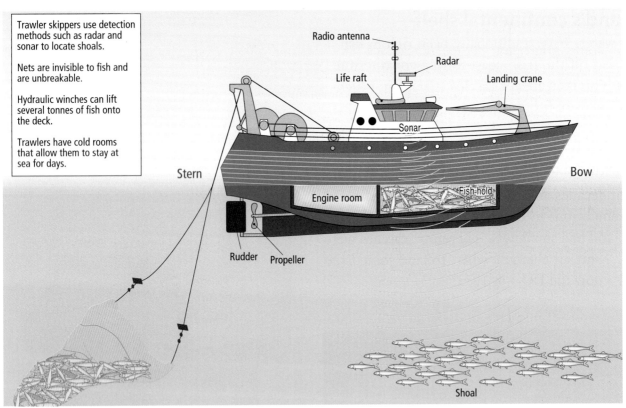

Trawler skippers use detection methods such as radar and sonar to locate shoals.

Nets are invisible to fish and are unbreakable.

Hydraulic winches can lift several tonnes of fish onto the deck.

Trawlers have cold rooms that allow them to stay at sea for days.

Fig 11.19 Modern trawler

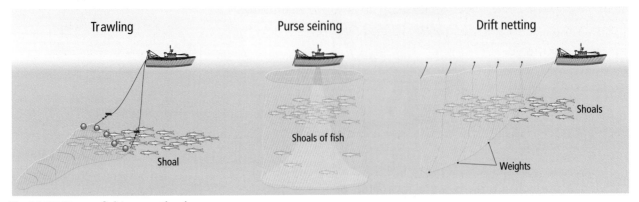

Fig 11.20 Ocean fishing methods

# Endangered species of fish

Due to overfishing **25 of the 56 species** of fish caught in Irish waters are in decline. These include **herring**, **cod**, **hake**, **haddock**, **plaice** and **sole**.

The reasons for overfishing include the following:

◎ Too many well-equipped trawlers are chasing too few fish.
◎ The seas around Ireland cover a wide area. It is impossible to stop illegal fishing.
◎ Many juvenile fish are being caught because some fishing trawlers use nets with a small mesh. This reduces the next year's catch.

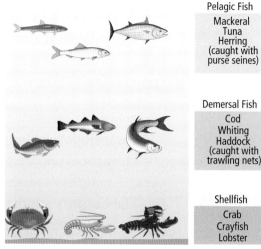

| Pelagic Fish |
| Mackeral<br>Tuna<br>Herring<br>(caught with<br>purse seines) |

| Demersal Fish |
| Cod<br>Whiting<br>Haddock<br>(caught with<br>trawling nets) |

| Shellfish |
| Crab<br>Crayfish<br>Lobster |

Fig 11.21 The main types of ocean fish

# The Irish Conservation Box

Some steps are being taken to reduce over-fishing. The **Irish Conservation Box** – an area of 100,000 km² – has been established. The Box is an important spawning ground for herring, mackerel, hake and haddock. Fishing is **severely restricted** in this area.

Other steps that are used to conserve fish stocks include the following:

◎ **Scientists** check the numbers of particular species of fish in the seas.
◎ **Quotas** are placed on the amount of each species that can be caught.
◎ The **number of trawlers** is being reduced. Fishermen can retire with an EU pension.
◎ The **mesh size of nets** is fixed so that juvenile fish can escape.
◎ The **fishing season** for some species is shortened.
◎ Trawlers from countries outside the EU, such as Russia, are not allowed to fish in EU waters.

**Conservation Zone**

Fig 11.22 A conservation zone has been created in the seas around Ireland

---

**SUMMARY**

◎ Modern trawlers use technology to locate and catch fish today.
◎ Many fish species in the seas off the Irish coast are overfished.
◎ Conservation measures are in place to try to conserve stocks for future generations.

**Definition**

**Quota:** A limit on the amount of fish that can be caught annually.

**QUESTIONS**

1 Explain two reasons for the decline in fish stocks within Irish waters in recent years. (JC)
2 Explain three steps that are being taken to prevent the collapse of fish stocks in the seas around Ireland.

**Geofact**

The Irish fishing industry is vital to the future prosperity of small coastal communities.

## 11.6 | Farming

Many primary economic activities may be examined as systems, with inputs, processes and outputs.

Farming is a primary economic activity. Farmers use many **inputs** in their farms. These include fertilisers and machinery.

The **processes** of farming include the tasks that farmers perform throughout the year. Examples of processes are milking cows, spreading fertiliser and cutting silage.

The **outputs** are the produce from the farm. These outputs may be vegetables, milk, beef cattle or sheep. Some farmers grow crops for cereal production such as wheat and barley.

### Mixed farms

Most farmers today specialise in one type of farming. There are dairy farmers, beef producers, market gardeners and cereal producers. However, some are **mixed farmers**. They are involved in more than one type of activity, e.g. dairy and beef producers.

## Case Study

## A mixed farm

We will now examine a 70 hectare mixed farm in the mid-Clare area. Up to 20 hectares are flooded under a seasonal lake in winter. The farm is a beef and sheep farm.

The farmer is called Pat. As a mixed farmer, he engages in two farming activities. His farm is under grass.

### The inputs in Pat's farm

#### Labour
◎ Pat works full time on the farm.
◎ His wife works as an office worker in Ennis. She keeps the farm accounts.
◎ One teenage son and daughter – both in secondary school – help out with herding and feeding animals during the holidays and at weekends.

#### Animals
◎ **Cattle:** Pat has a herd of suckler cattle. Each cow produces a calf every year. The calves suckle the cows for many months after they are born. They put on weight quickly.
◎ **Sheep:** Pat also keeps sheep, partly because it is a tradition and to have another source of income **when the price of beef drops**. Sheep lamb in early spring, a very busy time.

## Machinery and other inputs

◎ Pat has two tractors and several pieces of equipment including a fertiliser spreader, a trailer, a front loader and a tractor box.

◎ Other inputs include fertiliser, concentrated animal feed, seeds for reseeding grassland and electric fences.

## Specialist inputs

◎ The vet is called to attend to sick animals.

◎ The Teagasc representative advises Pat on farm management.

◎ Pat also attends IFA meetings and has gone abroad on farming tours to Germany and Denmark. He reads the *Farmers' Journal*.

A tractor is a vital machine on every farm

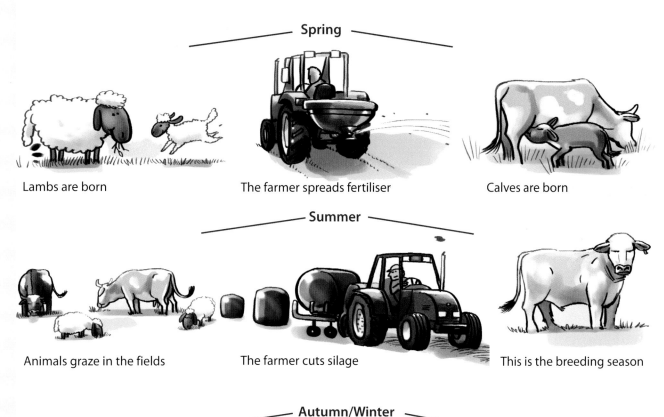

### Spring

Lambs are born

The farmer spreads fertiliser

Calves are born

### Summer

Animals graze in the fields

The farmer cuts silage

This is the breeding season

### Autumn/Winter

Cattle are housed indoors

Livestock is sold at the mart

Fig 11.23 Farm processes throughout the year

### Definition

Traceability: Beef and sheep can be traced back to the farms where the animals were raised.

### Question

Pat has two enterprises: cattle and sheep.
Can you think of one advantage in doing this?

## Outputs

◎ The major outputs of Pat's farm are cattle and lamb.

◎ **Pat sells the cattle** in Ennis and Sixmilebridge Marts **in the autumn**. Buyers come from cattle factories. Pat's name and address appears on meat products in Irish supermarkets because of the EU policy of meat **traceability**.

◎ **Lambs are bought by** local butchers. These are slaughtered and sold in butcher shops and to hotels in Co. Clare.

◎ **Slurry** from the winter sheds is spread on the fields as an organic fertiliser.

The scene at a cattle mart; this is the day that Pat gets paid for his year's work. Cattle prices are unpredictable

### SUMMARY

◎ Farming is a system with inputs, processes and outputs.
◎ In a mixed farm, a farmer produces more than one type of crop or produce.
◎ Farming activities vary with the seasons.

### QUESTIONS

1 Write down the farm inputs from the following list: silage, harvesting, diesel fuel for tractors, a sheepdog, daily herding of cattle and sheep, an electric fence, slurry, a visit from the vet.

2 Describe three important farming activities in Pat's work over the year.

3 Give one reason why traceability gives shoppers confidence in the meat that they buy.

4 'A farm operates as a system with inputs, processes and outputs.' Examine this statement in the case of any farm you have studied. (JC)

# SECONDARY ECONOMIC ACTIVITIES

## 12.1 Building Resources into Products

Secondary economic activities are those in which raw materials are processed. Any secondary activity may be viewed as a system of inputs, processes and outputs.

This chapter deals with manufacturing. In manufacturing, raw materials or semi-finished goods enter the factory as **inputs**. These materials are **processed** to manufacture a product. Finished products and waste are **outputs**.

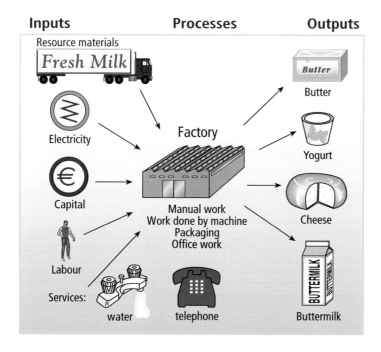

Fig 12.1 Inputs, processes and outputs in a dairy processing factory

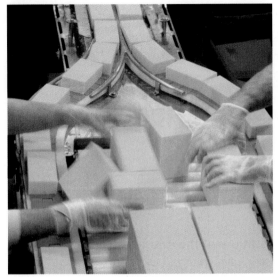

Cheddar cheese is wrapped on a conveyor belt in a dairy processing plant. Is cheese an input or an output?

## Manufacture of dairy products in the Golden Vale

The Golden Vale of Munster has a long tradition of dairying. The rich pasture lands of the Golden Vale support dairy herds. Milk is sent to processing plants in the towns of the Golden Vale. Milk is processed into butter, cheese and other dairy products in the co-op.

### Further processing

Some factories use components or parts to assemble a product. In a car assembly factory, hundreds of components are used to make a car. In a computer factory, workers attach many components together to make a computer.

A worker assembling the central processing unit of a Dell computer

### SUMMARY

◎ A factory is a system of inputs, processes and outputs.

### QUESTIONS

1  In a bakery, which of the following is not an input? Electricity, bags of flour, sliced bread, baking trays, plastic gloves.
2  What are secondary economic activities?
3  Can you name some of the components that are used to assemble computers?

## 12.2 Factory Location

The location of a factory is based on a number of factors.

## Resource materials

The raw materials, semi-finished materials or components that are used to make a product are called **resource materials**. The dairy processing industry requires fresh milk which is perishable. Therefore, dairy processing factories are located in the Golden Vale, close to dairy farms. Products such as butter and cheese **lose volume** when they are processed.

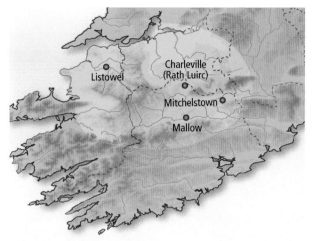

Fig 12.2 Dairy co-ops are located in the Golden Vale in Munster, near to milk supplies, which are bulky

## Transport facilities

Manufacturers choose locations for factories where the transport facilities are good. Manufacturers choose sites that are well served by road and if necessary, by rail. Many factories are located close to a ring road outside the city suburbs.

Some factories are located **close to a port**.

## Labour

Every factory requires a **labour force**. Manufacturers are influenced by the quality of the Irish labour force. Foreign companies, including Intel, Microsoft and Roche have plants in Ireland partly because the labour force is of a high quality and well educated.

Dublin, Cork, Galway, Limerick and other centres have **third-level colleges** and universities. Hi-tech manufacturers choose these cities as plant locations because large numbers of young graduates enter the urban workforce every year.

Fig 12.3 Bulky materials, such as milk, are processed close to where they are produced. Why is this?

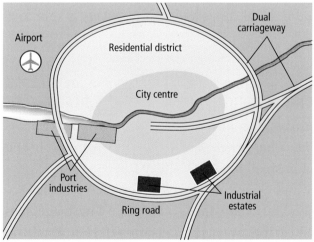

Fig 12.4 Many coastal cities have port industries. Industrial estates are located close to good transport links

### Questions

1 Suggest two advantages of locating factories close to ring roads.
2 Why are some factories located close to ports?

331

Industrial estates, such as Shannon, are attractive to **light industries** because they offer advance factories and excellent services

 **Definition**

**Light industry:**
Goods that are easily transportable, e.g. clothes and healthcare products.

## Services

All factories require electricity, water and telecommunications, including broadband. Electricity is available everywhere in the Republic of Ireland. Water supplies are adequate. Broadband does not yet cover the entire country, especially some smaller towns. Broadband is a vital service because of its communication speed.

Fig 12.5 Bakeries are found in market locations

## Markets

Some products **gain volume** after they have been processed, e.g. baking. For that reason, bakeries choose a **market location**, thus they are located in or beside cities. In this way, the transport cost of bread to local shops and supermarkets is kept low.

## Government policy

 **Definition**

**Multinational companies:**
Businesses that have premises in more than one country.

Irish governments have actively supported manufacturing in Ireland, whether it is through home-based companies or foreign **multinationals**. Governments give extra incentives to companies to locate a factory in areas that have high unemployment. Therefore, factories have been established in many western counties and in small towns.

Agencies such as the IDA and Shannon Development have been very successful in bringing multinational companies to Ireland. These agencies build factory bays in industrial estates to encourage companies to establish plants in them.

The Hewlett-Packard plant in Leixlip is one of many American companies located in the Republic of Ireland

## EU policy

Ireland is a member of the EU, which has a market of 490 million people. In the EU, free trade exists between all the members. Therefore, foreign companies are attracted to Ireland.

The EU – as well as the Irish government – has passed many laws relating to the health and safety of workers in the workplace.

**Geofact**

The use of English: Irish workers share a common language with American companies.

Fig 12.7 Some business ideas fail to win the support of the bank manager

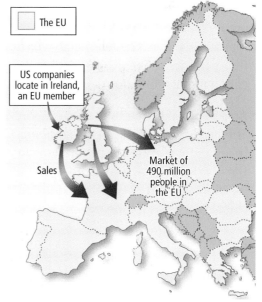

Fig 12.6 American companies in particular have located in Ireland because of Ireland's membership of the EU

## Capital

Entrepreneurs need **capital**, i.e. the cash to buy land, build the factory, and install machinery. Banks provide loans to entrepreneurs if they think the company is likely to succeed.

### Preferences of entrepreneurs and local communities

Local communities want to preserve a healthy environment. Some manufacturing activities use substances that are dangerous, e.g. toxic chemicals and asbestos. Some companies also require processes that communities dislike, e.g. incineration. For that reason, communities often object to a factory at the planning stages.

The following **two** case studies are to be studied by Higher level students only.

# Case Study

## A light industry: Intel Ireland Ltd

Intel Ireland is located in a **greenfield site** in Leixlip, Co. Kildare. Intel manufactures microchips for the computer industry. Microchips are the brains of a computer. In 2008, the Leixlip plant employed about 5,000 people both directly and indirectly. It is the largest Intel plant outside the USA.

Intel Ireland is very important to the Irish economy due to its large workforce and the contribution the company makes to Irish exports.

## Factors of location in Leixlip

### Government policy
The Irish government, through the IDA, actively supported the establishment of Intel in Leixlip in 1989 with grants and tax incentives. The IDA had already zoned the site for industrial use.

### An earthquake-free zone
The production of microchips requires the complete absence of vibrations in the rocks underneath the plant's location. The rocks under Ireland are stable (see Earthquakes, pages 11–14).

Intel, in Leixlip, Co. Kildare is located in a greenfield site

### Markets
Intel Ireland exports its microchips to markets in the EU, the Middle East and Africa as well as to other Intel plants throughout the world.

### Transport facilities
Good transport links are vital for Intel, as it exports most of its products. Intel products are small and valuable. Microchips are exported by air from Dublin Airport. Therefore, access to the airport via the M50 is important.

The Intel plant has good road access for its workforce. The site is located close to the M4, between Leixlip and Maynooth.

### Quality of labour
Intel is a **high-tech manufacturer** and uses scientific processes to manufacture microchips. Therefore, Intel needs highly-educated workers. More than 70 per cent of Intel's workers have third-level qualifications. Many are graduates from universities in Dublin. Intel actively supports science in Irish schools and universities.

### Definition

**High-tech manufacturing:** Industry that is heavily dependent on laboratory discoveries in science and technology.

## Processes and outputs in Intel

Intel workers manufacture microchips on polished silicon wafers. The wafers pass through more than 300 processing steps. Hundreds of millions of transistors are created on the surface of each wafer. This process is called **micro-technology** because measurements are very small. The microchips are then tested and packaged.

**Question**

Why does Intel support science subjects in Irish education?

Workers in an Intel clean room

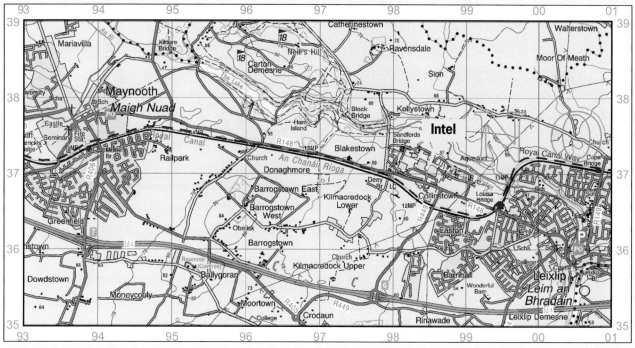

Fig 12.7 OS map of Leixlip and Maynooth

**QUESTIONS**

1 Draw a sketch map of the area shown in the OS map above and include the following:
 ◎ The M4 and the R148
 ◎ The Intel plant
 ◎ The towns of Leixlip and Maynooth
 ◎ The railway line
2 What evidence on the map suggests that Maynooth and Leixlip have large housing estates?
3 The railway line runs very close to the Intel plant.
 (a) Locate with a grid reference the location of a possible train station beside Intel.
 (b) Suggest two reasons why some workers might use the train to get to work in the Intel plant.

# Case Study

## A heavy industry: RUSAL Aughinish

RUSAL Aughinish is located in Aughinish Island, 28 km downstream from Limerick City on the Shannon Estuary. It is an **alumina refinery** that extracts alumina from the resource material **bauxite**. Alumina is a **semi-finished product**.

The alumina is exported to smelters in the UK and in Scandinavia where it is smelted into aluminium.

Alcan of Canada designed the Aughinish project in the 1970s. A Russian company, RUSAL, now owns the plant.

### Definition

**Heavy industry:** Manufacturing that uses heavy machinery and huge plants, e.g. iron and steel smelting and cement manufacture.

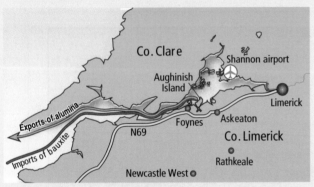
Fig 12.8 The Shannon Estuary

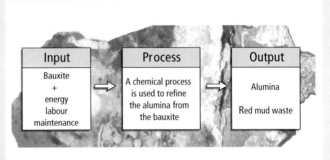
Fig 12.9 RUSAL Aughinish shown as a system of inputs, processes and outputs

## Why is the refinery located in Aughinish?

The most important factors for the location of Aughinish are:

1 **Source of resource material**: Bauxite, a bulky resource material, comes mainly from West Africa by ship. The product – alumina – is re-exported. Therefore, the refinery is on a coastal location.

2 **Transport**: The Shannon Estuary is a deep-water estuary with depths of 22 metres at low tide. This is deep enough to take very large ships known as **bulk carriers**.

3 **The site**: Aughinish Island is a very large water front site of almost 4 km². The site is large enough to store the waste material – an inert mud – from the refinery.

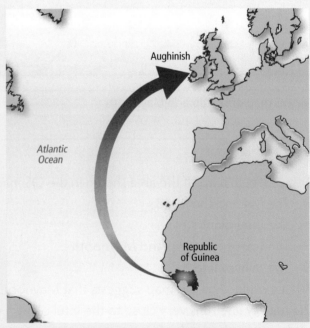
Fig 12.10 Transportation of bauxite from the Republic of Guinea, West Africa to Aughinish, Co. Limerick

## Government policy

The Shannon Estuary is a great national resource. For many years, Shannon Development has been responsible for the economic development of this region. The presence of RUSAL Aughinish on the banks of the estuary is a major success story.

RUSAL Aughinish operates with an Integrated Pollution Control Licence issued by the EPA – the Environmental Protection Agency. The licence controls all emissions from the plant.

## Labour

Employment is provided for about 700 people. Many workers live in nearby towns such as Foynes, Askeaton and Newcastle West. The alumina refinery is very important to West Limerick.

## Services

Services such as water, telecommunications and electricity are vital for a plant of this size. RUSAL Aughinish is one of the ESB's largest customers.

Bauxite

The refinery plant in Aughinish, Co. Limerick

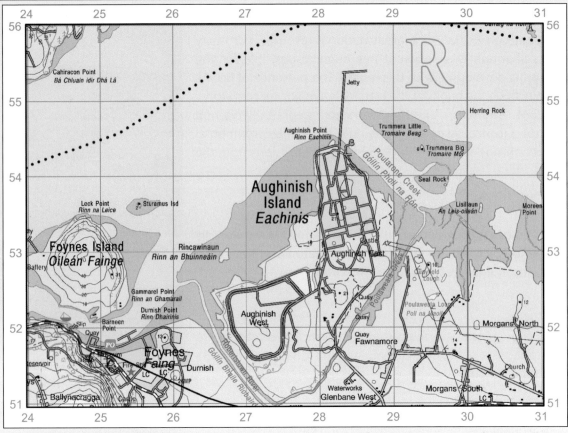

Fig 12.12 OS map of Aughinish (see page 183 for the OS symbol for electricity power lines)

## QUESTIONS

1   Draw a sketch map of the area in Fig 12.12 above and include the following:
    ◎ The mainland coast
    ◎ Aughinish Island and the jetty
    ◎ The settlement of Foynes
    ◎ The industrialised area of Aughinish Island
2   What is the approximate size of Aughinish Island in km²?
3   Why does the jetty extend outwards into the waters of the estuary?
4   Why do the two electricity power lines lead into the plant?
5   What evidence on the map shows that Aughinish Island is low-lying?

## SUMMARY

◎ An entrepreneur weighs up a number of factors such as the availability of resource material, transport costs, markets and labour before deciding where to locate a factory.
◎ Different types of industry are located in different places.
◎ Intel – an example of a light industry – is located in a greenfield site in Co. Kildare.
◎ RUSAL Aughinish – an example of a heavy industry – is located on the Shannon Estuary.

1 Explain two reasons why foreign companies have chosen Ireland as a location for a factory.
2 Define the following terms:
   ◎ Light industry
   ◎ Heavy industry
   ◎ Multinational companies
3 Explain two factors that caused Intel to locate in Leixlip.
4 Explain why RUSAL Aughinish is located on a waterfront site.
5 In relation to a named example of a manufacturing industry you have studied, explain how these three factors have influenced the location of the industry.
   ◎ Transport
   ◎ Labour
   ◎ Multinational companies. (JC)

# 12.3 Footloose Industry

Modern industry, unlike industry in earlier centuries, tends to be footloose.

## Industry in earlier centuries

The Industrial Revolution began in the 1780s in Britain. The major industries of the Industrial Revolution were iron and steel, textiles and heavy engineering.

## Coalfield sites

Heavy industries, such as the iron and steel industry, were tied to coalfield sites in Britain, Belgium, France and Germany. This was because coal became the energy source for smelting iron and steel.

The textile industry was also tied to coalfields because textile machinery used steam power. Water was turned into steam by burning coal.

Manufacturing in Britain, Belgium, France and Germany has not been confined to coalfields for many decades. This is because coal is no longer the only source of energy that powers factories.

## Earlier manufacturing sites in Ireland

Ireland had little or no coal. Therefore, water power on rivers was used to power small flour and textile mills along rivers throughout the country.

**Definition**

**Footloose industry:** Manufacturing business that is not tied to one location.

**Geofact**

In the nineteenth century, a cotton mill in Portlaw, Co. Waterford was located on the River Clodiagh.

The restored mill at Bealick, Macroom, Co. Cork is now a heritage centre

## Modern footloose industry

Many manufacturing industries are footloose today. There are several reasons for this:

◎ **Industrial estates** are widely dispersed both in Ireland and abroad. In Ireland, the IDA has encouraged many companies with light industries to set up plants in small towns.

◎ **Electricity** is widely available. Electricity is the main source of energy for manufacturing today.

◎ **Excellent transport** on national road and rail routes allows the transport of resource materials to factories in many locations.

◎ **Light industry products** – high in value and low in weight – can be distributed cheaply to markets.

◎ **The workforce** today is generally car owning. This allows factories in small towns to draw its workforce from rural areas.

◎ **Ring road**s around cities such as Dublin, Cork, Limerick and Galway attract footloose manufacturing industry.

The Schering-Plough pharmaceutical plant is located in a greenfield site in Brinny, Co. Cork

---

### 📄 SUMMARY

◎ In earlier centuries, much manufacturing industry was tied to coalfields and rivers.

◎ Today, manufacturing industry is widely dispersed.

---

### ✍ QUESTIONS

1 Why was textile manufacturing located beside rivers in Ireland at one time?
2 Explain the term 'footloose industry'.
3 Explain three reasons why much of modern industry is footloose.
4 Is RUSAL Aughinish a footloose industry? Explain your answer.

# 12.4 Industrial Location: Change over Time

Change generally occurs over time in the relative significance of locational factors, leading to change in distribution patterns. Industrial decline may occur in particular regions. However, for many reasons, an industry might not relocate, even though it is economically sound to do so. This is called industrial inertia.

The British iron and steel industry is to be studied by Higher level students only.

## The British iron and steel industry

### Early eighteenth century

Iron-making furnaces used **charcoal from forests** to smelt iron ore. Transport was very poor. Therefore, ironworks were resource-based, i.e. they were located where iron ore and forests were available. But forests were quickly cut down. Therefore, the industry relocated to a new energy source – coalfields.

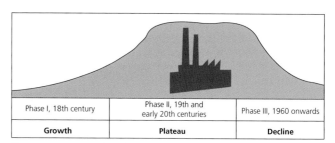

| Phase I, 18th century | Phase II, 19th and early 20th centuries | Phase III, 1960 onwards |
|---|---|---|
| Growth | Plateau | Decline |

Fig 12.13 Growth, plateau and decline in the British iron and steel industry

**Definition**

**Industrial inertia:** A factory remains although the reason for its location no longer exists.

### The nineteenth century

At the end of the eighteenth century, during the Industrial Revolution, the demand for iron and steel was very high. Ironworks were located **on or close**

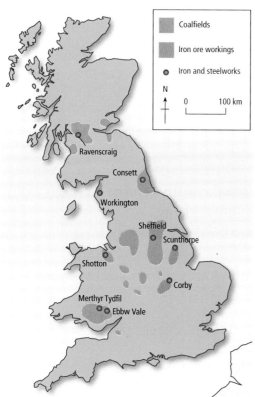

Fig 12.14a The iron and steel industry in Britain in the 1950s

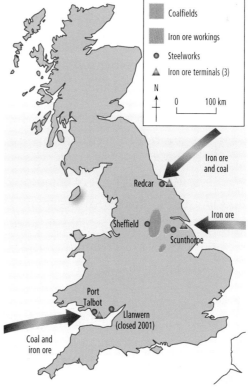

Fig 12.14b The iron and steel industry in Britain today

to **coalfields**. Canals, and later railways, carried iron ore to the iron and steel works. The coalfields remained the main location for iron and steel smelting until the second half of the twentieth century.

Port Talbot steelworks. Why are the steelworks found at a water-front location?

## Decline: 1960 onwards

The British iron and steel industry declined after 1960 for the following reasons:

◎ Coalfields were exhausted after generations of mining.
◎ New methods of working required far less coal to smelt iron and steel. Therefore, coalfields lost their importance as locations of iron and steel works.
◎ Foreign steelmakers in Germany and Japan were producing cheaper steel than British producers. Demand for British-made steel declined. British steel companies began to lose money.
◎ The coast of Britain became a more attractive location for steel plants. Iron ore and cheap Polish coal could be imported to coastal steel plants.

Therefore, inland steel plants closed with great job losses. For instance, the Corby steel plant closed in 1980 with the loss of 5,000 jobs in a single day.

## Industrial inertia in Sheffield

Most of the inland iron and steel plants in Britain have closed down. The iron and steel industry has **relocated** to the coast. However, Sheffield has continued as a steel producer for many reasons:

☞ **Definition**

**Niche product:** A good manufactured for a particular use, e.g. surgical instruments used in hospitals.

◎ The steel smelters of Sheffield have been **modernised** to make them more efficient. In this way, they can compete in price with imported steel.
◎ Sheffield cutlery is famous for its **good quality**. Today, it also specialises in **niche products** such as surgical instruments.
◎ Sheffield has a **highly-skilled workforce** that has a long and proud tradition of steel making.
◎ Sheffield has excellent **road** and **rail connections** to its customers.

Therefore, Sheffield steel has survived into the twenty-first century.

Surgical instruments are niche products

### SUMMARY

◎ The iron and steel industry was once tied to coalfields.

◎ The industry has moved from inland sites to the coast in recent decades.

◎ Steel making in Sheffield has survived – a classic example of industrial inertia.

### QUESTIONS

1 Explain why coalfields became the location of the British iron and steel industry during the Industrial Revolution.

2 Explain two reasons why the iron and steel industry declined in Britain after 1960.

3 Explain one reason why the British iron and steel industry moved to the coast.

4 (a) Explain the term industrial inertia.

    (b) Give three reasons for the survival of the iron and steel industry in Sheffield.

## 12.5 The Role of Women in Industry

The role of women within industry has changed in both developed and developing countries.

### Women in the workforce in Ireland: a developed country

One hundred years ago, women's roles in Ireland were very different to those of today. At that time, Ireland, apart from north-east Ulster, was an agricultural society.

◎ Many women's marriages were arranged.

◎ Very few women owned property.

◎ Women were tied to the traditional roles of wife and mother.

◎ Women in general did not plan their families.

◎ Very few women worked outside the home.

> **Geofact**
>
> In 1918, women over 30 were given the vote in Ireland for the first time.

A woman in a traditional role in Ireland in the past

Mary Robinson, President of Ireland, 1990–97, was the first woman to occupy the highest office in the Republic

**Geofact**

Women make up only 4 per cent of chief executives in the top 500 Irish companies.

## Changes in the role of women

Women today have lifestyles that are totally different to the lives of their grandmothers. Many women work outside the home. What has changed in 100 years?

◎ **Free secondary education** was introduced in 1967. This increased education levels for girls and boys. Today, girls enter third-level education in greater numbers than boys. Many women enter the workforce with degrees in law, business and architecture.

◎ **The Women's Liberation movement** of the 1970s – an international movement – led to many changes in the status of women.

◎ **Gender equality laws** gave women equal pay and equal status for equal work in the job market.

◎ Many women choose to work outside the home for **personal** and **economic reasons**.

◎ The great increase in the **cost of homes** means that in many homes both partners have to work to pay the mortgage.

◎ Mothers today have, on average, two children each. Therefore, women are **less tied to motherhood** and home-making.

◎ **Crèches** allow mothers to go to work.

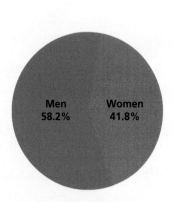

Fig 12.15 Ireland's workforce in 2005

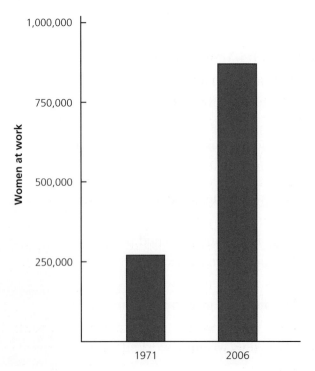

Fig 12.16 The number of women at work in Ireland has increased enormously in recent decades

## The work/home balance

Many women find it difficult to balance the demands of work and home. Therefore, many women do not seek promotion to senior positions. Some women also choose to work part-time or to take career breaks to raise their families.

Fig 12.17 Family friendly policies are essential for workers today

Fig 12.18 Women find promotion in the workforce difficult. Explain two obstacles to women's promotion

## Women in the labour market in China: a developing country

When the Communist Party took over China in 1949, the economy was agricultural. In rural areas women's lives were very difficult. As well as being wives and mothers they also worked in the fields. They had large families before the one-child policy was introduced in 1979.

### Industrialisation

China has experienced great change in recent years. Since 1980, the country has become industrialised very rapidly. Companies from Hong Kong and Taiwan have established factories in Export Processing Zones along the east coast. Many other companies, including American companies, hire Chinese sub-contractors in China to produce goods to order.

### Chinese sub-contractors

Chinese sub-contractors regularly fill orders for 600,000 pairs of socks, 300,000 pairs of runners and 50,000 ties for foreign companies. To fill these orders women work to strict deadlines, in cities all along China's east coast.

Women in the labour market in China is for Higher level students only.

### Geofact

There are more than 600 million females in China.

### Question

'When the multinationals squeeze the sub-contractors, the sub-contractors squeeze the workers.' What do you think this means?

Earrings

T-Shirt

Jacket

iPod

Belt

Jeans

Socks

Training shoes

Fig 12.19 Chinese-made goods are worn by teenagers in Ireland today. Check the labels on your own clothes

## The workshop of the world

China has now become the workshop of the world producing many of the goods that teenagers in wealthy countries buy. Millions of Chinese women work in these factories.

Women at work in a garment factory. Describe what you see in this picture

## Women's working conditions

China is a very big country and work practices vary throughout the country. However, the following statements can be made:

◎ Millions of female workers are recent migrants from the countryside who have come to the coastal cities to seek work.

◎ Women do not belong to independent trade unions. These do not exist in China.

◎ Millions of women work at dull, monotonous and repetitive tasks all day every day, sewing garments, stitching handbags and making shoes for Western companies.

◎ Wages are rising in China, but they are very low by Western standards. The average monthly wage in China was reported by one source as being Yuan 1,750 per month in 2008. Many women in low-skilled work earn less than this.

◎ Women are often obliged to do overtime to fill orders.

◎ Millions of women workers live with little privacy in crowded dormitories that are attached to the factories.

The push of poverty

Tianjin

Shanghai

Xiamen

Guangzhou

Shenzhen

Fig 12.20 In China, millions of rural poor are flocking to the east coast cities looking for jobs

 **Question**

If 1 euro equals 10.1 Yuan, what was the average monthly wage in euro in China in 2008?

## Life in China

Life in China is challenging. The east coast is intensely crowded. Cities and rivers are very polluted. People do not enjoy the same freedoms that we in the West take for granted.

Nevertheless, since 1949 women's lives have changed greatly. More than 90 per cent of girls are enrolled at school in China. Since 1949 life expectancy for women has more than doubled to 75 years, which is very close to European levels.

Many families live in large apartment blocks located in the industrial district of cities such as Chengdu

### SUMMARY

◎ Women in Ireland have broken away from traditional roles in recent decades.
◎ Many factors, such as education, have helped women to join the workforce.
◎ The work-home balance is a challenge for women.
◎ Millions of women work in factories in China owned by Chinese sub-contractors.
◎ Women in China's factories work long hours for low pay making items that they cannot afford to buy.

### QUESTIONS

1 Explain the following sentence: 'Women were tied to traditional roles up to a few decades ago'.
2 Explain three factors that have increased the number of women working in manufacturing in Ireland today.
3 Explain two pressures that face working women in Ireland today.
4 Why are millions of rural women migrating to China's east coast today?
5 Millions of women work at repetitive jobs in factories in China. Give two examples of that type of work.

# 12.6 Manufacturing on a World Scale

Industrialised, newly industrialised and industrially emergent regions may be identified on a world scale.

## Industrialised regions

The Industrial Revolution began in Britain about 1780 and spread to other European countries. By 1900, the USA and Japan were rapidly industrialising.

Today, Western Europe, the USA and Japan still dominate world manufacturing. However, other regions are catching up. This is partly because multinationals are transferring their factories to Asia and **Latin America**. Labour costs are cheaper in those regions.

A worker in a Lexus assembly plant in Japan; wealthy countries such as Japan have highly-skilled and well-paid workers

## Newly industrialised countries

Young people are aware from the labels on clothing and other items that much of what they buy is made in South-east Asia. Countries in this region are newly industrialised. These countries include Taiwan, South Korea, Singapore and China.

Some Latin American countries such as Mexico, Brazil and Argentina are industrialising quickly also.

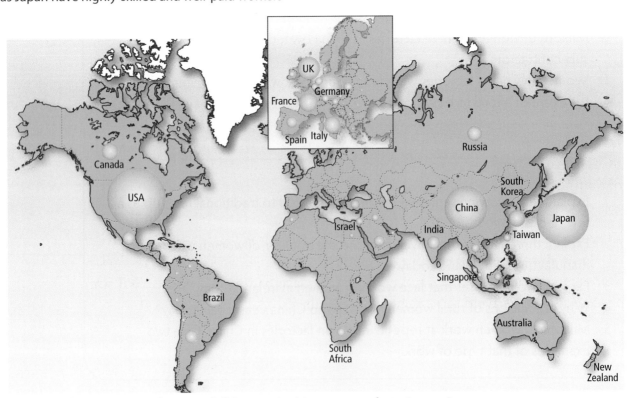

Fig 12.21 The USA, Japan, the EU and China are the biggest manufacturing regions

Fig 12.22 South-east Asia is a region that includes many newly industrialised countries. Japan was industrialised much earlier than other South-east Asian countries

**Geofact**

Many companies are closing their Irish plants and relocating to South-east Asia.

**Definition**

**Latin America:** The region spreading from Mexico south to Chile and Argentina.

## Low labour costs

South-east Asian countries are attractive to multinationals from the USA and Japan because of their low labour costs. Manufacturing brings jobs and a rising standard of living to these countries.

Vietnam is now a target of multinationals because their labour costs are even lower than China's.

## Industrially emergent regions

Industrially emergent regions have little or no modern manufacturing. Most of Africa, parts of Asia and parts of South America are in this position. Reasons for this include the following:

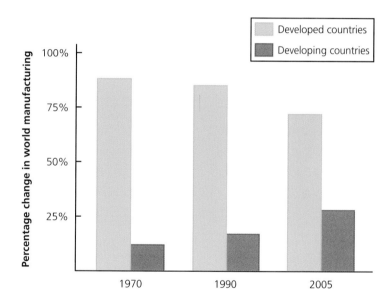

Fig 12.23 Manufacturing output in the developed and the developing world for selected years

◎ **Poor services** such as a lack of electricity and water supplies.
◎ **Badly developed transport systems** such as poor-quality roads and bridges.
◎ Some countries in Africa and parts of Asia have had many years of **civil war**. Multinationals avoid these regions as a result.

### 📄 SUMMARY

- ◎ Manufacturing is dominated by the USA, Western Europe and Japan.
- ◎ East Asia and parts of Latin America have industrialised in recent decades.
- ◎ Some regions, especially in Africa, have very little manufacturing.

### ✍ QUESTIONS

1 Study Fig 12.21 on page 348, and answer the following questions:
  (a) Name the two largest manufacturing countries in the world.
  (b) Which country is the largest manufacturing country in Europe?
  (c) Give one reason for the importance of China in manufacturing.
  (d) Name three countries in Africa that have some manufacturing.

# 12.7 The Impact of Industrial Activity on the Environment

Industrial activity may have important impacts on agriculture, forestry, tourism and the quality of life.

## Acid rain

Acid rain is a mixture of water and gases such as sulphur dioxide and nitrogen oxides. Water in the atmosphere that is not contaminated has a pH of about 5.6. Acid rain has a pH below 4.3. Acid rain can be as acidic as lemon juice or vinegar.

## The sources of acid rain

Power stations that burn fossil fuels, along with smelters, are major sources of acid rain. Coal is especially high in harmful gases. Vehicle engines also release nitrogen oxides. These gases release sulfur dioxide and nitrogen oxides into the atmosphere. They combine with water vapour to fall to earth as acid rain.

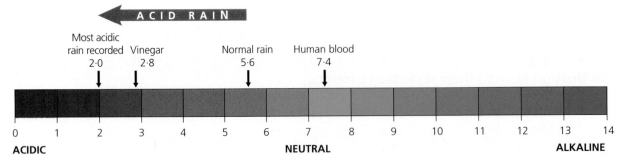

Fig 12.24 Acid rain on the pH scale

## The role of the wind

Since the 1970s, power stations have had high smokestacks to release gases. This was because it was believed that **dilution** was the solution to **pollution**. It was thought that if gases were dispersed by the wind over a wide area, they would be less harmful.

Unfortunately, diluting harmful gases was **not** the solution to pollution. Europe has so many power stations that millions of tonnes of gases are carried from one country to another. Thus, Swedish lakes and forests are damaged by acid rain from Britain and Central Europe.

Moneypoint Power Station is located in the Shannon Estuary, Co. Clare. It burns coal to generate electricity

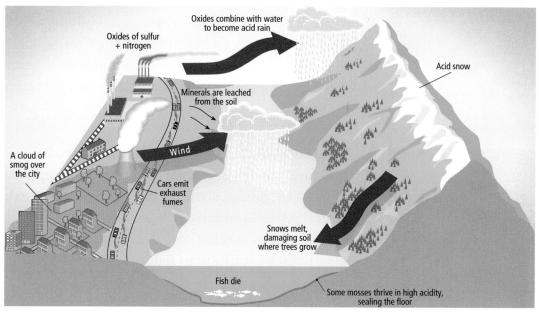

Fig 12.25 Acid rain falls over forests, lakes and farms and damages the natural world

# The damage caused by acid rain

## Forests

Acid rain **leaches** or washes away nutrients from the soil. Trees weaken because of a lack of nutrients. Acid rain also damages the foliage of trees. Damaged and weakened trees die from diseases and attacks by parasites.

## Fish life in lakes

Rivers carry acidic rainwater and melt waters from acid snow into lakes. Fish eggs are damaged when the pH falls below 4.3 in lakes. Fish no longer hatch and fish life disappears from lakes. Many lakes, especially in Sweden, are biologically dead.

A dead pine forest in Bavaria, Germany

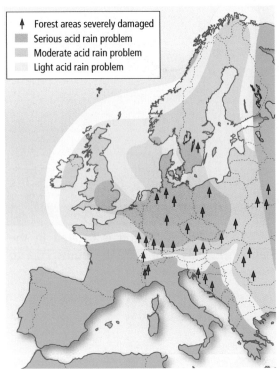

Legend:
▲ Forest areas severely damaged
■ Serious acid rain problem
■ Moderate acid rain problem
□ Light acid rain problem

Fig 12.26 The effects of acid rain on forested areas of Europe

The Parthenon in the Acropolis overlooking Athens has survived many earthquakes, but is now being weakened by acid rain

### Geofact

France produces more than 75 per cent of its electricity from nuclear power, an energy source that releases no acid rain.

## Quality of life

Acid rain also affects the quality of water supplies that come from lakes. The concentration of **metals** in lakes rises because they are washed out of the soil by acid rain. The polluted water can affect human health, especially the health of infants.

## Agriculture

Minerals and trace elements in soil such as copper and calcium are washed out of soil by acid rain. Soil loses its fertility. Farmers have to replace these lost minerals with expensive fertiliser.

## Historic buildings

Acid rain is very damaging to old stone buildings. The Parthenon in Athens, Köln Cathedral, the Colosseum in Rome and many other famous buildings are being damaged by the effects of acid rain. These sites are major tourist attractions.

## What can be done to curb pollution?

◎ Coal-fired power stations are gradually being replaced by modern power stations that use **natural gas**. Natural gas releases carbon dioxide only.

◎ Smokestacks in existing coal-fired power stations are being fitted with **filters** to reduce emissions of sulfur dioxide.

◎ Car engines release far fewer emissions today than in 1990. However, the continued increase in car numbers means that nitrogen oxide levels are still rising.

◎ Clean energy sources such as **solar and wind energy** need to be developed. Denmark is a leader in wind energy. Spain leads the way in solar energy.

◎ People must be persuaded **to use cars less**. Efficient public transport can help people to reduce their acid rain footprint.

◎ People can reduce their **personal use of electricity** in the home to decrease the output of harmful gases from power stations.

A solar energy farm in Spain produces electricity using photovoltaic cells. This sight will become commonplace in many countries around the Mediterranean in the years to come

Fig 12.27 Animal life and forest are affected by acid rain

## SUMMARY

- The release of emissions caused by burning fossil fuels leads to acid rain.
- Acid rain affects forests, lakes, agriculture and historic buildings.
- We can reduce the emissions of gases that lead to acid rain in many ways.

## QUESTIONS

1 How is acid rain formed?
2 Explain two effects of acid rain in Europe.
3 What can you do in your daily life to reduce your contribution to acid rain?

# 12.8 Conflicts of Interest

Conflicts of interest may arise between industrialists and others.

We will look at two conflict areas that can arise between industrialists and others:

1 The question of incineration
2 The shortening of working hours

# Case Study

# Incineration

In Ireland we generate up to 1 tonne per person per year of waste. The landfill sites are filling up. Some people claim that incineration – burning of waste – is part of the solution to waste. Incineration causes a lot of controversy.

## In favour of incineration

Incinerators burn waste at very high temperatures. **People in favour of the incineration** of waste make the following arguments:

◎ Incineration is necessary because our landfill sites are limited and filling quickly.

◎ All other countries in Western Europe use incineration to dispose of waste.

◎ Government agencies such as the Food Safety Authority and the Environmental Protection Agency say that if they are properly managed, incinerators do not present a danger to human health and to nearby farms.

◎ Incinerators can provide hot water to heat local homes and buildings.

◎ Incinerators have to be given planning permission by the local council and a licence by the Environmental Protection Agency.

An incinerator in Stoke, England

## Against incineration

**People opposed to incineration** make the following arguments:

◎ Incineration is unnecessary because if we **reduce**, **reuse** and **recycle** as much waste as we can, landfill will take the rest.

◎ Communities fear emissions from the smokestacks of incinerators. Some people claim that if materials are not fully burned, dioxins – very poisonous substances – will be released into the air.

◎ Incinerators release greenhouse gases because oil is used as the fuel in most incinerators.

◎ Lorry traffic on roads leading to large incinerators is greatly increased. This adds to local pollution levels.

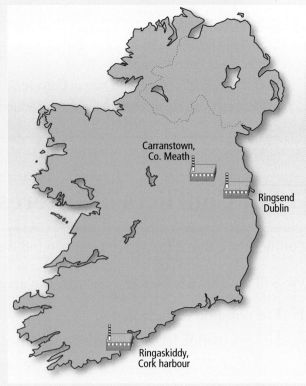

Fig 12.28 Three places where the location of incinerators has led to controversy

# Case Study

# The shortening of working hours

## Change over time

Here is a simple way of describing the change in working hours over time:

◎ Fifty years ago, people worked fifty hours per week, for fifty years.
◎ Today, people work forty hours per week, for forty years.
◎ It is believed that your grandchildren will work thirty hours per week, for thirty years.

## The role of trade unions

All through the twentieth century, trade unions sought shorter working hours for their members. Their efforts were successful. They also won the following:

◎ Paid annual holidays
◎ Paid sick leave
◎ Paid maternity leave
◎ Parental leave
◎ Earlier retirement

In the past, workers usually walked a short distance to their factory. Now, many workers commute from the suburbs to work. This adds several hours to their day.

## The attitude of factory owners

The priorities of factory owners and managers are different to those of workers. The concerns of owners and managers are as follows:

◎ They want bigger profits.
◎ They want to be competitive with rival companies.
◎ They fear that the parent company will close their factory and re-open in East Asia. In many countries in East Asia, the working week is longer and workers' pay is far less than in Ireland.

At present factories in Europe are closing because of competition from East Asian countries. In France, workers have enjoyed a 35-hour working week for several years.

However, in 2008 the French government introduced changes to this practice. These changes allow each company to negotiate the length of the working week with its workers.

**SUMMARY**

◎ Conflicts arise between industrialists and local communities on the question of incineration.

◎ Conflicts arose in the past between industrialists and workers on issues such as the length of the working week.

**QUESTIONS**

1 Explain two reasons why some people argue in favour of incinerators.

2 Why do some people object to incinerators that are close to where they live?

3 Study Fig 12.29 below and answer the following questions:

  (a) Name two commercial activities and two leisure activities in the picture.

  (b) From the evidence in the picture, explain two potential points of conflict between different groups.

Fig 12.29

4 Give two reasons why factory owners and managers might resist workers' demands for a shorter working week. (JC)

## Learning Outcomes

In this chapter you will learn that:

◎ In developed countries, most people work in services.

◎ Tourism is an example of a service industry.

◎ Tourism is an important industry in Ireland, because of Ireland's natural beauty and other attractions.

◎ The climate of Spain explains why it has a major tourist industry.

◎ As tourism grew in Spain, road, rail and air links were modernised to support tourism.

◎ There are some disadvantages to tourism, for example in Spain.

# 13.1 Services

Tertiary economic activity involves the provision of services and facilities. In a developed economy this includes a wide range of services.

In poor countries, very few people work in services. This is because people are too poor to be able to buy services that others provide.

As a country becomes wealthy, people demand personal services such as hairdressing, financial services such as banking and educational services for their children.

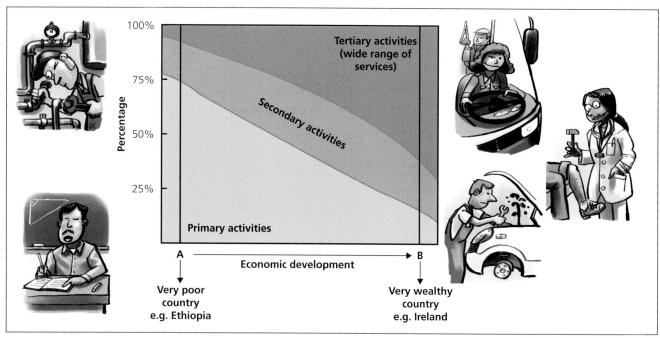

Fig 13.1 As the economy of a country develops, the tertiary or service sector expands

Fig 13.2 The range of services

CBDs in wealthy cities have a great many office workers

---

### 📄 SUMMARY

- ◎ Services expand as economies develop.
- ◎ Cities and towns provide a range of services.

---

### ✍ QUESTIONS

1   Look at Fig 13.1, on page 357, and answer the following questions:
   (a) In country A what is the percentage of people in the tertiary sector?
   (b) In country B what is the percentage of people in the tertiary sector?
   (c) Why is the tertiary sector very large in wealthy countries?
2   Where would you find administrative staff in your school?
3   In your town or city, name four different services that are available. Name the part of town in which these services are located.

# 13.2 Tourism

Tourist services and facilities tend to be located in particular regions which offer various attractions. Such regions include:

◎ Areas of natural beauty
◎ Regions offering recreational and sporting facilities
◎ Beaches and coastlines
◎ Cities

**Geofact**

In 2006, 91 per cent of overseas visitors to Ireland came by air.

The Upper Lake of Killarney; Killarney has attracted tourists to the region for generations

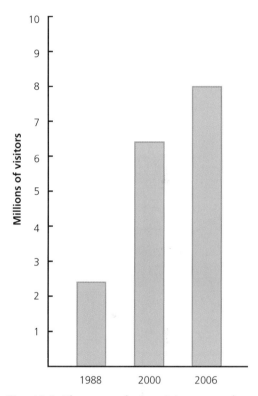

Fig 13.3 The growth in visitors to the Republic of Ireland for selected years

## The tourist industry in Ireland

Ireland is an important tourist destination with over 8 million visitors each year. Ireland is not a mass tourist destination, as are countries such as France and Spain. Nevertheless, the tourist industry is very important to the Irish economy in terms of jobs and income.

The cost of fuel will have an impact on the number of people visiting Ireland in the future.

Tourists visit Ireland for a variety of reasons.

### Areas of natural beauty

Ireland is a beautiful country and offers the tourist great contrasts in scenery.

◎ The Ice Age carved out many spectacular valleys in the mountains of Ireland, e.g. the Lakes of Killarney in Co. Kerry and Glendalough in Co. Wicklow.
◎ Many regions of Ireland are havens of peace and tranquillity, e.g. Gougánbarra in West Cork and the Glen of Aherlow in Co. Tipperary.

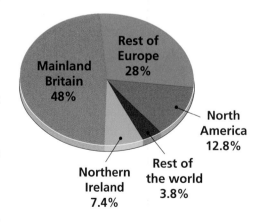

Fig 13.4 Where visitors to Ireland came from in 2007. Most came from Britain and mainland Europe

The beehive huts of an early Irish monastery can be seen on Skellig Michael (Sceilig Mhichíl) an island off the Kerry coast

## Beaches and coastlines

Coastal erosion and deposition have created a rugged coastline of great beauty. The west coast of Ireland is very spectacular.

◎ The Cliffs of Moher in Co. Clare rise to 220 metres. 750,000 people a year visit them.

◎ The peninsulas of the coast of West Cork and Kerry have spectacular cliffs and much bird life. Islands off the coast such as Skellig Michael are very dramatic.

◎ The west coast has many beaches; the east and south coasts are more noted for coastal deposition. Long-shore drift has produced excellent beaches such as Tramore in Co. Waterford. Long stretches of beach are found along the east coast from Wexford to Bray, and north of Dublin city.

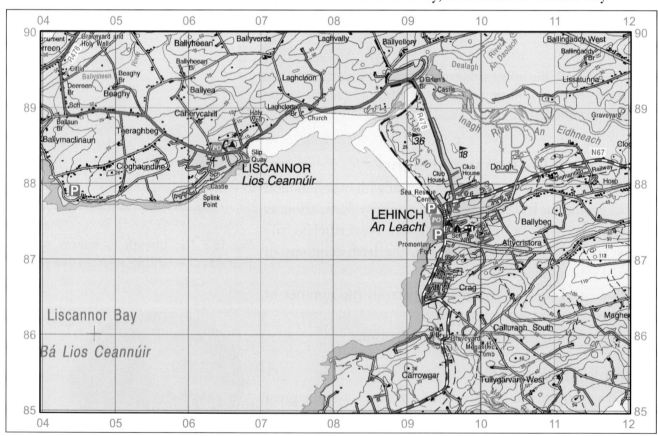

Fig 13.5 The coast of Co. Clare offers many attractions to tourists

### Question

Draw a map of the area shown in Fig 13.5 above. Mark and name:
◎ One national secondary road
◎ Two coastal settlements
◎ A beach

## Regions offering recreational and sporting facilities

Ireland is a playground for people who enjoy active holidays.

◎ Ireland has an ever-increasing number of golf courses and **links**. Links are playable for most of the year because of good drainage.

◎ **Angling** is an important **holiday activity**, fishing in freshwater lakes and rivers, as well as offshore. Many European lakes are no longer healthy enough to support fish life because of pollution. European anglers come to Ireland because of its unpolluted waters.

◎ **Waterways** such as the Shannon are used by people who enjoy cruising holidays. Tourists bring business to small towns along the Shannon from Killaloe to Carrick-on-Shannon.

◎ International **sporting fixtures** draw many tourists to the country, e.g. international rugby and soccer matches. The opening of Croke Park to international soccer and rugby has given these matches further publicity.

> **Definition**
>
> **Links:** A golf course located on coastal sand dunes.

> **Geofact**
>
> If the Irish Rugby Football Union is successful in hosting the Rugby World Cup in 2015 or 2019 it will bring many tourists to the country.

## Cities

◎ Dublin is the country's most visited city. This is partly because of its status as a historic capital. Dublin Airport has the best flight connections with British and European airports compared to other Irish airports.

◎ Dublin has many attractions that include the treasures of the National Museum, the Book of Kells in Trinity College, Grafton Street, the National Gallery and Georgian architecture.

◎ Cork is an excellent centre for exploring the surrounding region. Blarney Castle is just outside the city. Kinsale is famous for its seafood restaurants. The Queenstown Story in Cobh pays tribute to the great numbers of people who emigrated to the USA in the generations after the Famine.

An international rugby match between Ireland and France in Croke Park

A memorial to Irish emigrants in Cobh, where the story of emigration is showcased for visitors

## SUMMARY

◎ The number of tourists to Ireland has increased steadily in recent decades.

◎ The beauty of the landscape, Irish culture and niche holidays bring many tourists to Ireland.

## QUESTIONS

1 (a) Name the county in which you live.

   (b) Name an area of attractive scenery in your county.

   (c) Name one historic feature of interest to tourists.

   (d) Name an urban centre that provides tourist facilities.

2 (a) Using evidence from the OS map, Fig 13.5 on page 360, suggest three tourist activities that are available in the area shown on the OS map.

   (b) Write the grid reference of your choice of location for a coastal wind farm.

   (c) Explain two reasons why some people might object to a wind farm in this area.

## 13.3 | Tourism in Europe

**Climate is an important factor in making some regions attractive for tourists.**

Tourism is the world's largest industry today. Millions of people from Northern Europe have been holidaying in the Mediterranean since the 1950s. There are many reasons for this:

◎ Europeans could afford annual holidays when the economic boom of the 1950s started.

◎ The travel industry provided cheap package holidays for tourists.

◎ The introduction of large aeroplanes such as the Boeing 707 and cheap fuel made it possible to transfer millions of passengers quickly and safely to Mediterranean resorts.

The Boeing 707 became a workhorse of the jet age

◎ Mediterranean countries such as Spain, Italy and Greece developed tourist resorts in order to cater for large numbers of tourists.

◎ Sporting a tan was fashionable.

The result was that the Mediterranean became the largest tourist destination in the world.

> **Geofact**
>
> The Costa del Sol in southern Spain receives 3,000 hours of sunshine during the year. Ireland receives between 1,100 and 1,200 hours.

## Tourism in Spain

Spain developed its tourist industry very rapidly after 1955. At this time, it is the second most important tourist destination in the world with more than 56 million tourists annually. The **Balearic** Islands in the Mediterranean, and the **Canaries** off the coast of Morocco – both Spanish territories – are major tourist destinations.

### Sun, sand and sea

To the pale-skinned tourists from Northern Europe, Spain has enviable amounts of sunshine and high temperatures for many months of the year. Hotels and apartments are built along the coast close to the beach. Restaurants and discos are located along the seafront of every resort. Resorts welcome family groups. Almost every resort has a **marina**.

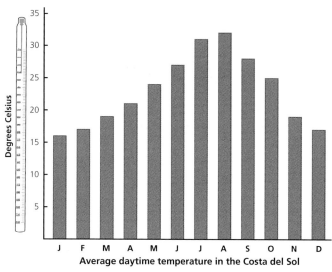

Fig 13.6 Midday temperatures in the Costa del Sol throughout the year

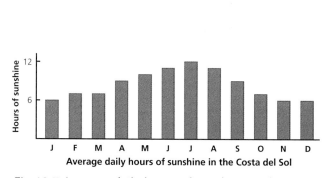

Fig 13.7 Average daily hours of sunshine in the Costa del Sol throughout the year

### Winter sunshine

Many people from Northern Europe, including Ireland, have bought apartments and holiday homes in Spain. Some retired people from Northern Europe spend part of the winter months in southern Spain or in the Canaries because of the mild winter temperatures. The Costa del Sol has an average of six hours of sunshine a day even in January. Niche holidays such as golfing holidays are popular in autumn, winter and spring.

> **Geofact**
>
> The average length of a tourist holiday in Spain is ten days.

Fig 13.8 The coastal and inland tourist centres of Spain

A sun-drenched beach in Majorca in the Mediterranean

## Inland tourist centres

Spain is marketing its inland attractions so that those regions can share in the tourist boom. Inland attractions include Seville, Cordoba and Granada in the south. As well as Madrid itself, historic cities such as Toledo, Segovia and Avila are well worth a visit.

The Court of the Lions in the Alhambra in Granada; the Alhambra is one of Spain's great cultural attractions. Tourists can combine cultural sights with good weather

### Geofact

More than 14 million British tourists holiday in Spain every year.

## Benefits of tourism to the Spanish economy

Many regions of Spain have greatly benefited from tourism:

◎ Tourism provides employment in hotels, restaurants, golf clubs and other tourist services. One in eight workers in Spain works in the tourist industry.

◎ Tourism also supports a major construction industry with the building of hotels, apartment blocks and other facilities.

◎ Farmers along the coast have a large market for fresh produce such as salad crops that are sold to nearby supermarkets.

◎ Airports have greatly expanded in eastern Spain and in the islands. These airports also provide employment.

◎ Local landowners have been well paid for land sold for tourist development.

However, as we will learn later, tourism has brought some disadvantages to Spain.

Plastic tunnels in eastern Spain are filled with vegetable crops that need vast quantities of water

---

### SUMMARY

◎ Spain is the world's most popular tourist destination after France.
◎ The Spanish climate is very attractive to tourists from Northern Europe.
◎ While the majority of tourists choose the coast, Spain has many inland attractions.

---

### QUESTIONS

1   Examine Fig 13.6 and Fig 13.7, page 363, and answer the following questions:
   (a)  For how many months of the year does the temperature reach 20°C or more?
   (b)  Name the three coolest months.
   (c)  Name the four months with the greatest number of hours of sunshine.
2   Draw a sketch map of Spain and Portugal and include the following:
   ◎  The border with Portugal
   ◎  The Costa del Sol and the Costa Brava
   ◎  The cities of Barcelona and Malaga
3   'Climate helps to make parts of Europe attractive to tourists.'
   Explain this statement, referring to one European country or region which you have studied. (JC)

---

# 13.4 Tourism and Transport Links

Tourism can lead to transport and communications links being improved.

The road and rail network in Spain existed before mass tourism began in the 1950s. However, these networks have been modernised to cope with tourist traffic, especially in coastal regions. New motorways have been built to cope with tourist traffic, especially along the Mediterranean.

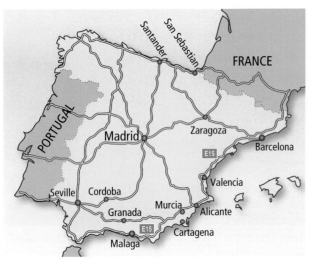

Fig 13.9 The Spanish road system radiates outwards from Madrid. The coastal routes are well served by roads

Fig 13.10 On Spain's high-speed train network it takes less than three hours to travel from Madrid to Malaga

Tourists flying to the south of Spain will see views of the landscape such as this

# The Spanish road network

Many tourists, especially the French, Swiss and Dutch, enter Spain by road. The **E15** is a great motorway along the east coast of Spain, which speeds French tourists on their way south. The E15 is a toll road because it was so expensive to build. The E15 is also used by truck traffic to supply the needs of the tourist industry.

Madrid has excellent road connections with all the provinces of mainland Spain.

# Spanish rail

The Spanish rail system is also used by tourists. The rail network connects all major cities.

## High-speed trains

High-speed trains, running at speeds of more than 300 km per hour, operate in many parts of Spain. Madrid has high-speed rail connections with the south and east coasts.

Many tourists use trains to take a trip to other tourist centres in Spain. Tourists staying in Malaga can travel to Seville, Cordoba and Madrid on a high-speed train. Tourists on the Mediterranean coast take day trips to Barcelona on high-speed trains.

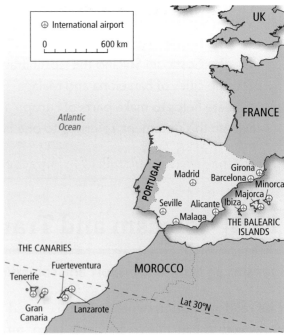

Fig 13.11 Spain has many international airports as tourists travel by air to Spain and its islands

# Airports

Great numbers of tourists from Ireland, Britain and Scandinavia travel to Spain by air. Therefore, most of Spain's airports are linked to the tourist industry. Apart from Madrid, most of Spain's international airports are close to coastal tourist resorts.

Airports are vital to the success of tourism in the Canaries and the Balearic islands. Irish tourists can reach the Canaries in less than four hours from Dublin, Shannon and Cork.

## SUMMARY

- Road and rail networks have been modernised in recent decades to keep pace with tourist growth in Spain.
- Spanish resorts are well served by airports.

## QUESTIONS

1  (a) If you were staying in Alicante, name two cities that you could visit by high-speed train.
   (b) Suggest one reason why British and Irish tourists might prefer train transport to hiring a car while on holiday in Spain.
2  (a) Name two airports on the Mediterranean coast.
   (b) Explain two reasons why airports are important for the Spanish tourist industry.
3  (a) Name two of the Canary islands.
   (b) What impact might a sharp increase in the cost of aviation fuel have on tourism in the Canary Islands? Explain your answer.

# 13.5 The Impact of Tourism

Tourism may have an unwelcome impact on society and the environment.

## Mass tourism

Mass tourism – where great numbers of tourists gather in the same resort – can bring some disadvantages. These disadvantages are evident in the Spanish resorts located along the Mediterranean coast.

## The social impact of tourism

Resorts on the coast of Spain have seen many social changes.

◎ Spanish culture is being hidden by the cultures of Northern Europe. British entertainers and DJs work in the club scene. English-language pop songs are played in discos. There are many American fast-food outlets. Irish pubs are also found in Spanish resorts.

◎ Many tourists do not learn any Spanish. Spanish tourist workers speak English and German.

◎ The resorts are losing their Spanish identity.

◎ Some holidaymakers behave badly.

◎ Petty crime and drug taking are problems in some resorts.

◎ The cost of land has risen along the coast. It is now too expensive for most locals. Young Spanish couples have to live in inland villages where property is cheaper.

## Tourism and the environment

Tourism has a great impact on the environment.

◎ Much of the Spanish coast is built up. A quarter of the land along the coast of the Costa del Sol is now covered in high-rise apartments and hotels as well as footpaths and roads.

◎ Modern high-rise buildings have swamped the traditional architecture found in local fishing villages. Some resorts have become **concrete jungles**.

◎ Agricultural land along the coast from Barcelona to Gibraltar is bought up by speculators. Some large holiday schemes have been built without planning permission.

◎ Pollution is a problem along the coast of Spain. Some partly treated sewage enters the Mediterranean Sea. This a shallow enclosed sea, with a very narrow entrance at Gibraltar. Therefore, it takes decades for the Mediterranean to renew itself through the Straits of Gibraltar.

◎ Water is scarce in eastern Spain because of very low rainfall during the summer. Meeting the water needs of tourism and irrigated farming is a major challenge.

High-rise buildings spread along the coast in Benidorm. These developments form part of the 'Great Wall of Spain'

## How should mass tourism be managed?

There are no easy answers to how mass tourism should be controlled. In Lanzarote, mass tourism is being managed in the following ways:

◎ Low-rise buildings use traditional designs and materials.
◎ Advertising signs are forbidden on road margins.
◎ Discreet shop fronts do not use plastic or gaudy colours.
◎ Gardens and parks use local plants and do not disturb the natural landscape.
◎ Planning laws are very strict and have wide public support among the 79,000 local people.

Traditional-style, low-rise buildings are evident in Lanzarote

### SUMMARY

◎ The Spanish coast has changed greatly over the last fifty years, both socially and physically.
◎ The disadvantages of mass tourism include bad planning and pollution.
◎ Lanzarote has tried to avoid the mistakes that were made in other tourist regions.

### QUESTIONS

1　Look at the picture of Benidorm and answer the following questions:
　(a) What are the high-rise buildings used for?
　(b) Suggest and explain two reasons for the high building density in Benidorm.

2　Look at the table below which contains information for a Spanish tourist resort. Answer the questions that follow:

| Month | Jan | Feb | Mar | Apr | May | Jun | Jul | Aug | Sept | Oct | Nov | Dec |
|---|---|---|---|---|---|---|---|---|---|---|---|---|
| Temperature (°C) | 9 | 11 | 13 | 16 | 21 | 25 | 26 | 27 | 19 | 17 | 15 | 12 |
| Precipitation (mm) | 71 | 55 | 28 | 19 | 5 | 5 | 3 | 0 | 6 | 16 | 60 | 79 |
| Daily hours of sunshine | 3 | 4 | 5 | 7 | 9 | 10 | 11 | 11 | 8 | 5 | 4 | 3 |

　(a) Name the months when the temperature is 19°C or higher.
　(b) What is the total rainfall in millimetres for the five driest months?
　(c) Which three months are likely to be the most popular tourist months?
　　　Give three reasons for your answer.

3　'Large-scale tourism can cause problems for busy tourist regions.'
　Describe three problems associated with large-scale tourism. (JC)

# ECONOMIC INEQUALITY

## 14.1 The Earth's Resources: Who Benefits?

In economic terms, the world can be divided into developed, quickly developing and slowly developing economies.

### Inequality

The world can be divided into the **developed world**, the **quickly developing world** and the **slowly developing world**.

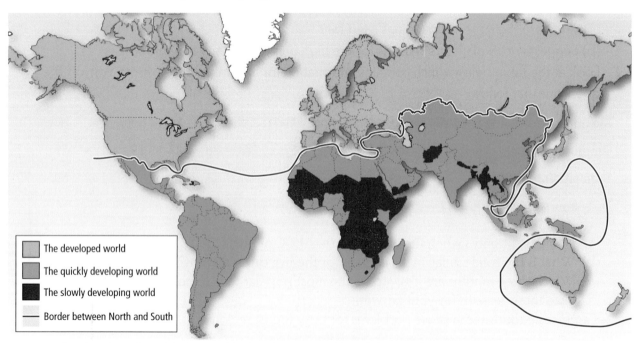

The developed world
The quickly developing world
The slowly developing world
Border between North and South

Fig 14.1 The developed world, the quickly developing world and the slowly developing world. Most of the slowly developing countries are in Africa

The **developed world** is made up of wealthy countries. Almost all of these are in the Northern Hemisphere. The developed world also includes Australia and New Zealand.

In East Asia, the countries of Japan, South Korea, Taiwan and Singapore are also in the developed world. These East Asian countries are major exporters of manufactured goods, such as computer parts, televisions and camcorders.

In the developed world, the majority of people work in services. People have high average incomes. Infrastructure such as roads, electricity and water supplies are of a high standard.

**Definitions**

**Developed world:**
Also known as the North (and the First World).

**Developing world:**
Also known as the South or the majority world (and the Third World).

Fig 14.2 Why is the developed world represented by an office worker?

Singapore, now a developed country, is one of the largest ports in the world

 **Geofact**

195: The number of internationally recognised countries in the world in 2008.

## Quickly developing countries

Countries that have **quickly developing economies** are found in the **developing world**, their economies are growing fast.

Most countries in Latin America are quickly developing. Countries in South-east Asia are also rapidly developing through the manufacturing of export goods. China, Indonesia, Malaysia, Vietnam and parts of India are in this group.

Oil producing countries of the Middle East such as Saudi Arabia and Bahrain are also developing rapidly.

A few decades ago, these regions were very poor, but living standards are rising for many people in quickly developing countries.

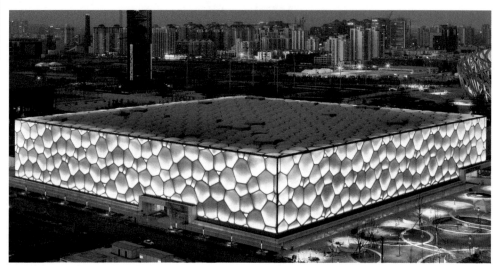

The National Aquatic Centre in Beijing; China was wealthy enough to host the Olympic Games in 2008. This indicates how quickly China is developing

## Slowly developing economies

At least fifty countries are very poor. **Sub-Saharan Africa** is the world's poorest region. It is located south of the Sahara Desert. Africa has more poor countries than any other continent.

In Asia, Afghanistan, Bhutan, Nepal, Bangladesh and Laos are also very poor.

## Some characteristics of the poorest countries

◎ Some of the world's poorest countries are landlocked, e.g. Mali.

◎ Many have experienced civil wars. These include Liberia and the Democratic Republic of Congo (DRC) – both in Africa.

◎ Many countries have crippling **foreign debts**. Repaying these debts forces countries to cut back on education and health spending.

◎ Corrupt political leadership is a problem. Some countries are ruled by criminals who steal from their own people.

◎ Slowly developing economies have high population growth.

◎ AIDS is a major problem in Sub-Saharan Africa and robs the region of many young adults as so many die as a result of the illness.

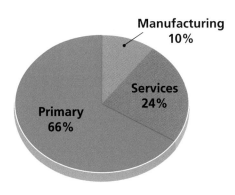

Manufacturing
10%

Services
24%

Primary
66%

Fig 14.3 The workforce in Bangladesh has a high percentage of primary workers. This is typical of slowly developing countries

A village scene in Bangladesh

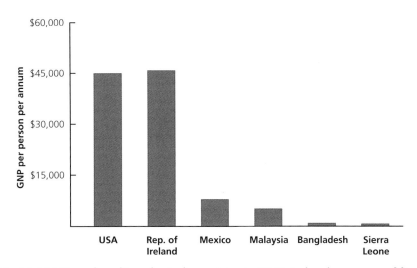

Fig 14.4 GNP per head in selected countries in 2006. Ireland, very poor fifty years ago, had become a very wealthy country in 2006

## SUMMARY

- The developed world is known as the North, although it also includes Australia and New Zealand.
- Many countries, such as China, are quickly developing.
- The poorest countries face very severe challenges.

## QUESTIONS

1 Study Fig 14.1 on page 370 and answer the following questions:
  (a) Name two developed countries on the North American continent.
  (b) Name two developed countries that are in the Southern Hemisphere.
  (c) Which continent has the greatest number of slowly developing countries?
  (d) Name two countries in Asia that are slowly developing countries.
2 Explain two reasons why China is a quickly developing country.

# 14.2 Exploitation of Poor Countries by Wealthy Countries

Throughout history, developed states have exploited less developed states. Even today richer countries dominate world markets. This makes it difficult for poorer states to develop economically.

**Definition**

To exploit: To take advantage of.

The rich and powerful have always **exploited** the poor and the weak. Wealthy countries with superior technology have taken advantage of poor countries. European countries did this in the past by a policy of **colonisation**.

## European colonisation

European countries began to colonise the American continents after Christopher Columbus discovered the New World in 1492. Spain and Portugal colonised Latin America.

Spain exploited the gold and silver mines of their colonies for generations.

Spanish and Portuguese colonists stole land from native people.

Fig 14.5 When colonists conquered territory, the native people were barred from their lands. Native people became poor immediately

## The scramble for Africa

Britain, France and other European countries rushed to divide Africa between them after 1875. The wealth of Africa – gold, diamonds, copper, cotton, mahogany and palm oil – was exploited for the benefit of Europeans.

Colonies were used as sources of cheap raw materials for the benefit of the colonial powers. In this way, European countries became wealthy while colonies remained poor.

We will now examine how Ireland was exploited in the past by Britain.

## Ireland exploited as a colony by Britain

Ireland's exploitation by Britain is for Higher level students only.

Britain colonised Ireland over many centuries. Ireland remained a colony until the twenty-six counties gained their independence in 1922. During colonial times, Ireland was exploited by Britain as a source of raw materials and food.

## The destructions of Irish forests

Centuries ago, Ireland was covered in forests that included oak – an excellent timber for shipbuilding. During the Munster Plantation, planters exported timber to Britain. In Britain, Irish oak was used to manufacture naval vessels.

Richard Boyle, a planter in the Youghal region of Co. Cork, used the forests of Co. Cork to make charcoal. This produced the energy for small ironworks in Munster that supplied the British market. The Boyle family became very wealthy, but the native Irish remained very poor.

## Ireland: a source of cheap food for Britain

Ireland, an agricultural country, supplied Britain with wheat, barley and oats for hundreds of years. Live cattle were exported cheaply to Britain, where beef was processed. Even during the Great Famine of the 1840s, food from Ireland continued to be exported to Britain.

After independence in 1922, the Irish state remained dependent on the British market. After 1922, 96 per cent of Irish exports – mainly live cattle and bulk butter – were sold very cheaply to Britain. Therefore, Ireland remained poor.

## Food processing in Ireland

Since 1960, Irish butter has been processed, packaged and marketed as a finished product in Ireland. Irish butter in this form fetches high prices abroad.

Cattle are also slaughtered and processed in Ireland. Irish factories provide employment and Irish meat products fetch high prices at home and abroad.

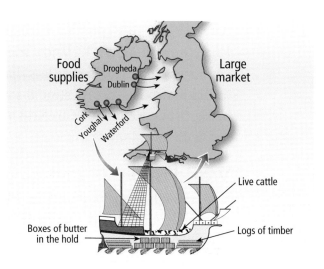

Fig 14.6 Britain used Ireland as a source of cheap food and cheap raw materials for centuries

A family search for potatoes in a field. At least 800,000 people died in Ireland during the Great Famine of the 1840s while Ireland was a colony

Kerrygold Butter is a famous Irish brand name

### EU membership

After 1973, the Republic of Ireland joined the EEC (now the EU). Ireland's trade with other countries increased. Today, less than 20 per cent of Irish exports are destined for the British market. The Republic of Ireland has broken the link with its colonial past.

## World trade

Even though former colonies in Africa have been independent for decades, most are still extremely poor. This is partly because countries of the developed world exploit poor countries through world trade.

Exports of processed meat are far more valuable than exports of live cattle

Many countries in the South still export unprocessed minerals and agricultural raw materials to the North. Apart from oil, prices of many raw materials have declined in recent decades. So the South must produce more to earn the same amount. The result is that Africa's exports are now valued at only 2 per cent of world trade.

### Dependence on one export

We have seen that Ireland was at one time dependent on the export of unprocessed agricultural goods. Today, the poorest countries in the world are dependent on the export of one or two unprocessed raw materials whose prices fluctuate or decline.

Most of these countries also have large **foreign debts**. They find it very difficult to repay debt because of the poor prices they receive for their exports.

> **Geofact**
>
> Agricultural raw materials include: cotton fibre, cocoa beans, coffee beans, raw rubber and palm oil.

We will now examine the coffee trade to show how world trade works to the advantage of wealthy countries rather than the countries that grow coffee.

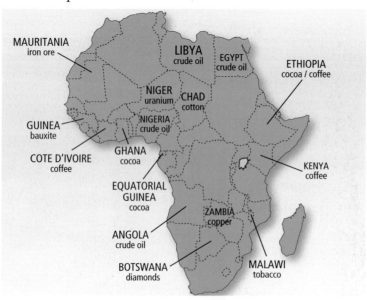

Fig 14.7 Many countries in Africa are heavily dependent on the export of one agricultural or mineral raw material

## Case Study

# The story of coffee

### Growing coffee plants

Coffee plants are very demanding in terms of climate:

◎ They cannot tolerate frost.
◎ Annual average temperatures must be above 21°C.

Therefore, coffee growing is confined to the Tropics.

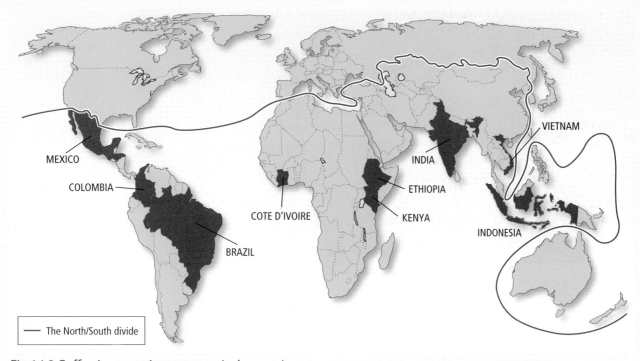

— The North/South divide

Fig 14.8 Coffee is grown in many tropical countries

### Coffee-growing countries

Coffee is an important export crop for many developing countries. Some coffee is grown on big farms called **plantations**. Small farmers also grow coffee as a cash crop. More than 25 million farmers and their families depend on coffee for their income.

### The price of coffee

Coffee beans are picked, dried and bagged. Most coffee is exported as unprocessed coffee beans. The growers have no control over coffee prices. The price of coffee beans fluctuates from year to year. A decline in price is disastrous for coffee growers and for countries that depend on coffee exports.

Coffee workers in Ethiopia. The harvesting of coffee requires much manual labour

## Supply and demand

The supply of coffee is often greater than demand. The reasons for this include the following:

◎ Many countries have large **foreign debts**. To repay these debts they have to increase exports. Therefore, farmers grow more coffee. This leads to a surplus of coffee. The price then drops.

◎ Vietnam has greatly expanded coffee production. Vietnam's exports flooded the world market with coffee beans. The result was that by 2003, coffee prices were very low indeed.

Coffee growers cannot suddenly change crops, because that is the business that they know. Changing to bananas or cocoa is not the solution either, because those crops suffer from the same price fluctuations as coffee.

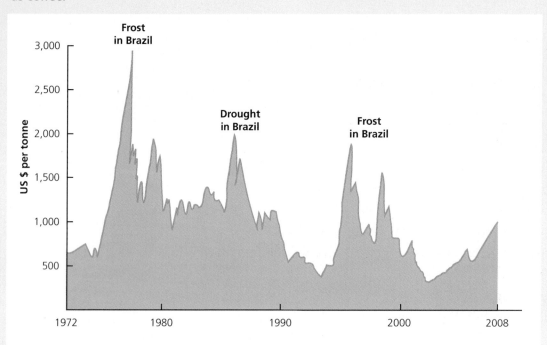

Fig 14.9 World coffee prices, 1972–2008. While the price of coffee fluctuates, the general trend over time has been downwards

## Tariff barriers in the North

A small number of multinational companies, including Kraft and Nestlé, dominate the international coffee trade. Coffee beans are roasted, ground and packaged in their factories in the USA, Europe and other developed countries.

 **Definition**

**Tariff barriers:** Taxes on imported goods which make them more expensive.

Governments in the North protect the interests of the multinationals and the jobs that they provide with **tariff barriers** on imported processed coffee from the South. Therefore, the North continues to take most of the profits from the coffee business.

We will see later in this chapter that the Fairtrade Movement is trying to correct the injustices that exist in world trade (see page 397).

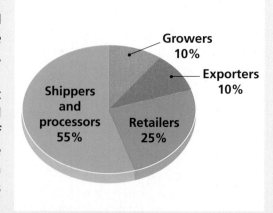

Fig 14.10 The division of money in the coffee business. Growers get a very small slice, which explains why they are poor

---

### SUMMARY

◎ Some European countries colonised other countries in the past and exploited their resources.

◎ Ireland's resources were exploited by Britain for centuries.

◎ The poorest countries depend on the export of one or two minerals or agricultural raw materials.

◎ Countries in the North make the largest profits in the coffee business.

---

### QUESTIONS

1  Name three European countries that had colonies in the past.

2  (a)  Explain two ways in which Britain exploited Ireland in the past.
   (b)  Explain two ways that the Republic of Ireland has become economically independent of Britain today.

3  Draw a sketch map of Africa. Mark in the location of the following countries: Kenya, Nigeria, Chad, Zambia, Ghana and Cote d'Ivoire.
   In each case, write in the main export of each country.

4  Name four countries that are major producers of coffee.

5  Study the pie chart in Fig 14.10 on page 378, and answer the following questions:
   (a)  What percentage of the money in the coffee business goes to growers?
   (b)  Explain the meaning of the term 'retailers'.

6  Explain how unfair trading may be a cause of poverty in the developing world.
   (JC)

---

## 14.3  Aid to the South

Rich countries give aid to poor countries. Disagreement exists concerning the effectiveness of aid programmes.

For several decades, wealthy countries have given aid to poorer countries. Aid can take many forms, for example:

◎ **Cash**: Money is given to build roads, hospitals, schools and water-filtering systems.

◎ **Skills**: Skilled people such as engineers, teachers and doctors from developed countries work for a time in projects in the South.

◎ **Goods**: Aid is often given as goods, such as food, hospital equipment and weapons.

'Give people a fish and they eat for a day. Teach them to fish and they eat for the rest of their lives.'
*Mahatma Gandhi*

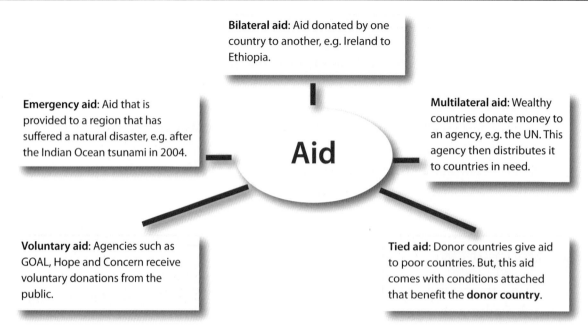

**Bilateral aid**: Aid donated by one country to another, e.g. Ireland to Ethiopia.

**Emergency aid**: Aid that is provided to a region that has suffered a natural disaster, e.g. after the Indian Ocean tsunami in 2004.

**Aid**

**Multilateral aid**: Wealthy countries donate money to an agency, e.g. the UN. This agency then distributes it to countries in need.

**Voluntary aid**: Agencies such as GOAL, Hope and Concern receive voluntary donations from the public.

**Tied aid**: Donor countries give aid to poor countries. But, this aid comes with conditions attached that benefit the **donor country**.

Fig 14.11 The different types of aid

**Definition**

**Donor country:** A country that provides aid.

**Question**

Can you name other Irish NGOs, besides the ones named on this page?

The Indian Ocean tsunami destroyed coastal villages and disrupted water supplies and communications. Emergency aid was provided in the months that followed

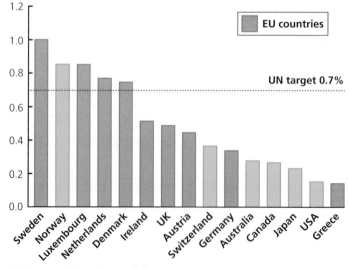

Fig 14.12 The aid donated by selected donor countries as a percentage of their GNP in 2006

# The advantages and disadvantages of aid

## Advantages of aid

◎ **Emergency aid saves lives**. Refugees, fleeing from war or famine, are fed, clothed and given shelter.

◎ Aid can contribute to people's quality of life. Aid used to bore wells, to filter drinking water, or to establish blood banks, improves local people's health.

◎ Aid that is targeted at certain groups can be very effective. Women who are trained in sewing skills can make items of clothing that they can sell in the market. This gives them independence.

◎ Some aid creates local employment, e.g. local building workers are paid by aid organisers to build schools and clinics.

◎ Aid can teach people **self-reliance**. Farmers are taught techniques such as crop rotation, fertiliser use and food storage. They can provide for their families and sell their surplus in the market.

## Disadvantages of aid

◎ Aid can create a dependent mentality among those who receive it.

◎ Many developing countries are led by corrupt politicians and officials. Dishonest people steal some aid given by donor governments.

◎ Tied aid favours the donor country. In tied aid, the donor country takes back much of what it gives in aid.

◎ **A lot of aid misses its target** – the poorest people. This is because the poorest are also the weakest and the least demanding. Many of the very poor live in remote rural areas.

◎ Some aid is not **appropriate** to local needs, e.g. lorries sent to parts of Ethiopia that have no roads or diesel filling stations.

Food aid is delivered to war-torn Liberia. Food aid is necessary in emergencies, but it can create a dependent mentality

Madam, where is the electricity?

There is no electricity. The nearest well is a 20 km walk.

Fig 14.13 Sometimes the North gives the wrong type of aid

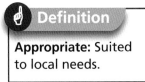

**Definition**

**Appropriate:** Suited to local needs.

After almost sixty years of aid, there are still 925 million people going to bed hungry every night. There is plenty of food in the world. The problem is that the poor cannot afford it. Therefore, aid has not eliminated poverty or hunger.

# Irish aid programmes

**Irish Aid** is the official name for the support supplied by the Republic of Ireland to developing countries. The Department of Foreign Affairs sends the aid to **recipient countries**.

## The aim of Irish Aid

The aim of Irish Aid is 'to help developing countries to find **sustainable solutions** to the problems of poverty that confront them'.

## Projects supported by Irish Aid

The Irish taxpayer contributes a lot of money to Ireland's bilateral aid programmes. It is important that the money is well spent.

Many Irish Aid projects are village based and are directed at improving the quality of people's lives. The following projects are examples.

# Aid to Ethiopia

Ethiopia is a very poor country. Eighty-five per cent of Ethiopia's people are involved in farming. Up to 7 million people are frequently short of food. Water shortages are a major challenge in Ethiopia. This is partly due to recent climate change. It rains for only two months a year.

> ### 👆 Definitions
>
> **Recipient country:** A country that receives aid.
>
> **Sustainable solutions:** Lasting long-term answers.

> ### ✍ Question
>
> Locate Timor-Leste (East Timor) and Vietnam on the world map on page 202.

Fig 14.14 Seven countries, all in East Africa, receive bilateral aid from Ireland. Ireland also gives bilateral aid to Timor-Leste (East Timor) and Vietnam, both in Asia

An Irish teacher working with a group of students in Africa

A classroom in Africa that receives financial support from Irish Aid

**Question**

How does education give young people choices in Ethiopia?

## Water projects

Irish Aid funds have been used in many parts of Ethiopia to bore deep wells for villages and to grow vegetables, fruit and potatoes under irrigation. By using irrigation, farmers can grow three crops a year in small plots.

## Hope for the future

Many Ethiopian farmers now have surplus goods that they sell locally. With this money, farmers have a year-round income. They can pay their children's school fees.

Having secondary education means that young people can better themselves and learn computer skills. Education is the key to the future because it gives young people choices.

Peter Power TD, Minister of State for Overseas Development inspects an Irish Aid project in Ethiopia

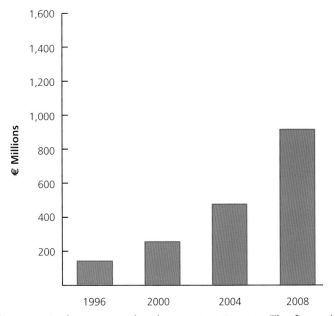

Fig 14.15 Irish overseas development assistance. The figure has grown very quickly in recent years

Land mine clearance in Mozambique

## Land mine clearance in Mozambique

Thousands of land mines lie hidden in parts of Mozambique. This is a legacy of a terrible civil war. Land mines can lead to grave injuries and even death.

When land mines are cleared, farmers can return to the fields, children can play safely and animals can graze undisturbed. Irish Aid is helping to fund mine clearance. It is slow, dangerous and expensive work.

## Assistance to HIV/AIDS victims in Africa

HIV and AIDS are major problems in Africa. There are now tens of thousands of orphans whose parents have died of AIDS. Irish Aid is used to support orphans and to provide drug treatment for HIV and AIDS sufferers. These drugs can prolong people's lives for many years and give parents the time to raise their children to adulthood.

## Education in Africa

Irish Aid funds are being used in many countries to train teachers and to help buy equipment for science labs in schools. These countries include Tanzania, Mozambique and Lesotho.

In several of Ireland's partner countries, Irish Aid is used to help students buy textbooks. Many city children who are homeless and whose parents are dead are also kept off the streets and put into full-time education.

The Niall Mellon project helps to build small dwellings in South Africa

# The work of Irish NGOs

Irish NGOs (non-governmental organisations) are voluntary organisations. They are independent of the Irish government. They collect money from the general public and spend it on projects in many countries in the South.

## People-to-people aid

NGOs get permission from governments to provide assistance to communities in poor countries. Their funds go directly into community projects. Therefore, this is called people-to-people aid.

NGOs work on small-scale projects such as village clinics and women's classes in literacy, dressmaking, nutrition and household budgeting.

## Education of the Irish public by NGOs

Many NGOs also raise awareness of development issues among the Irish public. For example, Concern, the Irish NGO, has conducted debates on development issues among pupils of secondary schools for many years. In this way, young people and their parents learn about issues such as poverty, debt, international trade and the arms industry.

This may help to explain why many Irish people spend time abroad on development projects.

Animals donated to farmers in Africa by Bóthar

---

### SUMMARY

◎ There are many different types of aid; these include bilateral and multilateral aid.

◎ Aid can make a great difference to people's lives in poor countries, but a great deal of aid fails to reach the poorest people.

◎ Irish Aid – the official name for the Irish government's official aid – has been increasing rapidly in recent years.

◎ Irish Aid projects target water supplies, health, agriculture, AIDS and education.

◎ Irish NGOs operate in many countries providing long-term assistance to communities.

---

### QUESTIONS

1  Explain the following terms with one example in each case:
   ◎ Bilateral aid
   ◎ Multilateral aid
   ◎ Tied aid

2  Would you classify emergency aid as short-term or long-term aid? Explain your answer.

3  Give one example of a natural disaster that occurred in recent years and that required an injection of emergency aid.

4  Write down and explain two advantages and two disadvantages of aid.

5  Examine Fig 14.12 on page 380 and answer the following questions:
   (a) Name the five countries that provided a greater level of assistance than the UN target.
   (b) About what percentage of its GNP did Ireland provide in 2006?
   (c) Name the only Asian country in the list of countries shown.
   (d) Of the countries shown, how many made a contribution that was below 0.4 per cent?

6  (a) Describe two examples of development assistance that Irish Aid provides in Africa.
   (b) Do you think that these projects help people to help themselves? Explain your answer.

7  Explain how NGOs provide people-to-people aid.

# 14.4 Factors that Hinder Economic Development

Many factors, such as climatic change, population growth, arms expenditure and war slow down economic development.

> **Definition**
>
> **Failed states:**
> Countries – mainly African – that are badly ruled and most of its people are trapped in poverty.

We have already seen that some countries are classified as slowly developing countries and that most of these are in Africa. Many are failing or **failed states**. These countries face very great challenges.

We will now examine the challenges facing Sudan.

## Case Study

### Sudan

Sudan is the largest country in Africa. It is also an extremely poor country, with a large proportion of its people living in poverty.

#### Climatic challenges

Northern Sudan forms part of the Sahara Desert. Therefore, that region receives very little rainfall. The land can support very few people.

Desert people live as nomadic herders. They travel from place to place with herds of sheep, cattle, goats and camels in search of sparse vegetation.

However, close to the River Nile, water is used to irrigate the land near the river. Here, the population density is higher.

Southern Sudan is less arid than the north. The south forms part of the Sahel where rainfall is low and very unreliable. Long periods of drought lead to the deaths of many animals and to crop failure. When this happens, people are forced to migrate to refugee camps for food aid. (See also Results of Desertification, page 112.)

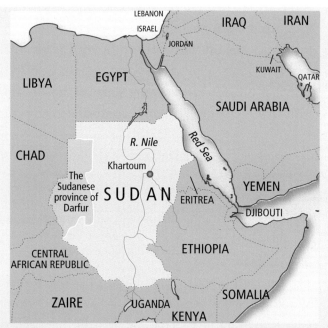

Fig 14.16 Sudan is Africa's largest country. It is located in the north east of the continent

Nomadic people watering their animals at a desert oasis near the Red Sea in Sudan. Even in this oasis area, vegetation is very scarce

## Rapid population growth

Sudan's birth rate is high. Mothers have an average of 4.4 children each. Population growth is very rapid, because the birth rate is far greater than the death rate. This means that, at the present rate of growth, the population will double in about thirty years.

As a result, providing schools for these children is a major challenge. Sudan also suffers from a shortage of teachers. The result is that many children do not attend primary school and very few go to secondary school.

Rapid population growth also places pressures on the environment. Sparse vegetation is cut for firewood. This leads to desertification, especially in the Sahel.

## Arms expenditure and war

Sudan has two racial groups: Arabs in the north and Africans in the south. The Arab majority control the government in the capital city, Khartoum.

## Civil war

Sudan experienced a civil war from 1983 until 2002. This was a war between the Arabs of the north and the Africans of the south. It caused the death of 1.5 million people. Education and health services were severely disrupted, especially in the south. Farming was also affected. Great numbers of people became refugees in neighbouring countries.

## Darfur

Darfur – a province in Western Sudan – became the focus of world attention when war broke out there in 2003.

Rapid population growth over many years meant that too many people put pressure on the water and land resources of Darfur.

Climate change reduced the rainfall of the region. In 2003, a mere 180 mm of rainfall fell in Darfur, causing vegetation to die and wells to dry up.

Arabs took possession of African people's land and wells. Africans were driven from their villages by force. Civil war erupted as a result.

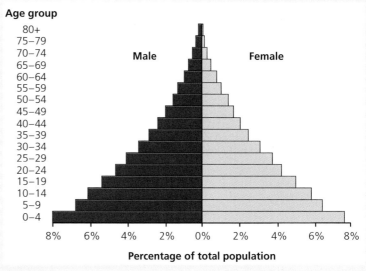

Fig 14.17 The population pyramid for Sudan shows that the birth rate is high

### Question

If the birth rate per mother in Sudan is 4.4 children, how many children will ten mothers have?

Fig 14.18 A cultural fault line divides northern Sudan from the south. The north is Arabic and Islamic. The people of the south are black Africans

A village in Darfur that was attacked and destroyed by the Janjaweed

The black population of the province has been brutally treated at the hands of the Janjaweed. These are Arabic volunteers who are assisting the Sudanese army to defeat the African rebels. Tens of thousands of people have been killed and 2 million people from Darfur have become refugees.

## Arms spending

For several decades, the Sudanese government has been spending vast sums of money on arms. This is far greater than the money spent on education and health. Education in particular has been starved of funds because of the high spending on arms and the military.

The Sudanese army is composed of 117,000 soldiers as well as civilian **militias**. Sudan also has an air force and navy in its Red Sea ports.

## A UN ban on arms sales to Sudan

The UN placed a ban on the sale of arms to Sudan because of the violence of the militias in Darfur. However, some countries are ignoring that ban. Sudan's oil exports are used to pay for these arms. Most of Sudan's oil is sold to Asian countries.

Sudan has also a large **national debt** as a result of the wars of recent decades.

 **Definition**

**Militia:** A military group that is composed of civilians who are trained in military tactics.

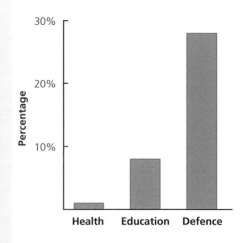

Fig 14.19 The percentage of government funds spent on education, health and defence

**Question**

Explain why the government of Sudan spends almost 30 per cent of its budget on defence.

📄 **SUMMARY**

◎ Sudan suffers from low and unreliable rainfall.
◎ Sudan's high birth rate is causing rapid population growth.
◎ Civil war has existed almost continuously in Sudan since 1983.

**QUESTIONS**

1 Explain how drought has hindered the development of one named developing country. (JC)
2 Study the population pyramid of Sudan Fig 14.17 on page 387.
   (a) What percentage of the population of Sudan is 14 years old and under?
   (b) Explain one way in which rapid population growth affects the economic development of Sudan.
3 (a) Describe recent events in Darfur.
   (b) Explain how the civil wars in Sudan have hindered economic development in that country.
4 (a) In which continent is Sudan located?
   (b) Name the countries that border Sudan.
   (c) Name the sea that is located along Sudan's eastern coast.
   (d) Name the river that flows through Sudan.

# 14.5 Economic Inequalities within the EU

Within states, differences exist between rich and poor regions.

Some regions of the EU are much poorer than other regions. The new member states of Eastern Europe are much poorer than older member states in Western Europe. However, over time, the wealth of many countries increases. For example, Ireland was the poorest of the members when it joined in 1973. By 2007, it was among the wealthiest.

## Wealthier and poorer regions within states

Even within each country, some regions are poorer than others, for example, the Republic of Ireland and Italy.

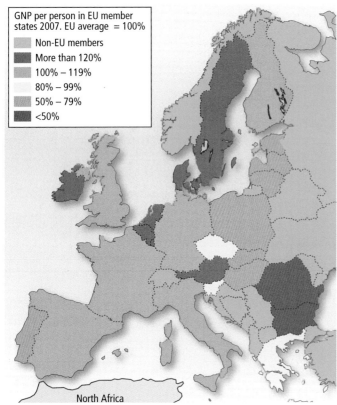

Fig 14.20 Economic inequality exists in the EU. The poorest members are Romania and Bulgaria

GNP per person in EU member states 2007. EU average = 100%

- Non-EU members
- More than 120%
- 100% – 119%
- 80% – 99%
- 50% – 79%
- <50%

North Africa

## Economic inequality in the Republic of Ireland

The Republic of Ireland can be broken into two economic regions:

◎ The more prosperous Southern and Eastern Region

◎ The less prosperous Border, Midlands and Western Regions called the BMW.

### The BMW

The BMW has a peripheral location. It is some distance from Dublin, which is the centre of political power and influence.

◎ The BMW contains much mountainous land especially in Galway, Mayo and Donegal. Mountainous land gives farmers a poor income.

◎ Because of soils, mountainous terrain and climate, farmers in most BMW counties concentrate on sheep and cattle farming. This is less profitable than wheat and barley.

◎ Many farms are small and have a high percentage of elderly farmers.

◎ The BMW is composed of thirteen counties. It contains only 1.1 million people. The BMW has a low population density. (See Low population densities in the West of Ireland, pages 226–27.)

◎ Apart from Galway, Sligo, Dundalk and Drogheda, the urban centres of the BMW are small. This makes the BMW less attractive for major companies to invest in the region.

◎ For generations, young people have migrated from the BMW to find employment. The population has grown a little since 1995, but many young people continue to move to other regions to work.

◎ Infrastructure in the BMW is not as good as in the south and east. The BMW has only one international airport, i.e. Knock, Co. Mayo.

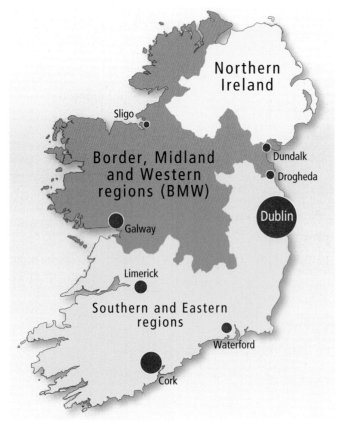

Fig 14.21 The Republic of Ireland's two economic regions: the BMW and Southern and Eastern Region

Co. Donegal has beautiful scenery, but much of its agricultural land is hilly and has poor soils

## The Southern and Eastern Region

◎ The south and east contain some excellent soils in river valleys such as the Barrow and the Munster Blackwater. The east has less rainfall. The south east has more sunshine than western counties.

◎ Many farmers in the south and east are engaged in tillage farming because the soil is suitable for ploughing. Profitable crops such as wheat and barley are grown. Farmers have very good incomes from dairy farming in the Golden Vale.

◎ The Southern and Eastern Region had 3.1 million people in 2006. This gives it a higher population density than the BMW. The region benefits from the inward migration of young people from the BMW.

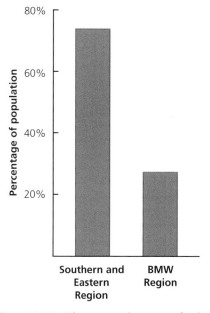

Fig 14.22 The population of the Republic of Ireland is unevenly divided between the BMW Region and the Southern and Eastern Region

A view over the rich agricultural lands of Co. Carlow

**Question**

Name three international airports in the south and east of Ireland.

◎ Apart from Dublin, large urban centres such as Cork, Limerick and Waterford are located in the south and east. These centres have attracted a lot of inward investment from foreign companies.

◎ The infrastructure of the Southern and Eastern Region is good. Three international airports and the largest seaports in the state are all located there. The main roads from Dublin have long stretches of motorway.

◎ Most of all, Dublin is the centre of the Republic's economy. Most Dubliners work in services. The headquarters of the country's largest banks, insurance companies and mortgage companies are in Dublin.

Economic inequalities in Italy is for Higher level students only.

# Case Study

## Economic inequalities in Italy

There are sharp differences in income between the North and South of Italy.

### The North of Italy

◎ Northern Italy has **a favourable climate**. It has a long growing season with summer showers.

◎ Agriculture in the **Po valley** is very productive. The valley contains rich alluvial soils, which are ideal for cereal production. The region produces excellent crops of wheat, rice, sunflowers, maize and vegetables.

◎ The North of Italy is one of Europe's greatest manufacturing centres. Companies such as **FIAT** (cars), **Benetton** (clothing), **Gucci** (leather goods), and **Zanussi** (electrical appliances) are located there.

◎ The **hydroelectric power** resources of the Alps are a major source of power for manufacturing.

◎ The north has excellent roads and railways. Tunnels and passes connect Northern Italy through the Alps to markets in France, Switzerland and Austria. Genoa is one of Europe's leading ports.

◎ The north has benefited from **inward migration** of young people from the south.

Fig 14.23 Italy's major cities; the red line indicates where the North-South divide in Italy begins

◎ The north has a great tourist industry with winter sports in the Alps, lake resorts, the coastal resorts of the Italian Riviera, and the jewel of the Adriatic – Venice.

Farmland in the River Po valley is flat. The terrain is ideal for operating farm machinery

The Grand Canal flows through the centre of Venice

## The South of Italy: the Mezzogiorno

The South of Italy is called the **Mezzogiorno**. This region includes the southern portion of the Italian peninsula, as well as the islands of Sardinia and Sicily. The South of Italy is a peripheral region. The region is much poorer than the North of Italy for many reasons:

◎ Much of the south has a **mountainous landscape**. This makes farming difficult.

◎ The south suffers from a **lack of rainfall** during the summer months. This severely limits agriculture.

◎ Agricultural output per hectare is much lower than in the north because of the terrain and summer drought. Many farms are too small to support a family. Irrigation is confined to small areas on narrow coastal plains.

◎ The south has suffered from **outward migration** for generations. This has drained it of many young people.

◎ Companies, both Italian and foreign, are less willing to invest in the south than in the north. The south is far from the markets of the EU.

◎ The south is infamous for **organised crime**, e.g. the Mafia in Sicily. This does not help inward investment.

The town of Matera in Southern Italy nestles against a background of rugged bare hills

◉ The south has many tourist attractions such as Vesuvius, Pompeii, the Isle of Capri and Sorrento. However, these have not been marketed abroad as successfully as the Spanish Tourist Board has done for Spain.

Tourists in Pompeii examine the body cast of a victim of the volcanic eruption of AD 79

 **Definition**

**Cassa:** An Italian word meaning fund.

**Question**

Look again at the picture of Venice on page 393. Explain why the city is a major tourist attraction.

## The Cassa

Southern Italy has benefited from a government agency called *Cassa* and from EU funds. *Cassa* has invested funds in irrigation schemes to help farmers.

In the last fifty years, southern Italy has been connected by motorway to northern Italy. This has helped agriculture, tourism and manufacturing. Farmers can now market their fruit and vegetables in the cities of the north, while tourists can reach the south quickly.

Farmers are educated in modern farming methods.

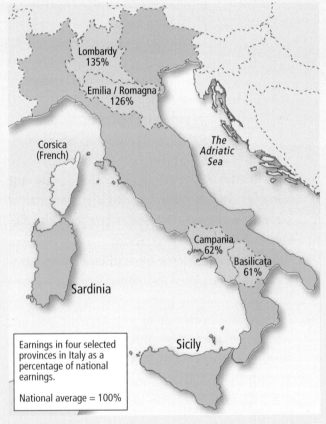

Earnings in four selected provinces in Italy as a percentage of national earnings.

National average = 100%

Fig 14.24 Earnings in four selected provinces in Italy as a percentage of national average earnings. National average earnings = 100%

## SUMMARY

◎ In the EU, East European members are poorer than older members of Western and Northern Europe.

◎ The Republic of Ireland has two regions: the Southern and Eastern Region is very wealthy, while the BMW is less wealthy.

◎ Northern Italy is very wealthy while southern Italy is considerably poorer.

## QUESTIONS

1 Study Fig 14.20 on page 390 and answer the following questions:

   (a) Name four countries where GNP per person is more than 120 per cent of the EU average.

   (b) Name the two countries where GNP per person is less than 50 per cent of the EU average.

   (c) Name the country in south-west Europe that is in the same category as Poland in terms of GNP per person.

   (d) How does this map help to explain why many migrants from Eastern Europe came to Ireland to find work?

2 (a) Explain two reasons why the Southern and Eastern Region is the wealthiest region of the Irish economy.

   (b) How has outward migration from the BMW slowed down the economic development of that region?

3 Draw a map of Italy and include the following:

   (a) The line that shows the northern limits of the Mezzogiorno

   (b) The islands of Sardinia and Sicily

   (c) The Po Valley

   (d) The Alps and the Apennines

4 Explain two reasons why northern Italy is a wealthy region.

5 How do the following hold back the development of southern Italy?

   (a) The terrain of the south

   (b) The summer drought of southern Italy

6 Explain one way in which the building of a motorway from the toe of Italy to the north is bringing economic change to the south.

# 14.6 Ending Economic Inequality

Disagreement exists as to how economic inequality can be resolved.

Wangari Maathai is an environmental and human rights activist from Kenya. She was awarded the Nobel Peace Prize in 2004. Does her achievement change your image of the developing world?

## The attitude of the North to the developing world

People in the North (the developed world) tend to think that all countries in the South (the developing world) are the same. Their view of the South is strongly influenced by images that they see on TV. These images include civil war, hunger, refugee camps and natural disasters. However, as we know, many countries in the South are making great economic and social progress.

## A developing world view of the North

People in the South are very conscious that European countries exploited them during colonial times. They believe that they are still being exploited.

People in the South want economic inequality to be reduced in the following ways:

1 Appropriate aid to the South must continue.
2 Trade must be fair.
3 The foreign debts of heavily indebted countries in the South must be reduced or cancelled.

### Appropriate aid

◎ Aid to the South must reach its target – the poorest people. Aid funds must be carefully supervised in recipient countries.

◎ Democracy must be nurtured in the South. Too many states in the South are ruled by gangsters and **kleptocrats** who steal from their own people. Democracy transfers power to the people. When a free press exists, an educated public can hold their leaders accountable for their actions. A free press can demand to see where the government is spending its money.

> **☝ Definition**
>
> **Kleptocrat:** A corrupt political leader who steals from his or her own people.

> **✍ Question**
>
> Give two reasons why ordinary people are powerless in a country ruled by a dictator.

Villagers in the developing world know what their needs are

◎ Military aid and tied aid to the South should cease.

◎ Aid must be appropriate to the South. People in the South are entitled to be consulted as to what their needs are. Aid organisations must listen to what local people have to say.

## 2 Changing the world's trading system

The world trading system is unfair. The North imposes tariffs on many processed goods from the South. That must change and to an extent, that is happening. The North has opened its markets to manufactured goods from China and other countries. But it continues to place high tariffs on processed coffee, tea, cocoa, chocolate, palm oil and processed minerals. This deprives many poor countries, especially in Africa, of billions of dollars in extra income.

Until this situation changes, countries dependent on the export of unprocessed goods will remain poor.

### Trade justice

The countries of the South make their case regularly at World Trade meetings. However, trade justice is something that governments in the North do not like.

**Geofact**

$100 computers that run on car batteries are now available for computer education in poor countries.

**Question**

Why do countries in the North use tariffs?

**Question**

What does trade justice mean?

**FAIRTRADE**

www.fairtrade.ie

**The Fairtrade Movement**

Fairtrade is designed to make the world trading system fairer to producers in the South.

Fairtrade works on the following principles:

◎ Decent and healthy working conditions for workers in the South.

◎ A fair price for producers.

Fairtrade puts people before profits. Fairtrade bananas, tea, coffee, chocolate and other products are for sale in many Irish shops.

Fairtrade is changing the lives of co-op farmers in the South. Because they receive more for their produce, co-ops can build clinics, schools and water treatment plants. These facilities improve the lives of local people.

**Geofact**

The South has for years repaid more than $4 in debt repayments for every $1 that it receives in aid.

**Question**

Do you agree that corrupt leaders should not have their countries' debts cancelled? Explain your answer.

# 3 Reducing the foreign debts of countries in the South

Many countries of the South have been crippled by debt in recent decades. In 2005, the South owed $523 billion to banks in the North.

Many debts were the result of military spending by dictators who are no longer in power. The ordinary people, who had no say in this, are now burdened with repaying huge debts.

## How debt affects people in the South

Up to 11 million children die every year in countries in the South because of poor healthcare, untreated water supplies and sanitation. Debt repayments cripple these countries.

## The Make Poverty History campaign

Two Irishmen, Bob Geldof and Bono, have led a campaign to have the foreign debts of governments in the South reduced or cancelled. In 2005, the world's wealthiest nations agreed to write off the debts of eighteen countries. Fourteen of these countries are in Africa and include Mali and Ethiopia.

Many developing countries with large debts were not given debt relief because of corrupt leaders.

Bono and Bob Geldof have worked with political leaders such as Tony Blair to make the world a more equal place

## SUMMARY

◎ People in the North have an image of the South that includes poverty, shantytowns, corruption and civil wars.

◎ The South is demanding that development assistance continues, that trade is made fairer and that debts are at least reduced and in many cases cancelled.

## QUESTIONS

1 Explain two ways in which aid to the South can be made more effective.

2 Give two reasons why democracy in the South should be encouraged.

3 Explain one way in which international trade continues to favour wealthy countries.

4 How does the Fairtrade Movement attempt to improve the quality of life of workers in the South?

5 Give two arguments in favour of cancelling the foreign debt that developing countries are burdened with.

6 (i) Reducing military spending
(ii) Increasing aid
(iii) Cancellation of debt
The three items above have been suggested as ways in which the differences between developed and developing countries might be reduced.
Choose two of the above and explain how they might reduce the differences .
In your answer refer to one example you have studied. (JC)

# Glossary

**abrasion**  Erosion caused by the load carried by rivers, waves and glaciers.

**acid rain**  Rainwater containing chemicals that occurs as a result of the burning of fuels such as coal and oil.

**aid**  Development assistance by rich countries and other organisations to projects in the developing world.

**alluvium**  Material transported and deposited by a river when it floods.

**anemometer**  Instrument used to measure the speed of wind.

**anticyclone**  An area of high atmospheric pressure (HP), usually associated with fine, settled weather.

**aspect**  The direction in which a slope faces.

**atmosphere**  The layer of gases, including nitrogen and oxygen, surrounding the Earth.

**attrition**  Erosion caused when the particles in the load carried by rivers and waves bump off one another.

**backwash**  Water returning to the sea after a wave has broken.

**biofuels**  Energy sources that can be extracted from crops and other organic matter.

**birth rate**  The number of live births per 1,000 people in one year.

**BMW**  The Border, Midland and Western Region in the Republic of Ireland.

**boreal**  Climate belt to the south of the Arctic Circle, with long, cold winters and short summers.

**boulder clay**  Mixture of clay and rocks deposited by a glacier.

**bridge point settlement**  A settlement that is located where a river has been forded or bridged.

**brown earth**  Fertile, well-drained soil that developed where deciduous forests grow.

**carbonation**  Chemical weathering where rocks such as limestone are broken down by acid in rainwater.

**CBD**  The central business district of a city.

**climate**  The average weather conditions of a region over a long period of time.

**cloud**  A visible body of very fine water droplets or ice particles suspended in the atmosphere.

**colonisation**  One country taking political control over another country.

**commuters**  People who travel some distance from their homes to their places of work.

**conservation**  The care, protection and careful use of resources and of the environment.

**convection currents**  Currents in the mantle move the heated molten magma upwards from the core towards the crust and cause the plates to move.

**crust**  The thin, solid outer layer of the Earth.

**DART**  Dublin Area Rapid Transit is a commuter railway line along the Dublin coast linking Malahide with Greystones

**death rate**  The number of deaths per 1,000 people in one year.

**deposition**  The laying down of the load transported by rivers, waves and ice.

**depression**  An area of low atmospheric pressure (LP), usually associated with wet, cloudy and windy weather.

**desertification**  The gradual spread of desert conditions into surrounding areas.

**developed countries**  Countries that are wealthy, have good services and a high standard of living, also known as the North or the First World.

**developing countries**  Countries that are poor, with few services and a low standard of living, also known as the South or Third World.

**development**  The use of resources and technology to improve people's standard of living and quality of life.

**doldrums**  Areas of low pressure and slack winds near the equator.

**dormitory town**  A town to which people return home after their day's work.

**drainage basin**  The area of land drained by a single river and its tributaries.

**earthquake** A sudden movement within the Earth's crust, usually close to a plate boundary.

**economic migrant** A person who has moved in search of work.

**emigrant** A person who leaves a country to live elsewhere.

**entrepreneur** A person who embarks on the risky business of developing and marketing new products and services.

**environment** The living conditions in which people, animals and plants exist.

**erosion** The breaking down of rocks and the removal of the resulting particles by rivers, waves and ice.

**export processing zones** Industrial estates, mainly in developing countries such as China, where goods are manufactured for export.

**feminist movement** A women's pressure group aimed at equal rights for women.

**fertiliser** Manure or a mixture of nitrates used to make soil more fertile.

**fold mountains** Mountains formed when rocks buckled and folded as two plates collided.

**food processing** The conversion of food resources such as meat and milk along with other ingredients into products such as sausages and cheese.

**footloose industry** An industry that is not tied to raw materials and has a wide choice of location.

**fossil fuels** Fuels such as coal, oil and natural gas that developed over time from the remains of plants and animals.

**freeze-thaw** Mechanical weathering where rocks are broken down due to water in cracks repeatedly freezing and thawing.

**front** The dividing line (cold front or warm front) between two air masses that have different temperatures and pressures.

**glacier** A large, slow-moving mass of ice flowing down a valley.

**greenhouse effect** The way that gases in the atmosphere trap an increasing amount of energy from the sun.

**heavy industry** The manufacture of goods in which heavy or bulky raw materials are used, such as smelting and oil refining.

**horizon** One of the layers into which a soil profile is divided.

**horse latitudes** Areas of high pressure and rising air, about 30°N and S of the equator.

**hydraulic action** Erosion caused by the power of moving water in rivers or waves.

**Ice Age** A time when vast areas of the Earth were covered by ice sheets.

**ice sheet** Moving mass of ice that covers a large land area.

**igneous rock** A rock that formed from the cooling of molten magma or lava.

**immigrant** A person who enters a country with the intention of living there.

**impermeable rock** Rock that does not allow water to pass through it.

**industrial estates** An area where several manufacturing companies are located, often on the edge of a town or city.

**industrial inertia** When an industry does not relocate even though the original reasons for its location no longer exist.

**industrially emergent regions** Regions and countries that have little or no modern manufacturing, e.g. Africa and Central Asia.

**infant mortality** The average number of deaths of children under one year of age per 1,000 live births.

**infrastructure** Networks such as road, rail, electricity, water, telephone and broadband.

**inner city** The area of the city with older housing and industries that is located next to the city centre.

**Irish Aid** Development assistance given by the Irish government to some countries in the developing world.

**irrigation** Supplying dry agricultural land with water in order to grow crops.

**karst** An area of limestone with surface and underground features that result from chemical weathering.

**landslide** The very rapid movement of earth and rock (regolith) down a steep slope.

**latitude** The angular distance north or south of the equator.

**life expectancy** The average number of years that a person in a given country is expected to live.

**light industry** Manufacturing activity, such as fashion and hi-fi equipment, that uses moderate amounts of raw materials .

**longshore drift** The zigzag movement of material along a coastline by waves.

**Luas** A light rail system linking Dublin city centre with Tallaght and Sandyford.

**magma** The molten or semi-molten material that makes up the Earth's mantle.

**mantle** The layer of molten rock between the Earth's crust and core.

**market** A place where goods are bought and sold or a group of people who buy goods.

**mass movement** The movement down-slope of loose material under the influence of gravity.

**metamorphic rock** A rock that has been changed by extremes of heat and pressure.

**Mezzogiorno** The South of Italy including the islands of Sardinia and Sicily.

**migration** The movement of people from one area to another to live or to work.

**mudflow** Moving rivers of rock, soil and water. They are the fastest forms of mass movement.

**multinational companies** Companies with a base in more than one country.

**navigable river** A river that has been deepened so that it can be used for barge traffic.

**newly industrialised countries** Countries that have become rapidly industrialised in recent decades, e.g. in South-east Asia.

**NGOs** Non-governmental organisations, e.g. voluntary agencies that provide assistance to projects in the developing world.

**nodal point** A city or town where natural routeways meet.

**nomadic herders** Farmers who move according to the seasons from place to place in search of food, water, and grazing land with their animals.

**non-renewable resource** A finite resource that will eventually run out or be depleted, such as oil.

**nucleated settlement** A cluster of buildings and inhabitants in a particular location.

**ocean current** Regular patterns of water flowing like giant rivers through the oceans.

**permeable rock** Rock that allows water to pass through it.

**pharmaceutical plant** A factory that makes healthcare products.

**plate** The separate sections into which the crust of the Earth is broken.

**plate boundary** The place where two plates meet. It is associated with volcanoes, fold mountains and earthquakes.

**plate tectonics** The theory that the crust of the Earth is divided into a number of moving plates, leading to folding, volcanic and earthquake activity.

**plucking** Erosion where blocks of rock are torn out by moving ice.

**polder** An area of land that has been reclaimed from the sea.

**pollution** Noise, harmful substances and dirt produced by people and machines that damage an area.

**population cycle (the demographic transition model)** Shows how changes in birth and death rates over time are related to a country's development.

**population density** The average number of people living in an area, usually per km$^2$.

**population distribution** The spread of people over an area.

**population explosion** A sudden rapid increase in the population in a region.

**population pyramid** A bar chart displaying the population structure of an area.

**population structure** The composition of a country's population by age and sex.

**precipitation** All forms of moisture from the atmosphere, including rainfall, snow, hail and fog.

**prevailing wind** The direction from which the wind blows most frequently.

**primary activities** Economic activities where resource materials are extracted from the land and the sea.

**pull factors** Things that attract people to live in an area.

**push factors** Things that make people decide to leave an area.

**QBCs** Quality bus corridors in cities and suburbs that are reserved for buses and taxis.

**relief** The shape and height of the land.

**renewable resource** A non-finite resource such as wind power or solar energy that can be used over and over again.

**resource** Any material or product that people find useful.

**Richter Scale** A scale by which the strength of an earthquake is described.

**scree** Loose pieces of rock with sharp edges. They are broken off by freeze-thaw and gather at the foot of a slope.

**secondary activities** Economic activities where raw materials are processed into products.

**sedimentary rock** A rock formed from sediments that were laid down and compressed over millions of years.

**seismometer (seismograph)** An instrument used to measure (and record) the strength of an earthquake.

**settlement** The manner in which an area is settled by people either as rural dwellers or in towns and cities.

**shantytown** A group of shacks or huts in an area of a city usually lacking electricity, water supply and a sewage system.

**soil** The thin layer of loose material on the Earth's surface.

**soil creep** The slow, down-slope movement of soil under the influence of gravity.

**soil erosion** The removal of fertile topsoil by wind, rain and running water.

**solar energy** Energy from the sun, giving heat and light to Earth.

**stratified rock** Rock that was laid down in layers or strata.

**Sub-Saharan Africa** The region of Africa that lies south of the Sahara Desert.

**suburb** A mainly residential area on the edge of the city.

**sustainable development** A way of improving people's standards of living and quality of life without damaging the environment or putting the wellbeing of future generations at risk.

**swash** The movement of water up a beach after a wave breaks.

**tariffs** Taxes placed on goods when they are imported.

**terrain** The physical features of a land area.

**tertiary activities** Activities that provide a service to people such as health and tourism.

**trade** The movement and sale of goods and services between countries.

**tsunami** A huge wave that is caused by an underwater earthquake.

**urban functional zones** Areas of a city where different types of activity take place, e.g. manufacturing, residential and retail.

**urban redevelopment** The demolition of old derelict buildings and homes in the inner city and their replacement with offices, hotels and apartments.

**urban renewal** The demolition of old sub-standard homes in the inner city and the construction of modern homes for the residents in the same location.

**urban sprawl** The expansion of a city into the countryside in an unplanned and uncontrolled way.

**volcano** A cone-shaped mountain formed by the eruption of magma from inside the Earth to the surface.

**water cycle** The continual recycling of water as it passes between the atmosphere, the oceans and the land. Also called the hydrologic cycle.

**weather** The day-to-day condition of the atmosphere, including temperature, precipitation, sunshine and wind.

**weathering** The breakdown and decay of rocks by mechanical (freeze-thaw) and chemical (carbonation) processes.

# Index

## Picture credits

The authors and publisher wish to thank the following for permission to reproduce photos: Alamy, Automobile Association (Publishing) Photo Library, Corbis, Inpho Photography, The Irish Image Collection, The Irish Times, Getty Images, National Library, Photocall Ireland, Press 22 (Liam Burke Photographer), Reflexstock, Royal Society of Antiquaries of Ireland, Science Photo Library, Shutterstock, Topfoto

### Aerial photography

European Photo Services Ltd (Peter Barrow Photographer): Glen of the Downs, page 70; Cavan, page 172; Drogheda, page 175; Swords, page 179; Claremorris, page 180; Trim, page 181; Westport, page 182; Kilkenny, page 186; Ardee, page 190; North Co. Dublin, page 221; Expanding Dublin, page 221; Strokestown, page 253; Dublin, page 254; Carlingford, page 256; Drogheda, page 256; Shannonbridge, page 257; Navan, page 269; Dublin, page 280; Blanchardstown Shopping Centre, page 287; QBC, page 291; Housing Estate, page 294; Tallaght, page 300; Adamstown, page 301; Intel, page 334

irelandaerialphotography.com (John Herriott Photographer): Poulaphouca, page 46; Lough Nahanagan, page 69; Glendalough, page 70; Wexford, page 169; Oblique aerial photograph, page 169; Kilmallock, page 171; Thurles, page 176; Lahinch, page 177; North Gate Bridge, Cork, page 178; Bandon, page 185; Clonmel, page 188; Macroom, page 192; Dublin, page 194; Galbally, page 257; Duncannon, page 262; Shannon Airport, page 275; Dooradoyle page 283; Doughcloyne Industrial Estate, page 283; Semi-detached housing, page 289; Ennis, page 297; Hewlett Packard, page 333; Mill at Bealick, page 339; Schering-Plough, page 340